WHAT IS ART?

WHAT IS ART?

AN INTRODUCTION TO PAINTING, SCULPTURE AND ARCHITECTURE
by JOHN CANADAY

ALFRED A. KNOPF NEW YORK 1980

A JOHN L. HOCHMANN BOOK

THIS IS A BORZOI BOOK
PUBLISHED BY ALFRED A. KNOPF, INC.

Grateful acknowledgment is made to Random House, Inc., and
Faber and Faber Ltd for permission to reprint "Musée des Beaux
Arts" by W. H. Auden. Copyright 1940 and renewed 1968 by W. H.
Auden. Reprinted from W. H. AUDEN: COLLECTED POEMS, by W. H.
Auden, edited by Edward Mendelson. Reprinted by permission
of Random House, Inc., and Faber and Faber Ltd.

Coming Home for Thanksgiving by Grandma Moses,
copyright © 1980 by Grandma Moses Property Co., New York.

Illustrations on the jacket of this book correspond to the following
figure numbers in the text: front, **30**; back, **4, 19, 68, 3, 101, 136,
186, 217, 239, 269, 305, 298, 363, 402, 438.**

Library of Congress Cataloging in Publication Data

Canaday, John Edwin, [date]
What is art?
"A revision and extensive enlargement of the Metropolitan seminars in art."
"A John L. Hochmann book."
Includes index
1. Art.   I. Metropolitan seminars in art.   II. Title.
N7425. C26 1979   701'.1   79-23256
ISBN 0-394-50320-1
0-394-32450-1 (pbk)

Manufactured in the United States of America
First Edition

To Katherine

CONTENTS

Introduction
WHAT IS ART?
3

WHAT IS A PAINTING?
11

SCULPTURE
33

ARCHITECTURE
53

REALISM
59

EXPRESSIONISM
95

ABSTRACTION
117

COMPOSITION AS PATTERN
145

COMPOSITION AS STRUCTURE
167

COMPOSITION AS NARRATIVE
195

THE PAINTER'S TECHNIQUES
219

PRINTS
263

THE ARTIST AS SOCIAL CRITIC
289

THE ARTIST AS VISIONARY
325

EPILOGUE
362

GLOSSARY
365

INDEX
379

This book is a revision and extensive enlargement of The Metropolitan Seminars in Art, a series of twelve monographs on the appreciation of painting written for the Metropolitan Museum of Art and distributed by the Book-of-the-Month Club. Sections on sculpture and architecture have been added, and those on painting have been enlarged to cover recent developments as well as revised in the light of changed attitudes toward art—my own, and those of the public this book is written for. Even so, the discussions of painting are for the most part adapted directly from the Seminars, and I want to thank the Metropolitan Museum for having generously given permission to draw upon that material so freely.

John Canaday

New York, 1979

WHAT IS ART?

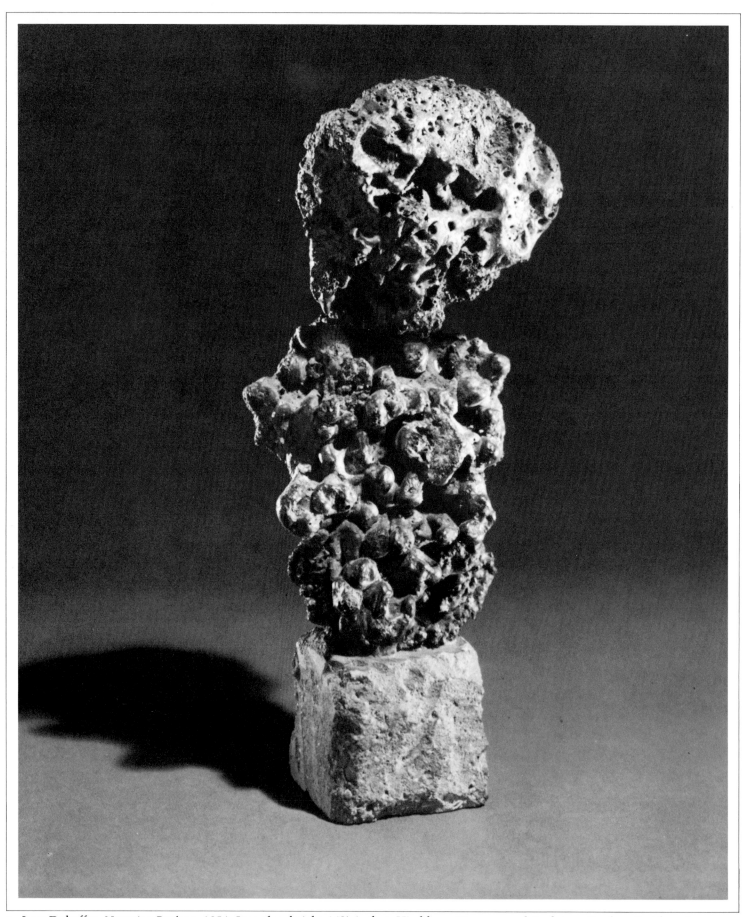

1. Jean Dubuffet. *Nourrice Profuse.* 1954. Iron slag, height 14⅝ inches. Hirshhorn Museum and Sculpture Garden, Smithsonian Institution, Washington, D.C.

Introduction

WHAT IS ART?

The only way to begin this book is to make clear that we are not going to arrive at any single answer to the question, What is art? Art has so many aspects, takes so many directions, serves so many purposes in such a variety of ways, that the question is almost as big as the biggest of all, What is life?

The two questions, in fact, overlap. The popular phrase "art for art's sake" implies that art can be an escape from life, but this—fortunately—is a delusion. Rather than an escape, art is an enrichment, and the underlying premise of this book is that art and living are inseparable and mutually sustaining, and always have been, ever since the appearance of human beings on our planet. "Creativity of man as distinguished from the world of nature" is the dictionary definition (one of many) that comes closest to answering our first question. This creativity and an awareness of history are the two characteristics most frequently cited as distinguishing human beings from animals.

For most people who enjoy it without knowing much about it, art's first function is to be "pleasing to the eye"—a sound enough idea as far as it goes. Art has served life as an embellishment from the day our prehistoric ancestors first smeared magical signs on their bodies with colored clays up to this moment, when no one reading this page is likely to be in a position to look away from it without seeing dozens of embellishments in one or another form of art—the patterns of rugs, bookbindings, and upholstery; the shapes of moldings, ashtrays, and knickknacks; the color and design of clothing—blue jeans being just as much an embellishment as are embroidered robes—and whatever pictures hang on the walls. Presuming that these objects were chosen because they were more attractive than others, the eye that chose them is pleased. But to stop with this pleasure is to deny ourselves the further ones of understanding why the eye is pleased and how these various forms and patterns evolved over the centuries and millennia of art history. The genealogy of virtually any painting or sculpture, no matter how modern, can be traced back to the ancient world or even to savage and prehistoric peoples.

The idea that art is created to please the eye leaves unanswered the question as to how an object like *Nourrice Profuse* (**1**) by the modern French artist Jean Dubuffet can please art critics even though it grates on eyes habituated to the beauties of more conventional sculpture. To such eyes, *Nourrice Profuse* looks like a lump of slag iron—which is exactly what it is. But it is not *only* a lump of slag iron. Nor can this ugly object—we will call it ugly for the moment, since we will be seeing it again—be very easily explained by a definition of the function of art widely accepted by estheticians, which is "to bring order to the chaotic material of human experience."

This definition is applicable enough when we test it on the Parthenon (**3**), a work

2. Michelangelo. *Last Judgment.* 1536–41. Fresco, 48 by 44 feet. Sistine Chapel, Vatican, Rome.

of art so perfectly ordered that even in ruins it is the consummate affirmation that life is a reasonable affair, that its goals can be formulated and achieved, that all confusion and ugliness can be vanquished in the creation of an ultimate harmony, a vital clarity.

But what becomes, then, of Michelangelo's thunderous *Last Judgment* (2) in the Sistine Chapel, which is all turbulence and terror? Even the martyrs, the saints, and the blessed on their way to Paradise seem to share the convulsions of the damned. On purely esthetic grounds we can rationalize that the *Last Judgment* is a carefully organized painting and thus "brings order" to its chaotic subject; but primarily this scene of universal damnation intensifies our experience of desperation and terror by investing these familiar human emotions with awesome grandeur.

So we extend the idea of bringing order to the chaotic material of human experience to form the second premise upon which this book is built, which is: The function of art is to clarify, intensify, or otherwise enlarge our experience of life. "Otherwise enlarge" affords a necessary catch-all that overlaps clarification and intensification but reaches into fields ranging from Dubuffet's *Nourrice Profuse* to the most acutely realistic paintings and sculptures ever created, with some of the most conventionally eye-pleasing in between.

Finally, every interpretation or analysis of a work of art in this book will be made within the all-embracing conviction that painting, sculpture, and architecture are the truest and most complete witnesses to the nature of the times and places that produced them. This is an argument that would have to be defended in debate with poets, musicians, dancers, playwrights, novelists, philosophers, and, above all, historians. Our defense would begin with the question as to which arts other than painting, sculpture, and architecture have left records dating back into prehistory and can bring the observer, or listener, or reader more vividly and immediately into the presence of immortal genius of all times and places without such obstructions as translation, notation, reconstitution, and guesswork. Fortunately, though, no art really has to be defended at the expense of another in the wonderful interplay of ideas by which all the arts make up the history of civilization. A knowledge of any art is an enrichment of the rest.

In its most obvious function as witness to centuries of change, art is a topical record describing how things, places, and people have looked, a function now preempted by the camera. *The Clock Tower in the Piazza San Marco, Venice* (4), by Antonio Canale, called Canaletto, tells us detail by detail how one wonderful spot in that always wonderful city looked when Canaletto recorded it about 1740. The picture is beautiful in the purest, least complicated sense of the word, and to say that it is "only" a topical record is both accurate and unjust. It is an impeccable technical performance by a master craftsman and certainly a work of art to delight any eye. Yet in the end it is a report, owing

3. Iktinos and Kallikrates. The Parthenon. About 447–432 B.C. The Acropolis, Athens. Photograph by Alison Frantz, Princeton, New Jersey.

4. Canaletto. *The Clock Tower in the Piazza San Marco, Venice.* About 1740. Oil on canvas, 20¾ by 27¾ inches. Nelson Gallery–Atkins Museum, Kansas City, Missouri. Nelson Fund.

5. Choir vaulting, Cathedral of St. Peter, Beauvais. Thirteenth-century. France.

more to the beauty of a fantastic city than to creative invention on the part of the artist. Canaletto applied technical prowess of the highest order—but here we come to the difference between highly developed abilities and innate creative genius.

This is not to say that Canaletto is a human camera insensitive to esthetic values or to the mood of his extraordinary city. His adjustments of perspective and his unification of the sky and all below it in a consistent half-magical light are the crucial difference between his paintings and those of studio assistants who helped turn out hundreds of Venetian views for tourists of the day. The dictionary's second definition of art is "Skill: craftsmanship," and by that definition alone Canaletto would be one of the great masters in the world rather than an admirable painter of enchanting views, which is a fair statement of the position given him today by art historians.

As a more profound record of its time, art rarely depends on topical reference, distilling instead the essence of the faith or philosophy by which people of that time lived, or tried to live. New art forms seem almost literally to invent themselves in response to changing ideals.

As an example:

Around the middle of the twelfth century a miraculous process of germination seemed to be taking place in the soil of Europe, beginning in France, then spreading through the continent and into England. Churches began to rise as if gigantic seeds of stone had sprouted and thrust new and wonderful forms into the light, growing higher and higher and more and more elaborate in competition with one another, becoming eventually the piers and columns of the Gothic cathedrals, slender stalks flowering at last into vaults supported by webs of ribs like the veins of leaves or petals (5). On the exterior, this upward striving was continued in spires that rose higher than any structures ever before imagined, tapering and finally disappearing in points that merged with the sky.

The Gothic cathedral summarized the spiritual aspirations of an age that had at the very least its full share of human evils—cruel wars, torture, superstition, ignorance, filthy poverty, political and religious persecution, and mass hysteria. Some of these abominations were perversions of the forces of faith, terrible facts that historians have recorded. But the cathedrals rise above terrible facts as witnesses to a glorious truth, the mystical faith symbolized by the soaring forms.

Contradictorily, this mystical expression was achieved by new feats of practical engineering. The great height of the cathedrals, with their hovering, apparently weightless stone vaults, demanded building methods more daring than any the world had yet known—for that matter, as daring as any the world has ever known. Cathedral vaults are ordinarily etherialized by the dim light in which we see them from the floor; it is only when they are brightly lit for purposes of photography (6) that their geometrical patterns are fully revealed, patterns that are continued on the exterior by the geometrical forms of the buttresses supporting them (**7**).

Geometry, of all branches of mathematics, is the one that clarifies and organizes our daily experience of lines, planes, and volumes, revealing their logical interrelationships in a way that inspired one poet to write: "Euclid alone has looked on beauty bare." Euclidian geometry held an honored position in the Middle Ages, being one of the four liberal arts (arithmetic, geometry, astronomy, and music) designated by scholars as the quadrivium, the higher division of the seven liberal arts completed by the trivium of grammar, logic, and rhetoric. But it hardly seems probable that the architect-builders of the Gothic cathedrals, faced with the practical problems of inventing vaulting systems to cover spaces of unprecedented height and width, were much concerned with philosophical interpretations of the Euclidian patterns that they employed in meeting the structural demands of weight and stress—and even less probable that they were conscious of the beautiful coincidence by which their engineering, their creation of mystical space by practical means, paralleled the philosophical exercises by which theologians set out to prove the existence of a mystical God in nonmystical terms.

Beginning with the premise of revelation, medieval philosophers constructed logical systems to prove God's existence, even while architect-engineers were constructing vaults to create the space that, for the Middle Ages, was the symbol of God, crystallizing the coincidence of medieval cathedral architecture with medieval thought. Integrating architecture with the arts then still subservient to it, the cathedrals were encrusted with sculptures expounding theological and scientific doctrines, while painting was represented by tapestries, murals, and the ultimate glory of walls of stained glass telling the history of the world as the Middle Ages conceived it.

We have considered Gothic cathedral architecture at some length in this introduction because it exemplifies so well our premise that the forms art takes are inevitably determined, as if self-invented, by forces within the times that demand appropriate expression. The more complex a civilization becomes, the less possible it is for a single work of art to summarize its culture. Regarded as a single work of art combining architecture, sculpture, and (as it originally did) color, the Parthenon is such a summary, created when Athens was a small city (100,000 people) with a corresponding unity and clarity of goals, in contrast with the modern city that now sprawls out around the Acropolis. There is no single Gothic cathedral that can be called the perfect summary of its time (Chartres comes closest), but the Gothic cathedral generically is that summary. After that, there are complexes of architecture, sculpture, and painting—St. Peter's in Rome, for instance—that come close to summarizing their times or at least vital segments of those times; but when we get to the nineteenth century, the prolixity of contrasting monuments is evidence of the

6. Choir vaults, Cathedral at Amiens. Begun 1220. France.

7. Flying buttresses of the nave, Cathedral at Chartres. 1194–1220. France.

complexity of an age that defies summary in a single expression. In France alone we would have to pit the Paris Opera House (considered later on in this book), with its brilliant transmutation of traditional themes, against the Eiffel Tower, with its denial of those themes, and even then we would not have dealt with a century of painting that was itself a series of revolutions.

As for our own time, our wonderful and terrible century, is there a work of art or assemblage of works of art that represents us at our best, as the Parthenon represents ancient Greece, the cathedrals the medieval world?

Perhaps the question belongs at the end of this book, but let us anticipate it and propose that the spectacle of New York City from the air at night is that composite work of art. We can even make a direct comparison with what we have said about the Middle Ages, a far from ideal period in terms of daily life that produced a glorious expression of faith. Similarly, New York seen from the air rises above the dross that surrounds us.

New York at street level (like the rest of our civilization) is often ugly, violent, sordid, dirty, noisy, confused, corrupt, and inhumane. It is a city where good living is the prerogative of those who can pay for it. But none of this is any more true of New York today than it has been of the representative metropolises of the past—ancient Rome, medieval Paris, seventeenth-century Rome, eighteenth-century London, and nineteenth-century Paris, which held its own well into the twentieth century. As the supermetropolis of the latter half of our century, New York has a vitality about it that for many people, even some of those who suffer most from the difficulties the city imposes, makes living there an indispensable condition of existence.

Artists who have set out self-consciously to express our century in its own terms have capitalized on materials and methods unique to its technology—all kinds of plastics, neon lights, computer-directed motion for computer-designed sculpture, and, at the other extreme, industrial waste products (here we come again to *Nourrice Profuse*) and the detritus of a consumer society. Sculptures have been made from crushed automobile hoods and fenders, and welded from discarded machine parts. In the late 1950's and early 60's artists of all kinds (painters, sculptors, musicians, dancers, writers, and their ringsiders) pooled their efforts in impromptu events called "happenings," performances improvised in studios or sometimes in experimental museums, that were supposed to invest the arts with spontaneous life by freeing them from consumer strictures. But no happenings ever approached in interest or spontaneity the spectacle of life on the streets of New York. Some artists, believing that the day of art for collectors and museums is finished, have theorized that the solution to the problems that have removed art from life and entombed it in private collections and public institutions is to create works of art in nature, built from the ground they lie on. Robert Smithson's *Spiral Jetty* (**8**), one of the most ambitious and more enduring of such projects, has become the standard example of in situ

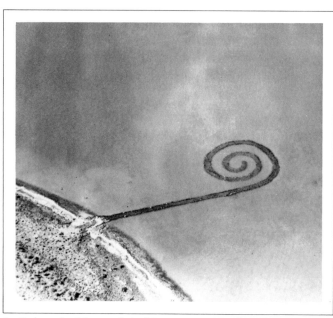

8. Robert Smithson. *Spiral Jetty.* 1970. Earth and minerals, diameter 40 feet. Great Salt Lake, Utah.

works of art that declare man's capacity for transforming nature even while recognizing nature as a basic fact of our lives.

While none of our efforts, some foolish and others serious, to create new art forms appropriate to our times can be more than fragmentary expressions of our inconceivably complex culture, all of them are fused in the single compound work of art called New York City—not as experiments and not as art forms, but in satisfaction of demands peculiar to our times that had to be met in practical terms.

Manhattan is a small island transformed by the works of man. Seen from the air at night, it is an anonymous man-made work of art, a phenomenon possible only in this century, the century of the airplane, glass-and-steel construction, the automobile, and electric light. Seen from above in daylight, the skyscrapers are spectacular enough (**9**), their towering clusters transformed from architecture into titanic sculptures—or titanic natural forms of a newly discovered planet. At night (**10**) they dissolve in their own light; neon signs become scattered jewels; the blazing crisscross pattern of streets surrounds a large, dark rectangle through which wind a few wavering lines of light—Central Park. The spectacle is doubly kinetic: its masses shift as our aerial point of vision moves across the island, and on the island itself the traffic flows in liquid light. Everything sordid, ugly, and trivial disappears in an astounding affirmation that the values our society lives by are ultimately valid, whatever their distortions at close range.

But all of that, we said, perhaps belongs at the end of this book. As a beginning, we will subdivide the question, What is art?, and deal in some of the particulars of that vast generality, beginning with the question, What is a painting?, and following it with considerations of sculpture and then architecture. The same order will be followed chapter by chapter.

This is the reverse of a traditional sequence by which architecture is recognized as the parent art, with sculpture closely bound to it and subject to its demands, while painting is semi-independent of the filial bond. The bond in any case holds firmly only into the Middle Ages, weakening in the Renaissance. In our times both painting and sculpture have long since left the fold and are totally independent arts. Their union with architecture, when it occurs, is a matter of collaboration on an equal basis, not of meeting predetermined parental requirements. We have reversed the sequence in this book because painting is the art that people have the most questions about today, and because the answers so often apply to sculpture and architecture as well.

9. Rockefeller Center, aerial view. New York City.

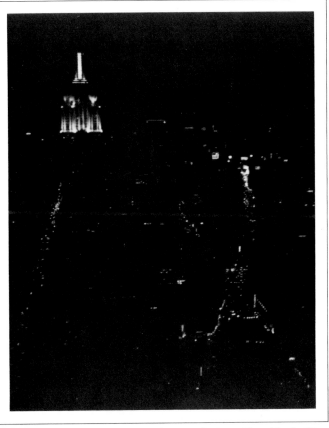

10. Midtown area, night aerial view. New York City.

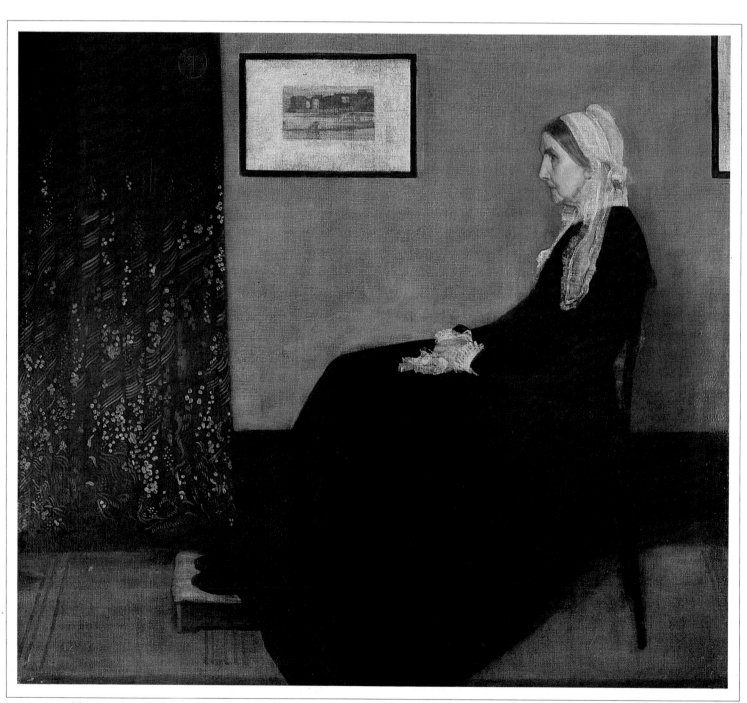

11. James Abbott McNeill Whistler. *Arrangement in Gray and Black, No. 1.* 1871–72. Oil on canvas, 56 by 64 inches. The Louvre, Paris.

Chapter One

WHAT IS A PAINTING?

A painting is a layer of pigments applied to a surface. It is an arrangement of shapes and colors. It is a projection of the personality of the artist who painted it, a statement—or at least a partial statement—of the philosophy of the age that produced it, and it can have meanings beyond anything concerned with the one person who painted it or the one period in which it was created.

For something like fifteen or twenty thousand years—that is, until our century and the revolution called modern art—a painting was also a picture *of* something, whether it was the work of Rembrandt or the sorriest hack alive, even though Rembrandt's painting of, say, an old beggar would be a profound philosophical comment on the human condition, and the hack's would be the tritest kind of picturesque sentimentality. In the nineteenth century, when art exhibitions first became a form of popular entertainment, art's new audience was not up to making that kind of distinction and felt safe enough in enjoying a painting simply as a picture (the words were virtually synonymous) *of* something—a man, a dog, a vase of flowers, the Madonna, a battlefield (in France, preferably Napoleonic), a small boy stealing cookies—and that was that.

To judge the merits of a painting by this standard was a simple affair. A picture was good first to the extent that the objects represented in it "looked real," and second to the extent that the artist's interpretation of the subject conformed to established ideas of what was entertaining (the small boy stealing cookies), or beautiful (the vase of flowers), or uplifting (the Madonna), or simply informative.

We like to think that all that has changed, and to a certain degree it has; but the twentieth century cannot look back smugly on the popular taste of the nineteenth. In spite of our proliferated museum and art education programs, this limited response to painting—not to esthetic qualities but to subjects that in themselves are entertaining, beautiful, uplifting, or informative in the most obvious ways—is not only persistent today but remains dominant outside a relatively limited circle. The American art public since about 1950, after decades of exposure to evangelism for modern art, is no doubt the most sophisticated in the world, yet the only artist to receive front-page headlines two days in a row in *The New York Times* on the occasion of his death was not Picasso but Norman Rockwell.

Norman Rockwell has been without doubt the general public's most beloved painter in the history of American art. Whether offering a humorous subject such as *No Swimming* (**12**), or the piously folksy Thanksgiving scene *Freedom from Want* (**13**), Rockwell's pictures are always easy to read, either as images, which are affectionately commonplace, or as ideas, which are so standard that preconditioned response is automatic. At this level of conception it makes no difference—in truth,

12. Norman Rockwell. *No Swimming.* 1921. Oil on canvas, 24¼ by 24¼ inches. Estate of Norman Rockwell.

13. Norman Rockwell. *Freedom from Want.* 1943. Oil on canvas, 45½ by 35½ inches. Estate of Norman Rockwell.

it is a help—that the expressions on faces are just as posed, as self-consciously assumed, as are the bodily attitudes, and that any stimulation of the imagination, any extension or enlargement of experience, is rigorously avoided.

Pictures of this kind are easily derided—too easily perhaps, in view of one important virtue: they please and art is meant to be enjoyed. The trouble is that enjoyment at their level is nothing more than a stirring up of stock responses to stock subjects, a form of picture enjoyment unrelated to the inexhaustible pleasures offered by exploration of the art of painting—deeper pleasures that can often be discovered beneath popular surface attractions.

Take, as an elementary exercise, a painting that has become so barnacled with Rockwellesque associations that its true character has become obscured—the painting universally but incorrectly known as *Whistler's Mother* (**11**). It comes off very well by the standards we have just mentioned. It "looks real" to such a degree that it suggests soft-focus photography (**14**). Its subject immediately calls into play the double reverence we feel for motherhood and old age. These associations are stirred up even more vigorously because this picture of a mother in her old age was painted by her son, adding filial devotion to the already impressive sum of virtues tied in with the subject. With such admirable connections, *Whistler's Mother* might have found its way into popular favor even if it had been a very bad painting. It happens to be a very fine painting, but *not* because it is a lifelike portrait of an old lady by her son.

The correct title is still the one Whistler gave it and always insisted upon: *Arrangement in Gray and Black.* And the real subject is a mood, a mood compounded of gentleness, dignity, reflection, and resignation. This mood may be suggested by the quiet pose of the old lady, but it is completed by the shapes and colors Whistler chose to use and the relationships he established among them. The disposition of form and color, termed "composition"—that is, the way a picture is put together—can be, as here, the most important single factor in the expressive quality of a painting.

Surely it is obvious that the quiet and tender mood Whistler had in mind could not be relayed through vivid colors and jagged shapes in complex or agitated relationships to one another. Hence the artist reduces the background to a few subtly spaced rectangles of subdued neutral tones, and against this background the figure of the old lady is reduced to a silhouette nearly as geometrical and just as uneventful. The head, the hands, and the scattering of luminous flecks on the curtain serve as relieving accents, lighter in tone and livelier in shape, in a scheme that might otherwise have been monotonous and melancholy.

At the risk of being unfair to an honest and proficient illustrator who never pretended to be more than he was, and in the certainty of offending his enormous public, let us imagine how Norman Rockwell might have gone about painting *Whistler's Mother.* In the first place, the picture would not be an arrangement in gray and black but a lively conglomeration of objects painted in cheerful colors, and the old lady would be *doing* something—not just sitting there. She might be knitting, in which case the immediate associative pictorial response of a kitten playing with a ball of yarn on the floor would be incorporated. A rag rug, affording an opportunity for maximum display of the artist's talent for precisely detailed description, might be included among other homely accessories in the sunny room to show how happy the old lady is in the modest family home where she lives. The pictures on the wall would lose their function as compositional elements and become narrative aids; perhaps the old lady's wedding photograph would be there, with some affectionately humorous pictorial comment on the groom's dandified moustaches. Any possible vestiges of

14. Detail from *Arrangement in Gray and Black.*

15. Jean-Auguste-Dominique Ingres. *Madame Leblanc.* 1823. Oil on canvas, 47 by 36½ inches. The Metropolitan Museum of Art, New York. Wolfe Fund, 1918.

the Whistlerian mood of loneliness and resignation would be removed by the introduction of a small boy or girl—or one of each—peeking into the room from behind the curtain at the left, and the whole thing would be polished off by a pair of granny-type spectacles over which the old lady would beam at her grandchildren. The fact that none of this would have anything much to do with life as it is has everything to do with why a vast audience would love *Rockwell's Mother*.

Why this same public loves *Whistler's Mother* must be explained on another basis. We have said that even if this had been a bad picture, it might have been a popular one. But it would never have become as widely known and loved as it is now, because even people who never doubt that their enjoyment comes from the subject matter of *Whistler's Mother* are being affected, whether they realize it or not, by the expressive composition of *Arrangement in Gray and Black.*

Composition affects our reaction to a picture, regardless of whether we think of it in compositional terms. If the arrangement of shapes and colors is successful, we respond as the artist intended us to, without asking ourselves why. But once we are aware of composition as an element in painting, we have the additional pleasure of discovering how the artist goes about evoking the response he is after. These two pleasures are perfectly compatible. In the same way, we may be moved by a great performance in the theater while simultaneously, quite aside from our emotional participation, we admire the actor's skill.

The structure of a composition can be tested by blocking off different areas with pieces of paper. Effective little pictures-within-pictures may be isolated in this way, but the fragments can never say the same thing as the total of a good composition, not because part of the subject matter is eliminated but because the relationships of shapes and colors have been disturbed. If everything in *Arrangement in Gray and Black* is blocked off except the central figure, you still have a picture of an old lady sitting in a chair. Nothing has been eliminated that tells part of a story or adds to what we know about this particular woman. But the picture's mood is gone. This picture, in fact, suffers in countless cheap reproductions where it is chopped off along the edges for convenience in putting it into a frame or onto a page.

We have said that a painting is a projection of the personality of the artist who painted it, and also a statement—or at least a partial statement—of the philosophy of the age that produced it. We will illustrate these points by comparing four portraits of young women, all of them fine or even great pictures, each of them different.

Ingres's *Madame Leblanc* (**15**) is more easily understood than the others because its intention is less profound. It has, superbly, what is usually expected in a woman's portrait—attractive grace, impeccable technique, and a personable sitter. It tells us nothing more about Madame

16. Detail from *Madame Leblanc.*

Leblanc than that she was a member of the prosperous upper middle class endowed with a pleasant combination of features.

Since it is the work of the most eminent portraitist of his day, we may take for granted that the likeness of Madame Leblanc has the required combination of veracity and flattery that a photographer achieves today by retouching. Madame Leblanc's features were probably less regular than they are shown here (**16**), her neck less elegant, and her fingers not so beautifully tapered. Without question, Ingres has made the most of her good points and minimized her shortcomings. The lady is further beautified by the presence of the exquisitely painted shawl, the jewelry, and the suggestions of fashionable interior decoration, since in a picture all the elements partake of the quality of all the others.

Madame Leblanc's is an utterly charming portrait. Perhaps it can suggest, too, the way of life of a certain class of people during a certain period in France, if we are already familiar with the period (the portrait is dated 1823); but as an interpretation, as an effort to present anything more than an entrancing effigy, it hardly exists, for it makes no attempt to explore the personality of the sitter. At most, we could say that this woman's individuality—her degree of intelligence, her capacity for emotion—has been concealed beneath the painting's exquisite surface in a way comparable to the way she herself perhaps concealed any strong individual characteristics in conformity to a social code of behavior.

Ingres's approach is, of course, a legitimate one in spite of its limitations. The picture has a virtue imperative to all good painting: harmony between what the painter wants to do and the means he uses to do it. Elegance, grace, and refinement disciplined by exquisite drawing and patterned by an artist with a genius for the creation of beautiful line—this is the recipe for an Ingres portrait. Further study could reveal complications and nuances, but essentially this is a picture we can accept at its most apparent values. It is all it appears to be—not much more, nothing less. Compositionally, it is a suave disposition of shapes whose contours have been designed into linear delights, and while this particular effigy is entrancing, it is not exactly an interpretation of the subject since Ingres applied the same formula to virtually all his portraits of women.

But not every picture, not even every portrait of a woman, wants to be or say the same thing. Madame Leblanc must have been delighted. She would certainly have been offended if she had been painted as Renoir painted his wife (**17**). Unlike Madame Leblanc's, this portrait holds deeper meanings beneath the simplicity of its apparent subject. This simplicity is extreme. A round-faced and buxom young woman in a hat and blouse sits facing us, smiling, her hands resting in her lap. That is all. There is no background of landscape, nor of a room, nor even of drapery. The entire image is there for us at a glance, without elaboration or distractions. Its appeal is immediate. It is bright, fresh, and happy.

Still, any number of pictures of young women are bright, fresh, and happy but are not in museums. What does this one have that any bright, fresh, happy magazine cover does not? What makes Renoir a great painter?

He was a fine technician, but so were hundreds of other painters of his generation who could do anything they wanted with a brush except paint great pictures. His life, as a series of events, holds nothing extraordinary. He lived through early struggles to see himself accepted at last as an important artist, but so did many of his contemporaries whose names have been forgotten, whose pictures now seem so dull and pretentious that they have been relegated to museum basements.

It is as simple as this: Renoir is a great painter because he had a joyous adoration of life and the ability to translate it into visual terms so that all of us may understand and share it. Many fortunate men have held the same joyous faith, but few other painters have combined it with Renoir's special gift for expressing it so richly. Other painters are great for entirely different reasons. This particular greatness is Renoir's own.

His art flows from an unwavering conviction of the world's goodness. He sees happiness, in its deepest sense, as the natural state of mankind, and finds it everywhere in the world around him. His art is direct, simple, and profound because it reflects a personal philosophy that was direct, simple, and profound. For Renoir, life was such a miracle that simply to take part in it gave meaning to existence.

His *In the Meadow* (**19**)—we will return to the portrait of his wife in a moment—sums up his joyousness in an especially fresh and delicious painting. The canvas shimmers with color. Everything glows with budding fertility. The grass, the trees, the landscape in the distance, the young girls, even the light and air that permeate the picture—everything blossoms and breathes in the perfection of a spring day. There is nothing unusual about the girls or the meadow where they sit. Renoir's subjects are never unusual. He paints in the conviction that the greatest values in life are, quite naturally, the simplest ones.

For Renoir these values are materialized and concentrated in woman—but not woman as a temptress, not even as an individual, and certainly not as a being with psychological quirks and fancies worth exploring. She is none of these things because she is something more: she is the source of all warmth and life in the world. Children, flowers, and fruit are natural adjuncts of this conception. Renoir's men, when they appear at all, appear as suitors, not with the aggressive force of the conquering male but as gentle idolaters of the female principle. It is this concept of woman as a basic universal symbol that makes the difference between the importance of a Renoir and the triviality of a merely attractive magazine cover, no matter how skillfully the magazine cover may be executed and no matter how successfully it fulfills its limited function.

17. Pierre Auguste Renoir. *Portrait of Madame Renoir.* About 1885. Oil on canvas, 25¾ by 21¼. Philadelphia Museum of Art. W. P. Wilstach Collection.

18. Detail from *Portrait of Madame Renoir.*

19. Pierre Auguste Renoir. *In the Meadow.* About 1890. Oil on canvas, 32 by 25¾ inches. The Metropolitan Museum of Art, New York. Bequest of Samuel A. Lewisohn, 1951.

And so, returning to the *Portrait of Madame Renoir,* the picture has a second and deeper meaning beneath the apparent one, by which it becomes the image of an earth goddess while remaining the tender record of an unexceptional young woman in a straw hat with a couple of roses pinned to it. In other words, the picture's message is universal, expressed in terms of the particular, a recipe for the interpretation of the world that in one variation or another has been effective for more than two thousand years and remains as vigorous as ever.

How does Renoir go about creating this universal symbol?

First, by using his subject as it existed in nature only as a point of departure, and by modifying it to suggest the eternal quality that woman, for him, represents. Artists of all periods, when they hunt for a meaning beneath the transient surfaces of things, have thought in terms of geometrical design. The fundamental nature of a symbol is somehow harmonious with the finality of a simple geometrical form.

Try now to see the *Portrait of Madame Renoir* not as a picture of a young woman but as a structure of strong, solid volumes.

These volumes, these forms, are much simpler than they would have been in a literal reproduction of the model's appearance. As Renoir has drawn them, the face and crown of the hat are combined to describe a solid, regular ovoid form. It is no accident that the hat brim repeats this oval in the opposite direction (**18**). And the mass of the figure, if we follow a line along the shoulders and arms, approximates half an oval or ovoid of the same shape, although it is larger and slightly irregular. The neck is a cylinder, and this same sturdy form is repeated, although not quite so obviously, in the arms.

If such an analysis sounds artificial, it is because the total effect of a work of art is more than the sum of the technical means used to achieve it. The point is that Renoir reduces his subject to large, solid, uncomplicated masses because such forms are suggestive of eternal values.

The danger Renoir runs in modifying the image in this direction is that it may become ponderous and inert. Hence he throws the figure slightly off balance (toward our right). As a kind of grace note, to relieve and accentuate the stability of the main forms, he combines the little bouquet of leaves and roses into a more broken silhouette, although he allows it at the same time to echo the oval forms. Finally he gives full freedom to the curling irregularities of the escaping locks of hair. The sharp V's in the lapels and the neckline of the blouse serve as contrast to the dominating rounded forms. The more the painting is studied in this way, the more apparent it becomes that everything in this deceptively simple composition is planned, and that to change any of it, for instance to make the button much larger or smaller, to change its position, or to make it one of a row of buttons, would put this detail out of its most harmonious relationship to the rest of the picture.

20. Detail from *Woman with Chrysanthemums*.

The image combines stability with a sense of vivid life. Much of this life comes from the rich sparkle of the pigment. The picture would be ruinously transformed if it were repainted with the almost chilly precision that is appropriate to Ingres's *Madame Leblanc* or with the softness of the Whistler. It is difficult to say why Renoir's paint is so alive; it is a matter of "touch"—the despair of the analytical critic, the defeat of the forger, the birthright of the natural painter, and for the observer a direct source of communication with the artist.

As for its reflection of a place and time, the picture is French through and through. Mystical or near-mystical veneration of woman is a constant factor in French art, expressed in forms ranging from medieval statues of the Virgin to allegorical portraits of eighteenth-century courtesans. Renoir is directly in line with this tradition, but he expresses it in terms of his own triumphantly bourgeois century. The nineteenth century placed its faith neither in

21. Edgar Degas. *Woman with Chrysanthemums* (*Madame Hertel*). 1865. Oil on canvas, 29 by 36½ inches. The Metropolitan Museum of Art, New York. Bequest of Mrs. H. O. Havemeyer, 1929, the H. O. Havemeyer Collection.

medieval mysteries nor in eighteenth-century refinements; a faith in the commonplace was basic to its philosophy. So was it to Renoir's. But he lifted the commonplace into the realm of the ideal, and in so doing became a spokesman for the love and respect for simple things that persists at the core of French life.

In discussing the Renoir as if it had achieved a kind of perfection, as indeed it has, we may seem to have left nothing for other portraits of women to achieve. But the glory of the art of painting is that instead of single perfections it offers multitudes of perfections. We will compare the Renoir with a picture by his friend and close contemporary, Edgar Degas, whose *Woman with Chrysanthemums* (21) was painted within a few miles and a few years of the Renoir.

We can imagine what Renoir would have done with the subject. Woman and flowers would have fused into a glowing symbol of bountiful fruition. But such an interpretation was impossible for Degas; he was as doubtful of life's goodness as Renoir was certain of it.

Degas's art reveals him as a man who is essentially a pessimist, who is not certain that he knows the meaning of life, not even certain that one exists. He is a doubter, except on one score: of life's fascination as a continuous, if haphazard, spectacle, he holds no doubt whatsoever. He is absorbed by the look of people, especially women, as they go about their daily affairs. He might be described as a passionate spectator. He is sensitive to human beings as psychological phenomena rather than (as Renoir's women must have seemed to him) as masses of protoplasm.

Like Renoir, Degas is a nineteenth-century Frenchman preoccupied with woman and the commonplace. But he is not the same kind of man as Renoir, and he is going to reflect this subject matter in a contrasting way.

Woman with Chrysanthemums is a brilliantly eccentric composition. Ordinarily the subject of a portrait holds the center of the canvas. Degas pushes this one far to one side. Ordinarily the subject either looks directly at the observer or regards some object within the frame or, at most, looks dreamily into space. This one looks out beyond the picture at something apparently familiar to her but unidentified and tantalizingly unidentifiable to us. The average portrait builds up its brightest colors and strongest contrasts in ways that ensure the subject its rightful climax of interest. But Degas not only gives over the center of this picture to a richly painted explosion of flowers while he crowds his subject against the frame; he also paints the woman in virtual monochrome and allows her to conceal part of her face with one hand (20). By violating all the conventions of portrait composition, he achieves a picture brilliant beyond anything most painters achieve by following them.

Why does Degas compose in this eccentric way? Because where Renoir composed to create an expression of eternal stability, Degas wants us to feel that we have come upon the woman with the chrysanthemums by chance. Where Renoir is enraptured by life in its wholeness, Degas is fascinated by its fragments. He composed the majority of his paintings as if they were segments of larger compositions. Paradoxically, though, the chance effect is meticulously controlled. Degas never falls into the trap of novelty for its own sake. His idiosyncratic compositions are always as sound as they are original, as satisfying as they are provocative.

We saw Renoir rejecting background in the portrait of his wife to enhance the universality of the image. A specific background tends to define place and time, thus reducing the timelessness and everywhereness appropriate to a universal symbol. Naturally Degas, interested in life as a transient spectacle, sharply defines the locale and the moment. In *Woman with Chrysanthemums* we can deduce such specific factors as the social level and financial bracket of the subject, just as we could with *Madame Leblanc.* But we are also aware of the woman as a person capable of thinking and acting in certain ways under certain circumstances.

Yet in the end she remains enigmatic, as Degas surely intended her to be. She half hides a half-smile, which may be half mocking. In her feminine elusiveness she is like another woman, known to us all in the most famous portrait in the world, painted four centuries earlier: Degas's *Woman with Chrysanthemums* is a nineteenth-century *Mona Lisa.*

Leonardo da Vinci's *Mona Lisa* (**22**), like the Renoir and the Degas we have just seen, is only secondarily a representation of the sitter, whose identity and personal relationship with Leonardo have inspired a great deal of romantic speculation. The woman we now call Mona Lisa was in fact the wife of a Florentine businessman, but there is no basis for the legend that the portrait commemorates an unhappy love affair (and even less for the argument, sometimes advanced, that the sitter was a man). None of this is of any real importance, since Mona Lisa, all other considerations aside, is a personality created by Leonardo da Vinci.

Some aspects of a picture that strike us as bizarre have been made bizarre by time. The eyebrows, if not shaved, have disappeared over the years. The hairline is raised far back by plucking or shaving in accord with a fashion of the day. The costume, richly theatrical to us, may also have been modish. As an additional difficulty, the picture has been too famous for too long; it is impossible to see it with a fresh vision. We never see it for the first time; it has always been around. It is no longer a picture; it is an institution.

Absurd legends have become attached to it—even such superstitious ideas as that the eyes "follow you around the room" and that the lips, stared at long enough, "begin to smile." It is unfortunate, too, that the picture has been called the greatest picture in the world. No picture can be

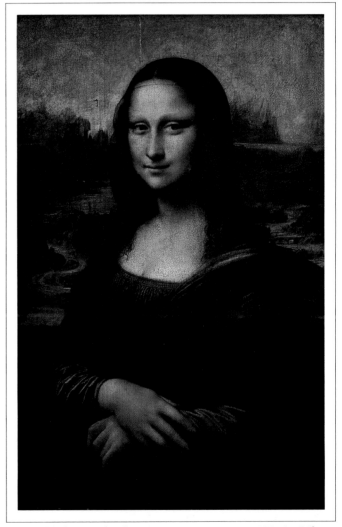

22. Leonardo da Vinci. *Mona Lisa.* 1503–6. Oil on panel, 30½ by 21 inches. The Louvre, Paris.

the greatest in the world because there is no single standard of perfection.

In spite of the obfuscations of legend and overfamiliarity, we can be sure that Leonardo set out to create a serene and timeless image, perhaps concerned with the mysterious origins of life and thought. The landscape background (in contrast with the snug domestic interior of *Woman with Chrysanthemums*) is a geological fantasy in which the works of man—roads and bridges—lead nowhere. And although the woman regards us directly, we know as little about what she is thinking as we do of what Degas's woman is looking at outside the picture. Nor are we supposed to know. *Mona Lisa* defies explanation; it is intentionally mysterious but hides no secret because it is concerned with imponderables.

Such difficulties explain why efforts at interpretation have a way of degenerating into literary maunderings like Walter Pater's notorious one, which has become the standard example of what art criticism should not be:

> She is older than the rocks among which she sits; like the vampire, she has been dead many times, and learned the secrets of the grave; and has been a diver in deep seas, and keeps their fallen days about her; and trafficked for strange webs with Eastern merchants, and, as Leda, was the mother of Helen of Troy, and, as Saint Anne, the mother of Mary; and all this has been to her but as the sound of lyres and flutes, and lives only in the delicacy with which it has moulded the changing lineaments, and has tinged the eyelids and the hands.

Be that as it may, our concern is with the similarities and differences, four centuries removed, between the *Mona Lisa* and the *Woman with Chrysanthemums* as examples of the way pictures reflect the times and places of their creation.

Degas's picture would have been inconceivable to a man of the Italian Renaissance. It would have been intellectual heresy to suggest to Leonardo that a painting like *Woman with Chrysanthemums*, deliberately emphasizing the transient, the casual, and the everyday, could be just as effective in suggesting woman's enigmatic quality as the *Mona Lisa* with all its idealization. Renaissance man sought an ideal, and this ideal was *order*. Leonardo was as fascinated by the world as Degas was, but being a Renaissance man he refused to accept its accidents, its imperfections, its confusion, and its discord. The *Mona Lisa* is purified of all suggestion of the temporary, the haphazard, or the commonplace. The picture exists with such calm that *Woman with Chrysanthemums*, alongside, seems vivacious; and it is so impervious to the moment that the Degas becomes by comparison a comment on life's evanescence.

Oddly enough, it is possible to make some fairly direct parallels between the *Portrait of Madame Renoir* and the *Mona Lisa*. What we have said about the oval of the head in the Renoir, the cylinder of the neck and arms, the mass of the rest of the figure, is applicable to the forms in the *Mona Lisa* too. But instead of Renoir's vigorous image, we have a subtle, almost sly, one. The forms in the Renoir face us directly; they are straightforward, while those in the *Mona Lisa* shift and turn. Leonardo presents us with the face from one angle, turns the body at another, shifts the arms to yet a third in order to return the curious, boneless hands to the same frontal position as the face.

Madame Leblanc, Madame Renoir, Madame Hertel (who posed for *Woman with Chrysanthemums*), and the forgotten Florentine immortalized as Mona Lisa—Ingres could have made any one of these women into a lovely effigy; Renoir, any one of them into an earth goddess; Degas, any one of them into a complete individual within a fragmented world; Leonardo, any one of them into an idealized enigma. The subject of a picture is only a point of departure for whatever the painter wants to say.

Once we have passed beyond the barrier of pure subject, our enjoyment of painting is limited only by our capacity to respond emotionally and intellectually to the infinitely varied expressions of the human spirit offered us in the art of all times and all places. This enjoyment is sometimes weighted on the side of thinking, sometimes on the side of feeling, and the artist works under the same double stimulus.

There is a popular and absurd conception of the "inspired" artist who works in a kind of hypnotic frenzy. His creations gush forth from some hidden reservoir of emotion without any effort on his part, although sometimes with considerable physical agitation followed by dramatic exhaustion. This simply does not happen. Or if it does happen, what gushes forth is formless and chaotic and hence not art.

At the opposite extreme are the few painters who have tried to eliminate all emotional and intuitive factors in an effort to work by pure calculation, even by mathematical formulas. This too is absurd, since even the most intellectualized painting must tie somewhere to the world of feeling, just as the most emotionalized must depend to some extent upon disciplined knowledge.

The words "romantic" and "classic" have so many meanings that we must define the way we will use them in this book: "romantic" will designate works of art that make their first appeal to the emotions or imagination, no matter how much calculation is involved; "classic" will refer to those making their strongest appeal to the intellect, no matter what emotional implications are present. We will look at two paintings comparable in subject (both being mountainous landscapes), the first treated romantically, the second classically—*Scene from Thanatopsis* (**23**), painted in 1850 by an American, Asher B. Durand, and *Mont Sainte-Victoire* (**24**), one of many versions of the subject, painted about 1904 by a Frenchman, Paul Cézanne. Not very long ago it would have been necessary to defend the Cézanne as a work of revolutionary modern art against the familiar

23. Asher Brown Durand. *Scene from Thanatopsis.* 1850. Oil on canvas, 39½ by 61 inches. The Metropolitan Museum of Art, New York. Gift of J. Pierpont Morgan, 1911.

24. Paul Cézanne. *Mont Sainte-Victoire.* 1904–6. Oil on canvas, 28⅞ by 36½ inches. Philadelphia Museum of Art. Purchased by The George W. Elkins Collection.

romantic imagery of *Scene from Thanatopsis*. If the tables are turned today, the important thing still is to remember that we limit our enjoyment if we refuse to tolerate contrasting conceptions and the mutually contradictory esthetic ideas that they entail. Either of these paintings is crippled if we try to force it into the other's category; neither is diminished by a recognition of the other's virtues.

Durand's imaginary landscape was inspired by one of the most admired poems of nineteenth-century America, by his friend William Cullen Bryant. "Thanatopsis" means "a meditation on death," but the poem, far from being gloomy, extols the grandeurs of nature as "thine eternal resting-place," "one mighty sepulchre" in which we may take comfort as members of the "innumerable caravan" of humankind. Durand's picturization of Bryant's "hills rock-ribbed and ancient as the sun,—the vales stretching in pensive quietness between; the venerable woods" reflects the spirit of excitement about the wonders of the American Far West, as new explorations revealed new grandeurs. Nominally, Durand was a member of the Hudson River School, which a generation earlier had been given its name because of its subject matter, stretching from the Hudson into the Adirondacks. But Durand and other "Hudson River" landscapists of his generation abandoned these relatively intimate scenes to celebrate the grandiose panoramas of the Rocky Mountains, where shadowy foregrounds receded into infinite distances studded with crags rising into dramatic lights. The majestic towering of trees, clouds, and mountains was set off by such intimate detail as grazing animals, men on horseback, people going about their little work (**25**). Ruined architecture on rocky peaks or small habitations in sheltering crannies suggested the infiltration of man into nature's vastness but remained diminutive or even spectral in the magnitude of their setting (**26**).

In *Scene from Thanatopsis* Durand is free to assemble all these trappings unfettered by the necessity of approximating the look of any actual view, and the painting becomes a kind of summary of all the devices he and his fellow romantics employed to invest nature with an air of mysterious powers. His imaginary mountains recede in ranges of pinnacles; a river stretches into the distance to culminate in the drama of the sun, hovering in space and illuminating the whole complicated spectacle by its colored light. Detail by detail the picture is explicit, but it does not seek so much to capture an illusion of nature as it does to intensify the awesome sensations we would feel if we could be confronted by the landscape itself.

Romantic landscape was nothing new. There is hardly a device in *Scene from Thanatopsis* that had not already been worn threadbare in European painting, but Durand uses them with all the enthusiasm of an explorer discovering a continent. If this excitement is diluted for us today by ease of travel and overfamiliarity through photographs and motion pictures, we can be all the more thankful that American nineteenth-century paintings have recorded the

25. Detail from *Scene from Thanatopsis*.

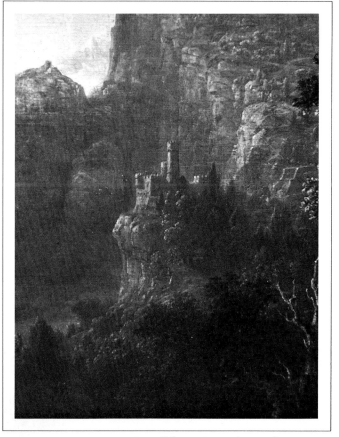

26. Detail from *Scene from Thanatopsis*.

27. Detail from *Mont Sainte-Victoire.*

sense of mystery, wildness, and grandeur that has so diminished during the past hundred years.

But mystery and wildness are exactly the opposite of the qualities Cézanne sought, and achieved, in his *Mont Sainte-Victoire.* Nature's romantic extravagances did not interest him; his first interest was to reveal the underlying clarity and logic that he sensed in the countryside he knew best, the fields and low mountains near his home and studio. If he had been faced by the Rocky Mountains that inspired American painters, this good Frenchman would simply have been appalled at the prospect of putting them into order.

In *Mont Sainte-Victoire* the sky is a curtain bounding the limits of the picture rather than an opening into infinite depth where the eye and the imagination are led and released. We do not wander away or escape from the Cézanne; we remain within its established boundaries, and even within them there is no exploring of nooks and crannies. Cézanne's mountain exists as one large, tangible, firmly integrated mass; Durand's mountains vanish here and there into suggestive shadowy recesses, or rise from them unexpectedly. The world within Cézanne's frame reaches us at first glance in its entirety; we discover Durand's bit by bit, led from detail to detail. Cézanne means his landscape to be complete. Durand means his to be inexhaustible.

Cézanne's subject happens to be an actual place, but he does not reproduce it. And if Durand could have sat beside Cézanne to paint the same scene, he would have found material for a landscape as romantic as Cézanne's is classic, as open as Cézanne's is self-contained. Nature in itself is meaningless; it is only as we interpret it that it has meaning. Durand seeks to open his landscape to the infinite reaches of the imagination. Cézanne seeks to contract his within the comprehension of the intellect. Through the two visions we may respond to both points of view.

Cézanne's art is difficult on first acquaintance. He was a revolutionary as far as technique is concerned, and his quality of order may not be apparent at first glance beneath the equally important vibrance, the quality of sparkling, all-permeating light that pulses from stroke to meticulously calculated stroke in the technique he developed. Nor will this order ever become apparent if the picture is regarded as an effort to imitate the appearance of nature. There is intentionally little expression of depth. The space is kept shallow, and the picture generally is highly abstract—that is, the forms in it tend to lose their identity as real objects and exist for form's sake (**27**). This, too, is the opposite of the Durand, where every form is recognizable in detail and surrounded by a host of associations. Durand regards nature as a manifestation of mysterious forces, while Cézanne regards it as an expression of the essential orderliness upon which the world must depend for its meaning. The basic contrast between the two pictures is between two points of view, romantic and classic.

· · ·

We have been talking so far as if certain general principles, once understood, can make all painting understandable. Happily this is more true than not, but some pictures carry their messages in disguises that must be penetrated individually.

The disguise in Edward Hicks's *The Peaceable Kingdom* (28) is no puzzle to anyone who has a nodding acquaintance with American colonial history and the Old Testament. In the foreground a congregation of animals and children illustrates three verses from the eleventh chapter of Isaiah:

> The wolf also shall dwell with the lamb, and the leopard shall lie down with the kid; and the calf and the young lion and the fatling together; and a little child shall lead them.
> And the cow and the bear shall feed; their young ones shall lie down together: and the lion shall eat straw like the ox.
> And the sucking child shall play on the hole of the asp, and the weaned child shall put his hand on the cockatrice' den.

The Pennsylvania Quaker preacher who painted *The Peaceable Kingdom* has followed these verses to the letter. Like other self-taught painters, he cultivates a meticulous technique. Unlike most of them, he is an inventive designer. He is an artist. If he does not always draw as well as he wishes he could, he never fails as a creator of patterns. The lack of conventional skills accentuates the innate artistry of the man and accounts for the arresting quaintness of his work.

So far the picture is only a biblical illustration invested with an agreeable air of fantasy by a charmingly awkward style. But in the background is a second illustration, William Penn concluding his treaty with the Indians (29). The picture now becomes a political or even sociological allegory. The peaceable kingdom of the Bible is reflected on earth through the concord of the red man and the white, and the Quaker preacher has left for us a confident statement of his belief that peace on earth and good will toward men is a realizable ideal.

It would be foolish to pretend that *The Peaceable Kingdom* rises to great expressive heights. It has charm rather than power; it is pious rather than profound, touching rather than moving. But it does enlarge our experience, as we have said a painting should do, by admitting us to a world of gentle faith that is no less true for being so small and so far away.

If we were ignorant of its historical and biblical references, *The Peaceable Kingdom* would be only a curious representation of animals, children, and men conducting themselves implausibly in a landscape. In this same way virtually everybody misses the significance of Jan van Eyck's double portrait of Giovanni Arnolfini and his wife, Giovanna Cenami (30). Probably not one person in a thousand among the tens of thousands who stop in front

28. Edward Hicks. *The Peaceable Kingdom.* About 1848. Oil on canvas, 17⅛ by 23½ inches. Philadelphia Museum of Art. Bequest of Lisa Norris Elkins.

29. Detail from *The Peaceable Kingdom.*

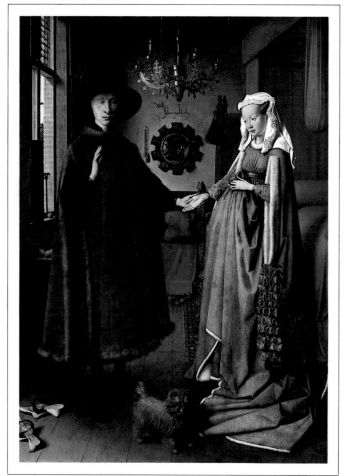

30. Jan van Eyck. *Marriage of Giovanni Arnolfini and Giovanna Cenami.* 1434. Oil on panel, 32¼ by 23½ inches. National Gallery, London.

31. Detail from *Marriage of Giovanni Arnolfini and Giovanna Cenami.*

of it where it hangs in London's National Gallery suspects that its details are anything more than fascinating curiosities.

Even so, it is one of the most compelling pictures in the world. This grave, beautifully costumed couple are such convincing personalities that once we have met them they persist in our memory as real people. We remember their air of consequence and solemnity, although it is odd that they should have chosen to be pictured thus, standing in a bedroom and surrounded by trivia: a little dog (**31**), pieces of fruit scattered on the windowsill, and a pair of wooden sandals discarded on the floor. It is odd that there is only one candle in the chandelier, odd too that it is burning in the daytime, and that the artist has inscribed his name so conspicuously on the back wall (**32**). This last is additionally surprising since at the time the picture was painted, more than five hundred years ago, it was unusual for a painter to sign his work at all.

The fact is that as we stand before this picture we are witnesses at a marriage ceremony. The air of solemnity is explained when we know that the hands are joined in the marriage oath. The painter is not only painter but witness and has inscribed his name on the wall in legal script of the kind proper to a document. And the picture *is* a document, in effect—a marriage certificate. These two fine and serious people first solemnized their own marriage in complete solitude, as was possible under canon law at that time. The picture records the renewal of vows, apparently on the occasion of the wife's pregnancy, and the "trivia" are not trivia at all but symbolic references to the sacramental nature of the scene before us.

The discarded sandals refer to the biblical command, "Put off thy shoes from off thy feet, for the place whereon thou standest is holy ground." This same symbol is used in other pictures, notably Crucifixions, to establish the holy or sacramental nature of the spot, which in this case is the nuptial chamber. The dog symbolizes the marital virtue of faithfulness, the fruit refers to the fruit of the Garden of Eden, and the single candle is a multiple symbol, combining overlapping references to the candle that was carried in wedding processions and the burning candle frequently required at the taking of an oath, which is also the candle as a symbol of the all-seeing eye of God.

The mirror on the wall symbolizes purity. The carved figure on the chair near the bed is Saint Margaret, the patron saint of childbirth. All of these symbols were standard ones, now half-forgotten but familiar five hundred years ago, and their combination within a single picture is too consistent to be coincidental. Their rediscovery in relationship to the subjects of this double portrait changed the *Arnolfini Wedding Picture* from one of the most curious pictures ever painted into a reverent expression of sexual love sanctified by marriage.

No introduction to painting can conclude without some consideration of the way ideas change as to what is good art and what is bad. We will compare two paintings as representative combatants in the pitched battle between modernism and traditional academic painting that has been going on in a mild way indefinitely but has been carried on with greatest violence in our century. While the battle continues, we will select an area where the dust has settled.

Pierre Cot's *The Storm* (33), representing the losers, was a tremendously popular picture well into the twentieth century, dropped to the nadir of critical esteem by mid-century, and recently has made a tentative comeback. It was painted in 1880. Oskar Kokoschka's *The Tempest* (34), painted in 1914, has an opposite history. At that time Kokoschka's art, praised by advanced critics, was still damned as degenerate by the public and by critics who could stretch a point backward to admire pictures like Cot's *Storm*. Today the Kokoschka *Tempest* cannot look very radical to anybody, and even the uninitiated layman would hesitate to damn it although he might be unable to respond with full sympathy. We will examine it first.

There is no actual "tempest" visible. We see a pair of lovers lying in what appears to be a frail barque, encompassed by forms like windy clouds or waves or a nightmarish landscape. The color, dominated by turgid blues and greens, suggests (but does not represent) a stormy sky shot through here and there with light. These swirling colors surround the figures of a watchful man and a sleeping woman, who are intertwined not only with one another but with the surrounding swirls of color as well. As a matter of historical fact, the lovers are identifiable portraits of Kokoschka and a prominent woman with whom at that time he was having an intense and scandalous affair. But the painting is only secondarily a personal document and loses much of its expressive force if regarded only in those terms. From a profound personal experience Kokoschka conceived a symbolical painting, in which specific reference is transmuted into universal statement by means of expressive distortions.

The lovers' bodies are twisted, deformed, and discolored, yet this man and woman are serene in the midst of all the surrounding violence. Whether or not the painter thought of his subject in exactly these terms, the picture says that human love is the sustaining miracle of goodness in the confusion and malevolence of life. The figures are "ugly" because they must participate in life; they are worn by it. They have not escaped from life, they have found a refuge within it.

The theme is an affecting one but could easily turn mawkish. Kokoschka expresses it with a vigor that would be weakened if his lovers were glamorous creatures immune to hardship or ill fortune and the normal difficulties of existence.

Such an unreal and idyllic immunity is suggested by the pretty lovers who flee the storm in Cot's painting. Like Kokoschka's, they are beset by the elements. Both painters express the oneness of the lovers by tying them together with interlacing lines and a billowing, surrounding form (in the Cot, the wind-filled drapery). Both suggest the

32. Detail from *Marriage of Giovanni Arnolfini and Giovanna Cenami.*

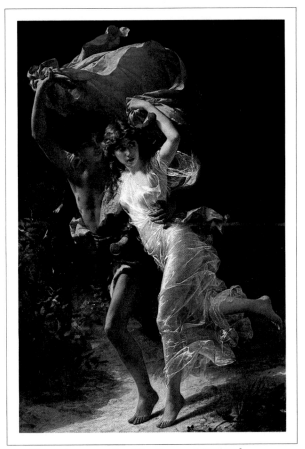

33. Pierre Auguste Cot. *The Storm.* 1880. Oil on canvas, 92¼ by 63¾ inches. The Metropolitan Museum of Art, New York. Bequest of Catharine Lorillard Wolfe, 1887.

34. Oskar Kokoschka. *The Tempest.* 1914. Oil on canvas, 71¼ by 86⅝ inches. Kunstmuseum, Basel.

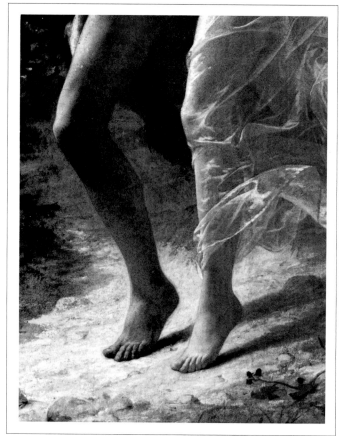

35. Detail from *The Storm.*

relationship of protective male to more fragile female. But beneath these similarities, the differences are extreme.

An important one is that the Cot is specific and detailed in such a way that it becomes an illustration of the plight of one particular pair of lovers, while the Kokoschka is generalized and abstracted. In a more emotionalized way, the Kokoschka is a universal image just as the portrait of Madame Renoir became one when we stopped regarding it as a portrait of a particular woman. Compared with the strength of the Kokoschka, Cot's picture seems today a flossy bit of picturemaking concerned with second-rate values. It is a wondrously slick piece of work, but nothing much goes on beneath this surface of technical display. For all the signposts such as billowing drapery and bodily attitudes pointing out that the figures are supposed to be running, there is no expression of flight. The lovers remain frozen forever on tiptoe (**35**), continuing to suggest models posed in the studio. Kokoschka's figures are integrated with the rest of the picture; Cot's stand in front of a photographer's backdrop. Our attention is constantly urged toward their prettiness, not toward their quality as human beings, and we are asked to admire the rendition of such props as the horn at the boy's belt, the girl's filmy gown, and all the incidental complexities of folds and curls, instead of being given a reason for their being there. These details say nothing except that the painter is skillful in representing them. We are offered a collection of accessories instead of a message.

There is fascination in watching any demonstration of acquired skill, which is why tightrope walkers are able to make a living, but unless the skill is directed toward an expressive or productive end it is only diverting. We are diverted by Cot's *The Storm;* our perception is deepened by Kokoschka's *The Tempest.* The Cot appeals by telling a little story; it is an anecdote. But the Kokoschka is the emotionalized expression of an idea.

Since we have said nothing favorable about *The Storm,* why is it included here? Only as a whipping boy? In that case, why is it given exhibition space in one of the greatest museums in the world?

For one thing, it is an absorbing picture to anybody interested in the history of painting because it is a perfect example of the attitude that dominated public taste, and most critical taste too, for half a century. We have said that one function of painting is to reveal to us what people have thought and felt and believed. If this is important, is it safe to ignore a picture that appealed so strongly to so many people for so long? Museums may set themselves up as arbiters of taste, but they also have a function as visual histories of thought and feeling, which is why the Metropolitan Museum pulled *The Storm* out of storage and gave it a respectable position once more. We do not exclude important villains and incompetents from books of political history just because we don't approve of what they did. The French Academy of Fine Arts, sponsoring a style perfectly represented by Cot, is nowadays regarded as the

villain of nineteenth-century art history for rejecting painters like Cézanne, Manet, Monet, and Renoir in favor of
painters like Cot and others now forgotten.

Aside from giving wall space to paintings like *The
Storm* as historical examples, we should ask ourselves why
a picture so easy to ridicule is so difficult to dismiss. Many
painters successful in their lifetimes, including the great
names of El Greco and Botticelli, have been dismissed by
one century and rediscovered by the next. Recently there
has been an enthusiastic renewal of admiration for a group
of sixteenth-century painters, the Italian mannerists, who
had been regarded with condescension.

If the meaning of a great painting is enriched with
time, while that of a poor one withers away, then *The Storm*
is still afflicted with all the symptoms of inferiority. But
time is a matter of the very long run, allowing for ups and
downs in reevaluations that seem impossible to us at the
moment. In the meanwhile, even "bad" paintings are
interesting as a counterpoint to the ones we call "good."

The most important—and the most disturbing—thing
to remember about *The Storm* is that it was conceived as
a serious work of art in accord with the dictates of the
majority of contemporary critics, teachers, and historians.
We have called the picture flossy and superficial, and
implied that it is silly, but it was not a tongue-in-cheek
product. Cot was making no effort to reduce his art to the
level of the nineteenth-century public that rewarded him
so generously; he was simply in tune with that public. So
far as he was concerned, he represented the most highly
developed esthetic standards of the day, backed up by the
Academy's notion of the progress of art through the centuries. It seems unlikely—impossible—that paintings like
The Storm can ever again be regarded with the seriousness
with which they were conceived, or that Kokoschka's *The
Tempest* will ever again look "degenerate," as it was called
when it appeared. But both paintings make the disturbing
point that it is never safe to leave unquestioned the dictates
of official taste in any age, including our own, when we are
so smug in our dismissal of any art that does not fall into
line with our certainty of our own excellence. Art critics,
on the whole, have a good record as evangelists but a very
poor one as oracles.

36. *Venus of Willendorf.* About 30,000–25,000 B.C. Limestone, height 4⅜ inches. Naturhistorisches Museum, Vienna.

37. Constantin Brancusi. *The Kiss.* 1908. Limestone, height 13 inches. Philadelphia Museum of Art. Louise and Walter Arensberg Collection.

38. Gaston Lachaise. *Standing Woman.* 1932. Bronze, height 88½ inches. The Brooklyn Museum. Frank S. Benson Fund and others.

39. Gaston Lachaise. *Torso.* 1930. Bronze, 11½ by 7 by 2¼ inches. Whitney Museum of American Art, New York.

Chapter Two

SCULPTURE

Much of what we have already said about painting applies as well to sculpture. We were speaking in sculptural terms when we called Renoir's portrait of his wife (**17**) "a structure of strong, solid volumes" appropriate to the concept of "woman as a basic universal symbol." In these terms the pretty young woman in a straw hat with flowers on it becomes a nineteenth-century earth goddess with ancestry dating back about thirty thousand years to a limestone carving not quite 4½ inches high found near Willendorf in lower Austria (**36**).

This fertility image, the oldest sculpture known, is also a structure of strong, solid volumes appropriate to the concept of woman as a universal symbol, in this case a symbol of fertility alone, with none of the tenderness, the personal response, of the Renoir. The parts of the body not associated with pregnancy and maternity are given short shrift; there is no face, and the tiny arms, folded above enormous breasts, are hardly noticeable. Whether or not by accident (but certainly not by the application of any esthetic theory), the grotesquely enlarged parts of the body associated with fertility are conjoined in a monumental composition (monumentality is not a matter of size alone), as if to declare once and for all that solid geometrical forms held in balance will thenceforth be sculpture's primary concern.

To an appreciable degree, the history of sculpture respects this unintentional prophecy; one school of sculptural theory holds firmly to it today, maintaining that "closed form"—the existence of a sculptured object as, essentially, a single solid mass, self-contained—is sculpture's natural province. An extreme example is *The Kiss* (**37**) by Constantin Brancusi, which leaves the original stone block virtually unviolated.

Before going into the opposing concept of "open form," we may see how, some thirty millennia later than the Willendorf carving, the French-American sculptor Gaston Lachaise paid homage to this and other paleolithic fertility images with his sculptures of women in which he idealized the female principle by similar exaggerations, sometimes in standing figures of almost arrogant sexual vitality (**38**) and sometimes in near-abstract forms of torsos that brought his sculpture even closer to Willendorf via the long detour of modern abstraction (**39**). Certainly more beautiful by any conventional standard than their grotesque paleolithic ancestress, these twentieth-century fertility images scarcely rival the sheer power of the Willendorf carving in spite of, or more probably because of, their technical sleekness, their sophisticated application of esthetic laws, and the philosophical eroticism that has taken the place of primitive superstition and magic.

The Willendorf and other paleolithic female figures are called Venuses, a doubly inaccurate sobriquet since that goddess had yet to be born, and because the sculptures

40. Archaic Athenian. *Kouros.* About 615–600 B.C. Marble, height 6 feet. The Metropolitan Museum of Art, New York. Fletcher Fund, 1932.

41. *Kouros.* Back of head.

42. Polykleitos. *Diadoumenos.* Antique replica of original. About 430 B.C. Marble, height 76⅞ inches. National Archaeological Museum, Athens.

are concerned with biological function rather than with ideal beauty. It was not until ancient Greece that the beauty of the human body, male or female, became a primary theme in sculpture, a theme so enduring that the history of sculpture from that time on could be told in terms of it alone. (We would meet limitations during the Middle Ages, but even in those times, when representations of nudity were taboo, exceptions had to be made for Adam and Eve and for the souls rising from their graves at the sound of the last trumpet, for they had to present themselves on Judgment Day as naked as on the day they were born.) The Greek veneration of the beauty of the male body was so profound that the phrase "Greek god" still denotes physical perfection, although Greek sculptures celebrate the beauty of athletes more frequently than that of deities.

Kouros (plural, *kouroi*), a Greek word for "young man," is the title conventionally given to the standing nude male statues of the Archaic period (600–480 B.C.). Kouroi vary considerably in proportions, as if an ideal type were being searched for; but all, like our example (**40**), are compact masses—"closed forms"—that continue to reflect the solid block from which the figure was carved, and all are emphatically geometrical, not only in the general masses of the body but in details such as the hair bound by a fillet (**41**), which is so conventionalized that it would be unrecognizable for what it is if we did not see it in context. Brancusi in our century was consciously working within the pattern of archaic sculptures like this one in *The Kiss.*

The kouros we have illustrated was carved about 600 B.C., early in the Archaic period. By the second half of the fifth century in Greece—the Golden Age—experiments and refinements had yielded a set of ideal proportions based on the normal proportions of an athletically developed body and set down as a canon by the sculptor Polykleitos. His *Diadoumenos* (**42**), an athlete with arms raised to bind his hair with a fillet (preparatory to being crowned with a victor's wreath), is less true to nature than it at first appears; details of musculature that would be strongly defined in an athlete's body are omitted, and those that are included are represented with an eye to design rather than strict adherence to anatomical truth. Some of these patterns had been set by the archaic sculptors. Our kouros and the *Diadoumenos* share several likenesses: eventful passages at the knees in contrast with the smooth volumes of the upper and lower legs; fleshy ridges separating the pelvis and abdomen; a central depression between ridges of muscle beginning at the navel and continuing to the neck; a winglike spread of the pectoral muscles and clavicles. The great difference is between the tense rigidity of the kouros and the grace and relaxation of the later figure—yet both conform to the basic sculptural goal of solid, uncomplicated masses in static balance. The balance in the kouros is as symmetrical as that of a column, while that of the *Diadoumenos* is more subtle, a matter of counterbalances—the outward thrust of the hip that carries the weight of the torso on the strong, straight right leg with the knee joint locked, as opposed to the relaxation of the left, bent at the knee, and the raising of the left shoulder in counterbalance to the thrust of the right hip. From the slight bowing of the head to one side on down through the curving torso and an imagined curving center line shared by the legs, an S-curve has replaced the straight vertical central line that runs from base to top of the kouros.

Approximately twenty-four hundred years later—in 1956–7—the modern Austrian sculptor Fritz Wotruba offered his version of the ancient model in another geometrical bronze, *Figure with Raised Arms* (**43**), where the classical stance of the *Diadoumenos* (and thousands of subsequent statues over the centuries) is reconciled with modern abstraction. (Abstract art, the subject of a later chapter, is art of pure form and color with only secondary reference, or none at all, to the representation of nature.) With its repetition of the simple geometrical solid of the cylinder, *Figure with Raised Arms* is a more obvious balance of formal units than either the kouros or the *Diadoumenos*. But look again. As in the *Diadoumenos*, one leg is straight, the other bent at the knee. The knees, in contrast with the simple cylinders above and below them, are relieving eventful passages; the pelvis and torso are separated by a decisive boundary. We can even find a specific reference to the *Diadoumenos* in that the missing portions of its two raised arms, long ago broken and lost, are reflected in the fragmentary raised arms of the Wotruba.

In terms of modern sculpture the Wotruba is only semi-abstract, especially with a figurative acknowledgment in its title. Forty years earlier Brancusi had already gone a few steps further with his *Torso of a Young Man* (**44**), consisting of three cylinders modifying the natural form of the tree trunk and two branches from which the piece was carved. (Brancusi later repeated it in bronze.) The question as to what has been gained and what has been lost in this passage from ideal realism to abstraction may be better answered if we omit the intermediate steps of the Wotruba and the Brancusi and compare the Greek statues with a totally abstract sculpture, one of David Smith's *Cubi* (**45**), a series of large stainless-steel sculptures burnished to reflect changing lights out of doors, and echoing—it is generally said—the heroic stance of monumental figure sculpture of the past without recognizable derivations of form.

Admitting of no compromise with the human figure, then, the *Cubi* combine volumes in counterplay with one another that must be enjoyed without associative ideas, for the beauty of the material and the balances of form against form alone. The balances are purely esthetic, for while we accept the skeletal and muscular structure of the body as explanation of the formal relationships assumed by a sculpture representing it, there is no explanation as to why some of the elements in the *Cubi* do not tumble to earth—except that we know they are welded together, which is not quite the same thing as being held together by a mechanism of bones and sinews. Possibly we have reached not an affirmation but a refutation of the Venus of Willendorf's proph-

43. Fritz Wotruba. *Figure with Raised Arms.* 1956–57. Bronze, height 75¼ inches. Hirshhorn Museum and Sculpture Garden, Smithsonian Institution, Washington, D.C.

44. Constantin Brancusi. *Torso of a Young Man.* 1922. Maple on stone base, height 19 inches. Philadelphia Museum of Art. Louise and Walter Arensberg Collection.

45. David Smith. *Cubi VII.* 1963. Stainless steel, height 9 feet 3⅜ inches. The Art Institute of Chicago. Grant J. Pick Purchase Fund.

46. Hagesandros, Polydoros, and Athenodoros. *Laocoön and His Two Sons.* First century A.D. Marble, height 96 inches. Vatican Museums, Rome.

47. Greek, early classical. *Battle of Lapiths and Centaurs.* From west pediment of the Temple of Zeus, Olympia. Marble, height of central figure 10 feet 2 inches. Archaeological Museum, Olympia. Photograph by Alison Frantz, Princeton, New Jersey.

ecy that the province of sculpture will be "solid geometrical forms in balance," for that balance presupposes logical responses to the law of gravity, which the *Cubi* often flout.

The refutation of solid, self-contained sculptural form was made, as a matter of fact, in antiquity, with such sculptures as the famous *Laocoön* (**46**), with its separated figures, its writhing serpent, its tortured bodily attitudes, its projections of forms into space, and the penetration of space into the hollows and voids carved in and through the solid marble. All of this is a general denial of the idea of sculpture as a self-contained mass. The group's unity is of a different kind; the various masses are knit together by sinuous lines of action that weave in, out, and around the prolixity of elaborately carved shapes.

Or for closer comparison and even greater contrast between open and closed form, let us compare a single figure, Gianlorenzo Bernini's *David* (**48**), an early seventeenth-century statue, with the other single-figure sculptures we have seen. There is balance here, but it is a balance of action in space rather than of self-contained masses at rest. The torso twists in one direction, the head turns in counterbalance in the opposite direction; instead of the gentle S-curve of the traditional classical stance, we have a spiral, or several spirals interwoven, that can be picked up and followed from any point. More important, it is not only that space interpenetrates the twisting and curling forms of the marble; the psychological focus of the sculpture is outside the sculpture itself. The tension of the figure culminates in the strained features of the face as David looks beyond us at his target, the giant Goliath. Standing in front of the *David*, we are as aware of the giant's existence as if there were another statue in the distance behind us. We have come to the opposite pole from the compact and self-contained Greek ideal to a sculpture that recognizes no strictures in its union with unbounded space.

The psychological attributes of closed and open form should be self-evident. Closed form has to do with finalities, with emotional or philosophical certainties, with clarity, repose, and proven truths. Open form is the natural vehicle for the expression of stress, emotional tension, philosophical contradictions; intensification is more important than clarity, action preferable to repose. Open form allows maximum leeway for exploration, invention, and argument; it presupposes no single, conclusive truth. For these reasons the Polykleitos and the Bernini that we have chosen for comparison are expressions of the times that produced them—the Golden Age of Greece and the intellectually tumultuous aspect of the seventeenth century that we call baroque.

In rebuttal it might be argued that the Greeks were certainly among the most exploratory thinkers of all time, that they, too, were inventive, argumentative, and inspired by a vital curiosity that made ancient Greece the morning of the world. All of this is true, but it does not refute the appropriateness of closed form as the inevitable expression of the Greek ideal—for this ideal was based on the assumption of an ideal clarity and harmony toward which all invention and argument must lead, if not by art, then by science. The contrast between the Golden Age of Greece and what we could call the Age of Turbulence in Europe is demonstrated by the difference between geometry and calculus, between Archimedes and Sir Isaac Newton, between a small world that could be thought of as the center of a finite universe and a large world that, as men of the seventeenth century were learning, is only a mote among astral bodies in infinity.

In our chapter on painting we said that a picture is an expression of its time and also of the personality of the artist who painted it. Sculpture, while emphatically an expression of its time, has been less permissive in its allowance for personal expression. We say "has been" because the twentieth century has liberated sculpture from an old alliance so strong that "sculpture, the handmaiden of architecture" was a popular cliché with nineteenth-century art historians.

Painters have always been relatively free to add a dash of personal flavor to their work, and for the last five hundred years—or nearly six hundred—that flavor has been increas-

48. Gianlorenzo Bernini. *David.* 1623. Marble, height 67 inches. Galleria Borghese, Rome.

49. Assyrian. *Eagle-Headed Winged Being Pollinating the Sacred Tree.* Wall panel from the palace of Ashur-nasir-pal II at Calah, modern Nimrud. 885–860 B.C. Alabaster, 90⅚ by 71⅜ inches. The Metropolitan Museum of Art, New York. Gift of John D. Rockefeller, Jr., 1913.

50. Greek, classical. *Young Horseman.* Fourth century B.C. From Rhodes. Marble, 18 by 12 feet. The Metropolitan Museum of Art, New York. Rogers Fund, 1907.

ingly demanded by patrons and an audience that now thinks of both painting and sculpture in terms of artists' individual personalities, their unique ways of translating the visual world into images. But in Greek temples, Roman forums, or medieval cathedrals, even in Renaissance palaces, it would have been unthinkable for sculptors to have said this is *my* idea of Athena, or *my* idea of Caesar, or *my* idea of Christ, or *my* idea of the King. The various images had to be materializations of *the* idea of each, and the nature of that idea was set by the priests, the clergy, or the rulers. In addition, sculptors often had to work within rigidly set architectural areas, such as pediments, which required utmost ingenuity in the design and placement of figures (**47**).

Primary among these dictates was the degree of relief—the degree of projection of carved forms from the flat surface—permissible as a harmonious adjunct to the forms of the architecture. On the long, flat, unbroken stretches of walls of ancient Assyrian temples and palaces, sculptured decoration was hardly more than carved drawing (**49**), with the edges of the very low relief picked out in sharp linear shadows by the brilliant sun. To have destroyed—psychologically—the solidity of these walls with sculpture in high relief would have been an unthinkable disharmony.

Sculptural relief is traditionally divided into four degrees, and we had best introduce the terms here. They are low relief, of which the Assyrian carving is an example, and for which the French term *bas relief* is frequently used; medium relief, for which the Italian *mezzo rilievo* is usually used, and in which figures and objects are represented at approximately half their true thickness; high relief, or *alto rilievo*, which approaches the full round; and finally, full three-dimensional treatment, in which sculptures are free-standing, even though they may be closely related to architecture in niches or alcoves where they are an integral part of the overall design.

Obviously it is impossible to make these classifications precise, since every degree and fraction of degree between very low relief and free-standing sculpture is met from example to example, including sculptures in which several degrees are interrelated. In a late fourth-century Greek sculpture of a horse and rider illustrated here (**50**), we have everything from very low relief in the rider's foot on the far side of the horse to the full three dimensions of the free-standing foot near us (now missing). Progressively fuller stages of relief correspond to relative distances as forms go from farthest to nearest us. The far hind leg of the horse, for instance, is in low relief but not as low as the rider's far foot behind it, while the hind leg nearer us approaches full relief in a kind of sculptural perspective. All sculptural relief other than the full round is a matter of compression of forms, as if front and back planes were closing in on one another.

Aside from instances where low relief is enforced by architectural circumstances, low relief offers potential for beautiful sculptures where no illusion of fuller form is sought—where the illusion is even avoided in order to capitalize on a special province of low relief, which is the play of linear rhythm and decorative form across a surface rather than into the volume behind it. A relief carved from the living rock of a cave in China about the year A.D. 522 (51) is an exquisite example reflecting the subtleties of Chinese painting of the period, which was very lightly modeled, in the gentle modulations of carved forms. It can be compared with a procession of Athenian maidens from the Parthenon frieze in a later chapter of this book (222), which falls within the area of medium relief.

Medium relief, or *mezzo rilievo*, probably offers the happiest combination of absolute integration with architecture along with sufficient freedom for independent creative expression on the part of the sculptor. And there is no happier demonstration of this union than the Royal Portal on the west façade of the Cathedral at Chartres (52 and 53). The anonymous master who carved the finest of the Old Testament kings, queens, and prophets on this, the main portal of the cathedral, can stand beside the great names of antiquity and the Renaissance. No sculptures, anywhere, are more respectful of the architecture with which they are integrated; each figure, carved on its own block of stone, is a structural as well as a decorative unit in the building. And as if to dispel any suspicion of sculptural independence, each figure in its extreme elongation and the arbitrary verticality of the lines composing it has the character of a column even while it is part of the wall. The figures are superbly designed as architectural sculpture—but something beyond design inspires the heads.

Here a great sculptor has created countenances as noble as any in the history of art (54). With their rich robes and their aristocratic mien, ranged on the jambs of doorways to the cathedral where those who enter must pass beneath their scrutiny, these personages are endowed with all the regality their exalted position demands. Expressions of royal hauteur would be understandable, acceptable, and impressive enough. But instead, the sculptor, not satisfied with so expected an interpretation, has invested the noble faces with a profound compassion prophetic of the divine forgiveness that a Redeemer will bring to the world. No sculptural formula and no model in painting (which sculpture at this time frequently followed) can be credited with this expressive innovation. It is the creation of an artist whose genius found expression without violating the bonds that medieval sculpture accepted in its union with architecture.

Most French Gothic cathedrals were built over such long periods of time that they were begun in one style and completed in a sequence of others. The chronological range at Chartres, partly by reason of rebuilding after two disastrous fires, is unusually wide, from an early eleventh-century crypt to an early sixteenth-century tower. The Royal Portal dates from about 1140–50, when the early medieval period called Romanesque (the eleventh century and most of the twelfth) was evolving into the one called Gothic. The north and south transept portals, fully Gothic,

51. Chinese, Northern Wei dynasty. *The Empress as Donor with Attendants.* From Pin-yang cave, Lungmen, Honan. About A.D. 522. Limestone, 6 feet 9 inches by 9 feet 1 inch. Nelson Gallery–Atkins Museum, Kansas City, Missouri. Nelson Fund.

52. Royal Portal. Cathedral at Chartres. About 1140–50. France.

53. Sculptures on jamb, Royal Portal. Cathedral at Chartres.

54. Head of statue on jamb, Royal Portal. Cathedral at Chartres.

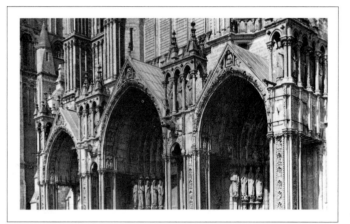

55. South porch. Cathedral at Chartres. Begun about 1200–1215. France.

56. Sculptures, south porch. Cathedral at Chartres.

are larger, deeper, more elaborate (**55**), following the usual course of development of style in all periods from solid and simple to more open and complicated—a course that holds for both architecture and sculpture. The sculptures on the south portal (**56**), about seventy-five years later than those of the Royal Portal, show changes quite in line with those we saw in Greek sculpture from the archaic kouros to the *Diadoumenos*. The later figures are more relaxed; still self-contained, they occupy space more easily; they are more realistic; they gesture freely, turn their heads this way and that. Nevertheless, they do not take full advantage of the flexibility inherent in these changes from the rigidity of the figures on the Royal Portal. Sculpture on the north and south portals is still quite consciously the handmaiden of architecture; the columnar form, even though much modified, is respectfully echoed.

Having already looked at sculpture in the full round, with its attendant variations of open and closed form, we may consider the conventional range from low relief to the full third dimension concluded. But two other forms of relief may be added, one at each end of this range. Even lower than the lowest low reliefs is *rilievo schiacciato* (the translation, "flattened relief," is seldom used), and we are going to suggest, somewhat hesitantly, and for purposes of argument, that there is a valid case for sculpture that goes beyond the familiar third dimension of full relief into the highly theoretical one called the fourth.

Rilievo schiacciato, invented by the Italian Renaissance sculptor Donatello, barely rises above the flat plane of two dimensions and is possibly even closer to drawing than it is to sculpture. In Donatello's marble panel *Saint George and the Dragon* (**57**), the relief of the arcade behind the princess is so delicately indicated that it is as much drawn as carved in linear perspective. Yet its definition is vigorous and specific in contrast with that of the *schiacciato* landscape in the distance, a mere veil of relief in which the marble seems to dissolve in an atmospheric mist. This beautiful form of relief—something like painting with a chisel and abrasive—is seldom employed for the double reason that it is difficult in its extreme subtlety, and because it needs a raking light at the proper angle to reveal it. In a direct light it can be literally invisible.

The fourth dimension? That one isn't easy. This dimension, or space-time, is a concept of modern physics that demands strained rationalizations when applied to art. The concept denies the Newtonian premise that space and time are independent realities (which all of us accept as an obvious fact of existence without wondering about theory) and proposes instead that space and time are indissolubly united. If that is true (some artists have argued), then we should be able to see all sides of an object at once, instead of sequentially as we move around an object in time. This idea has taken the form of cubism in painting, as we will see in a later chapter (**170**). In the meanwhile, is there such a thing, can there be such a thing, as a sculpture of which we can see all sides simultaneously?

Hardly. But the Italian sculptor Umberto Boccioni, leader of the movement called futurism, was working with some such idea in 1913 in his *Unique Forms of Continuity in Space* (58), with which he tried to illustrate in bronze his contention that no forms are finite: "No one can any longer believe that an object ends where another begins." Boccioni wanted to "break open the figure and enclose the environment within it." He demanded "absolute and complete abolition of definite lines and closed sculpture." We have seen that these ideas about open form and the interpenetration of sculpture and environment had been pretty well anticipated three hundred years earlier in sculptures like Bernini's *David*, but Boccioni also insisted that "objects never have finite ends, and they intersect with infinite combinations of sympathetic harmonies and clashing aversions." It was in this vital difference from the simpler idea of interpenetration of solids and voids—a sculpture and "the environment around it"—that Boccioni met his defeat, for his gleaming bronze *Unique Forms of Continuity in Space*, no matter what the theory behind it, remains a very solid and finite object—more so, even, than Bernini's marble. The fact that Boccioni's handsome, rushing figure also bears a strong, if coincidental, resemblance to the *Nike of Samothrace* (59), popularly known as the *Winged Victory*,

57. Donatello. *Saint George and the Dragon*. Relief below statue of Saint George. About 1415–16. Marble, 15⅜ by 47¼ inches. Orsanmichele, Florence.

58. Umberto Boccioni. *Unique Forms of Continuity in Space*. 1913. Bronze (cast 1931), height 43⅞ inches. The Museum of Modern Art, New York. Lillie P. Blixx Bequest.

59. Greek, Hellenistic. *Nike of Samothrace*. About 190 B.C. Marble, height 96 inches. The Louvre, Paris.

60. Naum Gabo. *Linear Construction, Variation.* 1942–43. Plastic and nylon thread, 24½ by 24½ inches. The Phillips Collection, Washington, D.C.

61. Alexander Calder. *Little Spider.* About 1940. Metal, painted, 55 by 50 inches. Courtesy Perls Galleries, New York.

and carved about the year 190 B.C., has also tended to take the edge off the modernity of *Unique Forms of Continuity in Space.*

It is difficult to see how any bronze object can be anything but finite by physical definition. Like the other traditional materials of sculpture, bronze stubbornly insists upon occupying space. The nearest thing to working with materials that do *not* occupy (or displace might be a better word) space, is to work with any that are transparent, as Naum Gabo does with clear plastic and nylon thread in *Linear Construction, Variation* (**60**). Made in 1943, this is one of numerous Gabos confirming a manifesto issued by the sculptor in 1920, in which he said: "We deny volume as the expression of space . . . we reject physical mass as a plastic element . . . a sculptural element, a material substance." It may still be necessary to walk around Gabo's "linear constructions" to get all views, but from any single view we do see intersecting spatial volumes—an approach, at least, to something like the fourth dimension, space-time, in static sculpture.

Kinetic sculpture, sculpture that moves, often approximates a space-time concept. Alexander Calder's mobiles (**61**), familiar to everybody today, with their component parts floating and turning in space in response to air currents, assuming new relationships between themselves and space around them as the lighter parts move more swiftly, the heavier ones more slowly, shifting and changing—these mobiles are indeed "unique forms of continuity in space," a description that fits them more accurately than it does Boccioni's bronze.

Calder designed his mobiles to be activated by natural air currents with consequent variations in speed. There is something very pleasant about the idea of this union between a force of nature and a piece of engineered sculpture, even though many of the mobiles set up in museums and other public buildings are animated by concealed fans. Other artists interested in mobile sculpture have depended on motorization in the first place. A pioneer in the field, and a highly influential theorist, László Moholy-Nagy, published a manifesto, *System of Dynamo-Constructive Forces,* in 1922, and included light among the sculptor's structural materials. To demonstrate the principle, he built his *Lichtrequisit,* a steel-and-plastic rotating construction from within which 140 electric light bulbs threw changing images and colors onto the walls around it.

Among motorized sculptures today, Nicholas Schöffer's "spatiodynamic" constructions, one of his many experimental forms, have as their declared aim "the constructed and dynamic integration of space into plastic work." A Schöffer motorized sculpture virtually dissolves when set in motion; its solid forms describe ethereal planes and volumes that we perceive in terms of flickering lights as they merge, interpenetrate, and emerge again, with no single aspect of the sculpture that can be thought of as its typical one—until a photograph freezes the action and thus belies the evanescent space-time relationships (**62**).

62. Nicholas Schöffer. *Microtemps 22.* Motorized sculpture, static and in action. 1966. Metals, approximately 35½ by 24 inches. Courtesy Galerie Denise René, Paris.

· · ·

There is surely something more significant than co-incidence in the fact that Gabo's and Schöffer's sculptures, striving for expression of a twentieth-century scientific and esthetic concept, are created in materials and by means peculiar to the century. (Schöffer has experimented with sculptures that are set in motion by reactions to sound and light, and has also designed computer-directed kinetic sculpture.) The revolution of modern art, initiated by painting, has changed the look—and definition—of sculpture more than that of any other art, largely because of the variety of materials that have become accepted as legitimate sculptural means. In addition to adapting the wide range of synthetic substances originally developed for commercial uses, sculptors now work in literally any material that may appeal to them, from junk machine parts to chewing gum.

But sculpture's heroic materials remain the traditional ones—stone, bronze, and wood (in special instances, terra cotta). None of them can be called neglected today in spite of the excitement over innovation and experiment. We will see that the painters' various mediums are reflected in the esthetic character of their work, but paint mediums are much less insistent in their demands on the artist than are the materials of sculpture. Paint is paint, easily manipulable, even submissive in the hands of a skilled artist, his means to an end. But the sculptor must admit stone, bronze, and wood, or the minor materials such as precious metals, ivory, and gems, to partnership in the creative act. They

63. German. Book cover, *Mondsee Gospels*. Late eleventh century. Silver, ivory, and rock crystal on gold ground, approximately 11 by 8 inches. The Walters Art Gallery, Baltimore, Maryland.

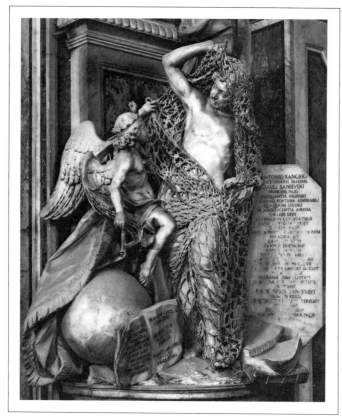

64. Francesco Queirolo. *Allegory of Deception*. Mid-eighteenth century. Marble, life size. Santa Maria della Pietà dei Sangro, Naples.

dictate how he may and may not employ them to best effect; they stay his hand, where the painter's hand is free to improvise. Marble, granite, limestone, sandstone, onyx, the dark Abyssinian marble called basalt, or the pure crystalline white marble of Carrara—each has its own potential and its own limitations in terms of grain, color, hardness, or softness, that must determine the sculptor's approach. Woods have their own textures, grains, and colors, almost as various as those of stones.

Ivory, a special case, combines workability, durability, and extremely fine texture that allows for precision in detail along with the warm white color in which that detail tells best. The gigantic statue of Athena in the Parthenon, long lost, was made of gold and innumerable pieces of finely joined ivory, but such sculptures were exceptions; part of ivory's charm is its adaptability to miniature scale. In medieval Europe, ivory was so precious as to rival gems, and carvings were set like jewels in small shrines, liturgical articles, and other religious objects where sumptuousness was a mark of devotion. The late eleventh-century Gospel book we are using as an example (63) is studded with miniature ivories of the four Evangelists, each, like the one of Saint Matthew shown here at full size, only 2⅞ by 1¾ inches (65). They surround a large cabochon crystal covering a drawing of the Crucifixion in gold.

The sculptor who ignores or violates the special character that his materials offer him in partnership is lost. A notorious example of the prostitution of material to the display of technical elaboration is Francesco Queirolo's *Allegory of Deception* (64), in which marble, the noblest of stones, is subjected to one indignity after another in the course of this eighteenth-century Italian sculptor's unintentional revelation of himself as a skilled artisan with no imagination, rather than a creative artist.

The one traditional material employed in monumental sculpture since antiquity that can be called flexible is bronze. It is "flexible" because the sculptor does not create in that obdurate material but casts in it, reproducing sculpture modeled in wax or clay, malleable substances that are literally sensitive to a personal touch, that are easy to change or correct, immediately responsive to the sculptor's intention, and versatile in the forms they are willing to assume under his manipulation. The special qualities of bronze, ranging from strength in the most delicate detail to the sleekest of surfaces—surfaces like those in the Lachaise and the Boccioni that we have seen—may be kept in mind while the sculptor works in clay or wax, and these qualities may be introduced or emphasized by the polishing, trimming, and sometimes addition of detail that the bronze receives after casting. Yet up into the nineteenth century large bronzes were conceived essentially in terms of carved sculptures. It was not until the late nineteenth century that the malleability of clay and wax, the direct touch of the sculptor, his personal impress, became a goal for reproduction in bronze.

Rodin's *The Age of Bronze* (66), compared with two

65. *Saint Matthew.* Miniature from cover of *Mondsee Gospels.* Ivory, 2⅞ by 1¾ inches. The Walters Art Gallery, Baltimore, Maryland.

66. Auguste Rodin. *The Age of Bronze.* 1876. Bronze, height 71 inches. The Minneapolis Institute of Arts. John R. Van Derlip Fund.

other realistic male nudes, the *Diadoumenos* and Bernini's *David,* is startlingly lifelike, so much so that it was attacked by French critics, who accused Rodin of having cast it from the model, a well-muscled and beautifully proportioned young soldier who was given leave from his company to pose for the sculptor. It is true that Rodin tried to reproduce the perfect body accurately, convinced that perfection in nature could not be improved by idealization in the studio. Yet the extraordinary effect of life comes not from accurate reference to reality, but from the feeling of suppleness in the rippling contours of muscular structure set off by the lustrous surface of bronze, a surface modeled with the sensitivity of the hand added to the perception of the eye. Possibly our knowledge that bronze enters the mold in a molten state has something to do with our feeling that this material, which is actually dry and hard, is sympathetic to the representation of a moist and flexible living body.

67. Auguste Rodin. *Colossal Head of Balzac.* 1897. Bronze, height 20 inches. Rodin Museum, Philadelphia.

The genius of Rodin's hands in contact with clay could respond to the sensuousness of a body, to the tenderness of a subject where tenderness was appropriate, and above all to the vigor of a personality as strong as his own. There is hardly a passage in his *Colossal Head of Balzac* (**67**) that conforms to actuality as does *The Age of Bronze;* the clay has been gouged, pushed, built up, pressed into ridges, smoothed flat with the thumb, manipulated in every fashion, always for purposes of expression, never imitation. In his early studies for a monument to Balzac, Rodin worked from a model who resembled photographs of the author. But after dozens of studies over some five or six years, the features had become only the raw material for a visionary conception of the man who wrote *La Comédie Humaine,* a man whose overwhelming creative energy paralleled Rodin's own. Originally Rodin had planned the monument as a gigantic nude with a thick, powerful body, but in the final version the head surmounts a vast all-encompassing cloak that swathes the figure from chin to toe (**68**). The two sides of Rodin's nature—everyone's nature, for that matter—are allegorized in the sensuous response to physical beauty in *The Age of Bronze* with its naked body, and the intellectual speculation upon the human condition in the bodiless *Colossal Head.*

The excitement that has greeted modern art in this century, expressing itself in applause, catcalls, and puzzled silence, was occasioned first by painting; but the transformation of sculpture was more extreme than that of any of the other arts. It was so extreme that we mean one thing when we say "sculpture" in the context of the thirty thousand years stretching between the *Venus of Willendorf* and Rodin, and another when we say "sculpture" in the context of the twentieth century. Objects now classified as sculpture are frequently neither modeled nor carved, but are glued or nailed or welded into a sculptural unit from odds and ends of material picked up here and there, with junked machine parts among the most popular. These sculptural "assemblages"—pronounced in the French fashion to rhyme with "collage"—have suffered drastically from their popularity with amateurs possessed of home welding kits and no acquaintance with design. In proper hands, the transfiguration of such material may take on the heroic stature of David Smith's sculptures, made from heavy machine parts, metal plates, and sometimes his own additions in forged iron (**69**). On a smaller scale, the ingenious forms of Richard Stankiewicz's sculpture revitalize scrap iron (**70**).

Individual bits of scrap metal or other industrial detritus of interesting shapes are sometimes mounted alone as "found objects" and can have an undeniable but rather tricky effectiveness, just as pieces of driftwood found on beaches may be mounted to set off their interesting shapes without modification. The found object has its art-historical ancestor in the "ready-mades" of Marcel Duchamp, the iconoclast of modern art who, by violating and mocking all

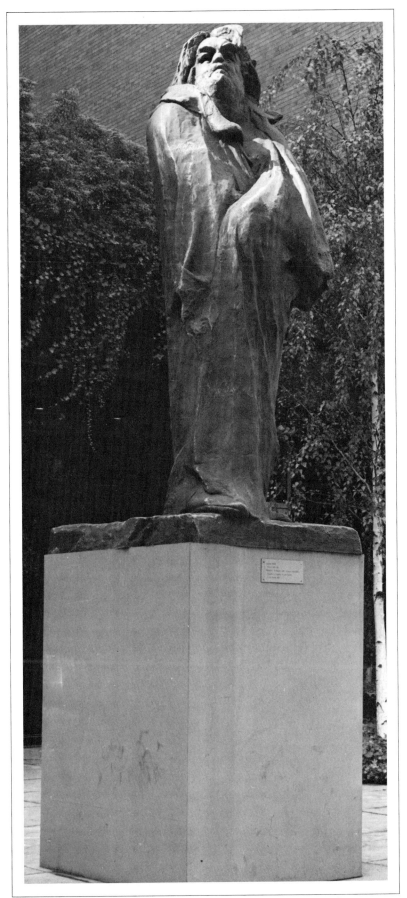

68. Auguste Rodin. *Balzac.* 1893–97 (cast 1954). Bronze, 8 feet 10 inches. The Museum of Modern Art, New York. Presented in memory of Curt Valentin by his friends.

69. David Smith. *Volton XV.* 1963. Steel, rusted, height 75 inches. Estate of David Smith, courtesy M. Knoedler & Co., Inc., New York.

70. Richard Stankiewicz. *Construction.* 1957. Welded iron and steel, 12½ by 13¼ by 8⅝ inches. The Museum of Modern Art, New York. Philip Johnson Fund.

71. Photograph of bottle rack ("ready-made" sculpture) included in valise with other photographs, replicas, and color reproductions of works by Marcel Duchamp. The Museum of Modern Art, New York. James Thrall Soby Fund.

traditional art values, helped to clear our eyes of habitual ways of seeing and our responses from habitual ways of feeling. An ordinary bottle rack (**71**), when we see it displayed in a museum as sculpture, becomes an arrestingly designed object. It was not Duchamp's purpose, however, to increase our sensitivity to the interest or beauty of ordinary objects, but only to deflate the pretensions of the pundits who had dictated taste during the nineteenth and into the twentieth century. "Dada," the movement in which such deflations were promulgated during the débâcle of World War I, was an anti-art art movement that soon died but left Duchamp as its vital symbol and occasional practitioner until his death in 1968. Impertinence was a major weapon in Dada, and if the example of the bottle rack is not strong enough, there is the primary example of a urinal that Duchamp exhibited under the title *Fountain*.

We will see other departures from sculptural tradition as this book goes on. For the time being, we might point out that our drastic change of ideas about what sculpture is and what makes it interesting is tied up with the dominant single element of our civilization—the machine.

Today, with our responses to machines toughened by the prolixity of forms from dishwashers to spaceships, it is difficult to imagine the degree of fascination machines held for the public a hundred years ago. In the great international exhibitions—world fairs—of the end of the nineteenth century in Europe and America, the halls where machines were displayed were the most sensational. In 1889, celebrating the centenary of the French Revolution, Paris held the largest of these exhibitions, but its machine exhibit had had a precursor in Machinery Hall in Philadelphia, where the Centennial Exhibition of 1876 celebrated the signing of the Declaration of Independence. The Centennial halls dedicated to art were crowded with visitors self-consciously absorbing culture (**73**); but in Machinery Hall (**72**) the excitement was genuine and spontaneous, a contrast exemplified by one of the most popular sculptures, *La Première Pose* (**75**), and one of the most amazing machines, the I. P. Morris Blast Engine (**74**).

La Première Pose—a marble by Howard Roberts, a Philadelphian who had studied in Paris—capitalized on the disguised lubricity of a subject dear to the French since the eighteenth century, a young woman posing nude for the first time in an artist's studio, which combined the pleasures of genteel voyeurism and artistic connoisseurship. The carving of the fringe and embroidery on the fabric draped on the model stand was as widely admired as the slick forms of the body, and in the minds of the day both were sanctified by the classical tradition.

But there was no tradition to explain the logical yet fantastic new forms in Machinery Hall. It could not have occurred to the crowds who were amazed by the blast engine (which could deliver 10,000 cubic feet of air a minute to a steel-making furnace) that the machines they admired for their sheer size and power would one day be cited by twentieth-century art historians as harbingers of an esthetic

72. General view of south nave of Machinery Hall, Centennial Exposition, Philadelphia, 1876 (Krupp cannons in foreground). Wood engraving from Frank Leslie's *Historical Register of the U.S. Centennial Exposition,*" published 1877.

73. A view of people at the arts exhibit, Centennial Exposition, Philadelphia, 1876. Engraving from McCabe, *Illustrated History of the Centennial Exposition,* 1877.

74. I. P. Morris blast engine. Wood engraving from J. S. Ingram, *The Centennial Exposition* (Philadelphia, 1876).

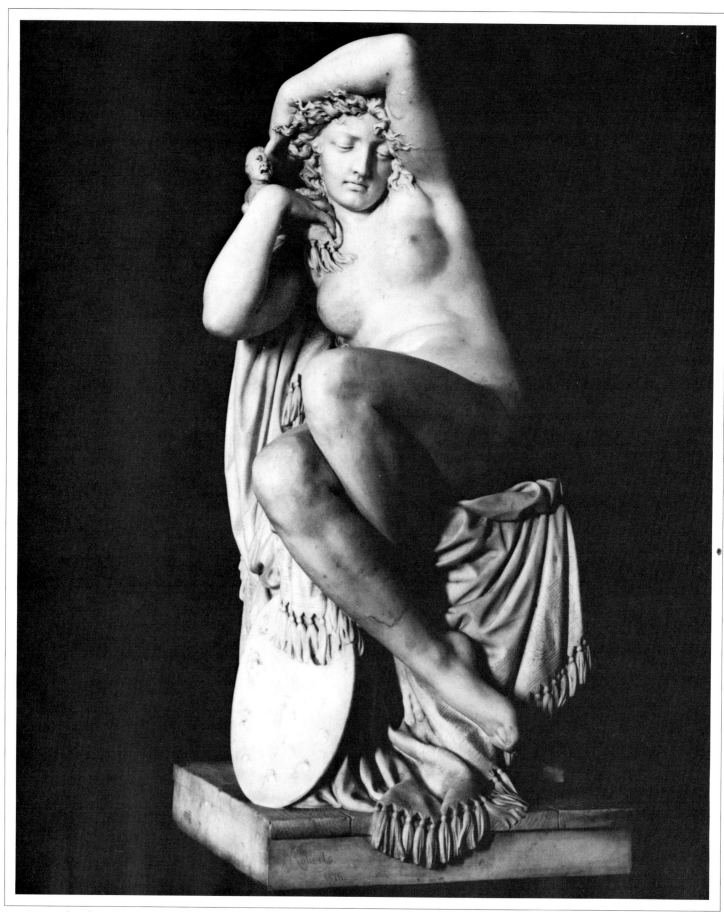

75. Howard Roberts. *La Première Pose.* 1875–76. Marble, life size. Philadelphia Museum of Art. Given by Mrs. Howard Roberts.

revolution—a revolution that would annihilate the values they had been taught to hold most dear in sculptures like *La Première Pose*. But today, the few antiquated nineteenth-century machines that have survived (mostly in science museums) seem to art historians to be the ancestors not only of modern machines that have become more sleek, more powerful, and in a way more impersonal and hence less interesting, but also to hold the genes that produced a varied school of modern sculpture. We have seen examples by David Smith and Richard Stankiewicz, in which the primitive heaviness and varied shapes of discarded machine parts were recognized as elements of a new sculptural esthetic, and by Alexander Calder, himself an engineer turned sculptor, whose mobiles, shifting and floating in the air, are machines etherealized.

The sources of modern sculpture are infinitely varied throughout the history of art; we have already compared the oldest sculpture known, the *Venus of Willendorf,* with the female nudes of a twentieth-century master, Gaston Lachaise. We can also compare that ancient so-called Venus with the first work of art shown in this book, Jean Dubuffet's *Nourrice Profuse* (**1**), to which we promised to return.

Nourrice is French for "wet nurse," a woman hired to suckle another's child. *Profuse* being self-explanatory, this lump of slag iron becomes a multi-breasted fertility image in a special way connected with *art brut*. The term, invented by Dubuffet, can best be translated as "art in the raw," and applies to his theory that such sources as the drawings of very young children, psychotics, the insane, and the per- petrators of graffiti on public walls are more vigorous and closer to art's most expressive sources than are all the rules and refinements that artists have developed and observed over the centuries. Extending the "raw" idea to materials, Dubuffet on occasion has used cinders and ashes for paints, just as, in *Nourrice Profuse* and a series of sculptures on the same order, he finds sculptural qualities in slag iron.

But *Nourrice Profuse* has another connection with the past that makes it a hypersophisticated transformation of "art in the raw" into art as a witty historical comment. Among the most curious sculptures from antiquity is the multi-breasted *Artemis of Ephesus* (**76**), a bronze and ala- baster Roman copy of a Hellenistic cult figure whose confused attributes include her position as goddess of wild animals. Thus the ancestry of *Nourrice Profuse,* stretching from prehistory through antiquity to our century, becomes one instance among innumerable others (although not often so eccentric) of the ramifications that make an acquaintance with art history inexhaustibly rewarding.

76. *Artemis of Ephesus.* Roman copy of Hellenistic ori- ginal. Bronze and alabaster. Museo Nazionale, Naples.

77. John Russell Pope. Jefferson Memorial. Dedicated 1943. White marble. East Potomac Park, Washington, D.C.

78. Stonehenge. About 2000 B.C. Height 13 feet 6 inches. Salisbury Plain, England.

Chapter Three

ARCHITECTURE

All the arts—including poetry, music, and any others not discussed in this book—satisfy needs of the spirit and offer exercises for the intellect. Of them all, architecture alone is called upon to satisfy practical demands as well.

A building may satisfy practical demands without regard for esthetic effect. As instances, there are factories, warehouses, and hundreds of other modern buildings that unfortunately offer nothing more than adaptable space and protection from the weather for machines, stored goods, or office workers, although the same practical demands could have been—and in some instances have been—satisfied in ways that also offer esthetic pleasure.

At the opposite pole is the architectural monument subject to no practical demands at all, unless, as in the case of the Jefferson Memorial in Washington (**77**), the protection of the statue of a great man from the weather can be called a practical function. The Jefferson Memorial is the direct descendant of a long and aristocratic line of shrines to gods, heroes, kings, savants, and politicians. And in the broadest possible historical view it is even a descendant of another circular temple, the grandest prehistoric structure in existence, Stonehenge (**78**), built about four thousand years ago on Salisbury Plain in England.

The megaliths of Stonehenge were quarried (with who knows what primitive tools?) about twenty-five miles from the site and, weighing up to 50 tons each, were dragged (by what primitive means? perhaps rolled on enormous logs?) and erected as supports for the megalithic lintels that were somehow (here the imagination fails) lifted into place. Geometry, the mother science of architecture, was united with astronomical observations by which the great stones were spaced in such a way that at sunrise on the summer solstice the first rays of light cut through to an altar, the celestial cue for the performance of the rites of spring.

Compared with the primitive majesty of Stonehenge, the classical forms of the Jefferson Memorial in Washington may seem a bit threadbare, anemic, and chilly. The monument was not well received by critics when it was dedicated in 1943. But there were arguments to justify its design. It is companion to another monument in classical style, the Lincoln Memorial, and Thomas Jefferson himself was not only a classical scholar in the eighteenth-century mode but an architect, who designed the University of Virginia in Charlottesville and the Virginia state capitol in Richmond as adaptations of monuments of classical antiquity.

Are there any standards flexible enough to help us understand and enjoy an art that has as many facets as the history of mankind? Between the extremes of the practical functional building and the decorative monument, the story of architecture includes every degree of interrelationship, each affecting the other, one sometimes supporting the other, sometimes demanding a compromise, as in every successful partnership. Thus, the first questions we will ask in evaluating some buildings selected as examples will be: How well does the building satisfy the demands of its function? and, How satisfying is it esthetically? Ideally, the union should be so harmonious as to be indivisible.

Indivisible, too, in the esthetic success or failure of a building, are the uses made of materials and the integration of design and site. An exceptionally dramatic example is the famous residence in Bear Run, Pennsylvania, designed by Frank Lloyd Wright, Falling Water (**79**), where cantilevered porches spring out over the natural stone ledges of the ravine site with its waterfall, while behind them the less conspicuous portion of the house, with thick walls of native stone rising from the raw stone itself, seems to have grown from the site rather than to have been built upon it.

Less spectacular and for that reason perhaps esthetically more satisfying in the long run, Taliesin East (**80**), one of Wright's own studio-residences, is a rambling structure designed to echo the long, low lines of the countryside around it. The structural materials are native stone and natural wood. With flagstone terraces continuing without a break as indoor floors, and with large areas where glass screens from floor to roof are the only division between indoors and out, house and site are perfectly mated.

Finally, and perhaps most rewarding for us as heirs of the past and witnesses of the present, architecture is not only an expression of the age that produced it, as are the other arts, but is probably the most dependable of those expressions. Because it is the least personal and the most sociological of the arts, architecture is the likeliest to give us the most unbiased and most complete reflection of the age it served.

So, in summary, our bases for the judgment of architecture in this book will be:

> *Functional efficiency.* How well does the building work?
> *Esthetic quality.* Is it good to look at?
> *Materials and site.* Is the most made of their potentials?
> *Humanistic record.* Does acquaintance with the building clarify, intensify, or enlarge our experience through its character as an expression of its time?

These bases can apply whether we are looking at a Greek temple or a Roman bath; a medieval cathedral or a Renaissance church; a nineteenth-century opera house or the Brooklyn Bridge; a radically modern structure that opened in Paris in 1977, the Pompidou Center, or a primitive tribal shelter in New Guinea, which is where we will begin.

There is no word for "architecture" or "architect" in the vocabularies of the builders of the men's ceremonial houses in New Guinea—we show here the framework of one under construction (**81**) and the interior of another (**82**)—yet these soaring structures could hardly have been bettered if the most sophisticated architects at work today

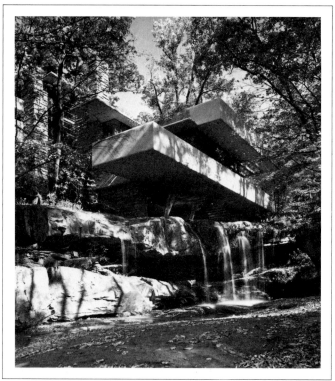

79. Frank Lloyd Wright. Kaufmann House ("Falling Water"). 1936. Bear Run, Pennsylvania.

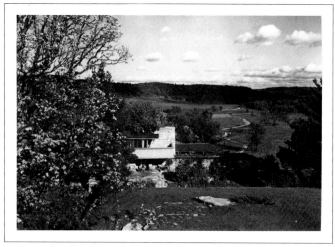

80. Frank Lloyd Wright. Taliesen East. 1925. Spring Green, Wisconsin.

had been set down in the forest and commissioned to design shelters for the specific function served by these houses, and to build them from the only available materials, those at hand in the forest.

The ceremonial houses are meeting places for the men of the tribe, where pubescent boys are secluded for a period of instruction before initiation into manhood. Any crude, low-roofed structure of sufficient size would satisfy the demands of space and seclusion, but it would not express the significance of mysteries central to the life of these people, or the importance of the rituals by which tribal secrets are transmitted from generation to generation. It is only coincidence that the pointed form made by joined bamboo poles resembles the vault of a Gothic cathedral, and that the interior is divided into a nave and side aisles, but the coincidence is at least appropriate, for in each case it is associated with the performance of rituals basic to the spiritual existence of a people. And if we marvel at the use of stone in cathedral vaults, we may also admire the ingenuity with which poles of bamboo (in that part of the world growing to a height of as much as 80 feet) serve as the exposed ribs for a covering of thatch. The beauty of the taut, energetic curve of the bamboo arch is the natural result of the plant's inherent strength and flexibility. By the standards we have set, the men's ceremonial houses are architecture of a high order: they are functionally efficient and esthetically satisfying; they make ingenious use of materials; and they are vivid expressions of the society that produced them.

These houses are, in effect, at least as old as Stonehenge, or older, in terms of the stage of civilization that they represent. Since these structures, thousands of years removed from our own time, fit so neatly the criteria we have set for understanding architecture, we should expect no difficulty in applying the criteria to a building of our own moment. But the "pure, direct, and forceful expression" typical of primitive art is denied a civilization as complex as ours, and the Pompidou Center (83) defies easy judgments.

The Centre National d'Art et de Culture Georges Pompidou is named for the French president, who in 1969 envisioned "a cultural center that is both a museum and a center of creation where the plastic arts would be side by side with music, cinema, books, and audiovisual research." Completed in 1977, the center is now generally called Beaubourg, from the area of central Paris that it dominates. Materialized, Pompidou's vision became an architectural behemoth of spectacular originality; as the latest development in the architectural story that began so long ago, it was controversial from the beginning, and offers a clear, unequivocal answer to only the last of our four questions: Beaubourg is, indeed, emphatically an expression of our time—although even here we must concede that it is not an expression generated in response to the inherent spirit of our civilization, but a design arrived at through a combination of theoretical reasoning and a talent for architectural dramatics.

81. Framework of a *davi*, men's ceremonial and clubhouse, under construction. Maipua, Papua, New Guinea. Photograph, about 1900, courtesy Field Museum of Natural History, Chicago.

82. Interior of a *davi*, New Guinea. Photograph courtesy American Museum of Natural History, New York.

83. Piano & Rogers; Ove Arup & Partners. Centre National d'Art et de Culture Georges Pompidou ("Beaubourg"). 1971–77. Paris.

84. Gustave Eiffel. Eiffel Tower. 1889. Height 984 feet. Champ de Mars, Paris.

Then, immediately, we have to make another concession: if time should prove that Beaubourg is only a monstrous tour de force, it nevertheless satisfies two conditions most important to the French government that commissioned it. First, in its size, its aggressiveness, and its compelling originality, it is a proclamation of French determination to regain leadership in modern art, a leadership that Paris lost to New York after World War II. Second, in its hybrid character as an amusement park and an art center, Beaubourg proclaims that art in France is no longer an élitist activity. The Louvre, nearby, is a palace to which the public are admitted as spectators. Beaubourg is a public building where visitors become participants in an exciting experiment, both inside the building and in the street-fair atmosphere that is encouraged in the adjacent plaza.

Generally speaking, the older a building is, the more adaptable it is to something like final judgment on its merits and shortcomings. We are using Beaubourg here as an extreme example where judgment must be approached warily, where conventional esthetic criteria can serve only as a basis for pro and con examination until time settles the debate. It should not be surprising that Beaubourg is somewhat upsetting when we try to apply criteria that apply pretty well to a wide variety of historical building types—for Beaubourg is literally a building turned inside out.

Biology supplies a good term for Beaubourg's design: "exoskeletal." Exoskeletons are the hard external supporting structures in nature, such as the shells of oysters or the cuticle of lobsters, as distinguished from endoskeletons, our own and other vertebrates' internal bony structure. Beaubourg's supporting skeleton of steel scaffolding, as well as the conduits for water, ventilation, sewage, wiring, and other engineering functions of a large building, which are normally concealed within or behind walls, are exposed all the way around the immense structure. What we think of as the building itself is suspended within this exoskeleton in the form of an enormous multi-storied, glass-walled cage of space that may be subdivided by lightweight movable screen walls where needed. It is a building without a façade: the bright color that dramatizes the exoskeleton is utilitarian in origin: it follows the engineering convention by which the conduits for different functions are identified by different colors, both in working drawings and in completed buildings, not intended for the decorative purposes they serve at the Centre Pompidou but only for easy recognition by builders, workmen, and repairmen.

Then there is the other way of seeing Beaubourg, not as a revolutionary structure but as the latest chapter in a long, uninterrupted story of engineering-as-architecture. Even the idea of an architectural exoskeleton is not quite new: the flying buttresses of the Gothic cathedrals, which we have already seen (**7**), are exterior continuations of an endoskeleton of piers and ribbed vaults. Perhaps flying buttresses looked radical on their first appearance, but they became so popular that later Gothic architects employed them in unfunctional proliferations. And like the piers and ribs of the exposed endoskeleton of the vaulting system, they were carved and patterned to increase their innate decorative character. The flying buttresses of Notre Dame are visible in the panoramic view of Paris from the upper levels of Beaubourg, as is another landmark in engineering, the Eiffel Tower (84), erected for the Paris Exposition of 1889 to demonstrate the potential of iron construction, and left standing after a narrow escape from protests that it disfigured the city—as does Beaubourg, to many eyes.

The catch in our set of qualities by which architecture can be judged is in the second of the four—esthetic appeal. No other art is subject to such extreme variations in style from epoch to epoch and hence to such extreme shifts in the esteem accorded a building as tastes change. It is chastening for an architecture critic to remember that in the eighteenth century, the Age of Reason when all things classical were revered above all things else, there was agitation in Paris to demolish Notre Dame as a barbarous eyesore. Nor need we go that far back. One of the finest monuments of nineteenth-century eclectic architecture in America, Philadelphia's City Hall (85), is standing today only because it is so solidly built that contractors would not offer firm bids for tearing it down in the late 1950's to be replaced by a more efficient building. The tower, including the statue of William Penn on top, is the highest building ever built without structural steel—that is, by putting one stone on top of another. The stones are massive, and the tower would have had to be disassembled stone by stone rather than knocked down with the swinging ball or dynamited; it was feared that the stones falling from such a height would go through the sidewalk and into the subway.

Having passed the dangerous age at which thousands of fine nineteenth-century buildings, especially residences, have been demolished, the Philadelphia City Hall is now conspicuous among buildings in a style that has been reevaluated upward esthetically, while the modern style of building with which it would have been replaced has taken a downward curve, as we will see in our next chapter. The tragedy of architecture is that while a painting or a sculpture may be relegated to basement storage during periods when its style is out of favor, nothing can bring back a destroyed building. If the judgment of a building as architecture is to be fair, we must take into consideration the terms that made it suitable for the time in which it was built. Again, as we go on in this book, we will see that terms usually applied only to painting or sculpture, such as "realism" and "expressionism," are also applicable to architecture, further complicating the standards by which architecture may be judged but, as a happy result, expanding the range in which it may be enjoyed.

85. John McArthur, Jr. Philadelphia City Hall. Cornerstone laid July 4, 1874. Completed 1901.

86. William Michael Harnett. *Music and Good Luck.* 1888. Oil on canvas, 40 by 30 inches. The Metropolitan Museum of Art, New York. Purchased by Catharine Lorillard Wolfe Fund, 1963.

Chapter Four
REALISM

A painting, a sculpture, or a building is a triple experience—visual, emotional, and intellectual. Since it is hardly possible to look at anything without reacting to it in one way or another, a certain amount of emotional response is inevitable. In character and degree this response depends on our willingness and capacity to respond to what the artist or architect offers us. But when it comes to intellectual enjoyment, our reaction is less immediate. It is more a matter of learning, and this is the point where many an interested person begins to protest his ignorance of what art is all about.

This protest is a natural defense in a time when art has been subjected to so much intellectual snobbery. The layman naturally takes refuge in the conviction that *all* intellectualization about art is snobbery. In its tiredest form, his protest is the familiar "I don't know anything about art but I know what I like." Translated into more formal jargon, the same thing can be said this way: "Intellectual understanding of art is not prerequisite to emotional response." Stated either way the proposition is only half-true, but, all other considerations aside, it is true that intellectual appreciation of art is a pleasure that need not involve snobbism.

This and our next two chapters are concerned with visual, emotional, and intellectual experience in the enjoyment of art—seeing, feeling, and thinking. Obviously what we see, what we feel, and what we think are so bound together they cannot easily be separated. But insofar as distinctions can be made, we are going to consider these pleasures separately under the titles, respectively, of realism, expressionism, and abstraction.

To begin, we will compare William Harnett's *Music and Good Luck*, a realistic painting (**86**); Raoul Dufy's *The Yellow Violin*, an expressionistic one; and Georges Braque's *Musical Forms*, an abstraction (**87** and **88**, p. 62). Their subjects are as nearly parallel as one could hope for in demonstrating such divergent results.

Harnett's *Music and Good Luck* is the kind of realistic painting the eager but unenlightened museum-goer encounters with relief. He knows that Harnett must be good because, after all, museums and collectors covet his work. But at the same time it is possible to enjoy Harnett without having to wonder what his art is all about. His pictures are guaranteed to be legitimate art, yet at the same time they are enjoyable at face value. In short, they are safe.

But confronted by Dufy's expressionist *The Yellow Violin*, our hypothetical layman may feel a little insecure. He may find the picture attractive enough in its way, yet it doesn't look as if it had been hard enough to do. Still, it is not too puzzling. You can tell what the images are supposed to represent, even if they are out of kilter.

Braque's abstraction is another matter altogether. By even the most relaxed standards of truth to nature, it defies every convention.

Yet the two paintings that are closest to one another as far as the artists' approaches are concerned, the two that can be enjoyed on most nearly the same basis, are the two that seem most unlike. The very realistic *Music and Good Luck* and the highly abstract *Musical Forms* are first cousins.

Music and Good Luck is an example of realism pushed to its ultimate extreme, illusionism; it sets out to please the eye by deceiving it, and is so sucessful that there are passages where different textures are simulated with such accuracy that it is hard to believe the texture is uniformly smooth over the entire surface of the picture, as of course it is. The illusion is intensified because the objects are painted at their exact size, but even in our small reproduction, it is as if we could take the violin off its nail; we can read the score of the music and the name on the calling card—which does double duty as the artist's signature; the horseshoe, violin bow, hasp, and piccolo hang so naturally that we can imagine lifting them off the picture; their shadows tell us just the distance between them and the door, and that the lower end of the piccolo touches the door while the upper swings away from it.

Any painter who has coped with the problem of illusionistic shadow—or any photographer concerned with fine printing that captures every nuance of tone between one shadow and another—will realize that Harnett's shadows, which are the least noticed element in his paintings, are the most subtly studied, their edges painted harder or softer in exact degrees according to their distances from the objects and the intensity of the light. It is next to incredible that the wooden frame around the rest of the picture is not a real one but an exercise in illusionism like the area it surrounds. The padlock is the giveaway here, once it is noticed. The date 1888 is "scratched" so realistically on the surface of the painted frame that it looks like a bit of vandalism. Actually, not scratched but painted, it is Harnett's way of dating the picture, just as the calling card is his way of signing it.

If illusionism were its whole content, *Music and Good Luck* would be a conglomeration of tricky simulations, nothing more, and would lose our interest once we had examined the imitated objects. But it continues to hold us. It holds us because it is more than an imitation of visual fact. This "natural" painting is not natural at all except from detail to detail. The arrangement of the objects, in the first place, is arbitrary. It is no accident that the bow is placed vertically, lining up with a system of other verticals including the axes of the violin and the hasp, the cracks between the boards of the door, and even the right and left borders of the picture, which we never think of as part of a painting although the artist is conscious that they must be incorporated into his arrangement. A second system of horizontals at right angles to the verticals is defined by the hinges, the top and bottom of the door, and, again, the top and bottom of the painted frame.

In memory, anyone would probably describe the violin as hanging in the center of the picture. It does not. It hangs just to the left, although it is the focal center of a beautifully adjusted balance of lines and shapes. Not one of these objects, or any of the smallest details (nail holes, for instance) is casually disposed. (In this illusionistic picture, the illusion of casual arrangement is the most deceptive illusion of all.) The angle at which the piccolo hangs is determined by its weight on either side of the supporting string, and the angle of the calling card is a natural one for a piece of paper stuck into a crack by one corner; but the angles are manipulated to coincide with one another and, at approximately 45 degrees, to relieve while conforming to the basic vertical-horizontal linear skeleton.

The page of music coincides with the vertical system in the top-corner-to-bottom-corner line of its hanging position; its top edge is another 45-degree angle, and its side edges split the difference between 45 and 90—all as a part of geometrical certainties determined by arbitrary placement. Against all these angles and straight lines, the crisp in-and-out curves of the violin and the simple curve of the horseshoe—music and good luck—make their full effect as the key objects in the group.

To test the nicety of Harnett's arrangement (we will use the word "composition" from now on), imagine adding to the picture, eliminating an object, or changing its position. Shift the sheet of music to a normal, upright position and the entire composition becomes expected and monotonous. Shift the angle of the horseshoe similarly and almost as much is lost. Move the brass match holder at the left up or down. Up, and it balances too obviously with the hasp on the right; down, and the composition begins to settle as if of its own weight toward the bottom. Try any other changes and it will become apparent how carefully every detail has been disposed—and how arbitrarily.

That is the point. Ultimately this naturalistic picture depends on not-natural elements. As a work of imitation, even at the amazing level that Harnett achieves, this or any other realistic picture is only second-best to the objects it imitates. As a work of art, it is an independent esthetic entity.

The idea in back of expressionism is that the actual appearance of objects may be distorted in any way, no matter how extreme, that the artist feels will best relay to the observer his own emotional reaction to a subject. Expressionism is usually associated with morbid, violent, or sorrowful subjects (Kokoschka's *The Tempest* is an expressionist painting), but need not be. Dufy's *The Yellow Violin* is bright, vivacious, happy; the color has nothing to do with nature but everything to do with what the artist wants to tell us. There is no interest in textures; the violin is sketched in a few quick lines against the solid yellow of

87. Raoul Dufy. *The Yellow Violin.* 1949. Oil on canvas, 39½ by 32 inches. Art Gallery of Ontario, Toronto. Gift of Sam and Ayala Zacks, 1970.

88. Georges Braque. *Musical Forms.* 1913. Oil, pencil and charcoal on canvas, 36¼ by 23½ inches. Philadelphia Museum of Art. Louise and Walter Arensberg Collection.

the tabletop, which continues on the wall and mirror above. Dufy's drawing is as fluid and broken as Harnett's is concise, and hence its effect is as animated as Harnett's is static. The notes on the sheet of music are a series of staccato accents with only the loosest connection with a readable score. Everything expresses liveliness, spontaneity, improvisation. As for being "too easy to do," it was easy for Dufy to do in the same way that a skilled pianist may appear to execute a dashing series of runs and trills without effort. The seemingly spontaneous fluency of this happy example of expressionism is as important to the mood it projects as is the feeling of swirling violence with which Kokoschka imbued the paint surface of *The Tempest* (**34**). Both paintings are antirealistic in Harnett's terms of literal reference to visual fact; both seek the deeper reality of the emotive nature of their subjects, with appropriate distortions as their means to that end.

In spite of distortion, the objects in an expressionist painting are usually recognizable. But in abstraction the objects tend to lose their identity and to exist as pure form. Braque's *Musical Forms* is no longer a "picture of" a violin, although a violin was the point of departure for some of the most conspicuous elements. Nor is it an emotional reaction to the idea of "violin," as Dufy's is. It is purely what it is: a composition of lines, shapes, colors, and textures combined arbitrarily for esthetic effectiveness.

Beneath their differences, Braque's abstraction and Harnett's collection of realistically painted objects have strong similarities. Both compositions are disciplined by systems of rigid straight lines, both are relieved by contrasting curved ones. The area enclosing the first five letters of the word *journal* in the Braque meets a compositional demand similar to that of the calling card in the Harnett. Within the two schemes there is a related interest in textures. Harnett simulates them; Braque utilizes actual, physical ones, including pasted paper and corrugated cardboard; charcoal's naturally grainy texture is deliberately emphasized, while paint, thick in some areas, is scrubbed thin in others for variety. The paint on the area of the violin has been scratched while wet with a comblike implement to create a texture resembling the grain of wood but not meant to imitate it. Whatever they suggest, these textures exist for themselves rather than as adjuncts to something else, while all textures in the Harnett simulate the textures of the objects.

Harnett, in his earlier pictures, sometimes "textured" his paint so that a match head, for instance, might be built up in relief from the surface of the canvas. The difference between doing what Braque does and building up a match head to look like a match head or imitating the surface of an old violin to look like the surface of an old violin, is the difference between realism and abstraction. Braque abandons the appearance of things because he wants to capitalize fully on the same abstract elements that interested Harnett (and others) without disguising these elements within the imitation of nature. Just why he chose also the further abstraction of breaking his forms up as he does is too long a story to tell here; as a phase of cubism it is better dealt with in a later chapter. In the meantime these three violins will serve as a reminder that although the subject of this chapter is realism, all painting—whether realistic, expressionistic, or abstract—involves the creation and combination of form and color according to the way the painter sees, feels, and thinks about the world.

Now "realism" is probably the broadest term in art, so broad that we must make our own working definition of it. We will call any painting or sculpture "realistic" in which a fairly close approximation of the look of things is retained. The realistic painter may considerably modify natural appearances, but he will stop short of the point where modification becomes distortion.

By this definition the bulk of painting and sculpture until the twentieth century is realistic. But the real world to one age is not the real world to another. The world around the artist changes, not only superficially in the obvious way of different buildings, different dress, and the like, but more fundamentally, since as times change artists see the world differently even when they begin by imitating the look of things. The visual world is only the raw material from which artists fabricate images reflecting the values fundamental to their times.

In the chapter on sculpture we saw a kouros and the *Diadoumenos* (**40** and **42**), examples of the ideal realism of ancient Greece, where the beauty of the perfect human body personified the ideal harmony envisioned beneath the accidentals and confusions of life. The creative method for this and other forms of ideal realism is to simplify and purify natural forms by eliminating accidentals, confusions, and other imperfections to an ideal standard of beauty that nature, unmodified, rarely if ever presents.

As inheritors of the Greek sculptural tradition, the Romans continued to imitate its ideal principles in many instances; but the Romans put less faith in an unattainable ideal world than they did in the practical world of power and politics, of personal achievement in a competitive society. One result was the most acutely realistic portrait sculpture in the history of art, in which, instead of idealizing or beautifying a countenance, sculptors reproduced every irregularity, every pouch and wrinkle, every sign of age and stress that marked a face, even such deformities as broken noses, toothless mouths, and tumors, in celebration of the uniqueness of every human countenance. (This extremity of realism is sometimes called "naturalism," but more often in literature than in painting and sculpture.)

In Republican Rome the family was a sturdy social unit wherein ancestral death masks were preserved and venerated. The realistic tradition of Roman sculptured portraits of living persons probably originated in stone copies of these fragile wax masks with their unrelenting veracity. Such sculptures depend for their effectiveness on the degree

89. Roman. *Portrait Head of a Man.* About A.D. 100. Marble, height 10²/₃ inches. The Cleveland Museum of Art. Gift of J. H. Wade.

of interest inherent in a face and involve no effort at revelation on the part of the sculptor. But there are Roman portraits of such force, such vivid reflections of personality, that we have to believe perceptive sculptors made small but revelatory modifications from literal reality in order to transform the record of a set of features into a record of character (**89**).

Having pointed out that "realism" is probably the most flexible term in the lexicon of art, and having spoken of "ideal realism," which is something of a contradiction in terms, let us go further and invent the term "mystical realism" to describe a salient aspect of the art of the late Middle Ages.

We have said that the function of art is frequently defined as the creation of order out of the chaos of human experience. This suggests a simplification and a purification of the raw material the visual world offers, which we have seen as the Greek way. But there is no one way, no best way, of achieving an expression of order and harmony appropriate to all places and times in history. *Saint Francis Receiving the Stigmata* (**90**), sometimes questioned, but also attributed reasonably to Jan van Eyck, goes about putting the world in order in just the opposite of the Greek way. Instead of simplifying, the painter multiplies detail. Paradoxical as that may sound, it was the reasonable approach for a painter of the late Middle Ages.

The medieval world was rich, violent, chaotic, complicated, swarming, colorful, and thoroughly contradictory. It was a world of cynicism and piety, of grossness and elegance. Licentiousness flourished. So did the cult of chastity. As we look back on the age, it seems to have been everything at once—except humdrum.

This welter of contradictions was unified by the assumption that the universe in its totality was a divinely ordained system of parallels in contrast. In this faith the age found its harmony. Heaven balanced Hell, winter balanced summer, sowing balanced reaping, birth balanced death. Each virtue balanced its corresponding vice. And in this universal harmony, ordained by God, the smallest detail of the world had its place. Nothing was accidental; everything was meaningful.

For medieval people the world of literal fact merged with the world of spiritual miracle and was frequently identical with it. This concept of the universe, reflected in painting, explains why the miracle of the stigmata could be represented in uncompromisingly realistic detail without contradicting its miraculous character. Within the small area of the picture, the complexity is enormous, a miniature world represented with staggering completeness, compressed into a few square inches (the picture is only 5 inches high) without any effect of crowding or jumbling. There are trees, flowers, crags, boulders, and pebbles. There is a river, a spring with its rocky basin of crystalline water. There are hills, clouds, and birds; a city with men on foot and on horseback around its gates; there are other cities in

90. Jan van Eyck, attributed. *St. Francis Receiving the Stigmata.* Date uncertain. Oil on panel, 5 by 5¾ inches. Philadelphia Museum of Art. John G. Johnson Collection.

the distance. There are roads and paths, a boatload of men. Lichens grow in miniature on miniature boulders and—so small that they are virtually invisible until magnified— there are woodsmen bearing loads of faggots in the hills. In the upper left corner (**91**) a man and a boy, smaller than fleas, walk on a rocky path, while tiny specks on and around a tree turn out to be a crow or some similar bird on the topmost branch with other birds in the air around it.

But breathtaking microscopic execution is not in itself of any esthetic merit. After all, the Lord's Prayer has been engraved on the head of a pin (a rather large pin) to no esthetic advantage. Certainly this tiny picture with its tiny details was painted with the help of a powerful lens; as a tour de force the execution is fascinating in itself, but in itself it could never have raised a stunt painting to the level of a work of art—which this painting undeniably is. What is meaningful is that the painter has combined the myriad details of the world into a picture where the total effect is one of unity rather than confusion, a world where rocks, grass, foliage, cloth, hair, and flesh retain their individuality and yet share a common quality of gentleness in the even flow of light that bathes the universe. The head of the saint can be covered with a dime; each bristle on the cheek, chin, and upper lip has been painted individually; individual hairs or small locks spring from the scalp with the same energy that invests the whole picture with a sense of life. But it is the sense of life that is remarkable, not the technical means by which it is achieved. Whether the head is the size of a dime or a dinner plate, it is a solid and forthright presentation of a person who exists with utterly convincing reality in a world both real and miraculous.

Does the miniature scale then serve no function at all? There may have been a practical reason; the picture might, for instance, have been part of a portable shrine. Whatever the case, the advantage for us is that here the eye rests on an entire world at once. The precision of minute realistic detail intensifies our reaction to the various objects by investing them with a magical concentration. Yet this could have been true of a much larger version also. The important point is that this medieval painter and inadvertent philosopher has seen the world as a place where every detail around him takes on spiritual significance because it has its place in the universal harmony. Detail by detail the picture is an assemblage of commonplace things painted quite literally—even, some critics have found, rather dryly. But as a whole the effect is not commonplace but miraculous. If any element in the picture is out of key it is, paradoxically, the un-commonplace apparition of the Cross. Against the elegant complication of the city, against the vivacity of the crowds of men and horses, the pattern of the rock ledges, and the shining water with its boat, the one obviously miraculous element, the Cross, seems extraneous. Its presence is not necessary to complete the impression of reverent spirituality already conveyed through the contradictory means of extreme realism. An age made up of contradictions achieved this final one in its painting.

91. Enlarged detail from *St. Francis Receiving the Stigmata.*

92. Filippo Brunelleschi. Santo Spirito. Began 1434. Florence.

93. Donatello. *David.* About 1430–32. Bronze, height 62¼ inches. Bargello, Florence.

· · ·

When the picture we have just seen was painted near the end of the Middle Ages in northern Europe, "the Age of Faith" had already given way in Italy to a period better described as an age of curiosity: the Renaissance. The fact that a thing existed was no longer any assurance that it had its own ready-made pigeonhole in an all-inclusive, divinely ordered system. The Middle Ages gave meaning to the world by filing every individual part of the universal clutter around us into a systematic harmony that already existed, and to which mankind was subject. But Renaissance man sought to discover a new harmony, more earthly, with himself as its center.

In art, this new attitude first took the form of passionate investigation of the world. Artists dissected corpses to learn anatomy and turned mathematician to codify the laws of perspective. They discovered that spiritually they were more closely related to the artists who had created the gods of ancient Greece and Rome in their own image than they were to the artists of the immediate past. They began to study the remains of classical antiquity, reviving its idealism and combining with it the factualism of their new knowledge. Renaissance architects labeled the soaring forms of the medieval cathedral an architecture of barbarians (thus christening the style "Gothic"). They synthesized a new church architecture from the columns, round arches, moldings, pediments, and other elements of classical antiquity, combined with the floor plan of the medieval church, scaling their new buildings to the earthbound human beings who would worship there, rather than aspiring to heavenly release (92). Sculptors rediscovered the human body as the paramount vehicle of expression that it had been for the Greeks, but modified Greek idealism with the new passion for investigative realism. Donatello's *David,* standing triumphant over the severed head of Goliath, is represented classically nude and in classical stance, but his bony young body, rather than being the ideal one of a boy-god, is that of a Tuscan shepherd (he wears the shepherd's identifying leather hat) in early adolescence (93).

Both of the examples we have just seen—the interior of Brunelleschi's Church of Santo Spirito, and Donatello's bronze *David*—are Florentine. Florence was the birthplace of the Renaissance, and produced during the fifteenth century an unparalleled concentration of artists (and art patrons) within a small city. Leonardo da Vinci, Florentine by birth and always a Florentine in spirit wherever he worked, was the supreme exemplar of the intellectual artist-genius.

Leonardo's *Virgin of the Rocks* (94) with its mysterious air may seem an odd choice to illustrate a form of realism that was concerned with the exploration of earthly things. A contradiction, if not quite a difficulty, for Renaissance artists was that mystical religious subjects continued to make up the bulk of commissions even in this nonmystical age. As a result, the age produced in its second-rate painters hundreds of pictures of madonnas where mysticism degen-

94. Leonardo da Vinci. *Virgin of the Rocks.* 1497–1511. Oil on panel, 74⅜ by 74¼ inches. National Gallery, London.

erated into sentimentality. Leonardo's *Virgin of the Rocks* is an extraordinary achievement of mystical expression by way of scientific study.

Among the thousands of pages of analytical drawings and tens of thousands of words in Leonardo's notebooks, kept for himself but happily preserved for us, the word "God" is all but absent. Again and again and again we find Leonardo speculating upon the physical origins of the world around him, analyzing the dynamics of air, water, and fire in the shaping of the earth. The grotto in which the *Virgin of the Rocks* is seated is an imaginary spot but not a flight of fancy; it is an invention worked out from knowledge of geological principles of erosion by wind and water, and the accretion of mineral deposits by evaporation, stalactites and stalagmites among them. We sense the cool dampness of the air, can almost hear the occasional drip of water that seeps through cracks in the natural vault of the grotto. Small plants flourish, but not with the encyclopedic profusion we saw in *Saint Francis Receiving the Stigmata.* These plants are few and botanically perfect.

More predictable examples of Renaissance realism can be seen elsewhere in this book (**231**, **236**, **273**, and **297**), yet none of them has foundations as deep as those of the *Virgin of the Rocks,* which is less concerned with the reality of the surfaces of things than with the scientific realities underlying them.

Nothing we have said about detecting the meanings beneath the surface of a work of art should be taken to imply that people in the past—the days of the "old masters"—had a livelier understanding of what art is all about than the average person has today. The opposite is the case. Until very recent times the art-minded percentage of the population even in the most creative periods of history was a very small fraction of the public at large. We tend to forget that most of the paintings and sculptures now available to everybody in museums were originally done for the private pleasure of connoisseurs. What we might call "public art"— art in places open to everybody, especially churches—was enjoyed or revered by the mass public for its subject matter and simple visual effectiveness. If some of these "public" paintings and sculptures were admired more than others, it was because they offered more intense vicarious experiences through their subject matter and its dramatic presentation. It was frequently to the advantage of a governing body or an individual—let us say, the Church or the State— to capitalize on the public's response to art *not* for art's sake ("art for art's sake" is a modern idea) but in order to stir feelings of reverence and loyalty through subject matter.

Artists of no other century have quite equaled those of the seventeenth in the creation of paintings and sculptures (and, for that matter, buildings) that could astonish and fascinate a lay audience while satisfying the most sophisticated demands of the most cultivated patrons. The phenomenon is most easily (a little too easily) explained as having originated as a tool of the Counter Reformation in the sixteenth century, by which the Catholic Church sought to check the inroads of Protestantism by dramatizing to the utmost an emotional Catholicism, with all the arts participating in a mighty spectacle to attract and hold a popular audience. Rulers could enhance the power of their images in the same way. But artists gave the same spectacular performances to other than Christian and political subjects, as Rubens did in *Prometheus Bound* (95), where he makes the most of the idea that an observer can participate in a pictured experience.

Prometheus, who stole fire from Olympus and gave it to mankind, was punished by the gods in the manner pictured. His liver was devoured by an eagle every day; every night it grew back, making his punishment eternal. Rubens treats us in as direct a way as possible to the spectacle of a giant writhing in agony as the voracious bird tears at his vitals through a wound in his side.

This was rich subject matter for a painter during a period when it was demanded that art appeal to the observer directly and forcefully through physical associations. Rubens offers us no invitation to divine meditation, nor to the contemplation of harmonious order. Here is an art that seeks to astonish. The spectator must, first of all, be shocked into an emotional response, must not be allowed to pass by. No chance may be taken with possible indifference. Any means of attraction is legitimate, no matter how spectacular, how violent, or, in some cases, how false.

Now, the quickest and surest way to shock is through physical experience. And since the artist who approaches us through astonishment cannot touch us with live coals, or dash us with cold water, or deal us a blow, he does the next best thing: he creates astonishing images so convincing that we share the pictured physical experience. In the case of this Rubens, the experience is offered directly but the same idea can be applied in ways not quite so obvious. Flesh or cloth or water or wind or hair or feathers or rock may be so painted or carved that they stir our associations of physical acquaintance rather than our ideological ones. An angel flying through the air is something we have never seen (any more than we have ever seen a giant chained to a rock), but if an angel can be painted or carved so that the flesh and cloth and hair and feathers are like physically real experiences to us, we are going to believe in the existence of that angel.

At least that is the intention behind dramatized realism of this kind. The appeal to our own physical experience of painful or pleasurable sensations is going to be most effective to the extent that the image is most tangible. For that reason there is no idealization in the figure of the powerful man who plays Prometheus. This is, actually, as realistic a painting as we have seen so far, for all its illusion of tempestuous drama and its fantastic subject. If Rubens had been a degree less skillful in maintaining the illusion, we would find ourselves imagining the model posed in the studio, illuminated by a spotlight and complaining that his left leg was going to sleep.

95. Peter Paul Rubens. *Prometheus Bound.* 1611–12. Oil on canvas, 95⅞ by 82½ inches. Philadelphia Museum of Art. W. P. Wilstach Collection.

We have been avoiding the term "baroque" so far in our discussion of seventeenth-century realism because the term is an ill-defined one, covering everything from forms of grandeur derived from classical antiquity to the kind of dramatic performance staged in Rubens's *Prometheus*. Rembrandt, the profound humanist, was a "baroque" painter by chronological definition; we will see later to what extent he fits into his century's love of dramatic representation (with *The Night Watch*, **254**), and where he is opposed to the sheer theatricality of the celebration of power that is a primary baroque ideal.

The seventeenth century—the baroque century—placed its faith in worldly power, whether the absolute power of such monarchs as Louis XIV in France, or the temporal power of the spiritual leader of the Church, the Pope in Rome. It was not an age that really believed in miracles, as the medieval world did; it did not really hope to discover harmony beneath confusion, as the early Renaissance did. The phenomenon of the age, as far as art was concerned, was that its artist-dramatists accepted the common denominator of appeal that painting and sculpture can present to the widest public—the appeal of physical experience at the expense of spirituality. Yet they managed to intensify that experience with such brilliance that any spiritual lack, or even much spiritual falsity, need not be forgiven but can simply be forgotten.

It was not too long ago that baroque painting and sculpture was dismissed as "in bad taste" by critics who judged it by the standards of the earlier periods of the Renaissance, with Leonardo da Vinci in the lead there. But all that has changed. It should already be apparent to readers of this book that to limit oneself to a single standard of esthetic values means cutting oneself off from the all-inclusive pleasure art has to offer, which is the sharing of ideas that have succeeded one another century after century up to our own.

It is true that by the standards of classical idealism baroque art often slips over the edge of drama into melodrama and bathos. Even at its most impressive, it has a strong element of the theatrical. Michelangelo Merisi, called Caravaggio, sometimes seems as much a genius of stagecraft as one of the great masters of painting. The miracles in the New Testament, he argued, happened to ordinary people, and to represent them ideally was to falsify them. Instead of idealizing, in the manner, say, of Leonardo, Caravaggio dramatized otherwise realistic scenes by means of brilliant artificial light, sometimes from a miraculous source. His most spectacular use of this device, *The Conversion of Saint Paul* (**96**), shows the moment when Saul of Tarsus (his Jewish name), on his way to Damascus to help suppress Christianity there, is struck by a blinding light and hears Jesus ask: "Saul, Saul, why persecutest thou me?" (Acts 9:4). Converted by the experience, he became the greatest of the missionary apostles, preaching in synagogues and marketplaces.

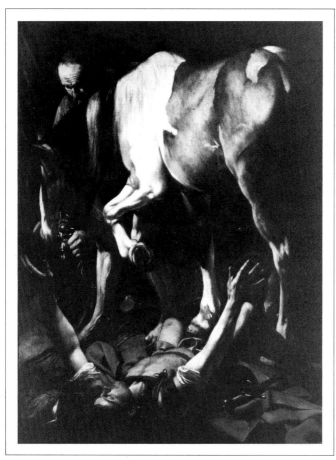

96. Caravaggio. *Conversion of Saint Paul.* About 1601. Oil on canvas, 90½ by 68⅞ inches. Santa Maria del Popolo, Rome.

It is impossible, surely, to look at this wonderful painting and see it only as a melodrama, or only as the breathtaking technical exhibition that it is. The light itself is a symbol of spiritual transfiguration—and is visible only to Saul. The attendant (who does not figure in the biblical account) is quite unaware that he is in the presence of a miracle; he remains commonplace, establishing the scene of the miracle in the everyday world that Caravaggio, as a militant realist, insisted was the artist's true domain.

Caravaggio's influence spread through all Europe, his contrast of light and dark, called *tenebroso*, being especially popular—but not often employed as expressively. Among Italians, Artemisia Gentileschi can serve as an example, partly because she is exceptional in being the first woman painter to attain her degree of prominence. In *Judith and Maidservant with the Head of Holofernes* (**97**) she capitalizes on the popular device of a logical, defined source of light, a candle that she employs in a combination of tour-de-force painting—she was a superb technician—and, to use the phrase again, theatricalism.

A few pages back we said that "The appeal to our own physical experience of painful or pleasurable sensations is going to be most effective to the extent that the image is most tangible." Sculpture, being literally tangible, flourished in seventeenth-century Italy with a vigor unmatched since the Middle Ages in France. Add to tangibility an effulgent theatricality, and it becomes apparent why Bernini's *Ecstasy of Saint Theresa* (**98**) can be called the superexample of Italian baroque dramatic realism. Tons of marble appear to float in the air, backed up by brass rays of light and illuminated by real light from a concealed opening above the group where the saint swoons in ecstasy as an angel prepares to pierce her vitals not with Cupid's dart but with one remarkably similar. (The scene is a sculptural transcription from the saint's own written description of the experience.) In addition, the sculpture occupies a chapel where the side walls are treated like those of a tiny theater, with members of the family that donated the chapel seated in boxes to watch the performance.

In a time of such violence and novelty as our own, people are not easy to astonish. But the power of an image is so great that the dramatic realism of seventeenth-century art continues to astonish even when we would expect it to pale in comparison with photographs of current events astonishing and painful beyond belief. Perhaps that is the clue to the effectiveness of baroque realism: it is *not* beyond belief. It brings the event close to us, makes us part of itself, in a way that idealism does not. We may strive for the ideal but we have experienced the real.

The seventeenth century produced armies of painters who were under no technical limitations at all; painters who could draw any figure, from any angle, in any curious or distorted attitude, whether or not they had anything to say. It is not surprising that the age produced the absolute

97. Artemisia Gentileschi. *Judith and Maidservant with the Head of Holofernes.* Early 1620's. Oil on canvas, 72½ by 55¾ inches. The Detroit Institute of Arts. Gift of Leslie H. Green.

98. Gianlorenzo Bernini. *Ecstasy of Saint Theresa.* 1645–52. Marble, height of group about 16 feet 6 inches. Cornaro Chapel, Santa Maria della Vittoria, Rome.

99. Diego Velázquez. *Las Meñinas* (*The Ladies in Waiting*). 1656. Oil on canvas, 10 feet 5 inches by 9 feet. Museo del Prado, Madrid.

100. Detail from *The Ladies in Waiting*.

realist of them all: Velázquez—Diego Rodríguez de Silva y Velázquez, who was content to pass his life as a vassal of the king of a declining Spain.

If ever painting, in its purest definition as the controlled application of paint to canvas, can be its own reason for being, it is so in the art of Velázquez. *Las Meñinas* (*The Ladies in Waiting*, **99**) shows a little Spanish princess, surrounded by her court attendants while, to one side in the background, the painter himself is at work on the picture we are seeing. Further back, reflected in a mirror, the king and queen watch him at work (**100**). The painting gives the impression of being executed in realistic detail, but when we look at a section of it, we discover that is not true. Here is a new kind of realistic vision. Whereas van Eyck would have painted individual hairs, Velázquez paints not a single strand or even a definable mass. Velázquez is not painting hair; he is painting the light reflected onto the retina of his eye by a substance that happens to be hair. He translates this reflected light into pigmented tones, giving us only the impression of the color, texture, and form of hair in terms of light (**101**). He does the same with the ornament of ribbon at one temple and at the neck of the dress. We could not describe these objects in precise detail because we are not familiar with them as specific objects. We know them only as light reflected over the considerable distance between the painter and his model, a distance that reduces the objects to spots of color with concentrations of lighter and darker tones in highlights and shadows.

In this kind of painting we see more than the artist puts there. Cover the upper and lower parts of the nose and you will see that its bridge is not described as form. We supply the missing description, just as we supply the individual hairs because we know they are there; just as we supply the lower lid of the little girl's far eye because we know it is there, though hardly suggested; just as we supply the division between the neck and the jaw near the hair, although as far as descriptive painting of form is concerned, that area is largely blank. On the other side of the face, the dividing line between cheek and hair is so softened that in places it cannot be precisely determined—but again we supply it. Velázquez paints the light reflected by an object across the distance between him and the object; he does not paint what memory or close-range inspection tells him the object looks like. If he had been painting the city in the background of *Saint Francis Receiving the Stigmata*, he would have painted it in blurs and spots, which is all the eye can see of a city at such a distance. He would never have painted the individual bristles in the beard of the saint, even if he had been painting the head at life size, since the eye does not see such details clearly except at very close range. Velázquez paints detail only to the degree that it is visible from where he, and hence the observer, stands.

The beauty of Velázquez's realism is its consistency. As objects recede into the distance of his pictures and become more vague, as they come into the foreground and become more sharply defined, every brush stroke, every tone, every modulation of color, is in perfect relationship—as a reflection of light—to every other.

All this sounds like the ultimate degree of mere imitation of nature, as if Velázquez were only a lens equipped with a paintbrush. But Velázquez the artist, as opposed to mere technician, selects, modifies, eliminates meaningless or confusing accidentals, slightly heightens or lowers intensities of light or shadow, to create a world of subtler visual harmonies than the one that serves him as a model. He creates a luminous world with its own abstract beauty in its order, its harmony, its consistency, its perfect relationship between every nuance of descriptive color.

Still, optical delight even at its maximum cannot explain the enduring appeal of Velázquez as expressive painter rather than supertechnician. Where does his expressive quality lie? It cannot be discovered in terms of Rubens's fleshly vigor or Caravaggio's miracles-on-earth. By these standards, Velázquez's religious paintings are meaningless collections of effigies, and his allegorical or mythological subjects end up as prosaic groups of patient models, beautifully painted. His expressive quality lies at the opposite pole: from Velázquez's world all passionate intensity, all mystery or symbolism, and all intellectual philosophizing have been distilled away as impurities. The images exist for themselves, always once removed from us, separated by an invisible barrier behind which they stand regarding us impassively, complete in their own being. When Velázquez paints an image of the Madonna we must accept it as the Madonna, just as literally as we accept, in *The Ladies in Waiting*, the room, the little princess, and her entourage. His art poses no questions and suggests no paths to solutions; it presents us with a *fait accompli*, as if the question having been asked and the solution found we need concern ourselves with neither; we must be content to accept without query the answer Velázquez offers without comment.

So far, in chronological sequence, as examples of different kinds of realism we have seen a Greek athlete, a Roman citizen, a mystical universe, the Virgin seated in a grotto, a Titan, a miraculous conversion, a Judaic heroine, a female saint's possibly hysterical vision, and a Spanish princess—all realistic images expressive of aspects of their centuries. After a list of such elevated subjects, the appearance of three apples, two pears, a mug, and a knife on a stone ledge might be taken to indicate that a new century has lost its sense of the grand and the noble. This is not so. In this picture the eighteenth century is discovering that nobility can exist in the commonplace.

The events of 1776 in our own country were a social manifestation involving the philosophical idea that nobility exists in the simplest things and the simplest people. Without exaggerating too much, we could argue that the Declaration of Independence and Jean-Baptiste-Siméon

101. Detail from *The Ladies in Waiting*.

102. Jan Davidsz de Heem. *Still Life with Parrots.* About 1646. Oil on canvas, 59¼ by 45¾ inches. John and Mable Ringling Museum of Art, Sarasota, Florida.

Chardin's *Still Life with a White Mug* (**105**, p.76) are first cousins under the skin.

Still-life painting is boring to many people; it is too often merely imitative. But a good still life can also be an expressive picture, and the range of expression can be fairly wide. It cannot compare with the range of landscape or the human figure, but even so it would be possible to tell the history of painting, on a reduced scale, in still life alone. Until Chardin, though, we would normally find still life either an incidental part of a larger picture or, when a picture in itself, an ornamental display of technical skill as in a canvas by Jan Davidsz de Heem, one of the most influential seventeenth-century still-life painters (**102**). With Chardin, still life becomes an independent expressive vehicle.

As far as accuracy of drawing is concerned, the objects in Chardin's still lifes are close to photographic, which of course is not enough. It is his way of painting them that transfigures surface facts into inner truths. Light and dark tones are adjusted, colors are modulated; even the rich, creamy surface of Chardin's paint is essentially a departure from exact imitation of nature. We commented on similar departures in Velázquez's way of working, but the two painters are not alike in effect. Velázquez was painting light; Chardin is painting form. Everything he does is directed toward one end, the expression of the weight, solidity, and repose that he feels in the objects he selects. The paint itself is heavier, richer, more firmly applied than Velázquez's, which by comparison is often only a veil of pigment.

The seven objects in our illustration are arranged very simply on the homely shelf, but very rightly. There are no set rules for this kind of pictorial composition, and thus no really good way to explain why one succeeds and another fails. The objects are placed in a kind of balance that cannot be calculated but can only "feel" right or wrong. The simpler such an arrangement is, and the fewer the objects included in it, the more difficult is the problem of adjustment of the parts to one another. Chardin's composition can be tested in much the same manner as we tested Harnett's (**86**), by imagining changes in the number or placement of the various objects. Take away the knife, and immediately the mug is divorced from the other objects. Or if we substitute another apple for the upright pear, or shift its position so that it leans toward the center of the picture rather than toward the left, we discover that we have to make other changes to compensate for the disturbed relationships.

In analyzing a Chardin in this way—as an exercise in formal relationships—we are seeing it from a twentieth-century point of view. In his own day in France (his dates are 1699–1779), Chardin's still lifes were admired for their illusionistic realism just as Harnett's were to be in nineteenth-century America, and were purchased at moderate prices by the prosperous bourgeoisie, while his scenes from daily life, such as *The Governess* (**103**), were so highly regarded that they were purchased for royal collections all the way from France to Russia. Chardin himself preferred still life, and painted nothing else during his last twenty-five years except when he would repeat one of his easily saleable early genre subjects to make a little money.

Within a few years of birth and death Chardin was a contemporary of François Boucher, his exact opposite, whose slick, artificial, frequently erotic art, exemplified by the *Toilet of Venus* (**104**), made him the reigning painter at the French court. That the same fashionable society should occasionally buy a Chardin genre scene like *The Governess* is less surprising than it seems; the attitude toward Chardin's subjects combined sentimentalism with a variety of semi-intellectualism in the appreciation of current concepts of the nobility of the common man propounded by the philosopher Jean Jacques Rousseau. Professed sympathy with the lower and middle classes took on a certain snob value among the aristocracy and its hangers-on; Boucher's paintings of shepherds and shepherdesses—sumptuously costumed in silks and satins—became as successful as his gods and goddesses, and were reflected in garden parties where dukes and duchesses came in similar pastoral finery. Chardin's scenes of bourgeois life were sentimentalized even by the upper bourgeoisie who, along with international royalty, collected them. When *The Governess* was reproduced as an engraving, it was accompanied by a verse to the effect that "Although this sweet-faced little boy pretends to listen obediently to the admonitions of his governess, I'll wager that he's thinking about getting back to his games," which demeans a painting that (as we see it today) is an affectionate reflection of respect for middle-class virtues, just as Chardin's still lifes celebrate the honesty of simple things.

It makes no difference whether or not "natural" man turned out to be as noble as the eighteenth-century philosophers hoped. We all know that near the end of the century in France noble heads were chopped off by the common man in a not very noble manifestation of his changed status. But the dignity of the common man was a noble ideal, it was in the air, and it found its way into Chardin's paintings of pots and pans.

The nineteenth century was, of all centuries, the practical one, the common-sense one, the respectable middle-class one. Whatever other qualities it had, its life was centered upon this substantial core. The eighteenth century's philosophical ideal of "natural nobility" became in reality frequently more vulgar than noble. In an age that was what we call "realistic about things" in its daily philosophy, realistic painting flourished over a range as wide as the century's own attitude toward the daily world: from crass to profound in its understanding of human life.

Jean-Léon Gérôme's *The Duel after the Masquerade* (**106**) is at neither the top nor the bottom of this range. We can begin to see just where it belongs by comparing its realism to Chardin's. When we say of the Chardin, "A pear on the left and a mug on the right binds three apples, another

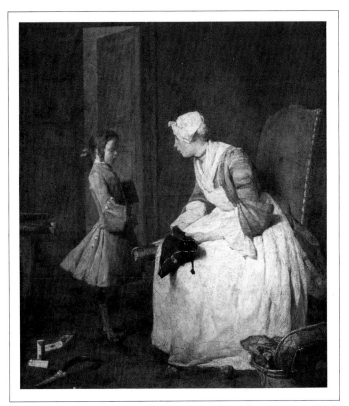

103. Jean-Baptiste-Siméon Chardin. *The Governess* (alternate title, *The Nursemaid*, formerly *The Admonition*). Oil on canvas, 13⅜ by 14¾ inches. The National Gallery of Canada, Ottawa.

104. François Boucher. *The Toilet of Venus.* 1751. Oil on canvas, 42⅝ by 33½ inches. The Metropolitan Museum of Art, New York. Bequest of William K. Vanderbilt, 1920.

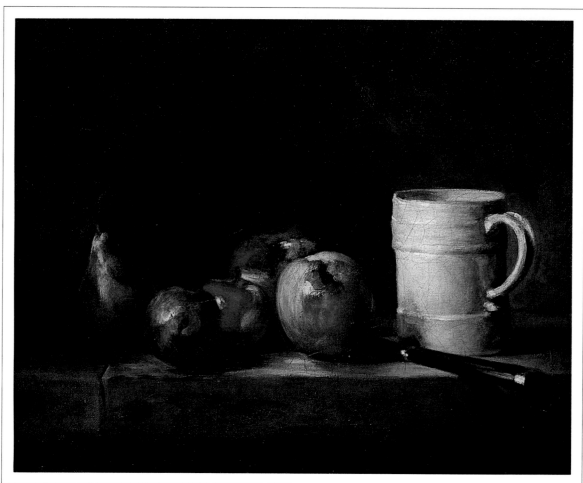

105. Jean-Baptiste-Siméon Chardin. *Still Life with a White Mug.* Date uncertain. Oil on canvas, 13 by 16¼ inches. National Gallery of Art, Washington, D.C. Gift of the W. Averell Harriman Foundation in memory of Marie N. Harriman.

106. Jean Léon Gérôme. *The Duel after the Masquerade.* About 1867. Oil on canvas, 15¼ by 22 inches. The Walters Art Gallery, Baltimore.

pear, and a knife on a stone shelf," we have said little about the picture. Its meaning lies elsewhere, as we have tried to explain. But when we say of the Gérôme, "After a duel in a snowy open space within a park, a male figure costumed as a seventeenth-century burgher supports another costumed as Pierrot, who, wounded, collapses, while a third, costumed as an oriental potentate, examines the wound, and a fourth in a rich velvet cloak clutches his head in grief; to the right the successful duelist, costumed as an American Indian, leaves the field accompanied by his second, costumed as Harlequin," we have described the essence of the picture, if we add that technically it is a faultlessly performed exercise. The picture is an anecdote. The anecdote may be pathetic, but the picture is not interpretive. It neither enlarges nor intensifies our experience. We cannot find anything else for the picture to "say" unless it says, as we already know, that when young men get into a fight after a dance, someone is likely to get hurt. With the young men in costume there is an element of fantasy for frosting. In other words, the picture is superficial.

This does not mean that a duel after a masquerade could not serve as a subject for a moving interpretation of some aspect of life. The anecdotal quality is inherent in the treatment, not in the subject. As mighty a subject as the Crucifixion could be reduced to anecdotal level by similar treatment—and has been, more than once. Any meaning we read into *The Duel after the Masquerade* must come from our reaction to the anecdote; it is not implicit in Gérôme's telling of it. And in the words "telling of it" we indicate that the approach is essentially literary, rather than painterly. The picture is an illustration, taking second place to something else rather than existing as an independent creation.

The painting's shortcomings are typical of nineteenth-century academic painting, the painting of the popular, successful artist who pleased the public because his art was easily understood, undemanding. But in making all these objections, we are not insisting that every painting should be a great one. Painting at second level has its place too, if it does not pretend to be anything else. If we accept the Gérôme as a stunning technical rendering, a pleasant bit of decorative color, a graceful combination of attractive figures, then it is an enjoyable picture. It hangs in a gallery full of nineteenth-century paintings of very high caliber and easily holds its own among them.

The nineteenth century was the one in which art first found a mass audience eager for culture. The ambitious bourgeoisie liked to think of art as an elevating experience, which, indeed, it can be, but never before or since has this experience been so identified with sentimentalism. A thriving culture-consciousness in the United States was often combined with the artistic celebration of homespun virtues that were supposed to flourish with exceptional vigor on native soil. Thomas Hovenden's *Breaking Home Ties* (**107**) is a superior example of the type of anecdotal realism that capitalized on popular moralistic values. The young man,

107. Thomas Hovenden. *Breaking Home Ties.* 1890. Oil on canvas, 52⅛ by 72¼ inches. Philadelphia Museum of Art. Given by Ellen Harrison McMichael in memory of C. Emory McMichael.

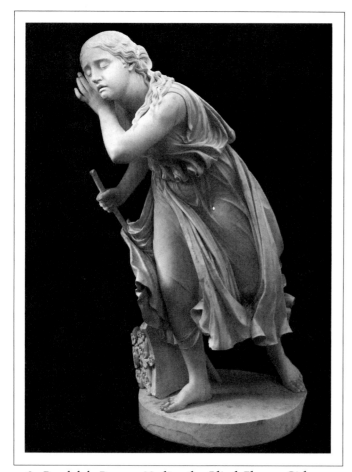

108. Randolph Rogers. *Nydia, the Blind Flower Girl of Pompeii.* 1856. Marble, height 55 inches. Museum of Fine Arts, Boston. Gift of Dr. and Mrs. Lawrence Perchik.

hat in hand, is leaving home for the first time; a male relative carries his bag toward the door at the right; the mother, concealing her grief in courageous recognition of the necessity of the situation, bids the boy goodbye, perhaps with a last word of advice. The grandmother sits stoically at the table; a young sister leans against the door; perhaps she will cry later. At one side another woman—a maiden aunt?—sits holding the boy's umbrella and a small package she has made for him. By her side the family dog is stoic in the prospect of bereavement.

When *Breaking Home Ties* was first exhibited in Philadelphia in 1890, people lined up to see it and, unlike the characters in the picture, were unable to restrain their tears. The picture's emotional force for its contemporary public is partially explained by a virtue still apparent: it is beautifully observant in the details of its setting, and beautifully painted in a firm, honest manner that bolsters the feeling of sturdy virtue, which is the picture's theme. If it no longer inspires tears, *Breaking Home Ties* can still inspire respect.

Anecdotal subjects were also popular in nineteenth-century sculpture, but time has been less kind to them than to pictures like *Breaking Home Ties.* Somehow the sheer tangible weight and mass of stone or bronze and the sheer physical labor of producing a work of sculpture accentuate the triviality of subjects that no longer seem worth the trouble. That a wide audience in the nineteenth century felt differently is proven by the popularity of *Nydia, the Blind Flower Girl of Pompeii* (**108**), by the American sculptor Randolph Rogers.

Nydia is the blind flower-seller heroine of *The Last Days of Pompeii* by the English historical novelist Edward Bulwer-Lytton. The book, published in 1834, was the *Gone With the Wind* of its day, and became so popular in America that Rogers virtually mass-produced copies of *Nydia;* nearly a hundred versions still exist. *Nydia* is the ultimate storytelling sculpture, totally dependent on a knowledge of the book. The volcanic eruption that destroyed Pompeii has blotted out the light in a city filled with smoke and ash; but Nydia, having always been blind, and knowing her way around the city in her own perpetual dark, is leading others to safety while she strains to hear the voice of her master, Glaucus. Our example was done in 1856, twenty-two years after the publication of the book, when Nydia's name was as familiar as Scarlett O'Hara's is today.

It is usually easier to explain what is wrong with a picture than to show what makes it good. The better a picture is, the more likely it is to communicate in terms that cannot be expressed as well in any other medium. This is true of other art forms, too. What Shakespeare says in *Hamlet,* for instance, has not been said as well in painting. Similarly, what Thomas Eakins says in his portrait *Miss Van Buren* (**109**) is said so completely in terms of a realistic image that when we come to discuss it, the temptation is to say no more than "Just look at it!" The picture is one of those great ones whose meaning is as obvious as it is unexplainable in specific comment.

Eakins was a life-long Philadelphian who at the age of twenty-two in 1866 went to Paris and studied for three years under academic masters, including Gérôme, the slickly proficient painter of *Duel after the Masquerade.* Fortunately Eakins was protected by a natural immunity to infection by this master, and returned home to become his country's soundest, strongest realist and, by many critical judgments, our greatest painter in any classification.

Even though the total effect of the portrait of Miss Van Buren is greater than the sum of its parts, leaving its greatness, as we have said, unexplainable, some specific virtues can be defined. As a realistic drawing (that is, as the expression by lines and shadows of a three-dimensional form on a two-dimensional surface), it is superbly skillful. Eakins is completely master of the craft of realistic drawing, which he inherits from the centuries of artists who worked before him. As a realistic painting (that is, a drawing that includes the re-creation of the colors of the represented objects), the picture is equally good. As creative realism, in its selection and modification from the visual material confronting the artist, it employs some devices we can be specific about.

The sitter has, first of all, been posed in an attitude natural in effect and expressively characteristic. From this advantageous beginning, Eakins goes on to exaggerations of the natural contrasts between light and shade. Without getting theatrical he creates a spotlight effect, a formula used in portraits by hundreds of painters (Rembrandt used it most insistently). By its use Eakins directs our attention to the salient passages of his subject, intensifying their effect by displaying them brightly against other passages that are relatively blotted out. But he does this so subtly that we are not conscious of the exaggeration, as Rembrandt makes us conscious of intensification for a more emotionalized statement. Eakins does not want to emotionalize his subject; the mood is one of contemplation but not of mystery. This mood is stated in the color, too, which is modified away from unexpected combinations or full intensities.

But not one of these devices is original with Eakins; we could find all of them combined similarly in any number of pictures that are nothing but proficient demonstrations of technique. Is the Eakins a greater picture because it does the conventional thing but does it better? No. Eakins employs these familiar devices with maximum skill, yet there remains an intangible quality in the art of every great painter, one that makes the difference in Eakins's case between this image of Miss Van Buren, which is so vital, and an image that is lifeless.

Whatever this intangible quality is, with Eakins it has to do with honesty. Feature by feature Miss Van Buren's face is not a beautiful one (110). It is even rather plain. But she is neither glamorized nor flattered. In terms of the average portrait, where the purpose is to produce an ac-

109. Thomas Eakins. *Miss Van Buren.* About 1889–91. Oil on canvas, 44½ by 32 inches. The Phillips Collection, Washington, D.C.

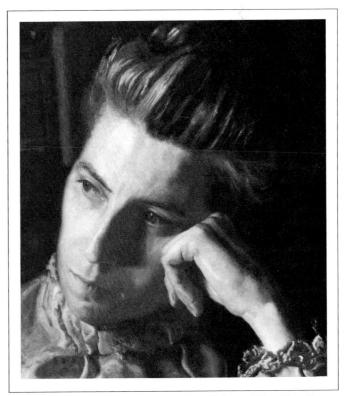

110. Detail from *Miss Van Buren.*

ceptably accurate likeness as beautified as possible, Eakins's picture would be mercilessly and pointlessly realistic. But a great Eakins portrait is a matter of neither cosmeticization nor documentation. It is a great painting finding within the substantial everyday world poetry of such strength that it needs no bolstering by prettification or ornament. Comparing this masterpiece with others we have been discussing, we see that it is not idealized (like the Leonardo), not dramatized (like the Rubens and the Caravaggio), not objective (like the Velázquez). Its everydayness is related to Chardin's; its greatest contrast is with *Saint Francis Receiving the Stigmata*. Whereas the painter of that wonderful little picture saw every fragment of the world taking on meaning as part of a great established scheme of things, Eakins sees that each fragment of reality must be accepted for itself, for whatever meaning it has in itself, independent of a divinely organized, an idealized, or a dramatized world. This idea was expressed more emphatically by a group of French painters—Eakins's contemporaries, but more experimental in their approach—who came to be known as the Impressionists.

Impressionism was a double revolution—an ideological one in which the chance moment became as interesting to an artist as were the eternal verities, and a technical one by which the "impression" of a chance moment was

111. Édouard Manet. *Boating.* 1874. Oil on canvas, 38½ by 51¼ inches. The Metropolitan Museum of Art, New York. Bequest of Mrs. H. O. Havemeyer, 1929. The H. O. Havemeyer Collection.

recorded. In order to achieve an impression of the light and atmosphere of a particular time of a day that might be rainy, snowy, foggy, or sunny, colors were applied loosely, even spottily, to be blended by the eye into the appropriate effect of sparkle or mistiness. Claude Monet, in his landscapes, epitomized this aspect of impressionism. But suggestion also took the place of exact statement in less systematic painting, going beyond the studious objective optical realism that we saw in Velázquez, to a kind of shorthand notation that approximates, rather than reproduces, what the eye registers at a glance.

Édouard Manet's *Boating* (111) is put together as if the subject had been caught by accident in a snapshot, as if it were a fragment of a larger composition. The effect is to increase our feeling of intimacy and participation in the scene. Harmonizing with this apparently offhand composition, the technique is sketchy; what we have already called impressionistic "shorthand" is used for the eyes and other features, for the details of clothes, particularly the hat and veil of the woman, for the expanse of water.

Living in a century when science had demonstrated that no one man can begin to know the universe, Manet was not interested in trying to make universal statements, ideal or otherwise. He seems to say: "Here is an instant in a day, to be accepted for what it is, without too much concern over its place in the vast, incomprehensible scheme of things." Thus Impressionist realism appeals because it so frequently discovers an idyllic quality in the commonplace and, above all, the transient. In the hands of trivial painters, the commonplace can be most trivial indeed; but in the hands of serious and sensitive painters like the great figures among the Impressionists, fragments of commonplace reality tell us that although the universal scheme of things may be beyond our comprehension, we can understand moments of it in terms of feeling and sentiment or enjoy their simple visual attraction.

The Impressionists fought their battles and won their victory—a total victory—in the last thirty years of the nineteenth century. But even as their century turned into the twentieth, a new generation was questioning their realistic premises. Expressionism and abstraction (the subjects of our next two chapters) fought new battles as the new century opened, followed by new victories. Shortly after World War II, with the triumph of a dazzling school of abstraction in the United States, it seemed possible to say that impressionism had been the last flower of realism, exhausting the possibilities of exploring alike the world of emotion and the world of intellect in terms of the world we see around us.

But this idea was mistaken. The 1970's saw a revival of realism in general, led by two extreme forms—photorealism and hyperrealism. (The term "superrealism" is also used; we are using the alternate "hyperrealism" to avoid confusion with "surrealism," which is an art of the fantastic

112. Isabel Bishop. *Two Girls.* 1936. Oil and tempera on composition board, 20 by 24 inches. The Metropolitan Museum of Art, New York. Arthur H. Hearn Fund, 1936.

and supernatural. We will encounter surrealism in a later chapter.

Realism had, in fact, persisted without interruption in the United States during the rise and triumph of abstraction. The Great Depression of the 1930's stimulated an approach called "social realism," marked by a sympathetic attitude toward the urban lower-middle class and the proletariat, who always bear the brunt of hard times. Artists discovered that the big city's subways, its park benches, its cheap movie houses, its hall bedrooms, and above all its business streets, were parts of a humanistic spectacle that had hardly been tapped as painters' material. Isabel Bishop's sensitive but unidealized observations of anonymous shopgirls and office workers (112) are among the enduring witnesses to the vitality of this twentieth-century American form of realism, while Edward Hopper's famous *Nighthawks* (113), in a different mood, plays a theme peculiar to our times— the loneliness of individuals in an urban society, a loneliness all the more poignant because it persists within a crowd. Painters like Isabel Bishop and Edward Hopper continued their careers during the years of the rise of abstraction, but by the nature of the contemporary art world, which demands recurrent excitement and novelty, something unusual was necessary to proclaim that realism was reborn.

Photorealism proclaimed something unusual indeed. Artists had used photographs for reference ever since the invention of the camera, but artists had not insisted that the camera's eye held a truth to which the painter must be subservient. The pioneer photorealists even claimed that the painter's only function was to "transfer information from the medium of photography to the medium of painting," and sought to eliminate all evidence of the artist's hand, all additional interpretive function, from their reproductions of

113. Edward Hopper. *Nighthawks.* 1942. Oil on canvas, 30 by 60 inches. The Art Institute of Chicago, Friends of American Art Collection.

photographs. And the more ordinary the photograph, the more certain was the escape from interpretation.

This escape, of course, was impossible—as well as rather dull for the artist and unrewarding for the observer, who quite justifiably might find more interest in a photograph than in a painted reproduction of a photograph. Even the most devout photorealists cleaned up the photographs in the process of transferal—sharpening edges, emphasizing important details, eliminating others. Richard Estes's *Supreme Hardware* (**114**) of 1973, while nominally photorealist, is obviously interpretive beneath its apparent objectivity. For one thing, his city street is abnormally deserted, with a resultant effect of unnatural silence. For another, although he seems to have included every detail of the clutter of this side street, including garbage bags, everything exists with an unnatural clarity. Our eye is carried from one familiar detail to another, yet each has more independent interest than it would have if lost in the conglomeration of details either in reality or in a photograph.

In a later picture, *Thom McAn* (**115**), by the same artist, the reproduction of photographic reality is hardly more than a starting point for invention. Each detail is perfectly, legibly, acutely defined in the rendition of multiple reflections in glass panes and shiny surfaces. Yet if we give the painting more than a glance, we begin to confuse reality with the reflection of reality, what is real with what is illusion. Which objects and planes are in front of us, and which are reflections of those behind us or at either side of us? The final enigma, of which we may be unconscious even while it affects our response to the picture, is that while we, as observers, are obviously standing in a position where our image would be reflected and re-reflected, we are quite absent. We stand as if invisible, or atomized, within a commonplace setting that has become unreal. In such a painting, "photorealism" is no longer an appropriate term; the artist's eye has rejected the eye of the camera in order to perform the eternal function of realistic art—to reveal the familiar world in a vision that affects our experience of it.

"Hyperrealism," by a dictionary definition of the prefix, would mean "more-than-the-normal realism," and its function, in the view of its contemporary practitioners, is to make us more than normally aware of visual realities we are so habituated to taking for granted that we only half see them. In terms of comparative realism, a head by Chuck Close (**116**) is exactly the opposite of one by Velázquez. We saw that Velázquez painted only what the eye perceived at a certain distance in a certain light. Chuck Close's heads are painted an enormous size—up to about 8 feet high—with proportionate enlargement of hairs, pores, small wrinkles, eyelashes, and all other details (**117**). It is as if our eyes had suddenly become powerful magnifying lenses; we become aware that we have never really seen a human face before, at least not in such explicit physicality. This is more-than-the-normal realism to an extreme degree, riv-

114. Richard Estes. *Supreme Hardware.* 1973. Oil on canvas, 40 by 66 inches. Courtesy of Allan Stone Gallery, New York.

115. Richard Estes. *Thom McAn.* 1974. Oil on canvas, 40 by 60 inches. Private collection. Courtesy Allan Stone Gallery, New York.

116. Chuck Close. *Nat.* 1972. Watercolor on paper, 67 by 57 inches. Neue Galerie, Aachen, West Germany. Ludwig Collection.

117. Eye from *Nat.*

118. Duane Hanson. Head of a man, detail from *Couple with Shopping Bags.* 1976. Polyester resin and fiber glass, polychromed in oil, with clothing and accessories, life size. Courtesy of O. K. Harris Gallery, New York.

119. Wit Stwosz (Stoss). *Saint Peter*, head. 1447–86. Wood, guilded and painted, life size. From the High Altar, St. Mary's, Cracow.

eting our attention on a facial landscape with all its erosions, cracks, ridges, and evidence of subterranean tensions.

The qualities that make hyperrealism a realism specifically of our time may be clarified if we juxtapose three realistically sculptured heads: first, that of *Saint Peter* (**119**) from the Cracow Altar, which was begun in 1477 by Wit Stwosz and remains in the Polish city where it was carved; second, a head of *Saint John of God* (**120**) by the seventeenth-century Spanish baroque sculptor Alonso Cano; and finally the head of the man (**118**, p. 85) from a two-figure sculpture group, *Couple with Shopping Bags,* by the contemporary American sculptor Duane Hanson. (The entire sculpture is illustrated and further discussed later on).

Saint Peter, carved in wood and painted in realistic colors, is only about forty years later than the painting of *Saint Francis Receiving the Stigmata* with which we discussed medieval realism. *Saint John of God* is contemporary with *The Ecstasy of Saint Theresa* and, like that sensational example, seeks to stir the observer by the tangibility of a religious image. Like Saint Peter's, the head of Saint John of God is carved in wood and painted, with the addition of real glass eyes. Originally it was part of an *imagen de vestir,* a type of statue popular in seventeenth-century Spain, clothed in real costumes, with real jewelry or other accessories, often symbols of martyrdom.

Hanson's twentieth-century martyrs to supermarket culture, an ordinary man and his wife, are cast from life in polyester resin. Their skins are painted with strict fidelity to nature; in addition to glass eyes and wigs for both, the man's arms are equipped with fuzz set into the vinyl hair by hair. Wearing real clothing and carrying real shopping bags filled with real products, here are examples of the *imagen de vestir* beyond anything previously seen—even in waxworks museums, for their fidelity to nature exceeds the most convincing of such effigies. With the exception of movement, the illusion of life is complete.

Saint Peter's seamed and wrinkled face, the pouches beneath his eyes, a small wart on the right side of his nose, the glint of upper teeth seen through the half-opened mouth, the curl-by-curl complexities of the hair and beard—here is an exaggerated and intensified realism that might have been called hyperrealistic if the term had been invented earlier. But everything is patterned with an eye to elegance that competes with the realism and, if we compare it with our twentieth-century shopper, triumphs over literal reality. And the spirituality of the saint's expression of compassionate concern is high drama, in contrast with the shopper's look of stultification and chronic despair.

It seems likely that *Saint Peter* is a portrait from life of some good citizen who lent his features (including the small wart) for the purpose. *Saint John of God* is a portrait of this Portuguese adventurer who turned to charitable works after his conversion—a portrait derived from paintings showing his traditional features. It is a strong face, making a first impression of great beauty that is accounted for, when we analyze it, more by the fineness of the noble, slightly melancholy expression than by the features themselves. The beauty of color reminds us that the tinting of stone and wood statues had been common practice from antiquity on through the very late Middle Ages, when it was often entrusted to eminent painters as being of equal importance with the carving. (The great Jan van Eyck was not too proud to accept commissions to tint other artists' sculptures.) The pure white marble statues of the Renaissance were left uncolored under the misconception that ancient statues, which time had bleached of their color, had never been tinted. Under this influence color was gradually abandoned, but the art of Alonso Cano shows how vigorously it survived in seventeenth-century Spanish religious sculpture. Cano was equally skilled as painter and sculptor, and thought of color as an integral part of his statues rather than a secondary addition.

Since the goal of the sculptor-painters of these three heads was to create as vivid as possible a projection of the life and the individuality of the subjects, and since both of the earlier sculptors employed departures from literal reality to enhance that vividness, is Hanson's sculpture "anti-art" (as it has been called) in its deliberate and insistently literal reproduction of the subject, even to the extent, as we have said, of casting from life? That is a reasonable question, but it is answered by the fact that whether you call it art or anti-art, the image of a weary supermarket shopper makes an impression *stronger* than life. By reproducing the commonplace with such staggering verisimilitude, the artist makes us examine this bit of life in the way he reproduced it—pore by pore, hair by hair. Because we are amazed by the technique, we are spellbound by the image of a person of exactly the kind that we pass by on the street without a glance. Thus the hyperrealist sculptor forces us into a more-than-normal realization of the character of life. He breaks our habits of seeing, clears our eyes, and by forcing this typical member of our society upon our attention, by amazing and fascinating us by the illusion of reality, leads us to look at that reality anew, and to speculate upon the nature of the society that produced this typical specimen of humankind. As we will see later, the inferred comment is not a flattering one.

Turning once more to the dictionary, we find that the first definition of realism is "a tendency to face facts and be practical rather than imaginative or visionary." This does not altogether conform to the more flexible ideas of realism in painting and sculpture, but does supply an affirmative answer to a question that naturally arises: Is there such a thing as realism in architecture?

There is indeed. Under the term "functionalism," architectural realism demands that the "imaginative or visionary" aspects of designing buildings be extraneous to "facing facts and being practical," and must be eliminated to give full play to the primary consideration of seeing that a building is designed to perform its function with maximum efficiency.

120. Alonso Cano. *Saint John of God,* head. 1660–67(?). Wood, painted, life size. Museo Provincial de Bellas Artes, Granada.

121. Church of Saint-Nectaire (Puy-de-Dome). Begun about 1080. France.

122. Walter Gropius. Bauhaus. 1925–26. Dessau, Germany.

As a corollary to that premise, a building may automatically take on forms that are esthetically satisfying as a result of the dictum that "Form follows function." The dictum belongs to modern architecture, but the principle is not peculiar to it, having been demonstrated in the past without benefit of theory. The exteriors of medieval churches, when not encrusted with sculpture and other carved ornament, are simply the defining skins of interior spaces designed for specific functions; yet these skins tell as solid volumes that seem to have been arranged with regard for their beauty, resembling, in effect, monuments of abstract sculpture(121).

The theory of functionalism, however, is applied only to modern buildings, and the argument goes that if a building serves the purposes of our time functionally, it will necessarily assume new forms, the forms of a uniquely modern style, as a kind of spontaneous stylistic autogenesis. Added to the modernism of these formal innovations will be the textures of building materials peculiar to our time. A good example of early-vintage functionalism is Walter Gropius's Bauhaus, built at Dessau, Germany, in 1926 (122).

The Bauhaus, a state school of architecture, painting, and sculpture, was formed in 1919 with the thirty-six-year-old Gropius as director. In a Germany suffering from the defeat of World War I, art was reflecting the neurotic tension, the pessimism, and the social chaos of the times. (As an example, see Ernst Kirchner's *Street Scene*, in the next chapter.) Gropius called for an educational program that would reestablish the unity of the arts, which were to be led out of the wilderness by an architecture that was positive and rational in spirit, a twentieth-century architecture that would be of its time in its adaptation to industrial civilization.

The industrial age supplied industrial products for building—modern concrete, steel, and glass—that were employed in the Bauhaus undisguised by overlays of traditional materials and undeformed by adaptation to shapes inherited from the past. Economy and function as the determining considerations of design yielded clean, spare forms that allowed maximum space and light for the studios and offices of the school. Familiar today (overfamiliar, in fact, and often misused), these forms in 1926 were strikingly modern, and virtually unheard of as the forms of a state building, where architecture is always most conservative. The projection of the upper stories beyond the ground floor, the elimination of the cornice except for a thin, narrow band, the opening of the interior to full view from the outside, the exposed construction everywhere, the elimination of ornament—all of this meant the rejection of standard architectural vocabulary and the creation of a new one.

The Bauhaus design, more than fifty years later, remains unusually satisfactory. Its simple clarity is the first reason, but this design was not, after all, determined entirely by functional demands. Such details as the size of the divisions of the panes of glass, the variations in size from square to long-rectangular, the variations in size and proportion of the interrelated blocklike units of the building's mass (if so open a building can be said to have mass), the purity of the long white bands of concrete, the play between solid structural elements and the voids between them—each of these was determined first by functional principles. But it is still true that every opportunity was taken to emphasize their inherent potential as elements in a controlled design. In its own way, this example of realistic architecture is an expression of an ideal, and an ancient one in architecture— the ideal of the rational spirit that has been persistent and recurrent ever since its consummate expression in the Parthenon twenty-five centuries ago.

The Bauhaus's twentieth-century ideal of absolute identification of form with function had been achieved in the middle of the nineteenth century by a building born of necessity in an emergency—the Crystal Palace (**123** and **124**), built to house England's Great Exhibition of 1851, the first international exposition. The requirement was for a vast building to house exhibits from around the world, with all the attendant problems of light, unencumbered space allowing for the construction of independent exhibition

123. Joseph Paxton. Crystal Palace, exterior. 1851, destroyed 1936. Line engraving.

124. Crystal Palace, interior. After a color lithograph, 13¼ by 19⅛ inches. From *Dickinson's Comprehensive Pictures of the Great Exhibition*. London, 1854.

125. Thomas Fuller. Parliament House. Ottawa. 1859–65. Chromolithograph by Burland, Lafricain & Co. Courtesy Public Archives of Canada, Ottawa.

126. Charles Garnier. Opéra. Paris.

127. D. H. Burnham & Co. Reliance Building, Chicago. 1894–95. Photograph, about 1905, courtesy Chicago Historical Society.

areas, and the accommodation of great crowds—plus the desperately complicating factor of quick and economical construction.

The taste of the time was for elaborate buildings in eclectic styles. The opposite of functional in their complex ornamentation of forms that often were themselves more decorative than functional, these buildings could be ludicrous. But at their best they were brilliant studies in design. Two of the finest examples, both contemporary with the Crystal Palace, will serve us. Parliament House in Ottawa, shown here (125) before being rebuilt in somewhat simpler style after partial destruction by fire in the twentieth century, was a major achievement, unsurpassed even in England itself, as an exercise in the favorite English eclectic style, neo-Gothic. The Paris Opera House (126) was, and remains, the supreme neo-baroque building. But the Paris Opera House took six years to construct, and Ottawa's Parliament House, eight. Quite aside from the expense of buildings like these, London needed its exhibition hall within a matter of months. Architects were at a loss.

The solution was reached by Joseph Paxton, a garden landscapist and greenhouse builder who had no training in either engineering or architecture. His iron-and-glass building, whose area of 753,000 square feet made it one of the largest buildings of its century, was essentially a gargantuan greenhouse built of standard units (the term today would be "prefabricated") that could be rapidly assembled and just as rapidly disassembled after the exhibition was over. Virtually every foundry in England was set to casting the standard units of hollow iron tubes, while glass factories rolled out the glass panes. Every functional requirement was met, and the building was completed in less than six months. In retrospect, the Crystal Palace is a landmark in functional architecture and the use of modern materials. At the time it was a sensational success as a kind of fairytale fantasy. And indeed it was a fantasy, a transparent building within which you could stand under the great trees of Hyde Park, where it was built, and look up beyond them and through the roof and into the sky. Within the building the light shifted and changed according to the time of day and with the passage of clouds.

In the seventy-five years stretching between the Crystal Palace and the Bauhaus, circumstances made one imperative demand on architecture that had never been made before. As cities grew bigger and bigger, with their business districts compressed within a central area, buildings could grow larger only by growing upward instead of spreading outward—and the skyscraper was born. Its early history included a battle of styles in which Chicago architects made the most prophetic recognition of the skyscraper as a layered steel skeleton that required no supporting walls and thus offered opportunity for the elimination of exterior wall space in favor of windows (127). This realistic approach was opposed by a continuation of eclecticism in which all the styles of the past were then juggled, twisted, stretched, and otherwise deformed in efforts to apply to an architectural form that was peculiar to the present.

The aspiring lines of the Gothic cathedral were best adapted to the skyscraper's verticality, and Cass Gilbert's Woolworth Building (**128**), built in 1913, must be called the masterpiece of skyscraper eclecticism. But following the lead of the Bauhaus and other forces that developed the spare, antiseptic, unornamented modern styles, the skyscraper assumed the form we now see repeated ad infinitum, that of a slab, frequently "walled" by only a glass curtain. The Seagram Building (**129**) is the most eloquent proof that exquisite attention to proportions in the linear divisions of the slab, plus the use of some of the most expensive square feet of real estate in the world as a plaza, can produce a beautiful commercial skyscraper and provide it with a beautiful site. For the most part, however, the skyscrapers that grew as thick as weeds (and almost as rapidly) in the post–World War II building boom were innocent of any serious esthetic considerations in their design. Design was determined by the builders' determination to make maximum commercial use of every square and cubic foot allowable under zoning regulations. This of course is "realism" of a definite kind, but hardly a desirable kind.

As early as 1950 the artist Saul Steinberg, whose satirical drawings of buildings in all styles are acutely perceptive critical judgments, anticipated other critics' disillusion in a prophetic drawing in which he used a sheet of graph paper as a skyscraper façade. Steinberg's prophecy was distressingly fulfilled during the next thirty years by building after building in what could be called Graph Paper Style, in which large glass boxes divided into the small, uniform squares of their steel skeletons became the monotonous norm for the skyscraper. What had once been modern had become rep-

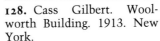

128. Cass Gilbert. Woolworth Building. 1913. New York.

129. Ludwig Mies van der Rohe. Seagram Building. 1956–58. New York.

130. Abandoned missile-tracking station, North Dakota.

131. Welton Beckett Associates. Hyatt Regency Hotel and Reunion Tower. 1973–78. Dallas, Texas.

132. First floor plan. Opéra, Paris. From "Le Nouvel Opéra de Paris," 1878–80. Courtesy The Museum of Modern Art, New York.

etitious, mechanical, unimaginative, and dehumanized in spite of the uneasiness of thoughtful architects. In the mid-1960's, the critic Ada Louise Huxtable expressed her misgivings as to what was happening to New York in an article, "Slab City Marches On."

Architects, critics, and historians began to suspect that the most exciting and possibly most distinctive structures of our time might be those whose forms followed specific functions that were satisfied not by architectural design but by practical engineering, such as our great refineries with their complexes of forms that had never been approximated by architecture of the past. Functionalism, in such cases, was the mother of invention. Unfortunately, obsolescence is also the death of architectural record, and these projects will be lost to the future except in photographs. An example is the $5.7 billion missile-tracking station in North Dakota (130), as eerie a group of structures as could have been imagined if fantasy and not science had dictated its forms.

Deliberate fantasy is an expensive indulgence in most building design, but efforts to create arresting effects in variations of the glass-box formula have been made when circumstances (which means financing) have permitted it. The Hyatt Regency Hotel and Reunion Tower in Dallas, Texas (131), by Welton Becket Associates, with its space-age overtones, is an example. In this case, the sacrifice of maximum use of ground space (and for that matter, air space) is worth the attractions the design holds for a public that by its patronage must support the project financially.

Disenchantment with the functional ideal that had been so enthusiastically received in its youth was not limited to the skyscraper, which was only the most spectacular example of the malfunction of a legitimate theory. Buildings large or small, residential or commercial, raised the same doubts. Was the human spirit being starved by the impersonality of the new styles? Was the eye becoming bored by formulas that, even when applied with taste and discretion, were monotonous in their repetition? Such questions were declared officially permissible in 1975 when the Museum of Modern Art, which had been a powerful influence in the popularization of modern architectural theories, took a revolutionary step with a sympathetically presented exhibition of the very kind of architecture that had been most reviled by the modernists, an exhibition called "The Architecture of the École des Beaux Arts."

The name of the École des Beaux Arts, the official French school of painting, sculpture, and architecture, had been synonymous for close to a hundred years with conservative or reactionary approaches to the arts. The reputation was well deserved, but the Museum of Modern Art's unexpected exhibition suggested that even so there were virtues in the nineteenth-century eclectic styles that had been too quickly dismissed as vices. Perhaps architects who in the nineteenth century had been thought of as creative designers along with painters and sculptors, had sacrificed this position to one in which they were subservient to all practical requirements. After all, the Paris Opera House, which exemplified the Beaux Arts style to perfection, was also a model of efficiency from a functional point of view. Even in skeleton outline, the Opera's plan and section (**132** and **133**) show that it accommodated one of the world's most beautiful auditoriums, with backstage arrangements for the most elaborately engineered spectacles, as well as offices, storage rooms, a multitude of foyers (we will see one doubling as a rehearsal room in Degas's painting, **261**), and circulation areas that not only allowed for heavy traffic in and out of the auditorium but made those passages delightful for the audiences. The Opera's Grand Staircase (**134**) makes one's entrance and exit a pleasure in itself, as opposed to the more practical but hardly fascinating escalators that perform the function of moving modern audiences but perform it with no recognition of the individual as anything more than a certain number of pounds, occupying a certain number of square feet, that must be got in and out of the hall.

In the 1970's at least one eminent architecture critic, Peter Blake, a former proselytizer for modern styles, reversed his stand in a series of essays entitled *Form Follows Fiasco: Why Modern Architecture Hasn't Worked*. Here he attacked various "fantasies," as he called them, that in addition to "the fantasy of form" included fantasies of function, of purity, of technology, of the skyscraper, of the ideal city, of mobility, of zoning, and of housing. Everywhere, by his arguments, "The spirit of architecture seems to have been lost."

This extreme rejection may be a necessary counterweight to the extreme commitment of the Bauhaus generation, but it cannot be accepted without some modifying recognition of modern architecture's achievements, including certain beautiful office buildings where the squared lines and glass curtain walls that have become so monotonous are employed with imagination. Lever House (**135**), built in 1950–52, is such a building, with its directional play of one volume in counterpoint to another, and its main unit hovering as if weightless above a terrace. But there have been proposals to raze the building or to redesign it with additions that would make it more practical—that is, increase the amount of rentable space at the expense of the esthetic quality of a building that is one of the delights of New York's deteriorating cityscape.

Architecture has always, perforce, been an art upon which realistic values must be imposed to one degree or another; but only in modern architecture have these values been allowed to overpower humanistic values that are at least equally important. Perhaps, in the post-1970's, realism in architecture will be as flexible and as various as we found realism in painting to be, early in this chapter. We will not be building neo-baroque opera houses or neo-Gothic parliament buildings, but we may find ways of giving warmth and variety to new patterns of places where we live and work.

133. Longitudinal section. Opéra, Paris. From "Le Nouvel Opéra de Paris," 1878–80. Courtesy The Museum of Modern Art, New York.

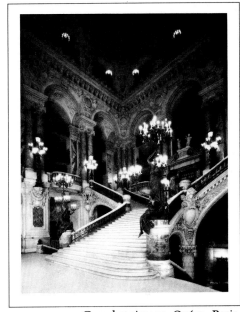

134. Grand staircase. Opéra, Paris.

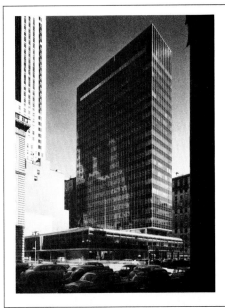

135. Skidmore, Owings & Merrill (Gordon Bunshaft). Lever House. 1950–52. New York.

136. Vincent van Gogh. *The Starry Night.* 1889. Oil on canvas, 29 by 36¼ inches. The Museum of Modern Art, New York. Acquired through Lillie P. Bliss Bequest.

Chapter Five

EXPRESSIONISM

No matter how much the realistic painters we have seen modified nature, we can still conceive of their painted objects existing in the real world. Harnett, Velázquez, and Chardin modified nature so subtly that at first glance their intentions seem only imitative. Others, like van Eyck, even when they are downright photographic from detail to detail, are not at all so in sum. And we found in every case that the *expressive* element of the realist's art comes from his modification of natural appearances rather than from his ability to reproduce exactly the look of the world around him.

Since this is so, it would seem reasonable that the less an artist is obliged to stick to the natural look of things, the greater his expressive range should be. This does not necessarily follow, but some artists have applied the principle, and this chapter is concerned with worjs of art where the modification of visual reality is so great that it reaches the point of distortion. We will see why the artists in question thought it necessary to violate the "real" look of things.

Our subject is expressionism, and the examples will be more intense and on the whole more personal than the ones we have seen so far. Every great artist has an individual style, but the expressionist's work is likely to be more sharply individualized than the realist's, more dramatically his own, sometimes to the point of eccentricity. Strong stylistic individuality is inevitable when an artist is more interested in probing his own soul than in reflecting the world of ideas, more interested in exploring a moody or tempestuous inner world than in revealing a basic harmony in the one around us. The expressionist may, in fact, be an individual who feels that the harmonies artists have always looked for beneath the chaotic surface of life have never existed, or have been vanquished by mankind's predilection for folly, and he cries out in resentment and horror. His world is one of intensified emotion, sometimes as a means of escape, sometimes as a means of release that brings personal salvation. In extreme cases, the very personal nature of expressionism may keep the observer from entering the artist's world because the artist may speak in terms perfectly clear to himself but puzzling to others.

As a working definition of expressionism, then: Expressionism is the distortion of form and color for emotional intensification. If we want to establish as neat as possible a dividing line between realism and expressionism, we can add to this definition that the distortions go beyond the point where we can accept the possibility of objects existing as the artist has represented them.

According to a dictionary definition, expressionism involves the "free" expression of emotions. We have been pointing out that all the forms in great art are organized into compositions that are far from free, if free means spontaneous and uncalculated.

137. Detail from *The Starry Night.*

So when we say that expressionist art is "free," we must still remember that what may look like a very free painting or sculpture may be a highly calculated one. A perfect example is *The Starry Night* (**136**) by Vincent van Gogh, painted in 1889 and now established as a classic of modern art.

The Starry Night appears to have gushed forth onto the canvas of its own volition; the whole picture swirls with a fierce, surging energy far removed from our ordinary associations with a starry night. The moon is as fiery as the sun (**137**), and the sky is filled with stars that seem to be whirling and bursting with the force of their own inner light. Through the center of this explosive firmament there winds a form that we cannot identify as a cloud or as the track of a comet or even as the Milky Way, which it is supposed to be. In such a sky, such a form really needs no explanation as a natural one. It is an expressive one, an invented one, far removed from the physical truth of whatever form may have inspired it.

The curling, rushing movement of this galaxy across the picture is repeated in an upward direction by the cypresses springing from the foreground as if they were tearing themselves free of the earth. Back of these trees, the fields and hills of the countryside surge and swell around the only quiet objects in the composition, a steepled church and some small houses, their windows yellow with lamplight.

The Starry Night is so highly charged with emotional fervor that it is tempting to think of it as the result of some kind of spontaneous creative combustion. Our knowledge of Van Gogh's life—his emotional torment, his unsuccessful search for peace with this world, his terrible loneliness—all this, as well as our awareness that he was subject to periods of irrationality, seems at first consistent with his having produced this fervid painting in an inspired frenzy or even in an almost hypnotic state.

The fact that we feel such immediacy in *The Starry Night* is a tribute to Van Gogh's genius for emotional expression. Our enjoyment comes in large part from our feeling of direct emotional communication with the painter. Although the picture is a personal revelation, it speaks in terms perfectly clear to the observer also. Van Gogh's paintings always seem to have come fresh from the easel; we seem to be in the painter's presence—even after we discover that this is a calculated picture, not a spontaneous production.

And very thoroughly calculated it is. For one thing, there is the way the upward twisting of the cypress forms is used as a counterforce, a kind of brake, to the forward rush of the comet-like form across the sky. Both forms benefit by the contrast since neither is allowed to overpower the rest of the picture, as either would have done without the balancing influence of the other. The most dramatic dark in the picture—again, the cypresses—is played in another balance against the most dramatic light—the fiery moon—on the opposite side of the picture. (Imagine the difference if either the moon or the cypresses were shifted into the center.) Among secondary elements the church steeple helps unify the composition, first by echoing the form of the cypresses and also by interrupting the insistent line of the hills against the sky. The rushing line of the horizon might otherwise carry us too swiftly to the edge of the picture and out of it. This steeple-and-hills relationship is a restatement of the cypress-comet relationship, a repetition of the main theme, and is a major reason why a painting of such violent force is complete and self-contained instead of chaotic. And all the other elements in the composition, including the direction of each brush stroke, are caught up in the flow of movement determined by these major forms.

All the organization, its balance, contrast, echo, and rhythmic flow, was of course perfectly conscious on the part of the artist. He probably painted the picture rapidly; it is so vividly direct that it is hard to believe he reworked any part of it, but the composition is so skillful that we could not believe it was accidental or "inspired" even if we had no evidence to the contrary.

We do have this evidence. We have Van Gogh's preliminary drawings for various parts of the picture, and at least one earlier study of the same subject, as well as his letters over a period of months with references to his plans for developing it.

In his letters Van Gogh talks again and again about his plans for pictures, describing his progress toward the expression he wants. He once wrote to a friend who had admired the intensity of feeling in one of his pictures of some gardens:

> ... that was not accidental. I drew them many times and there was no feeling in them. After I had done the ones that were stiff, came the others.... How does it happen that I can express something like that? Because it has taken form in my mind before I start on it. What I am doing is not by accident but because of real intention and purpose.

As for his color, which is so right and seems so pure that we feel he had nothing to do but reach for paint ready at hand, he tells elsewhere in his letters of the trouble he had in determining exactly the kind of black (greenish or bluish, in relation to the surrounding colors) for painting cypresses. And although he frequently used certain colors straight out of the tube, for maximum intensity, he did so only after experiments in color relationships that were no less complicated for having ended in the desired effect of extreme directness.

And so Van Gogh, like all great artists, was a theorist and craftsman as well as an emotional human being. But this theorist also describes himself as working in a "dumb fury" at times and once, after painting all day without even stopping to eat, he wrote: "I shall do another picture this very night, and I shall bring it off."

There is nothing really contradictory in this combination of feverish creation and the application of theoretical principles. Expressionist art like Van Gogh's, by the nature of its intensity and its personal quality, reaches its pitch of achievement at times when the artist is so "inspired" (for want of a better word) that his whole accumulation of knowledge and technical skill is at his command for immediate, as if spontaneous, use. But to think of an artist "inspired" to create a picture without preliminary spadework is as unreasonable as to imagine an actor giving an inspired performance without having learned his lines or a poet creating a masterpiece in a language he does not know. *The Starry Night* is an inspired painting if ever there was one, yet its creation was possible only because Van Gogh worked toward it for so long. (He wrote, "I wonder when I'll get my starry sky done, a picture that haunts me always.") The painting is so consummate an expression of Van Gogh's emotional nature that its creation must have been for him the most exalted and ecstatic release.

We have insisted that painting is an expression of its time. How does *The Starry Night*, as a work of modern art,

138. El Greco. *The Agony in the Garden.* 1590's. Oil on canvas, 40½ by 44¾ inches. The Toledo (Ohio) Museum of Art. Gift of Edward Drummond Libbey.

accord with this idea? We could say that in its extreme individuality it would not have been painted in a time other than our own, when individual freedom is a basic concept in our thinking. We could also say that in the need this lonely artist felt to communicate with his fellow man through painting, his art reflects the isolation of the individual that is a frequent corollary of his freedom. We could skate on very thin ice and suggest that in its violence, its agitation, its excitement, *The Starry Night* is a reflection of our age. All these arguments are at least partially valid; it is certainly true that stylistically (in its design, in its manner of paint application) *The Starry Night* cannot be imagined as belonging to any other time. But conceptually, as a personal expression, it is not much more of our time than of any other time—perhaps for the very reason that its creator was never able to become really a part of the life around him, as he so ardently desired to do.

139. Detail from *The Agony in the Garden.*

Expressionism is a new term, usually thought of in connection with modern art, but the expressionist principle of distortion of form and color for emotional intensification appears in the art of some of the old masters also. El Greco's *The Agony in the Garden* (**138**), painted in Spain just three centuries before *The Starry Night*, is every bit as expressionist as the modern painting and even makes its effect through similar distortions.

As far as subject matter is concerned, El Greco is obliged to conform to the letter of the Bible story; but he treats it in an individual—and expressionist—manner. Christ prays on the mount, his eyes lifted toward the apparition of an angel. Rocks, robes, clouds, and diaphanous shafts and veils of light intermingle until, in spots, one cannot be distinguished from another. The most curious element in the picture is the cavelike or mirage-like form beneath the figure of the angel that encloses the sleeping disciples (**139**). They lie in odd, unnatural attitudes, not at all suggesting the relaxed quality of sleep, but rather an enchanted or magically transfixed state that removes them as witnesses of the divine events in progress nearby. At the extreme right, within a mystically luminous landscape, we see Judas approaching with the Roman soldiers (**140**).

Compositionally, *The Agony in the Garden* and *The Starry Night* employ surprisingly similar devices. The various forms in both pictures are tied together by swirling, eddying rhythms continuing without interruption between landscape and sky, uniting earth and Heaven in ecstatic harmony. Both pictures are painted in vivid colors. In both, the rhythmic flow of line is picked out in supernatural lights. The distortion in the cypress trees is even similar to that of the robed figure of Christ; both forms are elongated into conelike shapes, swirling and twisting in the intensity of their upward striving.

The composition of El Greco's *The Agony in the Garden* is more complicated than that of *The Starry Night*, but the main flow of line that knits it together can be traced around the strange form enclosing the sleeping disciples, on up

140. Detail from *The Agony in the Garden.*

141. El Greco. *Burial of Count Orgaz.* 1586. Oil on canvas, 16 feet by 11 feet 10 inches. San Tomé, Toledo, Spain.

along the edge of the peaked boulder—the very summit of the mount—and then into the clouds that fill the upper right part of the picture. This sinuous line is very like the path of the Milky Way in the Van Gogh, although it is less obvious.

Behind all these surface similarities, however, the two pictures are totally different in the character of their emotionalism. Van Gogh's is a personal vision of overwhelming force. El Greco's intensity is somehow thinner, stretched to the breaking point. The El Greco has elegance—it makes its appeal in more sophisticated terms than the Van Gogh. Its mystical quality is the result of a colder and subtler calculation of staggering brilliance. This is a sumptuous painting, and although it is a religious one, its first appeal is through its sumptuousness, its elegance, its finesse, its intellectualism, and even its sensuousness. These comments are neither derogatory nor irreverent. The great art of El Greco makes sense in these terms as Van Gogh's would not.

El Greco is so individual a painter that the appreciation of his art has had a curious history as tastes have changed and ideas of what painting should be have shifted back and forth. In his own time, for that matter, one of his paintings was rejected by Philip II of Spain, who had commissioned it for an altar in the Escorial. But a select circle of intellectuals in and out of the Church recognized the mystical power of El Greco's style, and under their patronage he steadily increased the element of distortion, to the satisfaction of his aristocratic and ecclesiastical patrons.

Succeeding generations lost the understanding of El Greco's art until, not too long ago, he was either ignored or, at best, relegated to a minor place in art history as an interesting eccentric. His distortion was even explained as being the result of astigmatism, an absurdity that still pops up from time to time. If it is necessary to refute it, we can point out that astigmatic vision would not produce these distortions in the first place, and also that El Greco painted numerous pictures, particularly portraits, in which the degree of distortion is slight. In the *Burial of Count Orgaz* (**141**) he combines his more realistic style with his expressionistic one in the two parts of one picture.

The lower half shows the Count's body being placed in its tomb by Saint Stephen and Saint Augustine in the presence of surrounding relatives, friends, and dignitaries. There is a certain amount of elongation in the drawing of these thin-faced, melancholy aristocrats (**142**), but on the whole the figures in the lower half can be conceived of as existing in the form in which El Greco painted them.

In the upper half, however, we see first an angel who holds the soul of the Count in the conventional form of a naked babe, represented here as more shimmery and gauzelike than fleshly. The angel is more distorted than the human figures below it, and as we go on up toward the figure of Christ on his throne, the distortion becomes greater and greater. Saint John the Baptist, shown kneeling, is a fantastically elongated figure with a tiny head and

142. Detail from *Burial of Count Orgaz.*

odd swellings and contractions in the arms, legs, chest, and waist.

These distortions are repeated in the other celestial figures who surround the saint as he intercedes with Christ for the newly arrived soul. The scene takes place upon various levels made up of the same luminous, unidentifiable forms that twist through *The Agony in the Garden.* El Greco has harmoniously combined a realistic earthly scene and a visionary heavenly one, modifying his manner appropriately from realistic to expressionistic.

El Greco apparently developed his style objectively, calculating its effectiveness and making the most of it as a professional artist rather than as an emotional human being. With Van Gogh, expressionism was a personal release; with El Greco, it was an intellectual achievement.

The three expressionistic paintings we have seen so far are all visionary pictures, but the range of expressionism is wide. Our next illustration is at the opposite pole and brings us back to modern art. Georges Rouault's *Two Nudes* (**144**, p. 104) deals with brutal truth instead of rapturous hallucination, with degraded worldliness instead of elevated spirituality. It is the kind of picture that makes people say, "With so much that is beautiful, why paint something so ugly?" Not only the subject—two hideous, naked prostitutes—but the very look of the picture seems ugly to most people. The color, instead of being decoratively "beautiful," seems thin and acid, and the drawing coarse and heavy-handed.

Yet this is a painting by a man who on occasion draws with the most delicate precision, who has painted conventionally beautiful and reverent interpretations of mystical religious subjects, whose color frequently has the deep brilliance of stained glass. Why did he paint this "ugly" picture? If the man is a mystic, how can he choose this subject? And if he is an accomplished draughtsman, why does he draw like this?

Actually there is no paradox here. *Two Nudes* is noble in conception and its drawing is consistent with its message.

Two Nudes is an outraged cry against man's inhumanity to man, against corruption, meanness, and human degradation. In social and humanitarian terms it is a thoroughly moral picture. The painting is a condemnation, an accusation against a world that brutalizes and degrades. Secondarily, it is a condemnation in general of the animalism of lust.

Now, these ideas are impossible to present in a picture of conventional prettiness. Rouault slashes at his drawing in coarse, heavy lines expressive at once of his own anger and the brutishness of the women. He distorts the bodies into heavy, lumpy forms that are indeed ugly, as bodies. The color is scrubby, roughly applied, suggestive of fresh tints turned morbid, as if soured by the evil the painter reveals. And the answer to the question, Why paint this instead of something beautiful?, is that the whole world in any of its aspects is the painter's province. What he most deeply feels, he must paint, in the most appropriately expressive way.

But, of course, *Two Nudes* is a beautiful painting. Technically, it is beautiful in the absolute control of drawing. For all the appearance of coarseness and license, the thick boundaries of the forms are expertly controlled and designed to describe these forms, and to describe them with appropriate emphasis or, if you wish, exaggeration. Even the distortions are beautiful in their powerful expressive quality. They could not have been created by an artist who had not passed through apprenticeship in the kind of accurate, detailed drawing that looks more difficult. Finally, above all, the subject is neither base nor vulgar. It is noble, if faith in man's goodness is noble. The subject is not presented lasciviously. (Could vice be made more unattractive?) Nor is it presented in cynical acceptance of evil. It is presented as a protest, and to protest against evil is to recognize the possibility of good. In all Rouault's work there is a fundamental faith in man's redemption through his recognition of evil and his rejection of evil.

It is this implication that gives *Two Nudes* its meaning. We are shown ugliness in terms of such violence that we must recognize it—and reject it. From any other point of view *Two Nudes* is only a repellent image of two grotesquely ugly dehumanized creatures.

From what we have said so far it appears that expressionism must always be associated with the morbid, the tragic, or the visionary. To a large extent this is true. "Distortion for emotional expression" suggests violence and intensity, although the whole emotional range, including feelings of peace and quiet joy, can be expressed by appropriate distortions of form (into simple, quiet shapes) and appropriate colors (subdued, soothingly harmonious ones). In practice, however, these quieter emotions are expressed by poetic realism. Expressionism is given the field when subjects are intense rather than serene, agitated rather than peaceful. For a painting using expressionistic devices to interpret a scene more cheerful and familiar than most, we can look at John Marin's 1920's water color of New York City, *The Singer Building* (**145**, p. 105).

A photograph (**143**) or a realistic painting of the subject must be dominated by the rigid parallel vertical lines of the Singer Building and adjacent buildings, with their flat walls regularly punctured in a rigid pattern of windows. If represented in correct proportion to the buildings, the crowded traffic of automobiles and people would be diminutive and, if visible at all, clotted into masses not suggesting their turmoil of movement. Rigid horizontals (the street and sidewalks) and verticals (the skyscraper) suggest quietness, orderliness, permanence; they are the standard framework for pictures of static character.

Now, this is the opposite of the impression a city makes; a city is busy, pushing, noisy, excited, crowded, confused. Above all, it is dynamic, and this dynamism is immediately relayed by Marin's painting. If we try, we can

143. The Singer Building, January, 1908, New York. Photograph from Byron Collection, Museum of the City of New York.

144. Georges Rouault. *Two Nudes (Filles).* About 1905. Oil on paper, 39 5/16 by 25½ inches. The Metropolitan Museum of Art, New York. Gift of Mr. and Mrs. Alex L. Hillman, 1949.

decipher in the lower part some shapes recalling streets, shops, and the rest (including the elevated railway, long since razed). But the important thing is that the sharp, strong angularities that interrupt one another, breaking and shifting to other angles, are expressive of action and excitement, in contrast with the static photograph (although this particular photograph is enlivened by parts of buildings under construction, and the smoke or steam issuing just above street level). Much of the fascination of photography is that it can freeze action—freeze a baseball in midair inches from the bat, hold an athlete forever in suspension as he clears a hurdle. But to freeze action is the opposite of expressing it, as Marin wants to do. In the end, his expressionist vision of what a city is is "real-er" than a photograph can be, although—or rather, because—some of the most expressive parts are not even identifiable as objects. In the lower half many of the sharp, emphatic lines are simply that—lines, lines of force perhaps, not parts of buildings or other objects. Above center right a wavering oval of pinkish color represents nothing at all but serves as a transition, a symbol of dissipating energy, from the hectic activity of the lower half of the painting to the relative quiet of the sky.

The transition from confusion to clarity is the most important but least conspicuous achievement in this cityscape. We are embroiled in the action, the excitement, the dynamism of street level, which is expressed in proportions altogether unrealistic. As the buildings rise, the excitement diminishes, the forms are less interrupted, there is less contrast of dark and light, the colors are more delicately washed in, until finally the peaks of the skyscrapers escape into the open sky. In reality the Singer Building was capped with a dome and lantern (under construction in our photograph) that performed the architectural function of terminating the tower as a capsule, a self-contained volume clearly defined to hold its own as a material unit within the amorphous space of the sky. If it had been represented in that way in Marin's vision of the city, it would have been altogether discordant. Hence he has left the dome form recognizable but has shattered and opened it to make it a part of the all-permeating vital energy that suffuses every bit and piece of his city.

A generation later, in 1953, another American artist responded in much the same way to his city. Franz Kline, a leader of the abstract expressionist school, painted *New York, N.Y.* (**146**), a giant of a painting in which this same vitality is expressed in a lunging pattern of black and white without specific reference to pictorial matter. In its raw power and large size, *New York, N.Y.* could almost be an enlargement of a fragment of the lower part of the Marin. As a matter of fact, Kline began his career as an abstract expressionist by isolating and enlarging areas of his own realistic works, on the theory that the idea of "city" could thus be intensified by concentration.

Marin, however, went further in his exploration. Compared with Kline's, Marin's idea of "city" is panoramic. Just

145. John Marin. *The Singer Building.* 1921. Water color on paper, 26½ by 21⅝ inches. Philadelphia Museum of Art. Alfred Stieglitz Collection.

146. Franz Kline. *New York, N.Y.* 1953. Oil on canvas, 79 by 50½ inches. Albright-Knox Art Gallery, Buffalo. Gift of Seymour H. Knox.

as the forms in *The Singer Building* are graduated from violent dislocation in the lower part to relative quiet above, so Marin's colors are graduated from reds and oranges, "hot" colors psychologically associated with action and excitement, to blues and greens, "cool" and associated with quietness. Marin makes the transition from the strong, exciting colors to the quiet ones in several steps—including, for instance, a change in the colors he quite arbitrarily chooses for the window openings in the buildings. This color transition goes hand in hand with the transition from broken, shifting shapes and angles in the lower half to the quieter shapes in the upper part.

(Leonardo da Vinci used this warm-to-cool color progression in the landscape background for the *Mona Lisa* [22], going from golden browns to silvery blues, although the yellowing of centuries of varnish has obscured the original contrast, making the cool passages much warmer than Leonardo painted them.)

Finally, we must remind ourselves that like any good picture, *The Singer Building* is an organization of line, shape, and color into a compositional unit. The angular lines that express the excitement and confusion of the city also tie the composition together by repeating, buttressing, and echoing one another. Again we see that objective skill and technical control are the means to an expression (*not* a description) of a subject so agitated that objectivity and control might at first seem out of place. Realizing this, Marin makes a point of retaining effects of spontaneity. He is a first-rate water-color technician and carries the medium far beyond the delicate tones usually associated with it. Some of his color is applied from a full, wet brush; in other places he capitalizes on the grainy quality of the rough paper where he has dragged a nearly dry brush across it. These contrasting textures are an important element in the picture's variety and excitement.

The Singer Building plunges us into the city and surrounds us with its stimulating sound and movement. It is essentially a cheerful, vigorous interpretation, full of the optimism and sense of youthful power and flourishing growth that we like to think of as typically American. It was painted in 1921 when an American boom was under way and the chastening years of the Great Depression had not become part of our national experience. At almost exactly the same time (1922), a German expressionist, E. L. Kirchner, shows us a contrasting idea of "city" in *Street Scene* (147).

The mood of a German city in 1922, only four years after the nation's defeat and humiliation in World War I, was the antithesis of the American mood of triumphant vitality. The terrible period of shock and dislocation in Germany was producing some of the most vicious social deformities in the history of our civilization. *Street Scene* is full of morbid introspection, of melancholy brooding, of sinister foreboding and the soul-sickness of a hopeless and groping society. There is a haunted quality in the figures

147. Ernst Ludwig Kirchner. *Street Scene.* 1922. Color woodcut, 27¾ by 15 inches. The Museum of Modern Art, New York.

of the two women; their fashionable clothes have been turned into witchlike silhouettes, and although they are part of a crowd, we feel first of all their isolation in some private and unhappy world of disturbing preoccupations. The picture's colors are totally unreal, from the olive green of the skin to the brilliant red, blue, and yellow of the background. The angular treatment may somewhat suggest the angularities of Marin's city and may carry some of the same hint of noise and movement, but it is a very faint echo in a picture that, upon increasing acquaintance, relays a stronger and stronger feeling of unnatural stillness. The face of the central figure regards us uncomprehendingly, or suspiciously at best. She stands in an odd, half-crouched, retreating attitude. The strange little taxi behind her and the figures making up the crowd on the other side of the picture are as wooden and doll-like as toys, increasing the effect of unreality. The women are transfixed in a world without meaning, yet somehow threatening, filled with ominous portents of evil—exactly the opposite of the booming optimism of Marin's city.

Our present-day understanding of the art of children developed as a by-product of modern expressionism. Whereas children used to be taught to curb their natural exuberant expressiveness in painting, to "be neat," to "keep the color inside the lines," in short, to defeat every spontaneous release of their natural bent for putting ideas into pictorial form, they are now encouraged to paint exactly as they please, on the principle (quite sound) that they are unable to apply rule and theory in picturemaking but may have a natural response to psychological values of colors, lines, and shapes.

The nine-year-old who painted our third example of an expressionistic vision of a city (148) was no Marin, and as far as he was concerned, was simply painting a city the way it looks. Nor was the eleven-year-old who painted a hurricane (149) any Van Gogh. But the resemblance of these spontaneously invented forms to those in *The Singer Building* and *The Starry Night* is more than coincidental. The paintings say "city" and "hurricane" quite vividly because the children made direct translations of their feelings into images that seemed right to them. The adults have done the same thing, but not so innocently; their translations had to be conscious and studied, based on formal knowledge and theory that enabled them to distill the images from the depth and complexity of mature experience.

It is easy to overrate children's painting as artistic endeavor, which, of course, it essentially is not, and to credit many a lucky accident as an expressive intention. But at the same time it is good that we have learned that expression is often most effectively released through forms and colors that are not accurate transcriptions of nature, and that we have learned to understand the nature of painting done by children as well as the art of expressionism on this basis.

· · · ·

148. Nine-year-old child. *City Street.* Oil and crayon on paper, 14 by 19 inches.

149. Eleven-year-old child. *Hurricane.* Show-card color on paper, 14 by 19 inches.

150. El Greco. *Christ on the Cross with Landscape.* About 1610. Oil on canvas, 74 by 44 inches. The Cleveland Museum of Art. Gift of Hanna Fund.

If what we have said so far about expressionism leaves the impression that any intensely emotionalized presentation of a subject is ipso facto expressionistic; or that mystical subjects demand expressionistic treatment; or that expressionism is always an art of individual invention on the part of artists who relay their personal responses to a subject in a personal style—then let us say clearly that these impressions are mistaken, as we can see by comparing three versions of the Crucifixion.

The first of these, *Christ on the Cross* (**151**) by Rubens, was painted in the seventeenth century by a master who was under no technical limitations whatsoever. The laws of perspective and anatomy and other elements of realistic representation had been discovered and codified long since. For Rubens their use was second nature. He had at his fingertips the whole range of knowledge for the creation of effects of light and shade, the various ways of giving illusions of depth, of making forms look round and solid, and he saw no reason to abandon these methods for experiments in expressive distortion even when treating the most intensely emotional subjects, such as Christ's agony on the Cross. From what we have already said about Rubens's *Prometheus Bound* (**95**), it should be clear why Rubens paints the scene as realistically as he does. He appeals to the emotions through our own experience with sensations of pain or pleasure—which, from an expressionist artist's point of view, could raise the question as to whether this Crucifixion is an interpretive picture at all.

Rubens gives us a magnificently painted male nude who is Christ only by association of ideas. There is little or nothing to supply the mystical connotations of the subject; we ourselves supply them by foreknowledge. As far as the painter's contribution is concerned, there is nothing inherently divine in this figure of a man nailed to a cross. It is not irreverent to say that if we didn't already know otherwise, this might easily be some Olympic champion undergoing torture or, more accurately, a well-muscled actor caught at a climactic moment of a fine performance. The whole production is effectively staged; the lighting, the backdrop with its illusion of storm and distance, are marvelously dramatic. And so real! They almost make us feel we are there—and that, of course, is the whole intention.

There is virtually no distortion—expressionistic or otherwise. The features are twisted in agony, the muscles of the arms and chest are strained tight, but none of this is a distortion of nature. It is, on the other hand, a kind of extreme naturalism under given physical circumstances. Not only is there no distortion, there is hardly, even, any exaggeration. Everything in the picture is represented at highest dramatic pitch, but there is nothing in it that could not have been reproduced directly from nature. This is, in short, an emotionalized presentation of a subject without recourse to expressionistic devices; it makes its effect today in very much the same terms as it did when it was painted more than three and a half centuries ago in the now vanished context of the Counter Reformation.

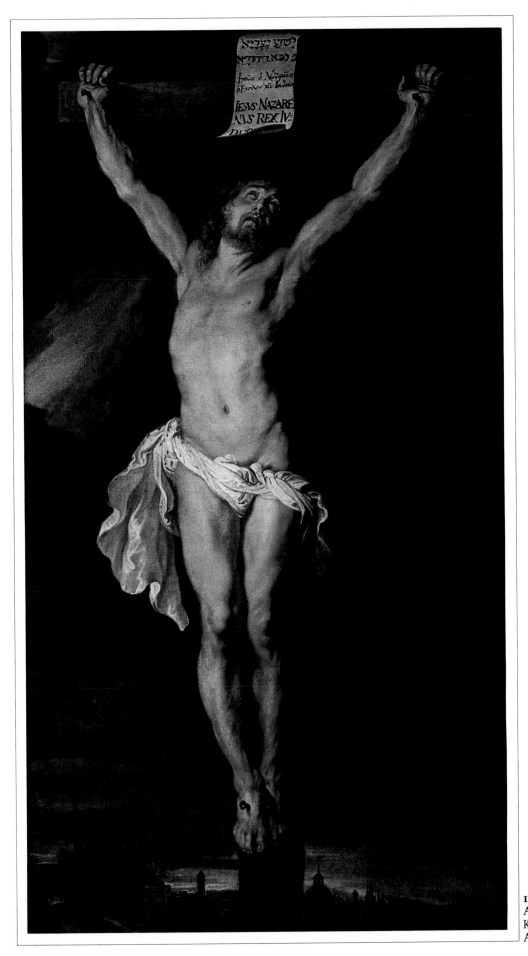

151. Peter Paul Rubens. *Christ on the Cross.*
About 1610. Oil on canvas, 87 by 47 inches.
Koninklijk Museum voor Schone Kunsten,
Antwerp.

152. Detail from *Christ on the Cross.*

153. Detail from *Christ on the Cross with Landscape.*

Now, returning to El Greco, the great expressionist among the old masters, we find in his *Christ on the Cross with Landscape* (**150,** p. 108)—painted at about the same time and perhaps even in the same year as the Rubens— that he is not content to let us supply the mystical and miraculous spirit of the event while he serves as stage manager. He wants to make mystery and miracle inherent in his vision of the Crucifixion, and to do so he must depart from real appearances. He creates as background an other-worldly space, shot through with ambiguous forms and supernatural lights such as never existed on earth or, for that matter, on stage. We can easily imagine the human being who posed for Rubens's Christ—in fact, we don't have to imagine him; we see him. But if we had to imagine El Greco's Christ as an existing human being, he would be a monster of grotesque proportions afflicted with skeletal deformities that would make it impossible for him to stand or walk, in contrast with Rubens's superbly athletic model. But there is no temptation to see El Greco's Christ in terms of physical reality; this is a sensuous transfiguration. Nor does it bother us that the body does not actually hang from or seem actually nailed to the Cross; rather, the arms might be extended in a gesture of mystical appeal; the figure seems magically suspended. A comparison of the hands of these two Christs summarizes the physical reality of one, the spiritual mystery of the other (**152** and **153**). We have said that, confronted by the Rubens, we supply the mystical connotations by foreknowledge of the subject; if we did not already know the story of the Crucifixion, we would still be aware that El Greco's haunting picture is no ordinary scene of torture, but the transcription of a divine event.

Whether the Rubens or the El Greco is the better picture is not a question. Some people will be more moved or more interested by one, some people by the other, some people equally but in different ways by both, and some may prefer—if it is a matter of establishing preferences—to either of them a painted Cross (**154**) by a follower of an unknown master of the Middle Ages, an Italian active at the end of the thirteenth century who is given the name "Master of the Saint Francis Legend." Such crosses were produced in large numbers in Italy during the latter part of the twelfth century and in the thirteenth, varying in size and quality according to the size and wealth of the church for which they were originally commissioned. The large ones were put over the altar (sometimes suspended from the ceiling) where, within the shadows of the vaults, illuminated by the flickering gleam of the candles below, they must have had the quality of a vision.

The figure on the Cross certainly looked much more real to the people it was painted for than it does to us. They did not demand, or even conceive of, realistic painting as we know it. Giotto's revolution (**275**) was still a generation away. The painter has made some effort to round out portions of the figure in a naturalistic manner, and this effort is fairly successful in the small figures. But even so, realism in the terms we have been discussing was beyond his conception. The loin cloth is primarily a decorative pattern in line (and a beautiful one); the hair is so highly conventionalized that it is out of the question to think that the painter tried for anything like realism; and the ear is snuggled in between the hair and beard like an afterthought (**155**). Nor is there any effort at realistic relationship between the various figures involved. There are four scales, descending in the order of the figures' importance. The largest is reserved for Christ alone; the Virgin and Saint John share the next largest; the two mourning angels at the ends of the arms of the Cross are a degree smaller; and finally the mere human being, kneeling at Christ's feet, is appropriately accorded the minimum size.

The figure of Christ, which would be merely inept in terms of realistic imagery, takes on a deeply moving spiritual quality precisely because it is *not* realistic, just as in the case of the El Greco; yet it is probable that this painter, a well-trained artisan but no revolutionary genius, was innocent of any idea of intensifying the emotional effect of the image by expressive distortions, and was being as realistic as he knew how. The apparent distortions are conventions inherited from generations of painter-craftsmen who were content to follow a set of patterns that had proven their effectiveness. But the rank and file of these journeyman painters turned out rather dry repetitions of studio formulas. This obscure follower of an obscure master has done more, within the indefinable area of creative art where we may feel the difference between one artist and another without being able to define exactly where that difference lies. It is possible that some of the effectiveness of this particular painted Cross among all the others came from this master's relatively advanced efforts to imbue the body of Christ with emotive power by exaggerating the angularities, as if the body had been broken on the Cross, and by striving for realism in such details as, for instance, the muscles of the abdomen. But need we worry about these questions. Except to the historian, do they make a great deal of difference? The artist's intention was to achieve an expression of the mystery of the Crucifixion, and he achieved it, by whatever means. The "distortions," whatever their origin, determine the character of the painting, and through them it speaks to us. We understand its visual language as well as we do today because our eyes have been attuned to it by modern artists who have expounded and demonstrated the principles of expressionism.

Expressionism in sculpture occurs less frequently than in painting, either modern or earlier. Perhaps this is because sculpture is so tangible an art that any drastic distortions are likely to become mere deformities when put into three dimensions. This is true of the *Venus of Willendorf* (**36**), that arch-ancestress of all sculpture, which, in spite of its towering anthropological importance, is unquestionably grotesque from any esthetic standard, expressionistic or otherwise. No painted fertility images comparable to the *Venus of Willendorf* are known; perhaps the same exagger

154. Follower of the Master of the Saint Francis Legend. *Crucifixion.* About 1280. Tempera on wood, 74 by 68½ inches. Philadelphia Museum of Art. Purchased by W. P. Wilstach Collection.

155. Detail from *Crucifixion.*

ations in two dimensions rather than the tangible third would have an advantage over this lumpy little object. In this respect we have already commented that El Greco's crucified Christ becomes grotesque only if imagined as a living body. Similarly, if translated into stone or bronze, it would be robbed of its ethereal, floating quality and would become monstrous. In addition, it is difficult to imagine a sculptural equivalent of the mystical, shifting lights in the background that account for so much of the mystical quality of the painting.

For a modern effort to create a sculptural monument calling on expressionist-related principles, there is Ossip Zadkine's *The Destroyed City* in Rotterdam, which is discussed later in this book in another context (386)—but its success is questionable. Expressionist distortions in sculpture are more successful at small scale, even intimate scale, as in a group of small German sculptures of the fourteenth century, where emotional intensification seems the product of a concentration of all the power of a large sculpture within an image only inches high.

As an example, the *Röttgen Pietà* (156), only 10½ inches high, and designed for private devotions, would be absurd enlarged to life size. At small scale the expressionistic exaggerations and distortions are poignantly affecting; the full range of expressionist devices can be employed. Christ's body seems to have come from the torturer's rack rather than the Cross; the neck is wrenched backward, the arms are frozen into rigid jointless rods, the chest protrudes as if paralyzed at the last moment of a supreme but impotent gasp for breath that leaves the mouth agape and the eyes half-closed. The blood has flowed from the five wounds in the body in rosettes like flowers.

But a Pietà is the Virgin's subject, dealing less with the pain and tragedy and glory of Christ's death than with his mother's human grief. To this end, the sculptor—in full control of his means—has concentrated on distortions that stimulate emotional response to the Virgin's agony. Realistic proportions have been discarded for expressive dimensions throughout; the Virgin's head is disproportionately large in order that her contorted features may tell to fullest effect, and the body of her son, which at normal size would distract from this effectiveness, is hardly larger than that of a boy. Each part and detail of this famous little sculpture is assigned its degree of emphasis in relation to the whole in order to complement a full dramatic realization.

If there are any questions as to the effectiveness of the expressionistic distortions in the *Röttgen Pietà*, they can be answered by putting it alongside another Pietà done about fifty years later, and not too far away, for the Seeon Monastery near Salzburg (157, p. 114). Comparing our comments on the *Röttgen Pietà* point by point, we see that Christ's body in the Seeon sculpture is peaceful and even comparatively graceful in death. The hands are gently folded, the eyes and mouth closed. The wound in the side, while realistic, is less effective for that reason; the blood has run, not gushed, from it, and the wounds in the hands

156. German, Middle Rhine. *Röttgen Pietà*. About 1370. Wood, painted, height without base 10½ inches. Rheinisches Landesmuseum, Bonn.

157. German, Salzburg. *Pietà* from monastery at Seeon. About 1420–30. Stone, painted, height 29½ inches. Bayerisches Nationalmuseum, Munich.

158. Antoni Gaudí. Casa Milá. 1905–10. Barcelona.

159. Arcade at street level. Casa Milá.

and feet are inconspicuous. The Virgin's pretty face in a head of normal size is unmarred by any agony of grief, although the corners of the mouth droop and the brow is slightly knit. The body she holds is also of normal size, with consequent difficulties. The Virgin's right arm has had to be unnaturally lengthened in order to support the corpse at the neck and shoulders, a deformation that is only awkward, not expressive. It is unconvincing as well; this delicate young woman could not support the body of the full-grown, if slender, man. Even the crown of thorns, to introduce another detail, is a spiked instrument of torture in the *Röttgen Pietà* that is reduced to an ornamental headband in the Seeon version. "Ornamental" is in fact a key word here, with emphasis on such incidental details as the lovely folds and fringed border of the scarf over the Virgin's head.

None of all this has to mean that the *Seeon Pietà* is inferior to the *Röttgen*. It is a matter of preference between contrasting styles or conceptions, and—such is the infinite variety of art—a devil's advocate could reverse our arguments in favor of a sculpture we have found wanting expressively.

Expressionism, involving as it does the willful distortion of form, is less compatible with architecture than with any other art. We have seen enough architecture so far in this book to know that architectural form at its most expressive is inextricably tied to the practical business of construction. As a primary example, the Gothic cathedral could never be called expressionistic, for all its originality and extreme expressiveness. The *invention* of forms is quite different from their arbitrary distortion. Rib vaults and flying buttresses were frequently ornamented, but they retained their strictly functional honesty undistorted beneath the frosting.

Early in the twentieth century, however, there appeared an architecture that can be called expressionist, growing out of a movement called *art nouveau*. *Art nouveau* was an effort to introduce into design the qualities of natural growth and movement in nature, the shapes of plants (particularly such sinuous ones as vines), the motion of water in the waves of the sea, and the eddies in the currents of streams or rivers. To design a solid building in terms of sinuous growth and shifting volumes is obviously an odd approach to architecture, exactly the opposite of what we called architectural realism in our last chapter, where form is disciplined by the practical demands of function.

The primary monument of *art nouveau* architecture is the Casa Milá (**158**), an apartment house in Barcelona by the architect Antoni Gaudí. Wavering, flowing forms are imposed not only on the exterior but also on the plan (**160**). The piers of the arcade at street level (**159**) are sculptured and roughened as if they were living stone entrances to grottoes. (The building is nicknamed "the quarry" in Barcelona.)

The Casa Milá was built in 1905–10. Later, in the

160. Plan. Casa Milá

161. Erich Mendelsohn. Einstein Tower (destroyed). 1919–21. Potsdam, Germany.

162. Eero Saarinen & Associates. TWA Terminal (Flight Center). 1957–62. John F. Kennedy Airport, New York.

163. Production still from *The Cabinet of Dr. Caligari*. 1919. Germany. Walter Röhrig, Hermann Worm, and Walter Reiman, designers. Photograph courtesy The Museum of Modern Art, New York.

1920's, corresponding to the rise of expressionism in German painting, there was a brief but lively growth of avowedly expressionist architecture, based on the idea that the form of a building should symbolize its function. (The important word here is "symbolize.") The design of the Einstein Tower at Potsdam (**161**), built in 1920, was rather indecisively connected with theories of relativity. It was also intended as a demonstration of plastic treatment of poured concrete in "sculptural" architecture—although, as things turned out, it had to be built of brick smoothed over with a skin of cement.

"Form symbolizes function" never became a popular idea, and the architect of the Einstein Tower himself, Erich Mendelsohn, soon abandoned it for a modern style closer to the realistic precept that form *follows* function. The triumph of functionalism reduced expressionist architecture to a trickle of small, special buildings—such as chapels—until suddenly one of the leading international designers of functional architecture, Eero Saarinen, temporarily reverted to expressionism in 1957–62 with a large commercial building, the TWA Terminal (**162**) at Kennedy International Airport in New York City. Using poured concrete, Saarinen sculptured the building in long, curved, flowing, and swelling forms like the wings of birds, forms that seemed buoyed up by the air beneath them, and managed at the same time to create interior spaces that satisfied the functional demands of an airport terminal—the waiting rooms, the ticket counters, the baggage reclamation area, lunchrooms, and access to and from planes. The TWA Terminal is the most successful expressionist architectural project ever built to satisfy utilitarian demands, and it proved that expressionist architecture could accommodate them; yet it has the air of a tour de force. Its uniqueness affirms the associations with eccentricity and arbitrary estheticism that make expressionist structures more interesting as sculpture—and, frequently, as fanciful stage sets—than as architecture. The very strong theatrical element in expressionist architecture, combined with effects borrowed from expressionist painting, is familiar to anyone interested in the history of movies in the famous German film *The Cabinet of Dr. Caligari* (**163**).

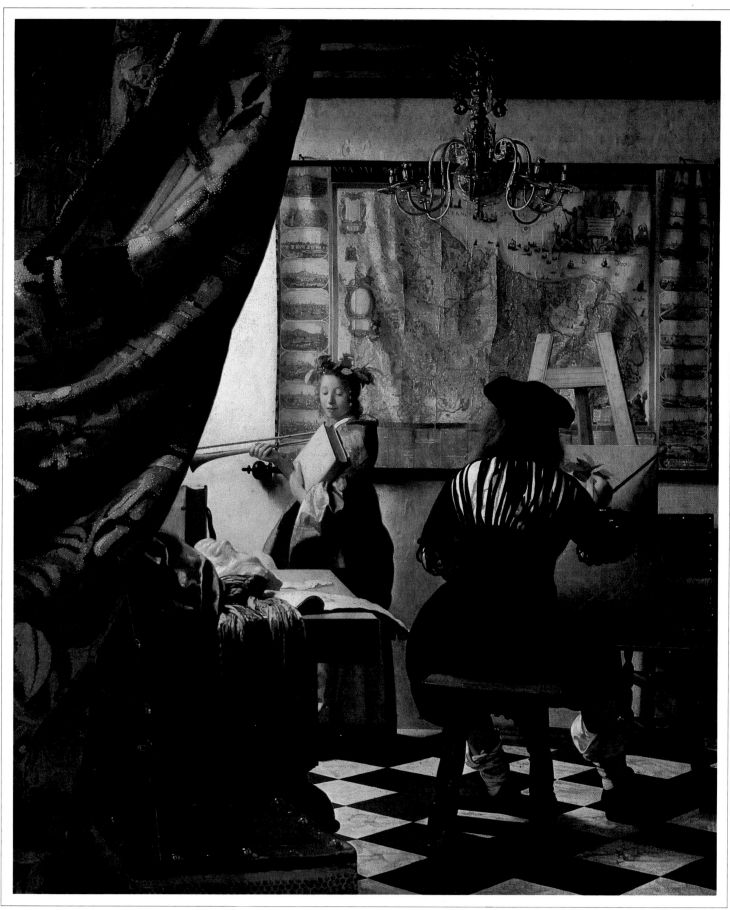

164. Jan Vermeer. *The Artist in His Studio* (*Allegory of the Art of Painting*). About 1665. Oil on canvas, 52 by 44 inches. Kunsthistorisches Museum, Vienna.

Chapter Six

ABSTRACTION

From everything we have examined so far, it must surely be apparent that the basic premise of this book is that if a painting or sculpture is of any consequence, the accuracy with which it reproduces the look of a person or thing is at best only a clue to something more important—even when the reproduction is as exact as Harnett's painting of a violin, a horseshoe, and other objects in *Music and Good Luck* (86) or Duane Hanson's sculpture of a pair of supermarket shoppers (380). The premise, always valid, became a truism in our century when totally abstract art came into its own.

We say "totally" because there are degrees of abstraction. As an art term, "abstraction" always implies a focus on aspects subsidiary to representation; but these aspects may be hidden within straightforward representational images and their arrangement, or may be apparent in formal and coloristic manipulations that violate the representational aspects of the subject while leaving it recognizable, or, finally, representation may disappear entirely, leaving the field free for totally abstract adjustments of form and color. The terms "nonrepresentational" and "nonobjective" are often used to distinguish this final stage of abstraction from all other art. "Semi-abstract," with its suggestion of compromise, is sometimes used to designate middle-of-the-road paintings and sculptures.

To show that principles of abstract art are involved in traditional, representational art, we began by pointing out that Whistler's title for his most famous painting, *Arrangement in Gray and Black* (11), insists on the importance of abstract premises as opposed to sentimental values that the public, as things turned out, discovered for itself in a picture it rechristened *Whistler's Mother*. We also argued that Renoir, in his portrait of his wife (17), transformed the image of a vital, blossoming young woman into a universal symbol by reducing natural forms to simple geometrical equivalents—an elementary kind of abstraction disguised, in this case, by an alluring realistic veneer.

Both of these paintings offer genuine rewards, but limited ones, when seen as nothing more than pictures of a sweet old lady and a healthy young woman. But when we come to Marin's *The Singer Building* (145), we find abstract elements dominating realistic ones. In the lower half Marin expressed the noise, the movement, the excitement and confusion of the city by a composition of slashing angles, lines, and colors that only half resemble the actual objects involved. Here we must recognize and accept abstraction to enjoy the subject at all. The artist seems to say that if a subject can be expressed through angles, lines, shapes, colors, arrangement, and other abstract elements, there is no reason why he has to depend any longer on even a ghost of reality. Is there then any reason to give us any recognizable images at all?

165. Pablo Picasso. *The Studio.* 1927–28. Oil on canvas, 59 by 91 inches. The Museum of Modern Art, New York. Gift of Walter P. Chrysler, Jr.

Perhaps abstract elements alone can tell the story. To carry the argument to its logical conclusion, why is it necessary even to have a subject? Why not just have forms, colors, and arrangement by themselves for their own sake?

This argument sounds reasonable enough, but it is also possible to contend that the abstract artist is defeating himself when he insists that recognizable images are of no importance in painting and should be left to the camera or (he might say) to those artists without enough creative imagination to get away from working like a kind of camera.

Without taking sides in this esthetic schism, we will examine some modern abstractions, comparing some of them with paintings by old masters or traditional artists who at first glance appear to be working almost photographically. We will begin by comparing two paintings of artists at work in their studios, one by the seventeenth-century Dutch master Jan Vermeer, *The Artist in His Studio* (**164**, p. 116), and another, *The Studio* (**165**), by Pablo Picasso, who hardly needs identification as the most conspicuous figure in the art of our century.

In Vermeer's painting we look into the cubelike space of an artist's studio, defined for us on all six sides. The back wall faces us directly. The front wall is expressed by the heavy curtain drawn aside to let us look within the space as if it were a stage. Without having to think about it or figure it out, we sense the windowed wall to our left by the flow of light onto the model and across the space of the room. The wall to our right is also defined by inference: the chandelier, which would be near the center of the ceiling, helps us locate it. The floor and ceiling we actually see.

Within this cube of space Vermeer arranges his figures and objects with exquisite care. We see the painter's back as he faces the canvas on his easel. He is using a mahlstick, an aid employed by painters to steady the hand while working on passages of fine detail. Without being able to see his other hand, we know that it holds his palette. He is glancing at the model, who is posed as an allegorical figure crowned with leaves and bearing a trumpet and a book. We see her across a table that holds, among other things, a cloth hanging off the edge nearest us.

The forms in this arrangement are not to be regarded as flat silhouettes, as it is possible to regard those in *Arrangement in Gray and Black*. They must be seen as solid volumes in three-dimensional space (the term is "spatial composition"). The little cube-shaped world is wonderfully self-contained; there is no feeling that the various objects are rigidly placed, but their relationships are so neatly adjusted that if we try to modify any one of them the serene balance of the picture is disturbed. We have said as much about still lifes by Harnett and Chardin (**86** and **105**); the difference is that the Vermeer is composed in space. Instead of playing from side to side and top to bottom of the picture area, as in the Harnett, or within the shallow depth of a shelf in the Chardin, the balances now play back and forth, around and about, within the spatial volume of a room. Testing the composition with this in mind, would you, for instance, want the model to turn her head so that, in profile, she looks out of the window? This would be a small change, but it would disrupt the picture by tempting us to follow the model's gaze into the imagined world outdoors, instead of remaining happily within the defined space of the studio. It would also tend to divide the picture down the middle, since the psychological connection between the painter and the model would be weakened. This connection is like a unifying structural element in the composition. If you can imagine the model looking out the window and the painter turned to regard us, thus divorcing the painter and the model and bringing the painter, so to speak, outside the room into the area on our side of the heavy curtain, you will see that the whole structure falls to pieces.

Other changes would be less disastrous, but any change would mar the picture's balance. Would you want to push the artist and his easel further back into the picture space? Or move them nearer to us, so that they become larger in perspective, leaving more depth between the artist and the model? Would you rather the objects on the table were tidied up, or removed, or added to? Would you like to see the curtain hanging in straight folds, rather than bunched as it is? Would you like to eliminate the series of beams that terminate the picture at its upper part with their succession of strong horizontal lines, and substitute a flat, eventless ceiling?

None of these changes except the elimination of the ceiling beams would make the individual objects any the less interesting. The picture would still be an assemblage of magnificently rendered textures bathed in light. We could still sense the brassiness of the chandelier, the nap of the curtain, the silkiness of the model's robe, the smooth, cool surface of the floor. But the perfection of the picture is not the sum of its wonderful details any more than the beauty of a musical composition is the sum of its individual notes. Its perfection lies in the harmonious union of these details as arranged in space, just as the beauty of music is the harmony of notes combined and arranged in time.

Our second picture, Picasso's *The Studio*, is such a close parallel to the Vermeer that it might almost have been painted to demonstrate how an old master can be translated into modern abstract terms. We have to begin by accepting Picasso's rejection of realistic imitation, and the first question is why he chooses to work in a way so radically different when perfection like Vermeer's can be achieved through an approach almost photographic in individual details.

Actually, the similarities between the two pictures are as great as the differences, and just as important although less obvious. The painter stands to the left in the Picasso; he sits at the right in the Vermeer. Picasso constructs the figure of the painter in a few dark lines played against the

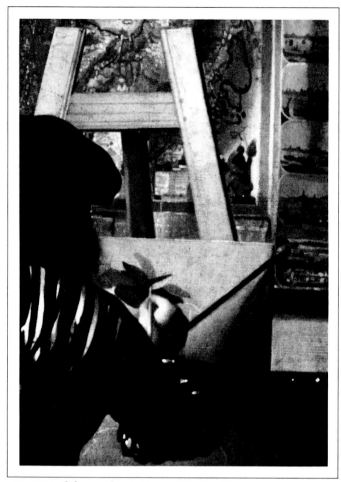

166. Detail from *The Artist in His Studio.*

bright yellow of the canvas he is about to work on; Vermeer constructs the figure of his painter as a dark silhouette, also played against the field of his canvas, upon which he has just begun to work (**166** and **167**). Both painters hold their brushes in a moment's pause. The "brush" in the Picasso is the short diagonal line terminating the "arm" that projects horizontally toward the right. Whereas Vermeer's artist has just stayed his hand to glance at the model, Picasso suggests by the extended line that his artist is sighting along his brush—a common practice in drawing—to measure the proportions of the object he is painting.

Picasso's painter's "head" is a long gray oval upon which is imposed an irregular white shape bearing three eyes arranged in a vertical row. Whether or not it was the artist's intention, we may hazard the guess that the painter is given this extra eye as a kind of symbol of the particularly acute, analytical vision developed by an artist in comparison with that of the rest of us, who see more casually.

The painters in both pictures hold palettes, although we see neither of them. In the Vermeer we sense the palette. In the Picasso it is symbolized by its thumb hole, a small circle just to the left of the painter's shoulder.

Vermeer's painter is working from a posed model; Picasso's from a still-life setup composed of a white sculptured bust (perhaps marble, perhaps a plaster cast) and a bowl of fruit on a table. A red cloth hangs from the side toward us, as in the Vermeer. The irregular white quadrangle is the base of the sculpture. Within the white oval of the general mass is a six-sided shape defined by a black line and bearing two eyes and a mouth—or perhaps two normal eyes and a "blind" one, suggesting the smooth blind eye of a sculptured face, arranged in the same way as the three eyes of the painter. The fruit bowl is reduced to two triangles, the fruit represented by a single green circle in the upper one. All four legs of the table and the round feet are visible, although they are placed arbitrarily, without regard to perspective. The red cloth, with its main lines accentuated by a wide hem, "hangs" in stiff angular folds reduced to flat patterns.

Flanking Picasso's painter on the side of the picture opposite him, there is a window or glassed door corresponding to the unseen window in the Vermeer, and on the back wall hang a framed picture and a dark mirror, rectangles only slightly more regular than the one of the decorative map hanging on the corresponding wall in the Vermeer.

These details add up to a close similarity between two apparently unlike paintings, even granting some leeway to their interpretation in the Picasso. The final similarity, and a most important one, is that each of the compositions is tied together by an invisible element—a cord of interest vibrating between the painter and the model. We have already commented on this in the Vermeer, saying that if the model looked out the window or if the painter turned his head to look at us, the beautiful integration of the cube of space would be disrupted. In the Vermeer, this connection between model and painter goes back into the depth of space. In the Picasso, it plays across the surface of the picture between the dominating lines and shapes abstracted from the figure of the painter and his still life.

But why has Picasso chosen to paint this way, instead of following a tradition that satisfied painters for so long? Picasso was something of a child prodigy. In his teens he had already mastered the conventional techniques of painting and drawing. Why did he abandon them? He had to sacrifice a great deal in order to work abstractly. First of all, he sacrifices the interest inherent in the objects making up the picture, an interest on which Vermeer capitalizes. Next, he sacrifices the fascination and variety of natural textures. He sacrifices the harmonies of flowing light, the satisfaction of building solid forms out of light and shade.

What has he gained?

He has gained complete freedom to manipulate the forms in his picture. He need not bother with the true proportions of objects or their parts. If for the sake of design or expression he wants to make a head three-quarters the size of the body beneath it, he may do so. He may adjust every shape within his picture area quite arbitrarily. If he has sacrificed the advantages of perspective, which would have permitted him to create an illusion, he has also gained freedom from its limitations, which would have forced him to show the table legs, the bust, or any of the other objects according to a rigid system. For perspective is after all only a systematic geometrical distortion by which objects are shown larger or smaller and in different relative proportions from their true ones in order to represent their position within a third dimension, all of this according to strict rules. Picasso's distortion is his own; abstraction has freed him from an imposed geometrical system, allowing him to improvise his own from one painting to the next.

But all these sacrifices and gains are only part of a means to an end. What is the argument in favor of the end Picasso has in view?

The abstractionist would argue that the enjoyment of a picture like Picasso's *The Studio* is more intense because it is purer than the enjoyment we take in the Vermeer. We more fully enjoy pure form, pure color, and pure arrangement because we are less diverted by incidental matters. In the Vermeer we are diverted by our interest in the map on the wall, by our curiosity about the details of the model's costume, by our surprise at the novel cut of the painter's blouse, and by all the other items that are curious or interesting in themselves. The traditional painter would argue that the enjoyment of the Vermeer is richer for the very reason that it may be enjoyed simultaneously on the double score of its abstract foundation and its associative overlay. But such discussion eventually boils down to the conclusion that a great painting is a great painting, regardless of its means.

Abstract art, which has been with us now for the better part of a century, continues to induce in some people the uncomfortable feeling that it is too easy because the painter

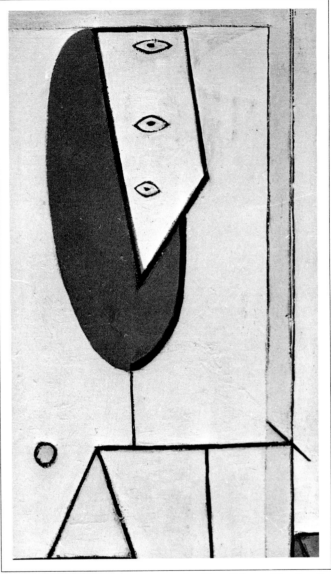

167. Detail from *The Studio.*

is not obliged to demonstrate a high degree of craftsmanship. The Vermeer, if considered as craftsmanship alone, would remain a gem. Technically and in details it is an extremely complicated picture, but in this very complication there is a degree of safety that is denied to the abstract painter. The Picasso is so simplified that any faulty relationship would be more glaring than one in the Vermeer. A second-rate picture along the lines of the Picasso is simply no good at all.

By examining the structure of the Picasso we can discover, if we have not felt it from the first, that the picture is as tautly constructed as Vermeer's is exquisitely arranged. It cannot be read in depth the way we read the Vermeer (although it is possible to discover some shallow recessions and projections of its flat planes), but we can apply something of the familiar test of shifting or changing forms and colors. The most obvious element tying the picture together is the repetition of strict verticals and horizontals. Then there are other parallels or near-parallels, such as the left edge of the red cloth, which parallels the right line of the main triangle of the figure of the artist, and the top left line of the plaster bust, which parallels the right side of the fruit bowl. The line of the artist's "neck," if continued downward, meets the intersection of two other lines and forms one side of a suggested square. The top of the fruit bowl, continued to the right, would meet the point of balance of the bust on its pedestal. A dozen similar relationships can be discovered; they form a kind of secondary, concealed but important, supporting structure. As in the Vermeer, every element affects every other one. The thumb hole of the palette, to take an example at random, seems just the right size and in just the right spot. Raised, it would seem to float; lowered, it would seem to be sinking—an observation we also made concerning the brass match holder in Harnett's *Music and Good Luck* (**86**). A change in color would affect the shape's psychological weight and would have to be compensated for by shifting its position, or changing its size, or both. This is bringing things down to a fine point, but a picture like *The Studio* depends on fine points. It leaves no room for accidental or unconsidered elements.

It would be fruitless to argue that the Picasso is better than the Vermeer or that the Vermeer is better than the Picasso. Both are superb achievements. You may prefer one or you may prefer the other, but to accept one and reject the other is to understand neither. Either picture, enjoyed through full understanding, increases our enjoyment and understanding of the other.

Having compared one realistic masterpiece with an abstract one, stressing their similarities, we will compare another realistic traditional painting with an abstraction to show how violently they can differ. About 250 years separate Vermeer's painting from the Picasso we have just seen, yet we found in them a fundamental kinship. Only seven years separate John Singer Sargent's *The Wyndham Sisters* (**168**, p.

124) from Picasso's *Les Demoiselles d'Avignon* (**169**, p. 125), which in terms of the chronological span of art history means that they were painted at the same moment. Yet they could hardly be more different.

The Wyndham Sisters, painted in 1900, is a stunning technical display celebrating aristocratic fashions. Sargent, an American expatriate in London and wildly successful internationally, was one of the most facile painters who ever lived; these yards and yards of satin, these geysers of flowers, these opulent glints of gold in the shadowy depths of a mansion, these delicately boned faces, and these graceful figures with their languorous hauteur and easy elegance, all are brushed across the surface of the canvas as if effortlessly. Everything is very cool, very expensive, and just a little patronizing in its suggestion that this privileged refinement is on display for us to look at, to marvel at, to admire, to envy, but not to touch. It is as if the ladies, having opened their mansion for charity, have had the further graciousness to incorporate themselves into the décor for the afternoon. Without this little seasoning of condescension the picture would not be the consummate expression of Edwardian fashion that it is.

The Wyndham Sisters is an extremely attractive picture, but it is virtually without abstract interest if we discount the pleasure we may take in Sargent's lithe acrobatics with his brush. The composition is casual—skillful enough, but not rewarding in itself, in no way comparable to the beautifully organized complexity of the two paintings we have just seen. The brushwork is breathtaking, in the same sense that it is breathtaking to see a magician pull a rabbit out of a hat. The painting's real interest, its real reason for being, lies in its stylish presentation of stylish subjects. There is no point in hunting for hidden depths, no point in exploring beneath immediate appearances. The merit of the picture lies not in its profundity, but in its finality; this is the fashionable portrait to end all fashionable portraits, a reflection rather than an interpretation of an attitude toward life. It is intended to be visually pleasing rather than emotionally stimulating or intellectually satisfying, and within that intention it is an unqualified success. It is a picture we may enjoy wholeheartedly for its obvious attractions, as we could not do if it pretended to offer anything more.

The Wyndham Sisters represented the apogee of fashionable good taste at the turn of the nineteenth into the twentieth century, and by its standards *Les Demoiselles d'Avignon*, painted in 1907, is a perfectly ghastly picture. The women are ugly, there are no dazzling technical fireworks, the drawing is so bizarre that you can't even tell where some of the forms begin and end. Above all, the whole thing looks inept, if not perhaps insane, by Sargent's standards. The most generous thing one of the Wyndham sisters might have found to say about the picture is that it must be a joke. Or if the artist was serious, the poor fellow must have lost his reason.

But if Picasso was insane, he certainly holds the all-

168. John Singer Sargent. *The Wyndham Sisters.* 1900. Oil on canvas, 9 feet 7 inches by 7 feet. The Metropolitan Museum of Art, New York. Wolfe Fund, 1927.

169. Pablo Picasso. *Les Demoiselles d'Avignon.* 1907. Oil on canvas 8 feet by 7 feet 8 inches. The Museum of Modern Art, New York. Acquired through the Lillie P. Bliss Bequest.

170. Pablo Picasso. *Nude Woman*. 1910. Oil on canvas, 73¾ by 24 inches. National Gallery of Art, Washington, D.C. Ailsa Mellon Bruce Fund, 1972.

time record for having remained conspicuously at large. And while there are still a few people who claim that modern art is an enormous hoax or a sensationalized bid for attention, *Les Demoiselles d'Avignon* single-handedly refutes such an accusation. This self-imposed labor of creative analysis was not even exhibited until thirty years after it was completed.

We have already said that while Picasso was still in his teens he had mastered the craft of drawing and painting as understood by Sargent's public. In his twenties he had already rejected it. *Les Demoiselles d'Avignon* was the prodigious effort of a twenty-six-year-old genius to discover new means of expression, not for the sake of their newness but for the sake of increasing the scope and intensity of the art of painting.

We need not pretend that *Les Demoiselles* is a completely successful painting. It is a masterpiece in the sense of being a landmark that everyone interested in painting should know, rather than a picture to be enjoyed out of historical context. It could hardly be a completely successful picture, for it was painted at the beginning of a revolution so great that it is still going on today. If we compare it with *The Studio*, which Picasso painted nearly thirty years later, we can sense that *Les Demoiselles* lacks the assurance, the final satisfying sense of completeness, of the later work. But it is still a painting of tremendous force and vigor. If it were not, it could not impress, irritate, and hold people as it does. What we must remember is that it is first of all an intellectual exercise in abstraction, an effort to evolve and apply new theories that were to crystallize as cubism, a new way of analyzing forms in painting.

Cubism was based on a double premise. The first of these was as old as art itself, that natural forms can be reduced or refined in the direction of geometrical equivalents, an idea that the Cubists forced to its extreme conclusion. The second, to which we have already referred in connection with sculpture (**60** to **62**), was that the "fourth dimension" of space-time should be recognized somehow in painting, allowing all aspects of an object to be seen at once. In *Les Demoiselles d'Avignon* the geometrization of the figures is surely too obvious to need pointing out, but the strangely broken geometrical forms of the head, shoulders, and arm of the seated figure at lower right have suffered less explicable dislocations. The nose and the eye to our right of it are a profile view of a face that is also seen frontally—an elementary space-time device—while the forms of the arm to our left break, change, and merge to the point of unrecognizability.

Recognizability all but vanishes in the full development of cubism's early stage, which was born with *Les Demoiselles* and is called analytical cubism. Analytical cubism continues the principles barely suggested in *Les Demoiselles* and is well exemplified by Picasso's *Nude Woman* (**170**), painted three years later. This extreme stage gave way to variations in which objects were represented with strong geometrical reductions but remained recognizable, as they do in the much later *Studio,* which we compared with the Vermeer.

To return, now, to *Les Demoiselles:*

The flaw in this painting that—in spite of its towering historical position, in spite of everything—keeps it from being completely satisfying, is exactly the fault that the layman is first likely to find with it: we are never able to break away from the fact that these *demoiselles* are, after all, five exceptionally unlovely female figures. No matter how hard we try to argue ourselves into seeing them as satisfactory abstractions, they remain thoroughly unsatisfactory women. They have not been "abstracted" to the point where we can dissociate them from our perfectly legitimate and inevitable ideas of what a human figure should be. Abstraction has merely deformed them, and the deformations are not of a kind to clarify or, as we saw in the case of the deformations in expressionistic painting, to intensify our response.

When *Les Demoiselles* was painted, artists were just discovering African tribal sculptures as fine art rather than anthropological specimens. Picasso's borrowing is clearly shown by comparing the head of the woman at upper right with an African mask of a type he certainly knew (**171** and **172**). The vigor of tribal sculpture appealed to young artists like Picasso, who borrowed, or adapted, its forms to give a transfusion to art, which they felt had grown anemic in its conventions. And vigor *Les Demoiselles* certainly has, even though at this early point in his career the young experimenter was not able to resolve the conflict between reality and abstraction, as we saw the mature man do in *The Studio,* where the objects retain a very real importance yet have a fully realized abstract character.

Many artists and estheticians argue that paintings like Picasso's *The Studio* where forms are abstracted from visible reality but remain recognizable are compromises, and that if art is to be abstract at all it should be totally so, having no recognizable connection with the world our eyes know. Such painting is sometimes termed "nonfigurative" or "nonobjective" to distinguish it from the kind of abstraction that retains a tenuous connection with the world we see. Piet Mondrian's *Lozenge in Red, Yellow and Blue* (**173**) is a nonfigurative painting that is best explained by asking a series of questions of the kind a puzzled observer might ask, and answering them with quotations or paraphrases from Mondrian's own recorded statements of his theories:

Question: Why do you call this a painting when it is only some black lines and a few rectangles of color?

Answer: All painting—the painting of the past as well as of the present—is made up of lines and color.

Question: Yes, I know, but in the pictures I like, the line and color are used to describe forms of things I recognize and like.

Answer: But all those things you recognize and like actually exist in nature as solid objects. The painter has to

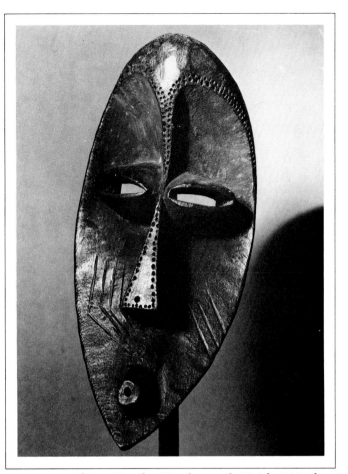

171. African, Itumba. Wooden mask. Height 14 inches. The Museum of Modern Art, New York. Purchased by Mrs. John D. Rockefeller, Jr., Fund.

172. Detail from *Les Demoiselles d'Avignon.*

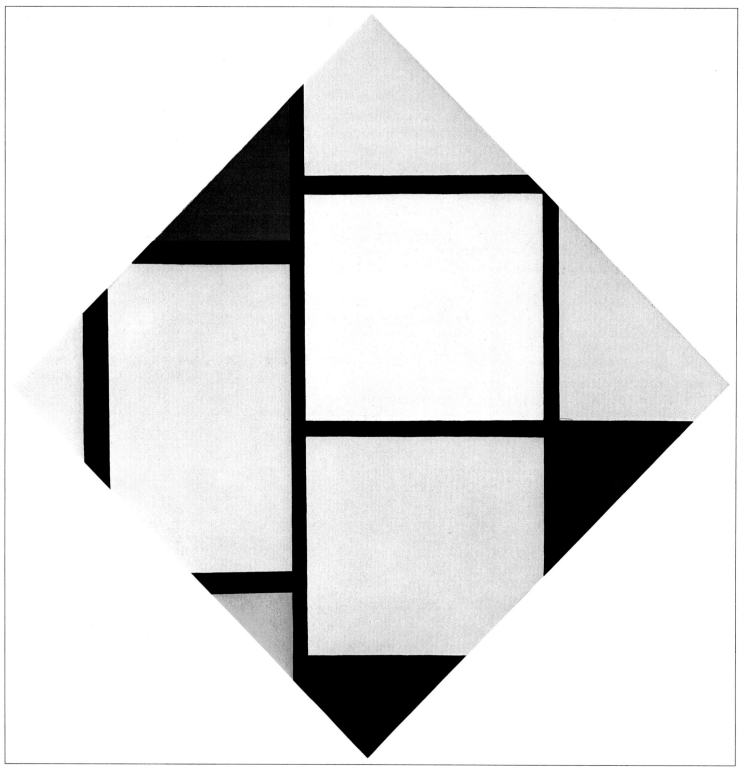

173. Piet Mondrian. *Lozenge in Red, Yellow and Blue.* About 1925. Oil on canvas on fiberboard, 56¼ by 56 inches. National Gallery of Art, Washington, D.C. Gift of Herbert and Nannette Rothschild.

reduce them to the flat plane surface of his canvas. If we forget about natural appearances, we can free line and color on this plane surface.

Question: A lot of painters paint rather flatly. Whistler's *Arrangement in Gray and Black,* which everyone calls *Whistler's Mother,* is made up of essentially flat shapes, and Picasso's *The Studio* looks completely flat to me. But those pictures mean something. Yours doesn't.

Answer: Those were steps in the right direction. But art should be a *universal* expression. Whistler's *Arrangement* is not universal because you can identify the forms as individual objects and the old lady as an individual old lady. Picasso's forms are more universal because they are more abstract. But mine are completely universal because I have used only a single universal form: the rectangular area in varying dimensions.

Question: It looks to me as if there are some angles in this *Lozenge* that aren't right angles—45 degrees and like that.

Answer: Ah! Yes, but you see this is a square picture hung diagonally stabilized by strict verticals and horizontals. The continuation and completion of the rectangular areas is sensed in adjacent space.

Question: The forms are still meaningless to me.

Answer: Not meaningless. Neutral. All associative values are annihilated, so line and color are completely freed.

Question: But it seems so cold, so mechanical.

Answer: I mean it to. I think that for the modern mentality, a work of art should have the appearance of a machine or a technical product.

Question: If you feel that way, I don't see why you wouldn't get more satisfaction out of being a mechanic rather than an artist.

Answer: I am not a mechanic. I am a living machine, capable of realizing in a pure manner the essence of art.

Mondrian has also stated that his art is not opposed to nature but quite the reverse, since he seeks a "dynamic equilibrium," which he calls the first law of nature. We can even discover that his nonfigurative painting developed from his early, fairly realistic works. His *Landscape with Farmhouse* (**174**) was painted about 1906. The house, and particularly its reflection in the canal, already gives a hint of his effort to find order by reducing forms to rigid, strongly defined rectangles (**175**). Also, the bare tree branches are beginning to resolve themselves into a tight pattern more interesting as pure pattern than as branches silhouetted against the sky (**176**). This means that his treatment is already half-abstract; he is well on his way to the much more abstract study *Horizontal Tree* (**177**), done in 1911. We can still find the general form of a tree in this abstraction, but it is the idea of tree, not the look of a tree, that he is analyzing here. Certainly the lines he has abstracted and combined express a rhythmic growth fundamental to the idea of a tree, part of nature's "dynamic equilibrium." In

174. Piet Mondrian. *Landscape with Farmhouse.* About 1906. Oil on canvas, height 34 inches. Anonymous collection.

175. Detail from *Landscape with Farmhouse.*

176. Detail from *Landscape with Farmhouse.*

177. Piet Mondrian. *Horizontal Tree.* 1911. Oil on canvas, 29⅝ by 43⅞ inches. Munson-Williams-Proctor Institute, Utica, New York.

178. Piet Mondrian. *Tree.* About 1912. Oil on canvas, 37 by 27½ inches. Museum of Art, Carnegie Institute, Pittsburgh. Maillol-Mondrian Fund.

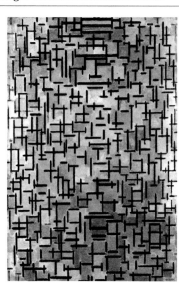

179. Piet Mondrian. *Composition.* 1916. Oil on canvas and wood strip, 47¼ by 29½ inches. The Solomon R. Guggenheim Museum, New York.

yet another *Tree* (178), done about 1912, the idea is abstracted in a vertical composition based on a tree's height rather than the spread of its branches.

When we follow through the idea in this way, Mondrian's abstractions are not puzzling at all—whether or not they are satisfying. The paradox in Mondrian's art is that his advanced theories produce paintings of an apparently elementary simplicity. The outcome of his logic, for the layman, is an art without content or structure, like the final stage of the tree sequence, his so-called plus and minus compositions, made up of short horizontal lines and small rectangular crosses that coincide with the forms of those two elementary arithmetical signs (179). We might read into this final reduction a philosophical premise or two concerning the basic and fundamental significance of plus and minus in life, thought, or what-have-you. Whether or not this deduction would be legitimate, it remains true that these plus and minus abstractions are the end result of an analytical process that began with the artist's response to the look of nature.

Mondrian was a member of the Dutch movement in painting, sculpture, architecture, and design called *De Stijl* (meaning The Style), pledged to an ultimate purity of form that would "serve a general principle far beyond the limitations of individuality." The group contended also that all arts are interdependent, with the result that their style, while limited, was one of the most closely knit in the history of art. Among sculptures, Georges Vantongerloo's *Construction of Volume Relations* (180) is self-evidently a three-dimensional equivalent of Mondrian's rectilinear planes.

It is more surprising to find that De Stijl's highly theoretical principles were applied successfully to the highly practical art of architecture. Gerrit Rietveld's Schröder house (181) in Utrecht, designed and built in 1924, was an early example of modern architectural style whose shock value at the time can hardly be appreciated today by people who have grown up with thousands of the Schröder house's legitimate and illegitimate modernistic descendants. Here Mondrian's planes and Vantongerloo's solid volumes are combined in an ingenious asymmetrical composition of rectangular slabs that interlock in space to create an interplay of hollow volumes. On the second floor, these volumes can be shifted in dimensions and relationships by sliding doors and movable screens.

There may be something chilling in the idea of living in a Schröder house surrounded by Vantongerloo sculptures Mondrian paintings and Rietveld chairs (182); the inhabitant of such an environment might soon be willing to sacrifice the ascetic purity and determined impersonality of De Stijl for a little chintzy, disorderly comfort—which may explain why De Stijl as an organized movement was short-lived. But we need only look at numerous examples of modern architecture, sculpture, painting, and furniture created since then to realize that De Stijl played a vital part in the creation of the "modern" style.

In an earlier chapter, we contrasted a Cézanne (**24**) with a Durand landscape (**23**), saying that Cézanne sought to reveal an essential orderliness in nature (without suppressing nature's vitality), while Durand regarded nature as a manifestation of mysterious forces. If we had to put all artists into one of two groups, one group would be made up of those who tend to intellectualize and the other of those who tend to emotionalize their subject matter. This contrast is even more true in abstraction, where the artist, unhampered by the associative values of subjects represented more or less realistically, may go the limit in expressing his bent.

The abstractions we have seen so far in this chapter are intellectualized conceptions, but a glance at Wassily Kandinsky's *Black Lines* (**183**, p. 132) is enough to show that the artist is not working with the calculation, the analytical approach, apparent in our other examples. *Black Lines* was painted in 1913, an extremely early date for the kind of emotive abstraction—abstract expressionism—that it exemplifies. It appears to be, and in fact is, an improvisation, a free invention. We are not supposed to interpret the lines and areas of color as abstractions of any actual objects; if we tried, we might find suggestions of large anemone-like flowers with black stamens, or of sunset clouds, of butterflies or exotic insects, depending on what direction our imagination took. But this would defeat the painter's intention.

Then what is his intention? Why doesn't he at least give us a clue by a more suggestive title? If he is trying to express a certain mood by using certain shapes and colors, are we expected to play detective to discover what the mood or idea is?

Quite the contrary. The painting is not an emotional anagram. The artist's idea is that a painting should be a creation independent of any outside supporting factors. If it is possible to translate the various combinations of shapes and colors back into real objects or to translate their "meaning" into words, then the painting fails, because it would then have derived its meaning in the first place from ideas or emotions that can be described specifically in something other than pure form and pure color.

Of course, while the painter is at work, his choice of shapes and colors and the combinations he puts them into is presumably determined by whatever complex of emotions and thoughts is stimulating him to improvise in that particular way at the time. But it is a mistake to try to pin the meaning down. We all know that red suggests excitement, that blue suggests quiet or melancholy, that a jagged line suggests action, while a curved one may suggest relaxation, and a twisted one turbulence, and so on, through a long list of ideas associated with color, shape, and line. But we cannot take the different shapes in *Black Lines* and decide what each one "feels" like, list them, add them up, and then say that the painting is a mood synthesized from

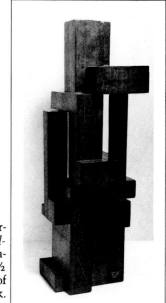

180. Georges Vantongerloo. *Construction of Volume Relations.* 1921. Mahogany, height 16½ inches. The Museum of Modern Art, New York. Gift of Silvia Pizitz.

181. Gerrit Rietveld. Schröder House. 1924. Utrecht.

182. Gerrit Rietveld. Red and Blue Chair. 1917. Painted wood. The Museum of Modern Art, New York. Gift of Philip Johnson.

183. Wassily Kandinsky. *Black Lines, No. 189.* December, 1913. Oil on canvas, 51 by 51¼ inches. Solomon R. Guggenheim Museum, New York.

184. Willem de Koonig. *Woman IV.* Oil on canvas, 59 by 46¼ inches. Nelson Gallery-Atkins Museum, Kansas City, Missouri. Gift of William Inge.

those factors. In his poem "Ars Poetica," Archibald MacLeish wrote:

> A poem should not mean
> But be.

Similarly this Kandinsky is what it is. It is "about" itself. What you get from it depends on your sensitivity to its shapes and colors and their relationships to one another. Here we are only a step away from the "gestural" or "action" and other paintings of the school of abstract expressionism that developed in New York in the 1950's and captured leadership in the world of modern art from France for the United States.

We have already seen one of the leading painters of the New York School, Franz Kline, whose *New York, N.Y.* we compared with John Marin's earlier semi-abstract *The Singer Building* (**145** and **146**). In what we described as its "lunging" execution, the Kline could be called "gestural painting," a self-explanatory term. So could *Woman IV* (**184**), by another reigning figure of the New York School, Willem de Kooning. Although not totally abstract, *Woman IV* goes in and out of recognizability from passage to passage, and its impressive projection of almost feverish energy is largely the result of the gestural application of the paint; we feel from stroke to stroke the hand of the artist, as if he were improvising the painting before our eyes. Oddly enough, we have something of the same feeling when we confront a painting that could hardly be more unlike *Woman IV* in spirit— Sargent's *The Wyndham Sisters* (**168**), which is brought to life by the exhibitionistic skill of great sweeping brush strokes, although Sargent devotes each stroke to a kind of sleight-of-hand indication of form, while each of de Kooning's is an abstraction of energy.

The apogee of gestural painting is pure "action painting," exemplified best by the work of its most conspicuous performer and cornerstone of the New York School, Jackson Pollock. Pollock's loops, blots, splashes, and skeins of color in a painting like *Convergence* (**185**) are flipped, dripped, or thrown onto the canvas (laid out flat on the floor during execution), but with much less dependence on accidental effects than the observer may suppose. Each splash, drip, or splatter is a controlled accident, the result of the artist's sensitivity—developed through experience—to the combination of his own motion (of both hand and body) and the weight and degree of fluidity of the paint in determining the nature of its fall as he moves around the borders of the canvas interweaving colors and rhythms with one another.

But why can't just anybody improvise abstractions like Kandinsky's or Pollock's? To a limited extent anybody can, and unfortunately too many people have. But the amateur is in the position of a person who sets about to prepare an elaborate dinner without ever before having so much as scrambled an egg. We can supply him with all the ingredients and recipes in the most complete detail, but the dinner is going to be inedible. The "recipes" in art are the accumulated knowledge and experience that every good

185. Jackson Pollock. *Convergence.* 1952. Oil on canvas, 7 feet 9½ inches by 12 feet 11 inches. Albright-Knox Art Gallery, Buffalo. Gift of Seymour H. Knox.

186. Joseph Mallord William Turner. *Burning of the Houses of Parliament.* About 1835. Oil on canvas, 36½ by 48½. Philadelphia Museum of Art. John H. McFadden Collection.

painter works from, whether he is modern, conservative, abstract, or whatever. For all its spontaneity, abstract expressionist painting is an application of this knowledge and experience. The paintings are often improvisations, but they are improvised from resources and disciplines that have become second nature to the artists.

In making comparisons between examples of realistic art and abstractions, we have been assuming that Vermeer's picture of a studio has wider appeal than Picasso's, that Sargent's fashionable sisters are more enjoyable to most people than Picasso's *Les Demoiselles,* and that any enjoyment of Mondrian's totally nonobjective patterns depends on knowledge of their ultimate sources in scenes from nature. However, abstract art has won such a large audience in the last twenty years or so that we find the reverse is true in some cases. J. M. W. Turner's *Burning of the Houses of Parliament* (**186**, p. 133), painted close to 150 years ago when abstract art was unheard of, was admired for its bright colors, which people always like, and because it was a representation of a spectacular event. But it has taken the pure colorism of paintings by abstract artists such as Mark Rothko (**187**, p. 136) to reveal what now seems quite obvious—that Turner, too, was at least as much abstract as he was realistic.

Turner's picture shows the conflagration that destroyed the Houses of Parliament in London in 1834. We see the spectacle from across the Thames. Crowds of spectators are eerily suggested; but the real play of interest is between the spectacular area at the left, its flames, smoke, air, and water, and the quieter, stabler form of the bridge on the right. As an illustration of an event, the painting is dramatic in the extreme. Everyone is fascinated by a good fire, and this one has the additional interest of involving an important place. We may be interested first by the fire and smoke because they are fire and smoke, and in the bridge because it is dramatically crowded—impromptu bleachers for the gigantic spectacle. But if we see the picture more than a few times, its enduring interest grows in other directions. *Burning of the Houses of Parliament* will always be a picture of a good fire. But it is a good picture of a fire because Turner has abstracted from the holocaust magnificent passages of pure painting, where incandescent yellows and oranges, purplish blacks and delicate grays, not only say fire, water, smoke, air, and stone, but can give pleasure in themselves as yellows, oranges, blues, and grays, in forms that range from solid, sharply defined ones to spreading, dissolving ones. This purely optical pleasure is a minor one; if Turner had done nothing more than turn a great fire into a passage of attractive color, he would have reduced a holocaust to an entertainment. Instead, he has transformed a specific incident of destruction into a cosmic vision of the elements in chaos, as if on the eve of the creation of the world.

At this point it would be easy to tie Turner's colorism to Rothko's by finding abstractions of fire and sunlight, or the dark of night, of summer skies or storm clouds, of rain, earth, or what-you-will in Rothko's sometimes glowing, sometimes somber, fields of color. Even easier, his paintings can be enjoyed for their decorative effect, a considerable pleasure in itself. By the artist's stated intention, however, his paintings are humanistic ponderings; he wanted to deal, he said, with human emotion and human drama, but found the human figure impossible for his purposes, after struggling to find a way of his own to use it. Rothko's suicide in 1970, at the age of sixty-seven and at the apogee of his international fame, is usually regarded as the result of his own feeling that the ultimate expression he sought escaped him. By "human drama" Rothko meant, of course, an inner drama, not the drama of life around us and our active participation in it. We have seen that the other abstract artists we have considered arrived at their abstractions by way of the visual world. Rothko was dealing with abstractions in the first place—such abstractions as hope, fear, love, all human emotions—that great artists of the past, with Michelangelo as a supreme example, had dealt with by personifying them in human figures. A complicated philosophical premise is suggested here, to the effect that although an artist may arrive at abstractions from reality, or may give material form to abstractions, it is impossible to create abstractions from abstractions as Rothko wanted to do. But it is never safe to say that anything in art is impossible; what one generation has thought impossible has been achieved by the next too many times.

A revolution as extensive as the one that has produced such quantities of abstract art in the past sixty or seventy years must affect the way we see the art of the past. Our understanding of the old masters is not a static thing; from generation to generation, new ways of thinking and feeling show us new aspects of ancient art and blind us to ways that were the accepted ones a generation, a century, or centuries ago.

One old master who has come into his own as a result of our century's preoccupation with abstraction is the Italian Renaissance painter Piero della Francesca. Piero has always been regarded as an important artist, but it is only within the last twenty-five years or so that his name has appeared on most critics' and painters' lists of the greatest painters of all time. We are reproducing one scene and two details of it (**188** to **190**, p. 137) from his series of frescoes painted between 1452 and 1466 on the choir walls of the Church of San Francesco in the small city of Arezzo. The series tells the *Legend of the True Cross.* Our illustrations show the Empress Helena directing the excavation of three crosses, that of Christ and those of the two thieves, on the hill of Golgotha outside Jerusalem. Later (at far right) the legitimacy of the True Cross is proven when its shadow falls on a dead man and brings him to life. What raises this storytelling painting to the rank of a world masterpiece?

First of all, we should be able by now to enjoy the arrangement of forms in the same general way as in the

187. Mark Rothko. *Orange and Yellow.* 1956. Oil on canvas, 91 by 71 inches. Albright-Knox Art Gallery, Buffalo. Gift of Seymour H. Knox, 1956.

188. Piero della Francesca. *Discovery* and *Proof of the True Cross*, from *Legend of the True Cross*. About 1453–54. Fresco. Church of San Francesco, Arezzo, Italy.

189. *Proof of the True Cross.*

190. Figure from *Discovery of the True Cross.*

Vermeer. The "stage" this time is extremely shallow, but within its limited depth the figures are arranged as solid, three-dimensional forms, not as flat shapes.

But the spatial relationship of the figures, which accounted for the intimate appeal of the Vermeer, does not somehow fully explain the powerful expressive quality of *Legend of the True Cross.* The rest of the explanation lies in the created forms of the individual figures. Each one has the solidity, the dignity, the quietness of a great natural object or the abstract beauty of a superb architectural unit. Some of the figures, with the regular vertical folds of their robes, are as much like fluted columns as like human beings.

Now, the events pictured here are dramatic, exciting, full of action—the discovery of the crosses, the proof by miracle. Yet the figures show no agitation, no surprise, no movement. They seem hardly to be taking part in these astonishing events. Another painter would have twisted them into every attitude of amazement, would have filled the scene with movement and contrasts, would have picked us up and carried us along as participants, taking advantage of every theatrical element the story offers.

But Piero does not want to illustrate spontaneous human reactions to spectacular events. He does not regard these miracles as mere exciting anecdotes. He deliberately removes his narrative from the plane of worldly experience and invests it with solemnity, grandeur, and reverence. His figures are not first of all human beings; they are first of all pure form. They are, in a word, abstract. From them we can read the story of the pictured events—but not in human, worldly, or emotional terms. We are held outside, denied the observer's role as vicarious participant. If it were possible for us to enter the picture, we would wander around in it unseen, and certainly out of place, among these stately, motionless forms.

This stateliness, this abstract reserve, explains why the art of Piero seemed stiff, cold, and limited not many years ago when people looked first of all for sentiment and emotional drama in religious painting. We now see in his art an abstract majesty that lifts the events to an appropriately noble level. By comparison, some of the religious paintings that were most popular a generation ago look superficial or even irreverent.

In color as well as in form, Piero is subtly unreal. Every color is modified or slightly neutralized. Instead of pure greens, he gives us sage and olive; instead of pure reds, rust or brick or plum. His whites, modified toward pearly grays and creams, are as rich as his colors.

A painting like this one, tremendous in size and painted directly on the wall of a church, must lose more of its true quality than other illustrations even in the best color reproduction. An illustration in a book is of necessity so reduced in size that we see all of it at a glance. The original in this case is so large that as we stand before it, our eyes do not see the entire picture quickly but must travel across it. Sensitivity to the individual forms is increased as they reveal themselves to us gradually. For that reason, the

191. Henry Moore. *Internal and External Forms.* About 1953–54. Elm wood, height 8 feet 7 inches. Albright-Knox Art Gallery, Buffalo.

illustration may bring you closer to the original if you cover parts of it and study only a few details at a time, or if you move a sheet of paper slowly across from left to right, revealing the figures in sequence. In this way you may become more aware of their variety and even get a somewhat better impression of their size and dignity.

We have already commented on the importance of abstraction in modern sculpture and have seen examples by Gabo, Calder, and Schöffer (60, 61, and 62). We will see other examples further on in other contexts. For the moment, we will pause long enough to be certain that one modern concept is clear—the concept of negative volumes, which can apply also to architecture.

We have already mentioned, in connection with Bernini's *David* (47), the interpenetration of space in "open form." The concept of negative volumes goes a step beyond that, by which space is not a mere void between solid forms but has shape, just as solid volumes do. As an example from everyday experience: when we think of the size and shape of a room, we are considering it as a negative volume rather than as a void created incidentally by the walls, floor, and ceiling that define it. In grander terms, when we stand under a dome we are conscious not only of the inner shell

193. St. Peter's, Rome. Colonnade by Gianlorenzo Bernini, begun 1656.

of the dome above us but of the volume of the space it shapes. The main reason that a photograph of, say, the interior of St. Peter's in Rome cannot approach the experience of actually standing within it is that space cannot be photographed as a volume since all the enclosing architectural elements cannot be photographed at once.

As a sculptural example, if we see Henry Moore's *Internal and External Forms* (**191**, p. 138) only as an arrangement of solids, we are only half experiencing it. But whether or not we have ever heard of negative volumes, we are "seeing" the voids that interlock with the solid forms on a basis of equal interest. To use another Moore as an example, one of his many sculptures abstracted from reclining human figures (**192**, p. 139), here we have hollows, pits, and other irregular voids resembling the kind of negative volumes created by the action of wind and water, a hollowing-out process directly comparable to the sculptor's creation of sculptured space. A final comparison with nature is appropriate here, since Moore thinks of his sculptures in terms of association with nature and natural forces: in a great cave we are equally conscious of the space that nature has hollowed out and within which we stand, and of the shapes and textures of the cave walls. The same double pleasure is offered by Moore's *Reclining Figure*—the pleasure offered by the beauty of the solid volumes and their material, and the pleasure of the intangible yet visible beauty of the negative volumes.

As an architectural abstraction, the idea of shaped space is not easy to grasp, and indeed we must not make the mistake of thinking that a space is "shaped" simply because it is enclosed. We are speaking of architectural space as the conscious, not the accidental, creation of the architect, which makes him a kind of abstract sculptor on the grand scale.

On the grandest scale of all, he may mold the space of nature itself, as Bernini did with the embracing arms of the approach to St. Peter's. A view from above (**193**, p. 139) gives us some idea of the majesty of the conception, but does not relay the sensation of being a participant in this vast spatial creation with its changing perspectives as one walks through the plaza or within the curved colonnades.

Changing perspectives are even more important to our full realization of the architect's conception when we mount or descend the staircase of the Trinità dei Monti (familiarly called the Spanish Steps), also in Rome. Again seen from above (**194**), the curving patterns of the steps and intermediate landings show how we, as participants ascending or descending the steep rise between a busy city street at the bottom and the church at the top, embody the factor of motion that was planned in theory by the architect. The steps are best seen on a busy day when crowds of people flow in directed currents and contribute to the variety and stimulation of our own experience as we follow the shifting, curving course of the staircase with consequent shifting perspectives on the architecture of the staircase itself, the buildings around it, and the view across Rome.

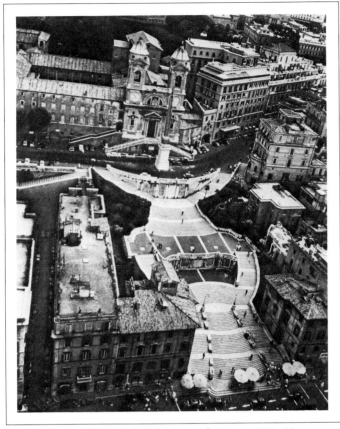

194. Francesco de Sanctis. The Spanish Steps. 1723–25. (Above them, the church of Trinità dei Monti, late sixteenth century.) Rome.

195. Francesco Borromini. San Carlo alle Quattro Fontane. Facade. 1665–67. Rome.

196. Interior. San Carlo alle Quattro Fontane.

197. Plan. San Carlo alle Quattro Fontane.

With the idea in mind that actual, physical motion is important to the full experience of certain architectural spaces, perhaps we can understand the idea of implied motion in others. In the small Roman Church of San Carlo alle Quattro Fontane, the idea of dynamic space is so important that the interior space seems almost to have shaped its enclosing walls, rather than the other way around. The wavering in-and-out façade (**195**), bulging forward in the center and reversing this movement at the sides, is really only a curtain rather than a direct result of the interior shapes (**196**), but it echoes the pulsating forms of an interior based on a plan of intersecting ellipses (**197**).

This little church, taking its name from its location at a crossing with four fountains, one on each corner, is difficult to see even in situ. And—for the last time, let us hope—it is imperative to say that this, of all interiors, defies the camera. The reader must try to combine the plan with our photographable fragment of the very small interior and put his or her best imagination to work.

In discussing the medieval cathedral, we spoke of space as the symbol of God. Some such symbolism was also attached to space in the design of seventeenth-century Italian churches, but the idea of dynamic space as an architectural abstraction is a baroque conception. Baroque is a term of sprawling definitions, but for our purposes here it means the period of the seventeenth century, extending into the early eighteenth.

The fact that our discussion of abstraction led us finally into a baroque church and up, down, and around a famous outdoor staircase is indication enough that abstract values are all-pervasive in the enjoyment of art. Many people who think of themselves as indifferent to, or even opposed to, abstraction in general are more receptive than they know to the enrichments it offers. The fervent proselytizing for abstract art by eminent artists, critics, educators, and editors of popular magazines in the United States since 1950 has frequently been opportunistic; even so, it has been salutary in its effect on the public. Familiarity often breeds a degree of understanding without study, and the boom years of American abstraction—say, 1950 to 1965—generated an atmosphere that vastly widened our appreciative range.

Those same years saw an insurgence of interest in Oriental art, an arcane field until then. It is true that institutions like Asia House in New York—with its series of beautiful exhibitions devoted to creating a wider public for the arts of China, Japan, India, and related cultures—were the major force in this insurgence, but it is also true that the increased receptivity to abstract art was helpful in the program's success. Oriental art even at its most nearly realistic has always stressed abstract values more strongly than has the art of the Western world, partly because it is traditionally an art for connoisseurs.

Up until 1950, an exhibition of Chinese calligraphy in America would have been regarded as a project for a very small audience of scholars and students; but in 1971 such an exhibition, organized by the Philadelphia Museum of

198. Mi Fu. "Sailing on the Wu River." Late eleventh or early twelfth century. Handscroll, ink on paper, height 12¼ inches, length of entire scroll 18 feet 4½ inches. Collection John M. Crawford, Jr., New York.

199. Ping-shou. "The Path at Pine and Brook." 1813. Handscroll, ink on paper, height 13¼ inches, length of entire scroll 53⅜ inches. Honolulu Academy of Arts.

Art and repeated at the Metropolitan Museum in New York, was a resounding success, crowded with people who, of course, could not read Chinese but stood absorbed by the abstract beauty of calligraphic handscrolls like the two illustrated here (198 and 199). Both are ink on paper, transcriptions of poetic nature subjects—"Sailing on the Wu River" in the late eleventh-century example, and "The Path at Pine and Brook" in the other, seven centuries later. Without knowing the poems, we can sense that the contrasting calligraphic styles—one so free, flowing, dashing, and joyous (in a style called "running script"), the other so determined, vigorous, emphatically defined—are as personal as painterly styles. To the literate, these Chinese characters do much more than transfer the words of the poems to paper; the styles are interpretive in themselves. The calligrapher recording the poem is comparable to an actor speaking the lines and investing them with whatever quality he thinks best. The remarkable thing about the success of the Chinese calligraphy exhibition is that the public, ignorant of this basic function of the calligrapher as "actor," enjoyed the interchange of purely esthetic ideas across seven hundred years between the art of calligraphers like Mi Fu and the "gestural" paintings of American artists like Jackson Pollock and Franz Kline.

We have said that Oriental art even at its most nearly realistic has always stressed abstract values. As an example, an eighteenth-century Japanese hanging scroll painted in color on silk (200), a compendium of plants and creatures of the sea, might have associative interest for a specialist in shells and coral but is essentially a combination of fascinating shapes and colors, which means that it is essentially abstract. We are very close here to an example of modern Western art in which the boundaries between East and West tend to disappear—Matisse's *Beasts of the Sea*, which figures in our next chapter (206). That chapter and the two following it are on the subject of composition— the way works of art are put together. In effect these three chapters on the patterns, the internal structures, and the inventive devices that lie beneath the surface of works of art, are continuations of this chapter on abstraction—an inexhaustible subject in any attempts to answer the question, What is art?

200. Itō Jakuchū. *Animals and Plants.* Edo Period, eighteenth century. Hanging scroll, color on silk, approximately 56 by 30½ inches. Imperial Collection, Japan.

201. Benozzo Gozzoli. *Journey of the Magi* (portion). About 1459. Fresco. Palazzo Medici-Riccardi, Florence.

Chapter Seven

COMPOSITION AS PATTERN

In discussing realism, expressionism, and abstraction, we have been dealing with the artist's point of view toward subject matter. We saw the realists reflecting the look of the world around them, but in different ways, according to what the real world, the visual world, has meant at different times and in different places. These differences aside, the realist, painting a tree, would give us a fairly accurate reproduction of the way the tree looks, leaving to us any emotional or intellectual reaction. The expressionist, in contrast, is less interested in reflecting the world around him than in revealing his responses to it; he explores these emotions in a personal and subjective way. Taking the same tree, he would distort its form and color as he pleased in order to tell us how he felt about it. The abstractionist has it both ways. Interested neither in reproducing the look of things, like the realist, nor in being specific about his emotional reactions, like the expressionist, he may be interested in the world as a complex of ideas and, if interested in trees at all, would ask himself what the idea of a tree might be, and would proceed to intellectualize a pattern revealing that idea. Or, if of an emotional bent, he might try to abstract from the *idea* of tree, rather than the *look* of tree, forms and colors that would express his response—which, we saw, would be a variety of abstract expressionism.

Of course these approaches are bound to overlap. The eye, the emotions, and the intellect all share in the creation of a work of art and in its enjoyment. All works of art of any consequence have an abstract element that many observers miss—their composition, the way they are put together.

Composition is so important that we began dealing with it in our first discussions. When we analyzed the reasons for the curious disposition of the elements in Degas's *Woman with Chrysanthemums* (**21**), where the subject of the portrait is pushed far toward one edge of the canvas leaving the most conspicuous position to a large bouquet of flowers, we were trying to show how one of the most skillful pictorial composers of them all went about saying what he wanted to say about his subject by compositional means. We discussed *"Whistler's Mother"* (**11**) as a combination of gray and black shapes arranged to create a mood. This is composition; what Whistler called *Arrangement in Gray and Black* could as well have been called *Composition in Gray and Black.*

Not every great painting is a great composition, but composition is so fundamental to the creation of pictures that a list of the world's greatest paintings would have to overlap a list of the greatest compositions in the majority of titles. Yet of all the elements in the art of painting, composition is usually the one least recognized even when it is playing a major part in one's reaction to a picture. By means of composition the artist directs the observer's eye, holds it on key areas, leads it away and back again, takes it slowly across some areas, quickly across others. To a lesser degree, sculptors do the same thing. Architects, working under the difficulty of meeting practical demands at the same time, are composing when they adjust dimensions and volumes into harmonious proportions.

It is quite possible to enjoy works of art without being aware of their composition, but our spontaneous enjoyment of subject, color, and form is deepened when we can recognize their interplay on a compositional basis. In a general way compositions fall into two broad classifications, two-dimensional and three-dimensional, with every transitional stage in between. Two-dimensional compositions recognize the canvas or panel for what it is, a flat surface, and are limited to arrangements of lines and flat shapes on that surface. Three-dimensional compositions eliminate the surface, so to speak, opening up the space behind it and arranging objects within that space so that the painter's and sculptor's fields overlap. We saw this distinction when we compared Picasso's *The Studio* with Vermeer's *The Artist in His Studio* (**164** and **165**). We followed the composition of the Picasso, which is quite flat, straight across the surface, but we looked into the depth of the Vermeer, into a cube of space created by the artist and occupied by the three-dimensional forms he arranged within it.

What enters into a painter's decision to conceive his painting in two dimensions or three? Ordinarily he may decide for himself, but occasionally the choice is dictated by special circumstances. If he is commissioned to do a mural painting, for instance, a painting actually covering the area of a wall as opposed to an independent picture merely hanging on the wall, his obligation is to make his mural harmonize with the architecture and, usually, to respect the flatness and solidity of the wall, in order to avoid leaving us with the uncomfortable illusion that a heavy ceiling is left unsupported because the wall is painted out from under it. To avoid this illusion, some muralists create another by incorporating painted columns or arches that seem to support the ceiling while we look through them into the distance. Andrea Mantegna designed a complete architectural scheme of supports and a vault on the four flat walls and ceiling of the Camera degli Sposi of the ducal palace in Mantua, and was then free to dispose his figures at will, either within the spaces of the architecture or against vistas of painted landscape (**202**, p. 148). But more generally, murals lie flat on the wall—like tapestries, we might say. Benozzo Gozzoli's *Journey of the Magi* (**201**, p. 144) in the Medici Palace, Florence, is such a mural.

The Medici Palace is a heavy stone structure, and the chapel interior shares in the feeling of solidity imparted by the thick walls. Gozzoli accepts the wall for what it is, a solid supporting area, and treats the *Journey of the Magi* flatly and decoratively, as if it were ornamental wallpaper. The rock shapes and tree shapes are designed for their interest as flat decorative shapes, not for their interest as representations of real rocks or trees, and certainly not as solid forms receding into and occupying space. Nominally this pictorial scheme begins with a procession immediately in front of us and goes back, back, and back across a fantasy landscape of rock ledges to a sky where clouds float. But nominally only. The distant forms are as clear, as precise and detailed, as those in the foreground. Ledges and figures, buildings and trees, grow smaller and smaller as we travel upward into the distance—but they are arranged in tiers as flat as sheets of paper, layer upon layer; they are not painted as solid forms receding into open space. In short, the painting respects the integrity of the wall.

A painter who composes in three dimensions would argue that it is as foolish for a painter to limit himself to two dimensions as it is for a composer of music to limit himself to a few instruments when he could write for a full orchestra. But another painter might respond that Beethoven said as much in his quartets as he did in his symphonies, and that Shakespeare said as much in the compact form of sonnets as Balzac did in all the volumes of *La Comédie Humaine.* And he would add that economy of means, the compression of subject into a quartet or a sonnet or a two-dimensionally conceived painting, results in greater clarity and greater purity, and thus intensifies whatever the artist has to say. It was some such argument that Mondrian was making about two-dimensional abstractions (**179**). And the French painter Maurice Denis, in a statement much quoted by other painters, once said: "Remember that a picture—before being a battle horse, a nude woman, or some anecdote—is essentially a plane surface covered with colors assembled in a certain order." The important words here are "plane surface." The implication is that there are both honesty and esthetic advantage in recognizing the limitations of a flat surface and capitalizing on them.

Two-dimensional composition includes the most elementary as well as some of the most sophisticated approaches to painting. The least experienced of us, given a piece of paper, a pencil, and a model, would place our image in the center of the space rather than in one corner. This is an instinctive recognition that a pictorial image needs a logical relationship to the flat area it occupies. We would also draw in two dimensions—necessarily, through ignorance of perspective and foreshortening and modeling, but also because the conception of space into the depth of a picture is a complicated one in itself. Yet even these unschooled approaches to the creation of a picture may produce a work of art when an artist's sensitivity is present, as in *Esther Tuttle* (**203**, p. 149) by Joseph H. Davis, a self-taught American painter of the last century.

In two-dimensional painting the artist's vocabulary is reduced to line, flat shape, and color. In each of these elements he must be inventive, but above all it is in their combination that he must be creative. Henri Matisse, generally recognized with Picasso as one of the twin fountainheads of modern art, once defined composition as "the art of arranging, in a decorative manner, the various ele-

202. Andrea Mantegna. Camera degli Sposi. Completed 1474. Fresco. Palazzo Ducale, Mantua, Italy.

ments at the artist's disposal." *Esther Tuttle* is a "primitive" painting—primitive in the art-sense of the word, meaning a painting by an untutored artist creating instinctively rather than working from a background of established theories, knowledge, and technical training. Primitive or not, the painter of *Esther Tuttle* has done a more than creditable job according to Matisse's definition of composition.

The rug, innocent of perspective, is drawn more like decorated baseboard than fabric lying flat on the floor. What difference does it make? Actually, a favorable difference: the rug's pattern is more vividly revealed for being free from the distortions that perspective would have introduced; the heavy curves are all the more effective in contrast with the crisp precision of the other forms. If we insist on photographic realism, we must admit that the artist has been unable to cope with the complications of the model's dress; but the important thing is that the simple bell-like shape of the skirt is combined happily with the nicely calculated irregular puffs of the sleeves. The intricacy of the lace-trimmed collar is set off by being played in fullest detail against the broad, undetailed silhouette of the dress. And the wavering line of the bottom of the apron is one of the least conspicuous but most successful bits of design in the whole arrangement: its gentle movement relieves the stiffness of the lower part of the figure without competing in interest with the upper part, where the face, drawn in profile with skillful delicacy, has to hold its own against all this strong pattern. We have no way of knowing how accurate the drawing is as a likeness—it somehow looks convincing—but the line is beautiful in itself.

Are we giving Joseph H. Davis, an obscure painter, exaggerated credit for knowledge or talent or sensitivities that he possessed only in small measure, reading into this little painting qualities that are not there? Certainly we are not. Thousands of primitive paintings were produced in nineteenth-century America, and for every one of such merit as *Esther Tuttle* there are a hundred that are merely dull, inexpressive, and awkward.

There was probably very little conscious application of esthetic theory or rule in the making of this painting; but every detail is carefully considered as part of the total arrangement, every detail is important to the total effect, and the total effect is good—too good to be a fortunate accident. The design is creative, even if it is arrived at through a feeling for rightness rather than by proven rules of what is right. Even when the most highly skilled artist applies rules and theories, it is still the feeling for rightness that makes the difference between a successful exercise and a work of art.

The attraction of a really good primitive painting is that the innate creative sensitivity of the artist speaks directly and purely. It would be a gross exaggeration to call *Esther Tuttle* a great work of art, but it is an extraordinarily appealing one. The extreme smallness of the hands and feet may be the combined result of technical limitations and the artist's effort to show Esther Tuttle as a lady of refinement and delicacy. But anyone who looks at such a painting with as much perception as Davis employed in executing it will recognize that its merits lie deeper than attractive quaintness. This primitive painter has, indeed, shown himself to be an artist in "arranging, in a decorative manner, the various elements" at his disposal.

By comparing *Esther Tuttle* with three other portraits of women, we will see that the two-dimensional vocabulary of line, shape, and color is a flexible one. Each of the three is the work of a master of such impressive reputation that if Davis could have known of them he would have quailed at the prospect of having to stand alongside them. Yet it is easy to believe that these men would have appreciated Davis's artistry and, fully aware of its limitations, would have recognized its kinship with their own. One of these men is a seventeenth-century Japanese artist; another, a sixteenth-century European court painter; and the third, a

203. Joseph H. Davis. *Esther Tuttle.* 1836. Water color on paper, 11¾ by 9 inches. The New-York Historical Society.

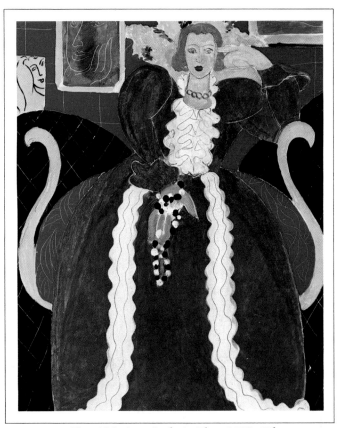

204. Henri Matisse. *Lady in Blue.* 1937. Oil on canvas, 36½ by 29 inches. Philadelphia Museum of Art. Collection Mrs. John Wintersteen.

205. Stages in development of *Lady in Blue*, February 26 to April 6, 1937.

great revolutionary of modern art. Their names are Torii Kiyonobu I, Hans Holbein the Younger, and Henri Matisse, who has already supplied our working definition of composition.

The quality of sincerity in a technically limited painting like *Esther Tuttle* is easily recognized; but why some modern artists like Matisse, highly trained in the dominant tradition of painting things the way they look, should discard that tradition with its perspective, its mastery of three-dimensional modeling, and all the other devices of realistic representation, requires some explanation. As a young unknown, Matisse augmented his income by copying old masters in the Louvre. These copies were irreproachable, and Matisse was capable of doing original work of the same technical caliber. But for him, original work in the manner of the old masters was no more satisfying than making copies. He set about to find means of expression that would be his own, something beyond traditional technical dexterity. It was necessary for him to discard the past (or at least this aspect of it) not because the past was faulty but because its modes of expression, suitable in their own times, were out of key in ours. We look for certain things in Rembrandt, certain others in Matisse (and certain others in both). "I am unable to distinguish between my feeling for life and the way I have of expressing it," Matisse said. His feeling for life, in that case, is one of gaiety, of elegance. These qualities, seductive if not profound, are represented at their highly civilized best in his *Lady in Blue* (**204**, p.149).

The freshness and deceptive air of simplicity of *Lady in Blue* suggest that it must have been a spontaneous creation, easily achieved. But during its painting a day-to-day photographic record was kept of the stages through which it passed (**205**), showing that *Lady in Blue* began as a semirealistic impression, went through many transformations, and became the picture we now see only after a series of drastic readjustments of its shapes and colors. Describing this method of work, Matisse said: "Supposing I want to paint the body of a woman: first of all I endow it with grace and charm, but I know that something more than that is necessary. I try to condense the meaning of this body by drawing its essential lines. The charm will then become less apparent at first glance, but in the long run it will begin to emanate from the new image." When it was painted in 1937, the charm of *Lady in Blue* was not apparent to a mass public that was still absorbing the shock of an esthetic revolution; but for most people today the "long run" has worked, and the charm does emanate from the final combination of shapes and colors that satisfied the artist.

The point we are making is that the unschooled painter of *Esther Tuttle* and the highly trained painter of *Lady in Blue*, working from the opposite poles of innocence and sophistication, separated by a century of time and an even wider cultural gap, share an essential similarity. The model, the dress, and the accessories in both paintings are only raw material for flat pattern that is ornamental and expressive in its own way in each picture. In both of them the bell-like skirt is relieved by the uneven lines and masses of the blouse. The contrast between the intricate lace-trimmed collar and somber robe in *Esther Tuttle* is comparable to the same elements in the Matisse, substituting the jabot for the lace. Other similarities are apparent after a little examination. Whereas the primitive painter, unable to cope with the problem of perspective, worked by necessity in two dimensions, Matisse, who of course was a master of perspective, discarded perspective in order to capitalize on flat pattern.

The American primitive portrait is composed as a spotting of solid areas; the Matisse is this plus a balance of curves. The lyrelike yellow forms derived from the arms of a sofa are reversed in the curve of the light trim in the skirt. A series of arcs—the sides of the skirt, the edge of the red seat of the sofa, the black shapes in the background— is tied in with these S-shapes. The hand holding the beads is startling in size, and at first it is not as easy to accept this bigness as it is to accept the equally exaggerated littleness of the hands and feet of Esther Tuttle. Yet if you cover up this hand, the picture looks empty. As a hand it would be grotesque; but it is not a hand, it is part of an arrangement of line and shape and color. Its extraordinary size and its conspicuous position in the center of the picture make it the major stabilizing element in this composition of curves and reverse curves. The picture, in its final effect, is static. It is tranquil. "What I dream of is an art of balance, of purity and serenity devoid of troubling or depressing subject matter," Matisse said. If ever he achieved that dream, he achieved it in *Lady in Blue.*

Matisse's stylistic history is a constant affirmation of the joy of life, expressed in vivacious patterns and exuberant colors with a constantly increasing emphasis on the two-dimensionality of his arrangements. His *Carnival at Nice* (207), painted about fourteen years earlier than *Lady in Blue,* shows spectators on a balcony overlooking a street where a parade stretches off into the distance, with hints of sea and hills against the sky. None of this, however, is treated with serious recognition of distance; at best it compromises with three-dimensional space by granting a token acknowledgment of perspective that is immediately refuted. The overall pattern of dots of bright color makes no distinction at all between things near and far. *Lady in Blue* rejects even any token acknowledgment; then finally, in 1950, thirteen years after *Lady in Blue* and four years before the artist's death at the age of eighty-five, we have *Beasts of the Sea* (206), a collage of bright papers cut with scissors into essentially abstract shapes derived from sea life, and pasted on canvas, Matisse's ultimate celebration of the beauty of composition as the arrangement of flat areas of pure color.

Before looking at the next portrait of a woman for comparison with *Esther Tuttle* and *Lady in Blue,* we might examine parenthetically some Eastern examples related to

206. Henri Matisse. *Beasts of the Sea.* 1950. Collage, cut paper on canvas, 9 feet 8⅜ inches by 5 feet ⅝ inches. National Gallery of Art, Washington, D.C. Ailsa Mellon Bruce Fund.

les bêtes de la mer...

H. matisse 50

207. Henri Matisse. *Carnival at Nice.* About 1923. Oil on canvas, 26½ by 37½ inches. The Cleveland Museum of Art. Purchased by Mr. and Mrs. William H. Marlatt Fund.

208. Mahmud Muzahib or pupil. *Bahram Gur in the Turquoise Pavilion on Wednesday.* 1524–25. Tempera and gilt on paper, 12¾ by 8¾ inches. The Metropolitan Museum of Art, New York. Gift of Alexander Smith Cochran, 1913.

209. Attributed to Torii Kiyonobu I. *Woman Dancer with Fan and Wand.* About 1708. Hand-colored wood-cut, 21¾ by 11½ inches. The Metropolitan Museum of Art, New York. Harris Brisbane Dick Fund, 1949.

our theme. Matisse was strongly influenced by Oriental art, and several resemblances between *Lady in Blue* and the Persian miniature *Bahram Gur in the Turquoise Pavilion* (**208**) show the kinship. There is the same emphasis on silhouette rather than solid, rounded form; the same use of pure, ungraduated color; the same flattening out of perspective so that the tile-paved floor in the Persian miniature reveals its pattern without distortion, just as does the crisscross pattern on the couch in *Lady in Blue* and the rug in *Esther Tuttle*. Another resemblance: both *Esther Tuttle*, with its identifying legend in ornamental script at the bottom of the picture, and *Beasts of the Sea*, with its conspicuous title and signature written by the artist, introduce script harmonious with the rest of the picture, just as the Persian artist incorporates a section of decorative script in the horizontal band above the conventionalized archway. Or, going back to Gozzoli's *Journey of the Magi*, the Persian miniaturist also designs rather than imitates natural forms, and both pictures recede into the "distance" from bottom to top in layered areas as flat, we have said, as sheets of paper. Of all these Western pictures, however, only the Matisse was painted with knowledge (and admiration) of the conventions followed by the Persian miniaturist. A further difference is that Matisse alone cultivates an air of improvisation, while the Persian, the American primitive, and the Renaissance Italian have called into play all the precision that they could muster.

In discussing Picasso's *Demoiselles d'Avignon* (**169**), we said that abstract and realistic elements in the same painting may conflict to such an extent that our enjoyment of either may be marred by the other—a possible objection, in some eyes, to *Lady in Blue*. No such difficulty can arise in *Woman Dancer with Fan and Wand* (**209**) by Torii Kiyonobu I. Never having developed our Western preoccupation with photographic reality, Oriental art at an early stage reached such a satisfactory balance between representational form and abstraction that our own extreme expressions of realism and our corresponding extreme reaction into abstraction never took place, or at least not until total abstraction was borrowed from the West in our century. Until then, Chinese and Japanese artists, working within a tradition many centuries old, perfected the expressive virtues of two-dimensional composition in which pictorial subject matter and abstract values are mutually supporting, not competing.

The sinuous yet strong lines and shapes of *Woman Dancer with Fan and Wand* are a superb expression of the studied, flowing postures of traditional Japanese dance. Each line is interesting, whether we take it for itself or as part of the system of lines making up the whole figure. Long curving arcs come to a point and turn quickly into almost straight lines; a series of lines like those around the waist looks at first like a knotted convolution, but unwinds into a system of clear, simple elements. We look at no single line for very long; each one catches us up into a stream of lines that move quickly here, slowly there, like flowing water or drifting smoke. The pattern of flowers and leaves on the sleeve is a delight in itself, but it too is like a line in its overall movement within a system of nearby lines. Some of the heavier forms act as weights or brakes to the quicker movement of others. Our constant and increasing pleasure in these patterns is fused with the idea of the dancer's movements; we have the double pleasure of an interesting subject and its abstract expression fused in indissoluble harmony.

If the picture is turned upside down, and especially if the face is covered, the design no longer represents a dancer's figure but becomes a purely abstract composition. It is quite changed, however, for it now billows upward into a climax of heavy forms. Right side up, the heavier forms lie in the lower half of the picture and curve up through lighter ones to the delicacy of the head with its terminating hat and the fillip of the orange bow. This is planned, of course; but the same thing happens, either by plan or by instinctive awareness of its rightness, in *Esther Tuttle*, where the delicate profile with its lightly painted bow at the neck and ornaments in the hair has a similar relationship to the heavier forms below.

As a brief aside before we see the Holbein, we can look at another Japanese woodcut, Torii Kiyotada's *Actor Dancing* (**210**). We do not need the grimace of the face, nor the paraphernalia of the swords that replace the fan and wand in the woman dancer's hands, to tell us that this is a dance of a contrasting character. We are told by line—sharp, angular line interrupted by other lines—and by shapes that are jagged and irregular instead of sinuous and flowing. The total silhouette has this same jagged character. The word "harmony" suggests, always, smoothness and grace. Actually, we have in *Actor Dancing* something like a harmony of conflicts—to be completely paradoxical—just as in music we may have a harmony of dissonances.

Compared with the extreme flatness and decorative conventions of the compositional patterns we have been analyzing, Holbein's realistic portrait of *Christina of Denmark, Duchess of Milan* (**211**) may seem to fall outside our two-dimensional bracket. But with its restrained modeling and shallow space, the composition is conceived more in terms of flat shapes than volumes. We are showing it in two versions, first as it was known before 1968, and then in its present state after cleaning, during which the oblong of white paper in the background was eliminated as a late addition and the background itself was discovered to have been varied, originally, by the cast shadow on the wall at the right.

Upon one of the occasions when Henry VIII was between wives, this habitual royal widower was considering as his fourth queen the eminently eligible and reputedly beautiful Christina, Princess of Denmark and recent widow of the Duke of Milan (she is still in mourning dress in the portrait). Henry sent Holbein to Brussels to participate in negotiations and to bring back a portrait of the princess.

210. Torii Kiyotada. *Actor Dancing.* About 1715. Hand-colored woodcut, 11¼ by 6 inches. The Metropolitan Museum of Art, New York. Harris Brisbane Dick Fund, 1949.

211. Hans Holbein the Younger. *Christina of Denmark, Duchess of Milan,* before and after cleaning. 1538. Oil and tempera on wood, height 70 inches. National Gallery, London.

212. Head of *Christina of Denmark.*

213. Hands of *Christina of Denmark.*

Holbein executed a study, now lost, and brought it back to London, where it evolved into the portrait we are now examining. It charmed Henry as it has charmed everyone ever since, but Christina was less charmed with Henry's record as a husband, and the union never materialized.

Until the 1968 cleaning, the composition as we knew it was dominated by three light silhouettes: The oblong of white paper pinned to the wall, the oval of the face, and finally the hands—all played against an eventless dark blue background and the gentle rhythms of the robe with its fur-trimmed edges and curving folds of the sleeves. The three silhouettes had a wonderful variety. The paper was a simple oblong; the hands, in contrast, an irregular flowering of curves and slender projections, while the oval of the face (212), terminated by the line of the cap and ornamented below by the lively frill of collar, blended the regularity of the oblong and the variety of the hands (213).

The three floating shapes were firmly anchored within the picture area on a horizontal axis established by the common center line of the face and the paper, and a vertical axis running through the center of the face and that of the hands. Coming at the intersection of these axes, the face was unequivocally established as the climactic focus of the picture—perhaps redundantly in view of its natural psychological dominance.

For anyone who had loved the picture in what proves to have been a modified state, the elimination of the white oblong was momentarily shocking. But it takes only a second look to see that the picture is even more subtly organized and more than ever revealing of personality by means of the original, and present, composition. We have more than ever the feeling that here is a real person, a person of great reserve, of acute intelligence—a subtle woman, a most attractive but not quite approachable one. The balancing function of the white oblong on the right, which counteracted the leftward lean of the figure, is now served, less intrusively, by the arbitrary band of cast shadow running along the margin at far right, leaving the lovely face and the lovely hands to tell even more effectively in their contrasting silhouettes.

Recalling the painting, even after having seen it frequently, most people would retain the impression that Christina is shown directly facing us in the center of the panel. If she had been so placed, however, the character relayed would have been that of a much more foursquare, more obvious, more everyday woman. As it is, the slight turn of the body and the variation from center constitute a removal from us, a reserve on the part of this beautiful woman that makes the direct gaze of the eyes all the more arresting. Composition, rather than the mere reproduction of a set of figures, accounts for our feeling that we are confronted by a fascinating personality.

To emphasize this point, we can compare the portrait of the Danish princess with *Anne of Cleves* (214), which Holbein painted the following year. The circumstances of its commission were the same: Henry, still shopping after

Christina's refusal, sent Holbein to portray this runner-up for the precarious honor of being queen of England.

It is an entrancing picture—possibly, in its elaboration of ornamental detail, more immediately attractive than the one of Christina. Presented with a different personality in his sitter, Holbein responds with a contrasting composition. Anne is presented in an absolutely frontal position, centered in the picture area, in a design as nearly symmetrical as possible without monotony. The sweet, prim, guileless, and unimaginative little mask faces us patiently, with a suggestion of gentle obedience (215). The hands are clasped in a meek and compact bundle (216), whereas Christina's were beguilingly patterned (213). Anne's elaborate robe, headdress and jewels, so different from the rich, subdued elegance of Christina's costume, manage to invest the ordinary little person with an air of circumstance; Anne's trappings are what we notice first, and remember best, while we remember Christina as a woman. As an expression of character, the portrait of Anne of Cleves is as successful a composition as the one Holbein devised to interpret Christina's more subtle personality; if it is less fascinating than Christina's, it is because it serves a less fascinating subject, showing us a sweet but unexceptional woman surrounded by and patiently accepting all the trappings of high position. These trappings flatter Anne. In a way, Holbein was too successful: Henry liked the portrait enough to contract the union but was so disappointed in Anne herself that he divorced her with indecent haste.

Now what are the rules for creating such compositions? There simply are none, except of the most general kind. Every artist knows that variety of shape makes for interest; that strong value contrast—that is, strong contrast between lights and darks—heightens dramatic effect; that a psychological balance can be created between a large, rather heavy area like Christina's robed figure and less conspicuous ones like the paper (or the shadow) on the wall back of her. But the final rightness of the disposition of the various elements in *Christina of Denmark* is the result of the same thing that made *Esther Tuttle* more than just another quaint primitive—the artist's individual sensitivity in applying general principles.

As we continue to analyze compositions we will find that certain rules, certain formulas, can be applied, but we can never set down rules and formulas that will entirely explain the power some paintings have to satisfy and move us while others that seem to follow the same formulas are nothing but dull and obvious products. From time to time some painter, critic, or esthetician sets out to discover the compositional secrets of the old masters and reduce them to a foolproof mathematical basis. The trouble is always that the systems work just as well when applied to commonplace objects and routine pictures as they do when tested on great sculptures and paintings. Precise theories derived from the beautiful shapes of Greek vases often work just as well when applied to ordinary coffeepots. In the

214. Hans Holbein the Younger. *Anne of Cleves.* 1539–40. Oil and tempera on parchment mounted on canvas, height 26 inches. The Louvre, Paris.

215. Head of *Anne of Cleves.*

216. Hands of *Anne of Cleves.*

same way, anyone who has taken a course in musical composition knows that it is possible to learn the rules of counterpoint and apply them correctly to produce a technically impeccable fugue that is downright ugly in sound. Composition in architecture, music, sculpture, or anything else is always a matter of creation, for which the rules are only a guide along tested paths.

We have analyzed the portrait of Christina as a two-dimensional arrangement because, in spite of the realistic modeling, it is so conceived. The modeling is slight, and although there is indication of shallow space, there is no great effort to create a spatial illusion, which is a different thing altogether. Logically explained, the piece of paper is pinned to the wall a foot or so back of the head, but compositionally the three light silhouettes perform on a single plane. However, we must always accept some ambivalence when a composition of modeled objects is conceived in what we might call "unmodeled space"; if you prefer to regard the picture in its shallow third dimension, the general analysis of its composition as we have given it can still be applied without very much modification.

In either case, Matisse—our spokesman in this chapter—could have been writing of Holbein's *Christina* when he said: "The whole arrangement of my picture is expressive. The place occupied by figures or objects, the empty spaces around them, the proportions—everything plays a part. All that is not useful in a picture is detrimental." For that matter, he could have been speaking of, or for, any number of artists who preceded him, but the emphasis he puts on "empty spaces" and his conclusion that anything not useful is detrimental call to mind one aspect of two-dimensional composition as a flat pattern of shape and color that has to be mentioned with a word of tribute to the artist responsible for it—the art of the poster as revolutionized by Henri de Toulouse-Lautrec in the 1890's. His *Aristide Bruant in His Cabaret* (**217**, p. 160) is in fact the purest example of two-dimensional pattern reduced to a minimal vocabulary of shape, color, and empty space that we have seen in this discussion.

Bruant was a singer of popular ballads in cabarets that corresponded, more or less, to our nightclubs. In a costume of black boots, black wide-brimmed hat, voluminous cloak, and scarf and cane, he sang songs of bohemian life (and low life, frequently bawdy) in the argot of Montmartre. Lautrec captures the essence of Bruant's professional personality with a vivid image that explains why it was said of his posters that they "take possession of the streets"—but without disfiguring them. In their inescapability, their compelling design, and their pungent characterizations of theatrical performers, Lautrec's posters were commercially effective. But wherever commercial expenses are involved in anything as variable and as personal as a work of art, there will always be opposition to risking money on anything new. Lautrec usually designed his posters free for his friends among performers and even bore some of the costs of printing to assure that they would finally appear exactly as he had designed them. His posters were the earliest to come into museums as works of art rather than period pieces, and the principles upon which they were designed—clarity, expressiveness, and esthetic appeal—have served as models for poster designers ever since, through one change of style after another.

The compositions we have seen so far have been analyzed as patterns of shapes and colors. The ones we will now see could be similarly treated, but are more strongly tied together by another compositional element—line. By "line" here we will usually mean the bounding edges of forms, either the total form as separated from the background or the contours of the various secondary forms within a main one. Secondarily, "line" may mean the general stance, the general direction, of a form. A detail (218, p. 161) of the group, the Three Graces, in Botticelli's *Primavera* exemplifies the rhythmic interlacing of linear systems either way you want to regard them—specifically, as the bounding edges of forms ("outlines" if you wish), or more generally as the stance of a figure, the angle or curve with which a neck rises from the shoulders or a head balances on the neck; the lift of an arm within its linear boundaries; the flow of a mass of curls composed of smaller rhythms within the mass.

Botticelli, generally conceded by art historians to be the consummate master of linear design in painting, worked in fifteenth-century Florence when the greatest excitement and the most modern art centered upon developing the techniques of three-dimensional realism—perspective, accurate anatomical structure, and the placement of realistically modeled figures in space—and he followed and employed these developments. But not wholeheartedly. He was a stylist to the point of eccentricity, and his passion was for line to the extent that in spite of everything else his drawing and his composition are most appropriately analyzed two-dimensionally.

The linear grace of the detail we have chosen, the flowing lines of bodies, gauzy draperies, and masses of ringlets and escaping locks of hair—all of these lines intermingling, separating, and meeting again, all with their own grace and logic as they flow into and away from one another—these could be analyzed indefinitely, but to little point, since any eye must surely take pleasure in being carried along the paths and currents that Botticelli set down so clearly. The picture is a lyrical celebration of the grace, refinement, and sensitivity to the beautiful that was cultivated (along with more hard-headed studies in power politics) at the Medici court. We can use the same words to describe the quality of Botticelli's line: grace, refinement, sensitivity. And, we must add, strength. The firmness and gravity of long, slowly moving lines serve as foils to the more fluid, rapidly moving linear arabesques nearby. It is this interplay of strength and delicacy that differentiates Botticelli's line from that of his imitators, which turns flaccid in comparison.

217. Henri de Toulouse-Lautrec. *Aristide Bruant in His Cabaret.* 1893. Color lithograph, 54½ by 39 inches. The Metropolitan Museum of Art, New York. Harris Brisbane Dick Fund.

218. Sandro Botticelli. The Three Graces from *Primavera*.

Line also holds the whole of the *Primavera* together as a unit that otherwise would break into three unequal divisions (**219**). The subject is an allegory that has been given various interpretations although the figures are individually identifiable. In the center stands Venus—a uniquely modest and maidenly conception of that goddess—framed by a natural arch formed by boughs within a grove of orange trees dotted with bright fruit. In a group to our right the wind god Zephyrus, painted in chilly blues and grays, urges his wife, the nymph Chloris, toward fulfilling her transformation into Flora, goddess of Spring. She looks back toward him as if reluctant, but flowers are already issuing from her mouth. The third figure shows her fully transformed and scattering flowers, as Flora. The group alone would be a wonderful picture. The English poet Robert Herrick invoked the Chloris-Flora metamorphosis in "Corinna's going A'Maying," in which he admonishes his mistress ("sweet slug-a-bed") to arise and usher in the month of May:

> Rise, and put on your foliage, and be seen
> To come forth, like the springtime, fresh and green,
> And sweet as Flora.

On the left, Mercury, who seems curiously uninterested in the events nearby, points upward with his caduceus. The

219. Sandro Botticelli. *Primavera.* About 1478. Panel painting, 6 feet 8 inches by 10 feet 4 inches. Galleria degli Uffizi, Florence.

Three Graces, handmaidens of Venus whose function it is to make life delightful, dance in a ring. (They are Euphrosyne, representing the grace of mirth; Aglaia, that of splendor; and Thalia, that of bloom.) They are, for whatever reason, the targets of blazing arrows from the bow of blindfolded Cupid, who flutters above the scene.

Compositionally the picture builds up to a tentlike peak at the middle, reaching an appropriate climax at the head of Venus. The angle of Chloris's figure is continued by foliage and tree trunks up to the figure of Cupid, whose arm and arrow direct us firmly downward at a corresponding angle. Interrupted by the complications of the group of the Three Graces, the angle is restated by Mercury's forearm. A swaglike course running downward can be followed from the wind god's arm along the lowered arms of Chloris and Flora and then up along the curve of Venus's robe to her raised hand, uniting Venus with the right side of the picture. On the left the continuations are more tenuous; this is, on the whole, a much more loosely organized picture than some we will see where composition is a firm structural skeleton for the unification of a number of figures.

Composition can also be a means of expression, and we will anticipate our chapter on that subject with one emphatically linear example here. The name of the artist, William Blake, is assurance enough that the picture will be in a linear mode.

Blake's *The Wise and the Foolish Virgins* (**220**) is a storytelling picture, told superficially by the images that act it out, but fundamentally by the lines composing them. On the left stand the five wise virgins, their lamps glowing with flames from the oil they have been sagacious enough to save against the coming of judgment. Ranged in righteousness, they reject the hysterical pleas of the five unwise virgins, who have squandered their oil and are now terrified by the sounding of the last trump in the darkened sky above them.

The two groups are characterized by contrasting lines. The lines of the wise virgins, followed from the left edge of the picture to the figure with the upraised arm, begin with the quite straight, almost rigid lines of the first two figures and gradually relax and curve until the fifth figure stands in a graceful arc, with a gown that flutters from the lower part of her body. Throughout the group the changing movement of line is steady, confident, and serene, as befits these women who by virtue of foresight now hold no doubts as to their salvation. But the lines of the group of the unwise five are wildly agitated, constantly interrupting one another, meeting at sharp angles and curling back upon themselves. The kneeling figure in front has a strong movement toward the left; the others move in contradiction to the right. The whole arrangement of the group expresses confusion and distraction.

Much of this story can be read purely in the attitudes assumed by the figures, although of course Blake invented the attitudes for the purpose of exploiting them in line. But the keynote of the narrative is that the unwise virgins

220. William Blake. *The Wise and the Foolish Virgins.* Water color with pen and ink, 14⅛ by 13⅙ inches. The Metropolitan Museum of Art, New York. Rogers Fund, 1914.

appeal to the wise to share their oil and are firmly refused; they must continue to suffer within their own foolishness. This idea is projected by line in the following way:

The kneeling figure appeals to the upright virtuous one, but this strong forward-rushing movement of appeal is turned back by the line of her own upraised hand, which swings us into the irrevocable line of the wise virgin's outstretched arm and back into the confusions of the group of unfortunates. There is no entering now into the fold of virtue; the foolish virgins are unequivocally rejected.

The paired linear systems, one serene, one agitated, are separated at their point of contact where the upward rush of the supplicating figure breaks against the standing figure and must return. In its arc shape, the upright figure seems to bend slightly as it receives the impact of the agitated rush, but does not yield. However, the picture must not be allowed to break entirely in half even though its two sides express opposing ideas. We cannot miss how the line of the supplicating hand is turned back along the extended arm, but, less conspicuously, this hand is also used to connect the two groups. The line of the hand is continued in the line of the wise virgin's scarf, though we must jump the barrier of the extended arm to follow it. The main line runs along the extended arm and back into the hysterical regrets of the foolish, yet through the secondary line we may reenter the linear system of the wise. Thus the two groups are united, as they have to be in a well-knit composition, but they are also divorced, as they must be to tell this particular story of wisdom and folly.

Matisse, whose ideas on pattern in painting have served us so well, was also a sculptor, and one who stood by what seems an obvious premise, that a three-dimensional art should not be approached in terms of a two-dimensional one (and vice versa). He declared this premise vigorously in sculptures where weight, solidity, and stress reverse the components we expect in his paintings—vivacity, grace, and charm. In his *Reclining Nude* (**221**) the parts of the body are violently distorted to express the counterbalance between load and support; the stress at the waist has all but wrenched the hip from the torso; the entire body is conceived in sections almost as if it had been built from raw boulders. There is nothing anywhere that can really be called a line. The smooth contours that allow for something like beautiful "line" in some sculptures we have already seen (**38** and **42**, for instance) have been rigorously avoided for rough surfaces and rugged forms that enhance the feeling of massive solidity.

In the field of low relief sculpture, however, the sculptor is frequently forced into an essentially two-dimensional approach. It is possible to create an illusion of depth in low relief sculpture just as it is possible to create an illusion of depth in painting, but the illusion is not always appropriate, as we have mentioned in connection with Gozzoli's *Journey of the Magi* (**201**). It would have been inappropriate in the Parthenon frieze (**222**), where it would have seemed to

221. Henri Matisse. *Reclining Nude.* 1907. Bronze, height 13½ inches. The Baltimore Museum of Art. Cone Collection.

weaken the structural reality of a band of stone uncompromisingly incorporated into the building's structural system. Originally running for 525 feet around the exterior of the sanctuary, 40 feet above base level, the frieze represented progressive stages in the Panathenaic procession, which every four years wound its way up to the Parthenon in celebration of the patron goddess. The section we illustrate shows maidens who will carry votive offerings being organized by stewards as the procession forms in the city below the Acropolis. The compression of three-dimensional figures into what could be called two and a half dimensions amounts to a hybrid between drawing and sculpture, where line is as important as volume, or more so. The arms of the maidens are virtually flat except at their edges. Everywhere, space and volume are indicated systematically, never imitated illusionistically.

To include an architectural example in a chapter on two-dimensional pattern and linear design may seem capricious, but the façade of the cathedral in Orvieto, Italy, is itself sufficiently capricious to justify its choice (223). With its sculpture in both full and low relief, its pictorial mosaics and their gold backgrounds, its marble colonnettes twisted like Christmas candies and banded with bright-colored mosaic patterns, also speckled with gold, and its fanciful carvings dividing areas from one another like elaborate picture frames—with all these, the façade is a single composition in what would be called mixed media today. In relation to the dimensions of the façade's beautifully unified total area, the relief of even the fully three-dimensional sculptures is much lower than that of the Parthenon frieze.

There is an inherent pretense in the design of this façade that, as with other Gothic façades, the decoration is subservient to architectural volumes that determine its divisions and subdivisions. But the pretense is exposed when the building is seen from the side—for the façade is a false front, a screen that has little architectural connection with the rest of the building except that it allows access to the comparatively severe interior. By the functional premises that underlie virtually all architectural esthetics to one degree or another, Orvieto's façade is a fib. But sparkling and gleaming against the blue Italian sky, it is one of the most joyful inventions in the history of buildings.

222. Greek, classical period. *Maidens and Stewards*, a fragment of the *Panathenaic Procession* from the east frieze of the Parthenon. Frieze completed 432 B.C. Marble, height about 43 inches. The Louvre, Paris.

223. Cathedral, Orvieto, Italy. Begun 1290. Facade by Lorenzo Maitani and others, begun 1310.

224. Leonardo da Vinci. *Last Supper*. 1495–97/98. Tempera or oil and tempera on plaster, height 13 feet by 9½ inches. Refectory, Santa Maria della Grazie, Milan.

Chapter Eight

COMPOSITION AS STRUCTURE

I f any painting in the world is more famous than Leonardo da Vinci's *Mona Lisa*, which we have already seen (**22**), it is his *Last Supper* (**224**), a great painting with a religious subject. That is not exactly the same thing as a great religious picture— which the *Last Supper* is not. In any mystical sense it is a religious picture only by association of ideas. Nor did Leonardo intend it to be one. He conceived of the moment when Christ says to his disciples, "One of you shall betray me," as a moment of unparalleled human drama. It was the psychological atmosphere of that moment that fascinated Leonardo, and he directed every element of his composition toward its expression.

The drama as he conceived it is an interplay of three states of mind and spirit: that of Christ, who makes his announcement in foreknowledge that the events leading to his Crucifixion have been set in motion; that of the faithful disciples, who are filled with confusion, astonishment, and incredulity; and finally, that of Judas, who has already made the bargain of betrayal. The expression of the total atmosphere of this moment, of the three contrasting psychological states fused into a unified whole, is achieved through compositional structure. Every element is studied individually, but each takes on its full meaning only through integration with the rest of the picture. Leonardo analyzed each of the disciples as a personality, drawing on biblical history and what legends and surmises there were about them; he invented for each one a set of features that he thought to be characteristic; finally after long study he gave each one gestures and facial expressions that would complete the psychological description.

Now, plenty of other pictures have been constructed just as carefully as the *Last Supper*, but it would be hard to find another in which the construction is so clear and simple yet so unobtrusive and expressive. Let us insist that the compositional structure of the *Last Supper* does much more than hold together a picture of great size. It is itself an expressive factor and (with the picture in its present ruinous condition) the strongest one. The facial types and expressions that Leonardo developed with such care are now so blurred they are only half-decipherable, and the original color harmonies have faded, thus modifying the psychological force that Leonardo intended them to have. Yet the picture still says what Leonardo wanted it to say because the overall composition remains clear.

The *Last Supper* was painted across the full width of the end wall of a long room, originally a refectory. Simple one-point perspective continues the lines of the actual architecture of the room. More importantly, though, these perspective lines are a concealed compositional device. A diagram (**225**, p. 168) shows that, continued, they converge at the head of Christ, or, if you prefer, they radiate from his head like rays of light. These lines are united by an arc, formed by the upper molding of a pedimented window above Christ's head. This arc, the only curved line in the painted architecture, is a segment of an invisible circle with its center on the point where the perspective lines converge. There are other relationships: two of the lines, those that follow the molding along the ceiling, pass through the ends of the arc, while the edge of the circle below the arc just touches the level of the horizontal line of the table on the side where Christ sits.

When we say that this invisible circle, with its center at the head of Christ, is like a halo, we do not mean to suggest that Leonardo had any such symbolism in mind. He has rather pointedly omitted the halos customary in paintings of the Last Supper, thus emphasizing the human drama rather than the divine mystery of his subject. But the fact that this circular form, the only one in the picture, does surround the figure of Christ tends to set him apart much as a halo would have done. If this was what Leonardo intended, however, he did not expect the observer to do this kind of detective work to notice it, any more than he meant that we should consciously follow the continuations of the perspective lines to Christ's head. He meant these lines to function structurally and psychologically as part of the total effect of the painting. And they do so, whether or not we are aware of them.

It might seem that once we have detected some of the devices the artist has used to create his drama, the drama itself would be rendered less affecting. This would be true if the *Last Supper* were nothing more than a kind of card trick. Once a trick is explained it has no further interest, since its only function is to puzzle us. But the *Last Supper* is not a card trick; it is a great painting. We may simultaneously enjoy its effect and the means that Leonardo has used to achieve this effect, just as we may be moved by great music and at the same time admire the musician's technique and be aware of the composer's inventiveness.

225. Diagrammatic scheme of *Last Supper.*

A second diagram (**226**) shows that the figure of Christ as it appears above the table is triangular in shape and closely integrated with the lines of the architecture. There could not be a more appropriate form: the triangle is the simplest, the most stable, and yet, with its apex, the most climactic of geometrical forms. This triangle, as a final, logical, and harmonious statement, is approximately equilateral. Its lines may be continued into the perspective lines of the floor pattern to form a larger triangle of the same proportions. (In addition, and Leonardo might have had it in mind, the triangle is a symbol of the Trinity.)

It is worth noticing that while the figure of Christ is closely integrated with the basic architectural scheme—the structural foundation of the picture—the figures of the disciples are not. This is one of several devices that not only draw attention to the figure of Christ but isolate him psychologically in this dividing moment of his life. Thus unified with the static architectural forms, Christ's figure is invested with a divine calm that contrasts with the human agitation of the disciples.

The disciples are clustered into four groups of three each. The two groups on either side of Christ echo the central triangle without repeating it exactly. The groups at the ends of the table also repeat the triangle but echo it yet more faintly, as is indicated in our second diagram. If these groups were as purely triangular as the central figure, they would compete with it. As it is, they come to a climax in the figure of Christ: vaguely formed at the far sides of the picture, more definitely formed on either side of Christ, they culminate in the purely formed triangle of Christ himself.

This is part of a scheme to build the picture in a current of excitement that moves toward the center, where it reaches its greatest intensity, and breaks against the serenity of the central figure like waves against a rock. Thus Christ is set off, in his noble acceptance, from the weaker human excitement surrounding him. An accelerating movement runs through the disciples, along their arms and the folds of drapery, growing more agitated as it approaches the center, where it is turned back by an uplifted hand on the right and, on the left, by the figure of John, the beloved disciple, who turns away in grief.

In most paintings of the Last Supper, John the Beloved is shown leaning toward or on Christ and being comforted by him. Leonardo abandons this convention to isolate Christ in this moment at the beginning of the trial, conviction, and execution that he must bear alone. Leonardo also departed from convention in putting Judas among the other disciples instead of by himself on the other side of the table, where he would have been too conspicuous for Leonardo's conception of the scene. As it is, Judas appears, clutching his bag of silver, in the group to Christ's right, the only one of the disciples who is not protesting the prophecy of betrayal that Christ has just made. Symbolically, also, his figure is a break in the symmetry of the triangle.

This outline analysis of the *Last Supper*'s composition could be enlarged to include any detail of it. For instance, the play of Christ's head against the light of the window is the strongest light-and-dark contrast in the picture. The hangings on the wall, because they diminish in perspective, are a series of vertical lines growing closer and closer together as they approach the center, just as the action of the figures grows quicker and quicker as it moves toward Christ. There are subtleties of balance at every turn. In the major one, Christ's head is bowed slightly off center to our right. Why? There are two reasons. The obvious one is that as an attitude it is expressive. But the head could have been bowed forward instead of to one side and been just as expressive. If it had, though, there would have been no relief to what would then have been a too rigid and obvious symmetry. The slight bending toward the right supplies the necessary relief. But it also creates a new problem. Such a variation in so conspicuous a spot must be countered

226. Diagrammatic scheme of *Last Supper*.

227. Raphael. *Trans-figuration.* 1517. Panel painting, 13 feet 4 inches by 9 feet 2 inches. Pinacoteca,

228. Nicolas Poussin. *Rape of the Sabine Women.* Before 1637. Oil on canvas, 60⅞ by 82⅝ inches. The Metropolitan Museum of Art, New York. Harris Brisbane Dick Fund.

elsewhere if it is not to throw the scheme too strongly to the right. Hence, Leonardo's emphasis on the chief secondary figures, Judas and John the Beloved, on our left.

Think, then, how much is involved in a factor as small as the bending of a head: rigidity and monotony are avoided and a place is made for a narrative comment (on Judas) that would not otherwise have been balanced, since there is no incident of comparable importance to put on the other side of the picture—and yet we are aware only that Christ's head is bowed in an appropriately expressive way.

The beauty of the *Last Supper* as a compositional structure is that it is original without being eccentric, highly calculated without being complicated. In it pictorial structure and intellectual conception are consummately unified.

As a contrast to the unity of the *Last Supper*, since a failure can be as illuminating as a success, Raphael's *Transfiguration* (**227**, p. 170) is one of the most confusing compositions in the world. It is impossible to tell exactly where in the group of excitedly gesturing figures in the lower half we are being asked to look. The eye is told to move in a dozen directions at once. No sooner does it begin to follow any one of the emphatically indicated routes along a pointing arm and finger than it is peremptorily checked and told to follow another. Figures point this way and look that; first we are crowded off to one side, then swung across to the other; we see a patch of landscape in the distance but are denied access to it. Why is it there? Apparently only as filler. If we escape into the upper half, we are in an area of forms so obvious, so much weaker than those below, that our interest is not held, and we reenter the jangling confusion we have just left.

An attempt to diagram the composition would result in an incomprehensible and irrational web of lines stretching arbitrarily from point to point. Something like a warped triangle with the ascending Christ at its apex would emerge, but the only figure that really holds its own against all competition in this confusion is the kneeling woman who dominates the foreground—dominates, indeed, the entire picture (**229**).

This figure is beautiful in itself, in spite of the strained artificiality of attitude and the draper's-display fall of cloth from one shoulder onto the ground. But this beauty is insufficient reason for the figure's prominence. As far as the miracles represented in the painting are concerned (Matthew 17:1–8 and 14–18), the figure is only an accessory, with no more significance than most of the others and with less than some. Its importance should have been given to the epileptic boy to the right, whose miraculous cure by Jesus so astonished the onlookers. In a sound, if obvious, bit of composition the woman points to the boy, but her gesture is nullified by the stronger line of her glance in the opposite direction. In short, the composition fails because it lacks unity and focus. The spasmodic crisscross, the

229. Detail from *Transfiguration*.

abrupt turns and interruptions, could have served effectively to express the excitement and agitation of the moment if they had been organized toward an appropriate climax; as it is, they only confuse the observer and obscure the narrative.

It may be argued that to compare this composition with the *Last Supper* is unfair since Leonardo's subject was a quieter one involving only thirteen figures instead of twenty-seven. But the problems solved in the *Last Supper* only seem simpler because the solution is presented with such clarity that it appears to have been inevitable. For the sake of argument, however, the *Transfiguration* can be compared, still to its disadvantage, with an even more complicated, even more violent subject that involves even more figures, Nicolas Poussin's *Rape of the Sabine Women* (**228**, p. 171).

As in the *Last Supper,* but used toward a different end, literally every detail, no matter how small, is integrated within the whole of *Rape of the Sabine Women.* The composition is built upon a triple interlocking framework. First, there is the strong diagonal movement upward from right to left stated by the warrior in the right foreground, a linear continuation of the figure of the old man grappling with him. A young woman, her torso bent in conformity with the diagonal, completes the interlaced group, which forms a slanted triangle (**230**). The diagonal is repeated in the middle distance by a rearing white stallion, in the foreground center by the back of the crouching old woman, and in the upper left by the staff held by the heavily robed figure (Romulus) standing on the portico of a temple. A dozen other repetitions are discoverable at a glance. In sum, the diagonal is a neat 45 degrees from the vertical.

Second, this surging movement is countered by another, less vehement, in the opposite direction; some of the elements of this upward movement from left to right are the uplifted folds of Romulus's robe, the raised arms of two women who struggle against their abductors, two swords in the background, the fleeing figures that move out of the picture at the far right, and, again, many others. These two systems overlap; most of the figures and groups carry elements of both. For instance, the white stallion is integrated with the first system, while the woman who is being carried away on its back is part of the second. Her abductor in turn is part of a third system, which is a stabilizing repetition of horizontals and verticals, most apparent in the lines of the architecture. Also, Romulus stands vertically, and there are strong horizontals in the clouds, and verticals or horizontals in various arms, legs, and draperies, and in small details everywhere.

Upon this skeleton Poussin has constructed a composition in which there are various elements that can be better understood when we reach the end of this discussion. We will look at the *Rape of the Sabine Women* once more at that time, returning now to the point at which we left our discussion of the *Last Supper.*

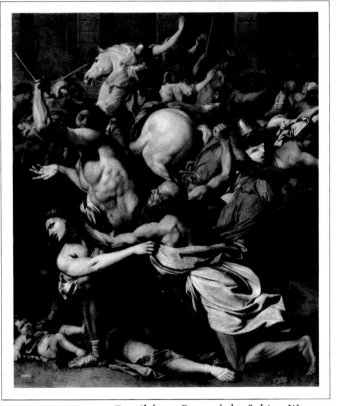

230. Detail from *Rape of the Sabine Women.*

231. Pietro Perugino. *Crucifixion with the Virgin and Saints.* About 1485. Oil and tempera transferred from wood to canvas. Center panel 39⅞ by 22¼ inches. National Gallery of Art, Washington, D.C. Andrew Mellon Collection.

When Leonardo used a triangle as the central element in the *Last Supper*, he was capitalizing on the most popular geometrical form in painting. A picture planned for a conspicuous central position in a building often demands a symmetrical composition that builds up to a climax at the center—and when we have said that, we have just about demanded the triangular form. This was so true during the Italian Renaissance, when altarpieces were the painter's stock-in-trade, that the triangular composition crystallized into a formula. The altar itself is the climax of the symmetrical scheme of a church. Everything leads inevitably to it, and thus, to the altarpiece. To cap the architectural scheme with a painting that would throw it off balance was unthinkable. The balance was usually achieved by symmetry. Perugino's *Crucifixion with the Virgin and Saints* (231) applies the triangular formula so purely that it could have been designed as a model demonstration.

Let us say immediately that an altarpiece is the kind of painting that suffers most by removal from its original location to a museum. Religious paintings lined up by the dozens along museum walls grow monotonous and sometimes we react by feeling guilty that they do. But we are quite right; installed in this way, they *are* monotonous.

Many paintings, especially modern ones, are executed with museum exhibition in mind. Each one is designed to compete for attention by its individuality. Each diverts us; each offers newer and more curious forms and combinations of colors. But an altarpiece never had and was never supposed to have the appeal of competitive novelty. Each one was painted to be seen by itself, not as part of a gathering of exhibition pieces. It was meant to be seen, frequently by candlelight, as part of the ensemble of a church or chapel.

Nor were altarpieces created in the knowledge that they would become items in a collection of historical specimens mounted for critical observation. That is exactly what most of them have become, and this is, of course, exactly the way we are treating Perugino's *Crucifixion* and Raphael's *Transfiguration* when we discuss their composition. But in so doing we should try to remember that altarpieces are particularly vulnerable when not seen as they were intended to be seen, as part and climax of a certain architectural scheme and emotional atmosphere.

The formula for the triangular composition, repeated hundreds of times in Crucifixions, Nativities, Madonnas with Saints, and similar subjects, calls for a central triangle with the picture's focal point at its apex and a secondary, weaker, inverted triangle to counter it. In his *Crucifixion*, Perugino uses the formula with particular grace (232). There is additional interest in that the formula unites three separate panels. Saint Jerome, in the left panel, forms one side of the triangle with the "line" of his upward glance directed toward the head of Christ. This line exists as strongly as if it were visible, like the dotted lines in old comic strips that lead from the eye of a character to the object he is looking at. This invisible but inescapable line

232. Diagrammatic scheme of *Crucifixion with the Virgin and Saints.*

not only forms a side of the triangle but unites the left panel with the center one by cutting across the dividing frame. The figure of Saint Jerome bends forward from the waist at the same angle.

In the right panel the Magdalene creates a similar line. Her body is not bent, but her head is tilted in the same direction as the line of her gaze toward the apex of the triangle. The forms of the rocks just behind her strengthen the line by echoing it, as does the fold of her robe from ankle to hip. The figure of Saint John, at the right of the Cross in the central panel, directs our eye to the apex in the same way. The Madonna, however, looks downward. (How repetitious and obvious it would be if she also looked upward.) But the head of Christ, bowed as if he were looking in her direction, suggests the missing line. The Madonna's bent head supplies a slight yet necessary variety among the four attendant figures and serves to single her out as the most important of them.

The inverted counter triangle is determined primarily by the landscape on either side of the Cross. It is also repeated in folds in the drapery of each figure and by Saint Jerome's staff. (The objects carried by saints in these pictures are always a great convenience to painters, who are free to tilt them this way and that for compositional purposes.)

There is nothing particularly original in the arrangement of this painting. Perugino is even notorious for the way he repeated his compositional devices from picture to picture, reassembling his figures from a stockpile. But he does satisfy beautifully the decorative demand for a painting that will not disturb the symmetry of an overall architectural scheme and the psychological demand for reverent peacefulness. There is even an agreeable clarity in the scheme's dependence upon the simplest and most apparent

233. Pablo Picasso. *Guernica.* 1937. Oil on canvas, 11 feet 5½ inches by 25 feet 5¾ inches. Estate of the artist.

principles of arrangement. Virtually every element in the three panels ties in with either the major or the secondary triangle or with the verticals—the Cross, the towers, the delicate trees that rise so quietly and so serenely upward. Finally, the strong horizontal rectangle of the arm of the Cross is stretched firmly across the top of the central panel as an emphatic conclusion to the artist's note-perfect performance.

It would seem unlikely that anything having to do with a picture as quiet and tender as Perugino's *Crucifixion* could apply to a picture as violent and complicated as Picasso's *Guernica* (233), but compositionally the two paintings have an unexpected similarity. Perugino's altarpiece is a triptych, that is, it is made up of three separate panels, each side panel measuring half the width of the central one (because the side panels of triptychs often are hinged to fold over and protect the main panel). Picasso's painting is not actually divided into panels, but it also is composed as a central scheme with two "wings" of half its width divided from it by vertical lines, yet at the same time united to it, like Perugino's, by repeats and continuations of the main lines of a triangular formula. These the reader should be able to trace for himself.

Guernica is an extremely large painting (more than 25 feet wide), so large that one tends to look at it in sections. The triptych-like division makes the picture more decipherable section by section, since each section can be seen as a separate entity, but at the same time the three sections are a tightly knit unit when the picture is seen as a whole, as it is in our illustration, or at a sufficient distance from the original.

But the similarities between the two pictures end with their compositional skeletons. Whereas Perugino is serene, Picasso is violent; whereas Perugino is content to be conventional, Picasso is explosively original. Perugino, through realism, synthesizes an ideal beauty; Picasso, through distortion, creates an expressive brutality.

Guernica is a passionate indictment of a shameful incident that presaged the worst horrors of World War II. On April 26, 1937, market day in the peaceful village of Guernica, this ancient capital of the Basque people was bombed with high explosives, antipersonnel shrapnel, and incendiaries by German planes in the service of the Spanish Fascists in rebellion against the Republican government, to which the Basques were loyal. The bombing was part vengeful, part a cold-blooded experiment in the effectiveness of attack from the air—although Guernica was not in any way a military objective, and was defenseless. The painting is a carnage of dead, dying, and mutilated animals and human beings. In the right "panel" a figure is swallowed by a flaming ruin (234). On the left, a bull, symbolizing brute force, rises triumphantly over a woman who shrieks in grief as she cradles her dead child (235). In the lower part of the central panel a severed arm holds a broken sword, a traditional symbol of heroic defeat. The head of the horse

234. Figure from *Guernica.*

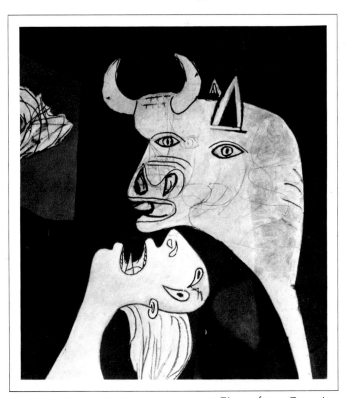

235. Figure from *Guernica.*

that rears from the center of the picture is grotesque, ugly, and, in a hideous way, ludicrous. But death by such violence is also grotesque, ugly, and even hideously ludicrous. *Guernica* is an overwhelming picture. There is every reason to believe that it will remain one of the half dozen masterpieces of twentieth-century painting.

Both Perugino's *Crucifixion* and Picasso's *Guernica* have as their subject social crimes of monstrous proportions. The difference is that the Perugino represents a social crime resolved into the divine blessing of man's salvation; hence it is painted with the serenity of divine confidence. But nothing can resolve the crime of Guernica into anything better than a staggering demonstration of viciousness and brutality—hence it is painted in terms that are as ugly and nightmarish as the crime itself.

Having seen the foregoing examples, we should immediately recognize the triangular formula in Antonio Pollaiuolo's *Martyrdom of Saint Sebastian* (236). The executioners' bows and arrows define the scheme like direction pointers. The arrows of the two men standing in the foreground point toward the apex of the triangle, while their bows, at right angles to the arrows, are part of the counter scheme, which is more conspicuously stated by the figures and arrows of the two executioners in center foreground.

But in this composition we have an important variation on the formula: here the composition demands to be read in depth, in three dimensions, if it is to be most effective. The executioners form a ring around the stake, and we read it as a ring. Thus, instead of a flat triangular composition, we have what would be better described as a tent-shaped or cone-shaped or pyramidal composition. It is as if the flat triangle had been spun on its pivot (the stake), and all the forms arranged in the spatial volume thus defined. Pollaiuolo insists on the spatial character of his composition by the sweep of his landscape, which opens into depth rather than hanging behind the bowmen like a tapestry on a wall.

He leads us into this depth by a series of transitions between the foreground, middleground, and background. A small plain with men and horses leads us to the river and hills, then into the horizon and the limitless sky. Admittedly the transition from foreground to middleground is rather abrupt. In dealing with a new concept of space in picturemaking, the unification of foreground and background in three-dimensional compositions was one of the most vexing problems painters had to solve.

Now, it may be asked why painters developed an interest in three-dimensional space when the possibilities of two-dimensional expression are so great; it could even be argued that a painter is working on a two-dimensional surface and should respect it as such, leaving three-dimensional design to the sculptor, the architect, the stage designer, and any other artist whose medium legitimately and unavoidably involves the third dimension. It may be asked why the Japanese and the Chinese, with their infi-

236. Antonio del Pollaiuolo. *Martyrdom of Saint Sebastian.* Completed 1475. Tempera on panel, 9 feet 7 inches by 6 feet 8 inches. National Gallery, London.

nitely cultivated traditions in painting, never felt the necessity of creating spatial illusions but were content to express entire mountain ranges in a few washes upon a surface that was allowed to maintain its integrity.

A proper answer to these questions would require a volume of philosophical and historical explanation. But somewhere within it would be an examination of this point: that the Western scientific spirit, which insists upon knowing the world by investigating its tangible realities, was born to all intents with the Italian Renaissance. Artists in harmony with their times were no longer content with pictorial symbols but sought instead to paint the world in images as nearly as possible real in a tangible sense. To this end they studied anatomy, invented perspective, and explored the laws of movement, light, and color. It is obvious that objects drawn and painted to express a third dimension, to look solid, could not compete successfully with the constant physical denial of a panel's (or a canvas's) two-dimensional surface. Hence this surface was "done away with" to create space in which solid objects could exist. When this happened, the artist's problem as pictorial composer ceased to be one of arranging flat shapes on a flat surface and became one of arranging spatial relationships between objects in depth.

We have just said that in the *Martyrdom of Saint Sebastian* Pollaiuolo was unable to make an entirely satisfactory transition from foreground to middle distance. He compromised by placing the foreground action upon some kind of ambiguous promontory that terminates—not satisfactorily, not quite understandably—and breaks the background in half. How successfully later artists finally achieved the full integration of space is apparent in Jacob van Ruisdael's *Wheatfields* (**237**), painted in the mid-seventeenth century. The transition from foreground to infinity is easy and uninterrupted. As we enter the landscape and go deep into it, space is all about us—beyond us, behind us, to every side, and infinitely above. Space, rather than the objects within it, is the dramatizing and unifying component of the composition.

From the foreground, which we see as though we were standing upon a slight elevation, we are led down a road into a clump of trees, through them, and into the vast, cloud-filled sky. The trees, even though they partially obscure the horizon, are a zone to be entered and passed through, rather than a barrier. We are invited through natural alleyways between their trunks; we discover an area enclosed by an old wall, but it does not constitute an obstruction since we are faced by a wide opening (**238**).

As if to make certain that we feel free to enter and explore all this space, a man walks into the picture toward two figures in the middle distance, a woman holding a child by the hand. The forms of the landscape radiate around this pair like the spokes of a vast wheel around its hub, an effect emphasized by the outward lean of the trees at the right and by the dead branch in the left foreground.

237. Jacob Isaacksz van Ruisdael. *Wheatfields.* Date uncertain. Oil on canvas, 39⅜ by 51¼ inches. The Metropolitan Museum of Art, New York.

238. Detail from *Wheatfields.*

There is nothing particularly unusual about the fields and objects making up this landscape, nor is there intended to be. It is a rather ordinary bit of countryside, even more ordinary to the people for whom it was painted than it is to us, since time has given the costumes a fillip of the quaint and foreign. Space, the place these objects occupy, the infinite depth to the horizon and beyond it, the infinite upward reach of the sky, is the artist's subject. The earth, the trees, the clouds, exist more to create this space than for their own inherent interest.

You may remember that in an earlier chapter we compared two paintings, Cézanne's *Mont Sainte-Victoire* and Durand's *Scene from Thanatopsis* (**23** and **24**), commenting that Durand sought to create limitless expanses stimulating to the imagination, while Cézanne sought the opposite, a contracted and enclosed landscape that could be comprehended by the intellect. These are the two basic approaches to spatial composition, whether the subject is a landscape, a "roomscape" like the Vermeer of the artist's studio (**164**), or a figure composition. The picture we have just seen, Ruisdael's *Wheatfields,* belongs in the same group as Durand's imaginary landscape. Of course it is a gentler, more realistic scene, but like the Durand it suggests that space is infinite, not defined, extending on every side beyond the limits of the frame. Vermeer's roomscape, on the contrary, keeps us securely within a small, well-defined cube of space, where everything is so neatly disposed that a sense of order, harmony, quiet, and security is relayed to us.

These two contrasting space concepts can be called closed space and open space, or classical space and romantic space, comparable to closed and open form in sculpture. As an example of a close-knit composition in classical space, we will examine Piero della Francesca's *Madonna and Child with Saints and Angels Adored by Federigo da Montefeltro* (**240**), a formidable title for which we will substitute here the more convenient one of the Brera altarpiece, taking the name from the gallery in Milan where the painting now hangs.

The Brera altarpiece is so important that we will approach it through an earlier painting, *Madonna of Mercy* (**239**), in which the artist is working toward the kind of spatial composition he so magnificently achieves in the later example.

The *Madonna of Mercy* shows us the figure of Mary geometrized into a form approximating a channeled column, surmounted by a head and neck of even more geometrical character. She extends her arms to make a shelter of her cape for the figures at her feet. Considered in two dimensions, this is an impressive painting; its air of contemplation and gravity is characteristic of all Piero's art. But as a composition in three dimensions, its impressiveness is increased. The cape then forms a semicircular enclosure; we look into it as if it were a niche behind the column-like figure. Seen in two dimensions the worshippers on either

239. Piero della Francesca. *Madonna of Mercy,* center panel of triptych. 1445–55. Oil and tempera on wood, height about 57 inches. Communal Palace, Borgo San Sepolcro, Italy.

240. Piero della Francesca. *Madonna and Child with Saints and Angels Adored by Federigo da Montefeltro (Madonna of the Egg).* Tempera on wood, height 8 feet 2 inches. Brera Gallery, Milan.

side are only rows of figures, but in three they form two half-circles into the depth of the picture, curving away from us into the niche of the robe. Thus the worshipful band surrounds the central figure instead of merely flanking it in clusters at either side.

This is a fairly elementary arrangement of forms, but in calling it elementary we must remember that Piero was a pioneer in three-dimensional composition. Also, the arrangement loses much of its three-dimensional effectiveness because the gold background is flat and tends to flatten the figures in front of it. Hence there is a contradiction between the three-dimensional arrangement of the figures and the two-dimensional background, a contradiction that could have been remedied by a background of painted forms harmonizing with the spatial forms in the foreground. Such a background could have repeated the column-like and niche-like forms to emphasize rather than nullify them.

This is exactly what has been done in the Brera altarpiece. Here, about twenty-five years later, Piero amplifies the virtues and corrects the shortcomings of the *Madonna of Mercy*. The Brera altarpiece is completely three-dimensional in conception, so much so that if we analyze it as an arrangement of surface lines and shapes, it is an indifferent composition—tending to divide into two parts, with its upper half occupied by an architectural background of some beauty but not much point.

But when the figures and background are regarded as a combination of solid objects and shaped space, the composition is firmly and beautifully unified in all its parts. *We have to remember that the voids are as important as the solid forms.* These voids are sometimes called negative volumes (as we have already seen in sculpture, where the concept is a bit easier to grasp).

The various forms, positive or negative as volumes, combine to create an impression of majestic repose. Again the Madonna is encircled by saints and angels, but this time the ring spreads out in the foreground so that in a ground plan the figures would be standing in an arrangement like the letter omega (Ω). The niche in the background is thoroughly integrated with this curving plan; from its back the form of a shell curves outward toward us. An egg (often a symbol of resurrection) suspended from the tip of the shell is the solid core of a series of spatial volumes surrounding it (**241**). These volumes are defined and enclosed by the projecting canopy, the niche, and the arch above it. Two other arches at the sides curve toward us, suggesting limitations of space instead of leaving us free to wander beyond this compact scene. If one figure breaks from the scheme it is that of Federigo da Montefeltro, the armored man who kneels at the right. This divorce is intentional, for he alone among the congregation is neither saint nor angel but merely the patron of the artist, and it is right he should be a little separated from the holy band.

Compositionally, the Brera altarpiece is so much an exercise in solid and spatial geometry that it is no surprise to learn that Piero della Francesca was as interested in

241. Detail from *Madonna and Child.*

mathematics as he was in painting. (He combined these interests to formulate the laws of perspective.) There are critics who feel that his late works, including the Brera altarpiece, are concerned too much with mathematics and too little with human sensitivities. Whether you agree will depend upon what you look for in painting. The Brera altarpiece does have an extreme reserve, but for those who respond to Piero's analytical approach, the geometrical forms suggest a nobility and a steadfastness appropriate in such a picture, lying beyond the too-human weaknesses and indecisions that harass all of us. This removal from the trivialities of daily life is expressed also in the curiously grave facial type that Piero repeats again and again (242).

When we say that the quality of this painting is architectonic, we are not referring to actual architectural elements like the niche and the arches that happen to be included in its composition. We mean the scheme is conceived and arranged in terms of structure. In this case the creation of spatial volumes, a primary conception in real architecture, does depend to a large extent upon the architecture in the picture; but the same architectonic attitude is present in the volumes created by the ring of worshippers, the egg, and the figures of the Madonna and Child.

Piero della Francesca's Brera altarpiece, which employs pictured architecture as an aid in creating architectonic values, may help us perceive architectonic values in Cézanne's *The Card Players* (243), which does not. Cézanne painted several versions of this subject with varying numbers of figures; all of them share the same solid and enduring quality so marked in this one. The direct comparison to architecture should not be pushed too far, but it is easy to see that the three men around the table, leaning forward over their cards, suggest domelike space, while the standing figure suggests the strength and stability of a column.

The Card Players lends itself to comparison with architecture, but with no loss of warmth. Where does this warmth, this human quality, come from, and how does it manage to exist in harmony with abstract values like the architectonic ones we have been talking about? Why is the quality of human warmth present here, while it has been distilled out of the Brera altarpiece, which we analyzed in much the same compositional terms?

Cézanne's idea was that the fundamental dignity of human life, the fundamental order that gives meaning to life, could be best expressed by geometrical forms of great solidity and simplicity arranged in organized space. In his paintings these forms are sometimes human beings, sometimes mountains, sometimes merely fruit and simple bowls and vases disposed on a tabletop. Ornate, precious, or unusual objects could have been used in the arrangements, but less successfully. (One critic, Sir Charles Holmes, commented that in a Cézanne, a crumpled tablecloth could take on the majesty of a mountain.) Cézanne's importance as the father of modern abstract art is so impressive that too little attention is paid to his subject matter. He may not be

242. Detail from *Madonna and Child*.

243. Paul Cézanne. *The Card Players.* 1890–92. Oil on canvas, 25½ by 32 inches. The Metropolitan Museum of Art, New York. Bequest of Stephen C. Clark, 1960.

interested in his card players as personalities and he is not interested in them as members of a certain social class with certain problems; but it is important in this picture that the men are simple, earthy people. One of them wears a peasant's smock. The picture might be almost—but not quite—as effective if the players were doctors, lawyers, or successful businessmen. Cézanne chooses to make them simple people for the same reason that he painted apples and pears in his still lifes instead of rare exotic fruits.

The Card Players is not first of all a picture of four honest men of an unpretentious social level. It is first of all a structure of solid volumes that interlock with spatial volumes. But it is wrong to argue that the subject matter has no importance at all. Many contemporary painters do so argue. They try to eliminate subject altogether, dealing with pure forms, as we saw in our discussion of abstraction. But Cézanne is a major figure in the history of art because in pictures like *The Card Players* he achieved a perfect fusion of abstract and realistic values.

It is difficult today, even for those who dislike modern art, to understand why Cézanne was so viciously attacked in his own time as an incompetent or degenerate artist. The figures in *The Card Players* are downright realistic in comparison with abstraction today, but to Cézanne's contemporary audience they looked appallingly crude. Popular taste demanded slicked-up, semiphotographic images. Even the more liberally educated art public regarded Renoir's *Portrait of Madame Renoir* and Degas's *Woman with Chrysanthemums* (**17** and **21**) as pictures that had pushed modernism just about as far as it could go. Cézanne's spatial structure was beyond the understanding of more than a very few critics; it is still the aspect of his art least recognized by a public that has learned to enjoy him without analyzing his methods.

244. Caravaggio. *The Musicians.* 1594–95. Oil on canvas, 36¼ by 46⅝ inches. The Metropolitan Museum of Art, New York, Rogers Fund, 1952.

245. Théodore Géricault. *Raft of the Medusa.* 1818–19. Oil on canvas, 16 feet 1 inch by 23 feet 6 inches. The Louvre, Paris.

The two paintings we have been comparing may leave the reader with the impression that three-dimensional compositional structures are always concerned with the majestic and the monumental. Let us, then, compare *The Card Players* with Caravaggio's *The Musicians* (**244**, p. 187), a seventeenth-century example. Like *The Card Players*, it is composed of a main group of three closely related figures, with a fourth, subsidiary figure in the background. The Cézanne is powerful; the Caravaggio, elegant. The Cézanne is concerned with the basic values of human life; the Caravaggio, with sophisticated ones.

Both pictures, however, are conceived as arrangements of volumes within a block of space. The forms of the Caravaggio weave in and out, back and forth, carrying us into little pockets of space and leading us out of them, offering us a series of sensuous delights in the rich fabrics, fine woods, ripe fruit, and handsome youths.

The Cézanne, on the other hand, does not lead us from form to form but focuses on the completed structure as a whole. We may examine either picture detail by detail, of course, but our interest in the details of the Cézanne does not last long; it is its wonderful completeness, its total unity, its cohesiveness, that gives *The Card Players* its monumental strength.

The clashing forms of Picasso's *Guernica*, for all their violence, are held within an evenly balanced scheme; they are motionless, as if revealed in an instant of blinding illumination. Pollaiuolo's *Martyrdom of Saint Sebastian*, which also illustrates a subject of some violence, is without movement. The archers are frozen at the precise moment when they are about to release their arrows or just about to complete the action of reloading their bows. We have commented on the wave of action in Leonardo's *Last Supper*, but the wave passes along a series of essentially static poses and goes only across the surface, not into the depth, of the picture. The Caravaggio *Musicians* has something of this same flowing quality except that, as we have seen, the flow is into and out of and around and about rather than across the surface. The musicians are not actually represented as being in motion, but the sinuous lines, which keep the eye moving within the picture, suggest motion.

How one painter solved the problem of composing a picture that is at once a firm structure and an expression of violent motion is demonstrated in Théodore Géricault's *Raft of the Medusa* (**245**, p. 187), painted in 1818, where the survivors of a shipwreck are crowded on a raft in a stormy sea with others who are dead or dying. The main path of action boils upward and across from the lower left to the upper right, where the figure of a young man, supported by a struggling group, waves a cloth in an attempt to attract the attention of a ship in the distance.

It is at once apparent that again we have a composition that builds up to a climactic figure by means of a triangle. The usual devices of outstretched arms, the direction of some glances, the disposition of draperies—all play their conventional roles. The difference is that the triangle is pushed off center so that it leans far to the right instead of resting in the center of the picture. This unbalance does not constitute action in the literal sense of the word, but the composition nevertheless creates the effect of action. You need only imagine the climactic figure at the top of a symmetrical triangle, centered in the space, to see that the effect, or impression, of motion would be lost or reduced, no matter how much the individual figures writhed and twisted in an attempt to create a feeling of movement.

This lopsided triangle leaves the picture overweighted on the right. Géricault brings it back into balance with a counter triangle leaning in the opposite diagonal direction, defined by the mast of the raft and the ropes that support it. This is a strong shape with echoes throughout the composition (the strongest one being the body of the dead youth in the foreground, which lies half off the raft), but the mass of struggling survivors holds our interest against the strong counteraction. To make certain that it does, the artist has weakened the counter triangle and strengthened the main one by a simple device: he interrupts the strongest line of the counter triangle by cutting the line of the rope against the sky with an arm that points toward the peak of the main triangle.

The result is a composition that creates an effect of action by its off-balance climax, but retains its strength as a pictorial structure by a neat counterbalance. And the whole scheme is a variation of a fundamental formula, the triangle and its inverted echo, that had been effective in one treatment or another for several hundred years.

The *Raft of the Medusa* is a conspicuous landmark in the history of painting because it became a battle cry for the famous romantic movement, which stressed emotionalism and individual invention instead of the intellectualism and observance of convention that dominated the arts at that time. We have already made the distinction between closed (or classical) space and the open space of romanticism. Actually, the *Raft of the Medusa* does not quite fit the romantic definition. The scene is played against open space but the figures are not united with it; they are arranged like an independent monument against a distant horizon. A later picture, Eugène Delacroix's *The Abduction of Rebecca* (**246**, p. 190), painted in 1846, is a fuller expression of romantic composition.

The Delacroix swirls from the foreground deep into the background, from the cyclonic forms of the horse, the abductors, and the victim to the excitement around the burning fortress, so that the principal figures are not only played against depth but also integrated with it. Can we analyze the tempestuous forms of the main group? Not with the same clarity as in our earlier, more static compositions. But we can see that the raging excitement is expressed by the constant turns, reversals, and interruptions of forms and their directions. The rider twists backward into the picture while the figure of Rebecca is thrust forward toward us. The horse is ready to charge in a third direction,

246. Eugène Delacroix. *The Abduction of Rebecca.* 1846. Oil on canvas, 39½ by 32¼ inches. The Metropolitan Museum of Art, New York. Purchased, Wolfe Fund, 1903.

and the rider's head is turned in the opposite one. Through the whole group lines snake and twist without rest. Color explodes in fragments over the turbulent forms.

This fragmented color is in direct opposition to the decisively confined color areas of Poussin's *Rape of the Sabine Women*, to which we are now ready to return. Several questions arise in the light of what has been said since we first saw this painting. Is it a composition in three-dimensional space? We analyzed its framework in two dimensions across its surface. What about the emotionalism of the subject and the apparently contradictory controlled definition of the arrangement? And what about this static composition for a subject of such violent action?—the mass abduction of the women of the Sabine people to supply wives for the womanless followers of the Roman Romulus.

The thing to remember about the Poussin is that it is in no sense an illustration, nor is it an emotionalized expression. It is an intellectual synthesis devoted to the classical idea of ultimate clarity.

The depth of the Poussin is a defined block of static space like that of the Cézanne and the Caravaggio, rather than a portion of swirling limitless space as in the Delacroix. The figures don't seem to move (**247**) as Delacroix's do; their passion, terror, and rage are not emotionalized for the observer, but objectified. We do not participate in the abduction of the Sabine woman as we do in the abduction of Rebecca. Instead of participating, we contemplate; instead of feeling, we reflect; instead of being in a world of action and conflict, we are in a world where all indecisions have been resolved. This is the classical world, where order has been imposed upon chaos, and to some temperaments it will always seem too static, a little cold, and impossible of reconciliation with themes of violence. But for others there is more satisfaction in this harmoniously disposed world of Poussin's, a world of complex balances and multiple relationships distilled from human experience. Poussin's composition says that all human experience is meaningful beyond its moment, that the moment may be overpowering in the immediacy of its joy or anguish, but there is an eternal order within which the moment is absorbed.

In looking at paintings in this chapter we have been dissecting them to discover their structural systems, sometimes only as the skeletons that hold them together (as in the case of Pollaiuolo's *Martyrdom of Saint Sebastian*) but usually, in addition, as an artist's means of interpreting pictorial subject matter, with Leonardo's *Last Supper* as an exceptionally clear example. It has been a matter of looking beneath surfaces for the increased pleasure that an understanding of a painter's methods can give us.

In sculpture and architecture the situation is often reversed. When structural systems are exposed and self-explanatory, unencumbered by any overlay, they may become the immediate source of the pleasures we are offered. Kenneth Snelson's *Audrey I* (**248**)—the title is a form

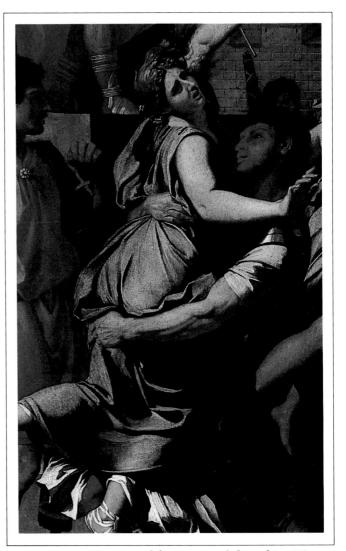

247. Detail from *Rape of the Sabine Women*.

248. Kenneth Snelson. *Audrey I.* 1965. Porcelainized aluminum and steel, height 7 feet 2 inches. The Cleveland Museum of Art. Gift of Kimiko and John Powers, Aspen, Colorado.

249. Mark di Suvero. Untitled. Steel and wood, 19 feet 11 inches by 6 feet 9 inches.Greenville County Museum of Art, South Carolina. Gift of Elaine de Kooning.

250. Pierluigi Nervi and A. Vitellozzi. Palazzetto dello Sport, exterior. 1956–59. Rome.

of dedication, not a subject, for the sculpture has no other subject than itself—is a structure of porcelainized aluminum tubes and steel wires held in a complex of interdependent balanced stresses. "Tensegrity" is Snelson's term for his form of engineering, and brilliant engineering it is. But it is engineering employed in the creation of sculpture of a very high order, coming close to full realization of the paradox of dematerialization declared as a sculptural goal back in 1920 with Gabo's "We deny volume as the expression of space . . . we reject physical mass as a plastic element." Gabo often called his sculptures "linear constructions," and we have seen one example (**60**). Snelson's tensegrity sculptures have been called line drawings in space, but he is in no way a follower of Gabo, who thought in terms of transparent planes. Snelson's aluminum tubes seem to float; contradictorily they are held in a system of extreme tension and compression. These static structures, filled with a sense of vibrant internal life, are defamed if compared to skeletons. They are more like nervous systems.

But to qualify as a work of art, this sculpture should "say" something beyond its amazing visual effectiveness as an engineered structure. Does it? Compare it with an untitled sculpture by Mark di Suvero (**249**). In contrast with Snelson's sleek, spare, hollow cylinders and thin wires, di Suvero's sculptures are compounds of ponderous, crude, found materials: heavy, weathered, scarred raw-cut beams, old chains, hawsers, cables, now and then such oddments as old tires or inner tubes. They seem (deceptively) to have been assembled on a semi-improvisational basis, one heavy piece added here to prop or buttress another there, a chain or hawser introduced as a provisional support that could be supplanted by another arrangement, one idea suggesting the next, in a process of asymmetrical growth that might change or continue, while Snelson's structure is finite. Di Suvero's structure is primarily a matter of weights; Snelson's entirely a matter of tensions. But regarded as expressive works of art, the two sculptures become more than contrasting structural exercises. They are expressions of the bilateral nature of all art, the reciprocal relationship between the intellectual and the emotional, between calculation and impulse, between what we call the classical and the romantic spirits. Both are wonderfully alive, with the difference that if we can compare Snelson's sculpture to a nervous system, di Suvero's has the character of muscles and tendons.

The biological metaphor of nerves, muscles, and tendons could apply to that form of building that has been recurrent in this book—the Gothic cathedral, where the structural systems of rib vaults and flying buttresses are fully exposed. We have also referred to the "exoskeleton" of the Pompidou Center (**83**), and have seen how structure, exposed and unornamented, was synonymous with fantasy in that landmark building, the Crystal Palace (**123**). These are conspicuous rather than isolated examples in the history of construction-as-architecture (a near-relative, but not identical with, form-follows-function), and of the architect-as-engineer or engineer-as-architect. One of the latter who has had a strong influence on modern building is Pierluigi Nervi, who capitalized early on the innate architectural qualities of ferro-concrete construction. Unlike Saarinen, who, in his sculptured TWA Terminal (162), took advantage of concrete's plastic quality in a largely arbitrary design, Nervi, a purist, insistently observed the principle of making the most of the beauty natural to this form of construction. His Palazzetto dello Sport in Rome (250 and 251) is an example.

The engineering of bridges, whether from the vines and bamboo of primitive jungles or the girders and cables of today's suspension spans, has produced probably the most beautiful examples of nonarchitectural construction over the ages. One example of this form of civil engineering, where architectural principles of harmonious proportion and the practical solution of a problem are inseparably fused, demands our attention: the Pont du Gard near Nîmes in southern France (252), built by the Romans shortly before the birth of Christ as a viaduct combining the functions of roadway (in which capacity it is still sound) and aqueduct.

Modern engineering could have supplied pumps for this transfer of water, but the height of the Pont du Gard was determined by the necessity of observing a proper slope from the hills to the city, hence the two arched courses over the one supporting the roadway. The splendid second course is marked by protruding blocks of stone that supported scaffolding during construction and would ordinarily have been cut away; here they were left in case scaffolding was needed in the future for repairs. For the final course, the water channel proper, any crude stone casing would have done; but the architect-engineer terminated his design with the small arches, four to each of the large ones below, to make the Pont du Gard a masterpiece from the always fruitful union between structural engineering and architectural design.

Today we are more conscious of the Pont du Gard as architecture than as engineering because we are more accustomed to thinking of the stone arch as an ornamental form than as a functional structure. But we are also conscious of the beauty of a modern structure like the Verrazano-Narrows Bridge (253), even though its design and proportions were determined entirely by engineering in the service of practical demands. Between such structures and the structural schemes of paintings like Leonardo's *Last Supper* and others we have seen in this chapter, there could hardly be a wider difference in conception. Yet logical structure—whether in a purely functional bridge, the exposed engineering of a cathedral vault, the arbitrary balancing of weights and tensions in sculpture, or the abstract scheme that underlies and binds together the pictorial surface of a painting—has a profound psychological effect upon us as observers. Whether or not we realize it, we are being reassured that order can be distilled from the chaos of human experience, and this, by a definition we have already offered, is a primary function of art.

251. Pierluigi Nervi and A. Vitellozzi. Palazzetto dello Sport, interior forms. 1956–59. Rome.

252. Roman. Pont du Gard. First century B.C. Near Nîmes, France.

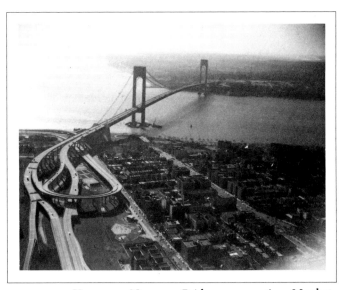

253. Verrazano-Narrows Bridge, connecting Manhattan and Staten islands, New York. Main span 4,260 feet, height of towers 690 feet above water. Construction started August 13, 1959; bridge opened to traffic November 1, 1964. O. H. Ammann, engineer.

254. Rembrandt. *The Company of Captain Frans Banning Cocq and Lieutenant Willem van Ruytenburch* (*The Night Watch*). 1642. Oil on canvas, 11 feet 5¾ inches by 14 feet 4½ inches. Rijksmuseum, Amsterdam.

Chapter Nine

COMPOSITION AS NARRATIVE

In analyzing pictorial compositions first as patterns, and then as structures, we have also been seeing composition as a means of expression. Leonardo's *The Last Supper* is one of the most logically constructed of all pictures, but the compositional system that binds the picture together as a firm structural unit serves composition's second and equal function of expression. The graceful, swinging arabesques that tie together the various figures in Botticelli's *Primavera* could never have served Leonardo as a substitute for the geometrical framework of the *Last Supper*, nor, in turn, could this framework have been anything but ruinous if the *Primavera* had been forced into its general lines. Yet both compositions, along with the others examined in the last two chapters, are built on general rules that apply to the majority of pictorial schemes where balances and counterbalances must be adjusted to give the desired relationships—psychological and structural—to the component parts of a picture.

Basic compositional rules have served artists for centuries without inhibiting invention or individual interpretation, but frequently an artist will depart from the rules or deliberately violate them to satisfy special demands. Degas's *Woman with Chrysanthemums*, one of the first paintings we discussed (**21**), is an instance of such violation. In this chapter we will see other instances remarkable for their ingenuity as means of expression or narration, as well as some less radical instances that will help to clarify the special examples—beginning with three paintings: Rembrandt's *The Company of Captain Frans Banning Cocq and Lieutenant Willem van Ruytenburch*, more conveniently if inaccurately known as *The Night Watch*; Charles Willson Peale's *The Peale Family*; and Degas's *The Bellelli Family*. Painted respectively by a seventeenth-century Dutchman, an eighteenth-century American, and a nineteenth-century Frenchman, they contrast strongly with one another. Yet they share a common problem in composition, which they solve in different ways. All are group portraits, and the group portrait is as vexing a compositional problem as a painter is ever required to solve.

In a group portrait each member must be awarded his proportionate share of interest and prominence. Obviously this condition limits the artist's freedom in arranging his material, since ordinarily he is free to assemble as many or as few figures as he wishes and to dispose them at will to build up whatever focal climax he wants. In a group portrait where all the members share equal interest and importance, his problem is to involve them in a composition that will be interesting in itself, rather than being merely a line-up of figures like, say, the usual graduating class photograph.

Rembrandt's problem in *The Night Watch* (**254**), as we will call it, was to catalogue the features of the individual members of an organization (which was

255. Rembrandt. *The Anatomy Lesson of Dr. Tulp.* 1632. Oil on canvas, 66¾ by 85¼ inches. Mauritshuis, The Hague, The Netherlands.

essentially social in spite of the military connotations of its name) and to create at the same time an inherently interesting picture. With some twenty figures to be included, he chose the device of showing them at the moment when they respond to the commander's order to get into parade formation. Individual psychological studies were not attempted, as being less appropriate here than in another kind of picture, say a call to arms in which every man would respond to the emotional moment in his own way. In an earlier and smaller group portrait, *The Anatomy Lesson of Doctor Tulp* (**255**), Rembrandt gave the individuals their own psychological identities as they react to the dissection, but in *The Night Watch* it was more reasonable to subordinate identity to activity. This was, in fact, the only feasible approach to such a large and complicated subject. *The Night Watch* is primarily a rendering of light and movement organized in space, and would be disrupted if our attention were called to a variety of psychological factors within it. For that matter, the call to parade formation would not stir a very interesting variety of individualized responses.

The Night Watch has been a much misunderstood picture. It was long obscured by coats of yellowed varnish and layers of dirt that reduced its color to a murky gloom punctuated by figures, some of them only half-visible, others revealed here and there as if by torchlight. Thus it acquired its inaccurate popular title—and the subject was thought to be a call to arms. It is not a night scene at all. During World War II the canvas was dismounted (it is a huge picture, more than 13 feet high) and hidden for safekeeping. After the war it was cleaned before being put back on exhibition. Cleaning revealed details in the background that had been obscured, brought minor figures into proper relation with the others, and above all brightened the yellow glow to reveal the members of the "night" watch occupying a spacious room in which cool daylight flows.

The members of the company are awarded varying degrees of prominence, but each is clearly visible. The fact that some of them had all but disappeared under layers of varnish and grime helped give rise to the legend that when Rembrandt completed the picture it was rejected by the company, ruining his career and beginning his long decline into poverty and relative obscurity after early success. This decline—in success, not at all in Rembrandt's power as an artist—did in fact take place. But the reasons for it must be found elsewhere; there are no factual circumstances to support the legend that *The Night Watch* was a disastrous landmark in the painter's career. The introduction of incidental figures, especially the girl so conspicuous in the pool of light to the left, was by the same legend arbitrary on Rembrandt's part. He was supposed to have used these figures as convenient elements in the creation of his dramatic composition, in spite of the fact that they had no justifiable relationship to the shooting company whose members had paid to have their likenesses recorded. But these figures are now believed to have emblematic significance.

256. Charles Willson Peale. *The Peale Family.* 1773 and 1809. Oil on canvas, 56½ by 88¾ inches. The New-York Historical Society, New York City.

257. Edgar Degas. *The Bellelli Family.* 1859. Oil on canvas, 78¾ by 99½ inches. The Louvre, Paris.

However, if cleaning and historical reconsiderations have brought us back to a more proper understanding of the picture, it has suffered one irremediable disfigurement. The canvas was at some time cut down on both sides and at the bottom, crowding the figures at left and right in a way that is obvious at a glance, and making a less apparent but more serious shift in the relation of the two central figures to the rest. As the picture now exists, these figures are too obviously centered. Originally they were off center; this placement emphasized the feeling of movement and excitement of the composition, a device already familiar from previous discussions, especially in Géricault's *Raft of the Medusa* (**245**).

As a solution to a problem, *The Night Watch* was a skillful consolidation of a given number of figures into a group portrait and, under the conditions of this particular assignment, seems to have been satisfactory to the clients who commissioned it. In our two other examples, the Peale and Degas family groups, the drama and monumentality of *The Night Watch* would of course have been altogether inappropriate. Family subjects demand intimacy rather than dramatic excitement, an intimacy based on the psychological interplay between individuals whose lives are closely bound together. Yet the two family groups contrast with one another just as strongly as the pair of them contrast with the Rembrandt. In both pictures the painters employ composition to express contrasting psychological values.

Peale began work on the group portrait of his family (**256**) about 1773. Nine of the people in the picture are family members by birth or by marriage. The tenth is a matriarchal family nurse who stands in the background, hands folded, with all the dignity of a great natural monument. For good measure Peale includes three familial portrait busts on the shelf to the right, and as an afterthought adds the portrait head of a member who joined the family after the picture was half-finished, the dog Argus.

Argus, as a pup, was left to the Peales by a grateful old Revolutionary soldier who pulled him out from under his blouse in return for a free meal. The Revolution had come and gone since Peale began the picture. For many years he kept it unfinished in his studio as a kind of demonstration piece. In finishing it, he added the portrait of Argus, by then venerable, and the following inscription at center right: "C. W. Peale painted these Portraits *of his family* in 1773. wishing to finish every work he had undertaken— compleated this picture in 1809!"

A little arithmetic shows that the picture was completed thirty-six years after it was begun. This explains why Peale, who was sixty-eight years old at the time, appears in it as a young man of thirty-two. He stands to the left side, holding a palette and bending over to inspect a drawing on which his brother, St. George Peale, is at work.

The Peale Family is a delightful painting. John Adams, who saw it in 1776 in the painter's Philadelphia studio, wrote in a letter: "There was a pleasant, a happy cheerfulness in their countenances, and a familiarity in their air towards each other." And the intention of the picture is no more complicated than that. It presents an ideal façade of family life, informal, affectionate, harmonious, and secure. The canvas on the easel in the background, the picture-within-a-picture upon which Charles Willson Peale has been at work, originally bore the phrase *Concordia Animae* as a clue to the meaning of the whole painting. But Peale later eliminated these words, "the design being," he wrote to his son, "sufficient to tell the subject," as indeed it is. A glance at *The Peale Family* is enough to show that the ten people in it are happily united as a group. They are pleasantly disposed and share the limelight without competing for it (although Argus, it must be confessed, remains what he was when he was introduced into the composition, a postscript).

Compositionally, the subjects are divided into two groups, six figures clustered at the left and three at the right side, or, if you include the nurse, four. She stands in a nicely selected relationship to the family proper, expressive of her position in the household, closely allied with the other figures yet slightly removed, painted as she is in more subdued tones and standing as she does in the only attitude not physically bound to the rest by contact of a hand or a shoulder.

If all the figures had been massed together, they would have looked crowded and monotonous. Hence the division into two groups. But this is a family, a harmoniously united family, so it is necessary that we also be conscious of the two groups as a unit. And we are: the two halves are united by a slight overlapping and by a scattering of fruit across the table, a trivial detail, yet an important one in binding the two halves together—as well as a pretty bit of still life gratuitously offered (**258**). The halves are even more strongly held together by the fact that St. George (extreme left), sketching his mother as she holds a grandchild (extreme right), glances toward her as he draws. This play of interest across the breadth of the picture is a psychologically effective tie, nullifying any feeling of disunity that might have been produced by the physical division into two groups.

Within this firmly knit composition each figure is pleasantly varied. We are conscious of each one as an individual, but we cannot look long at one without being led to another. The composition is not brilliant or complicated; it need be neither to fulfill the painter's conception, which is direct and simple.

Peale's style has a suggestion of dryness in it, like a pinch of salt in a dish that might otherwise have been too bland. There are occasional awkwardnesses in drawing—the hands of the sister standing at the left, one resting on the shoulder of Charles Willson Peale, the other on the shoulder of his wife, are a touch oversize. These hands are not quite as fortunately incorporated as the rest. They remind us that the picture is a group of separate studies synthesized into a whole. Also, the arm of the grandmother

258. Detail from *The Peale Family*.

cannot bear close examination. Instead of terminating as it should, it continues as a tubelike form and disappears into the shadows a moment too late to conceal from us that it is overlong, and handless. But these imperfections have their own appeal; they account for the suggestion of engaging provincialism that distinguishes the work of this early American painter from that of the facile English portrait painters he would have liked to emulate.

Pictures of this general type, which go by the name of "conversation pieces," are frequent in eighteenth-century and early nineteenth-century painting. Based on the assumption that life is a matter of agreeable surfaces, they are usually built around a theme with incidental reference to some pleasurable activity associated with the subjects, like the exercise in drawing that occupies St. George and Charles Willson here.

The picture is a happy interpretation of family life but not a very searching one, even for a pre-Freudian age. Families are more complicated than this. Family relationships produce frictions and irritations as minor evils, agonizing psychological conflicts as major ones. The brothers, sisters, and in-laws gathered around the Peale table were human beings, and certainly not immune to these difficulties. Just as certainly, in other aspects of their family life they rose to joys more intense than the casual affections so uniformly expressed in the group. Peale does not hint that these human beings have more than an agreeably tepid experience of life, nor does he make much effort, if any, to differentiate one from another psychologically. He was certainly aware of the psychological individuality of his sitters and of the crosscurrents of emotional relationships, but if it even occurred to him that it would be interesting to explore these in a painting, he rejected the idea as inappropriate in a family portrait.

The particular circumstances of individual relationships in all their psychological subtleties fascinated another artist, a young Frenchman who painted a family group in 1859 when he was less than thirty years old. This, you may remember, is younger than Peale was when he began his family portrait. But at that age this Frenchman, Edgar Degas, was already an urbane cosmopolite. He was a doubter, a speculator upon human nature, and basically a pessimist. He spent the better part of a year in Italy in spite of his father's repeated insistence that he return to Paris, for Degas had begun work on a large painting of his aunt, Baroness Bellelli, his two young cousins, and the Baron. In this family there was a less happy state of affairs than the one Peale would have us believe existed in his. Degas reveals it through a composition as original as any in the history of painting, and, as Peale said of his own, "sufficient to tell the subject." "Sufficient" is an understatement. Superlatives are dangerous, but there is less danger than usual in describing *The Bellelli Family* (**257**, p. 197) as the finest psychological group portrait ever painted. The temperament of each of the four members is individualized for us, and, beyond that, their interrelationship is analyzed. Before you read the following paragraphs, you may want to ask yourself on the evidence of the picture what these people were like. In that case try to decide what the relationship of the father to the rest of the family might be, what the emotional tie of each of the little girls is to each of the parents, and what the difference is, temperamentally, between these two children. The chances are that you will learn as much from the picture itself as you will know when you have read the following summary, with the exception of specific historical facts.

From references in family letters we gather that the Baron was a man of uneven temperament, given to moods and, at least during the time Degas visited the family, conscious of frustrations and discouragements both in his personal life and in his career. His only son had died (the family is still in mourning in the portrait) and the Baron was marking time as a political exile from his native Naples. His disturbed life made him half a stranger in his own household, a condition aggravated by an increasing rift with his wife. Social conventions of respectability in the mid-nineteenth century placed limitations on a woman in the Baroness's situation. A reserved, intelligent, and patient woman—if we can accept the judgment of her young nephew—she seems to have shouldered even more of the responsibility for the home and the children than did the average wife of her time. Of the two little girls, the elder, Giovanna, was placid and closely attached to her mother, whereas the younger, Giuliana, was more energetic and restless, temperamentally sympathetic to her father but, by force of circumstance, more securely bound within the lives of her mother and sister.

The most casual observer must notice that in Degas's portrait the father is separated from the rest of the family by a series of vertical lines, which, violating normal compositional rules, separate a generous third of the picture from the rest. In addition, he sits unconventionally, with his back toward us and his profile in shadow. His features are painted less decisively than those of the other figures (259). He is the only one of the family who is not completely revealed to us as a person; we are left with the feeling that we do not know him as we know the mother and daughters. He has a life beyond this room; perhaps he leads a life more important to him than the life we are seeing here; he is an outsider.

But this vagueness, incompleteness, and isolation are reversed in the figure of the wife. She stands with decision, dignity, and forbearance, dominating the room by her quietness. Of all the figures, hers is the simplest and strongest in silhouette; that is why we return to her always, no matter how interesting the rest of the picture may be in its greater detail and variety.

Her right hand rests on the shoulder of Giovanna, the more placid daughter, who was like her and closest to her. This little girl is held within the larger silhouette of the mother's figure; her way of standing echoes her mother's,

259. Detail from *The Bellelli Family.*

as does her general silhouette—and she stands quietly. She is the only one of the family who looks at us, although the others are aware of our presence. She looks at us unquestioningly, content to stay within her mother's support and protection.

But the other child, Giuliana, partially breaks away from the pair. She occupies the side of the picture separated from the father, yet we feel strongly her connection with him. She is the only one whose glance could, and in a moment might, meet her father's. She sits restlessly, one leg tucked up under her, as if impatient with sitting for her artist-cousin, unable to remain still, the volatile member of the group. Just as she is divided in her loyalty to her mother and her father, so she does not belong wholly to either in the composition of the painting.

It is apparent, then, that Degas set about expressing a specific set of circumstances with the help of appropriate compositional means. When we know the circumstances, the picture takes on some peripheral interest; but it is a great picture because it is expressive of the interrelationships of four people, whether or not we know the specific circumstances. The picture has a life of its own beyond the immediate reasons for its creation. If the identity of the painter and the family were unknown to us, any meaning *The Bellelli Family* might lose would be of little consequence.

The Bellellis are not important to us as individuals. It makes no difference how they looked. Their troubles were never of any significance except to themselves. The relationships so brilliantly revealed were neither unique nor on the grand scale. The picture's greatness lies in its ability to stir us to thought beyond the limited considerations of a single family's not unusual circumstances. And it does so because Degas has crystallized his material into forms of perfect order, rid of all confusions, incidentals, vagaries, and distractions. In the resultant clarity our sensibilities and understanding may expand.

Degas was one of the greatest of all pictorial composers, and *The Bellelli Family,* an early painting, is only one (though one of the best) of a succession of startlingly original compositions. Degas is preeminent in this unconventionality without freakishness. Other great masters of pictorial composition time and again demonstrate their ability to use conventional devices more skillfully than their contemporaries. But Degas invents compositions without direct precedent, and each of these compositions is so special to its subject that none is directly useful to followers hunting a formula. The composition of *The Peale Family* might be adapted to any number of group portraits, but that of *The Bellelli Family* could not.

At the same time Degas was a master of what we call classical composition, although even here he was original in his use of traditional devices. We will compare Poussin's *The Funeral of Phocion* (**260**), a standard example of classical composition at its zenith, and Degas's *Rehearsal in the Foyer of the Opera* (**261**), an exceptional classical composition although it is seldom thought of as one. Beneath their surface dissimilarities, the pictures have much in common.

Poussin's masterpiece, painted in the seventeenth century, is an arrangement of architectural and landscape forms, completely imaginary, beautifully disposed in space, studded here and there with some small human effigies of no very great interest or individuality in themselves. On the other hand, Degas's *Rehearsal* is an arrangement of human beings drawn from life and sharply individualized, in an identifiable interior of the Paris Opera. The Poussin looks backward through centuries to the half-legendary world of classical antiquity for its subject, a subject involving the great and the mighty. Degas chooses a subject at hand, involving nobody more important than a few second-string ballet performers, their rehearsal master, and the fiddler who supplies practice music. These people are not even involved in a performance with its attendant excitement and glamour; they are engaged in a routine rehearsal, and some of the dancers are apparently a little bored with the whole thing. Yet both pictures, for all their contrasts, are organized in terms of classical order.

Ultimately the subject of any classical composition is order. We have already seen that all composition is order of one kind or another, but in classical composition order is associated with the idea of repose and may exist almost for itself. What we call a classical composition is conceived in limited space, bounded space, rather than imaginative reaches into infinity. We made this contrast between Cézanne's *Mont Sainte-Victoire* and Durand's *Thanatopsis* (**23** and **24**). We saw other classical compositions in Poussin's *Rape of the Sabine Women* (**228**), taking place in architecturally bounded space, and Vermeer's *The Artist in His Studio* (**164**), where space was limited to a small room defined on all sides.

Poussin's *The Funeral of Phocion* is designed on the same principle: the satisfaction it gives us is based on the sense of order within a limited world. True, this is a panoramic landscape in contrast with the forum of the *Rape of the Sabine Women* and Vermeer's small room. But the sky is treated more as a backdrop terminating a stage set than as a continuation of space in nature. And even though we have no walls at the picture's sides, we are not offered temptations to wander beyond the frame. We may, however, wander at will within the landscape. Space exists all around the architectural and landscape forms. To enjoy the picture fully we must think of it in three dimensions, not as the flat surface of a canvas.

Actually, we do not wander: we are led. The contour of a hill, the angle of a low stone wall, the placement of a tree, the direction in which a cart moves—all these elements direct us as we explore this microcosm, this small, complete world. We are never allowed to escape from it, any more than we are allowed to escape from Vermeer's small room. Yet the elements composing the world are so harmoniously ordered that we do not feel imprisoned.

260. Nicolas Poussin. *The Funeral of Phocion.* 1648. Oil on canvas, 45 by 69 inches. Collection Earl of Plymouth, Oakly Park, Leidlow, England.

261. Edgar Degas. *Rehearsal in the Foyer of the Opera.* 1872. Oil on canvas, 12½ by 18 inches. The Louvre, Paris.

Such a picture is the result not of rules but of the artist's feeling for what is right. This feeling, of course, is developed through study, contemplation, and practice. If the means used to achieve its order were too obvious, the picture would be less satisfying. Some of these means, however, are definable and can be pointed out without marring our spontaneous enjoyment.

There is the device of "repetition of the picture plane." The picture plane is simply the plane defined by the frame or the surface of a canvas; it can be compared to the curtain of a stage. When the curtain is raised, the "plane" where the curtain hung still exists psychologically. On a stage this plane would be repeated by, let us say, a piece of furniture facing the audience directly rather than at an angle. Likewise it would be repeated by any actor who stands directly facing the audience. It would be repeated finally by the terminating backdrop or set wall.

In the Poussin the picture plane is repeated again and again as objects recede toward the final "backdrop," the sky. It is repeated by the facing surfaces of walls, by various buildings, and is suggested by long, low hills or mounds disposed across the picture space parallel to the picture plane.

A second series of planes at an angle to the picture plane is suggested first by the side plane of the stone wall at the right. We enter the picture from the lower left corner and move across it, but are kept from moving out by the tall tree at the right and by this plane of the wall, which is turned to deflect the "current" of our movement back into the picture. It is not noticeable that this plane is, in fact, a distortion of true perspective. In true perspective we would not see the side surface of a wall whose front plane parallels the picture plane, but Poussin turns this (and other planes that repeat it) slightly inward to create a series of checks to our movement, like objects placed on a stage to keep our eyes from wandering off toward the wings.

A corresponding but weaker set of planes serves the same function in the other direction. The rigidity of all these forms is alleviated by the curvings of streams or paths or pathlike areas winding backward and forward, around and about. Although the small figures represented as seated, standing, walking, riding, and carrying the sheeted corpse also turn us in directions in which the artist wants us to move, they themselves are not invested with motion. Essentially they are as static as the natural and architectural forms around them.

We commented in our discussion of Poussin's *Rape of the Sabine Women* that the static quality of figures represented as if in motion is the element in classical composition that, to many people's way of thinking, limits its effectiveness. Degas, with his customary ingenuity, finds a way to avoid this difficulty in his *Rehearsal in the Foyer of the Opera*. The figures in the *Rehearsal* are classically static and classically balanced, but at the same time they are convincingly engaged in an activity based on a premise of motion—dancing.

Degas resolves this contradiction by choosing an instant of repose in the midst of continuous action. The ballet master, in the white suit at the right side of the picture, has just held up his hand and tapped the floor with his stick. Responding to this command, the dancer (extreme left) whom he has been rehearsing stops stock-still, holding the attitude of the moment as she listens for the comment or correction he is about to make. The violinist has lowered his bow, taking the opportunity for a moment's rest. Most of the other dancers, attracted by the tapping of the stick, pause to glance and listen, but others in casual attitudes chat with one another or stand waiting their turn for rehearsal. Thus the picture is full of life; it is, in a way, full of activity. But it is quite natural that every figure in it is perfectly still, and Degas is free to use each one as an object for disposition within a static, classical composition as if they were the walls, buildings, shrubs, and trees that served Poussin in *The Funeral of Phocion.*

Degas has also turned his space at an eccentric angle. To increase the effect of informality in a paradoxically formal arrangement, he abandons the picture plane idea. But his pictorial space is still precisely defined. The chair in the foreground, which appears to be so casually placed, repeats the angle of the walls, thus becoming a major factor in defining in the foreground the volume of space that the walls define in the background. The chair also serves as a barrier to keep us from entering the void in the center of the picture; it deflects us either to the ballet master and the group around him or to the dancer at the left.

To build a composition around a large central void is another eccentricity, but Degas is not interested in novelty for novelty's sake. In physically isolating the dancer from the ballet master, he is unifying them psychologically. The tension of interest that vibrates between them would be weakened by any interruption of the space. This is the same device, more inventively employed, that Peale used when he bound his family portrait together by the glance St. George casts toward the figure he is sketching.

By all the rules, Degas's *Rehearsal* is overbalanced on the right side, where a mass of figures occupies one end of a kind of compositional seesaw whose other end must be held down by the lone figure of the dancer. But the two sides are in what is called "psychic balance" (or "occult balance"). The dancer's isolation attracts our attention in a composition where the other figures, massed, compete with one another. The curious attitude of her legs and feet, opposed to the more ordinary gestures and attitudes of the several members of the group on the other side, also sets her apart. And finally, the "seesaw" is at the angle in space defined by the chair and the walls, so that the dancer's end of it is thrown nearer to us. Thus she is not only in a more conspicuous location but by reasons of perspective must be drawn larger than the figures she faces. For all these reasons she holds her own against superior forces.

The Degas is everywhere as neatly and beautifully balanced as the Poussin. Both painters set for themselves the problem of balancing static objects within defined space. They contrast in that Poussin invests his subject with majestic implications that seemed valid in a century that accepted the divine right of kings, while Degas, living in the century of the triumph of the bourgeoisie, accepts the authority of the commonplace. Yet both seek meaning through order. Neither one is much concerned with his apparent subject. The Poussin's sheeted corpse happens to be that of an Athenian general wrongly convicted of treason, and executed, who must therefore be buried outside the walls of the city. But the picture would not be much changed if the object on the stretcher were, say, the drum of a column being carried to a building site. The Degas has a much closer connection with its subject matter, yet the longer we know the picture, the more our satisfaction comes from the disposition of the objects rather than from our interest in who they are or what they are doing.

Degas admired both Poussin and Vermeer, and the gentle flow of light in the *Rehearsal* is similar to Vermeer's. Similar, too, is the device of implying a wall by showing objects illuminated by light coming from a window not seen but clearly sensed.

In arresting his figures between moments of action, Degas has a classical precedent in a Greek sculpture of the fourth century B.C., the *Discus Thrower* (262), which we know in several versions copied from a lost original by the sculptor Myron, representing an athlete engaged in violent action. The sculptor seizes the instant when the arm has reached the apex of the upward motion of its arc, the instant before it starts the downward motion that begins the act of throwing. This is also the instant when the body has reached the extremity of its twist in one direction and is ready to reverse this motion.

But every great work of art is new, no matter what its connection with the past. Other painters have imitated Vermeer, have imitated the *Discus Thrower*, have imitated Poussin. Degas imitated nobody. If we made a long catalogue of the sources of the art of Degas and an equally long one of the sources of the art of some mediocre painter, these sources might be the same; yet Degas would still be an original artist, and the other would remain an imitator, an eclectic.

Of all the paintings discussed thus far, only a few have told stories. When they did, as in the cases of Gérôme's *Duel after the Masquerade* (106) and Hovenden's *Breaking Home Ties* (107), we found them lacking in interpretive power. This is understandable since by its very nature the storytelling picture is likely to be a compromise between pictorial art and verbal art, or narration. You may argue that Rubens's *Prometheus Bound* (95), which pictures a classical legend, and Delacroix's *Abduction of Rebecca* (246), which takes its subject from *Ivanhoe*, and the various Crucifixions we have seen, which tell that great story, are all narrative paintings. This is true, on the face of it; but it is also true, and much more important, that these

262. Myron. *Discobolus* (*Discus Thrower*). About 450 B.C. Roman copy of bronze original, life size. Vatican, Rome.

paintings are conceived as pictures of ideas. We do not have to translate them back into their original form of narrative in order to give them meaning. The medium of images is not playing second fiddle to the medium of words. When an artist wants to tell a story as vividly in images as it has been told elsewhere in words, his most vivid narrative device is composition.

Saint Anthony Tempted by the Devil in the Form of a Woman (**263**), painted by the Sienese artist Sassetta more than five hundred years ago, is as economical and expressive a bit of storytelling as can be found in any medium. Instead of showing us the incident as a kind of glorified snapshot of an actual happening (in the manner of *Duel after the Masquerade*), Sassetta creates a dramatic and psychological atmosphere through the abstract means of color, line, and arrangement. It might be objected that the temptation of Saint Anthony could hardly suggest a snapshot since the incident is a fantastical one, but an unimaginative painter could have treated it as literally as if it were the factual record of a commonplace event. Even such a painter might be able to tell the story clearly enough, but we all know that a story told effectively by one person may fall flat when told by another. In this little picture, it is not so much what Sassetta says as the way he says it.

What he says is that when the saint, who lives in the wilderness dedicated to a life of ascetic contemplation, returns to his cell one evening he discovers waiting near the door a woman, delightfully beautiful, who tempts him to the pleasures of the flesh. And the way he says it is this:

The saint, walking toward the door of his shelter, has just discovered the woman. In a wonderfully expressive attitude he hesitates, half turning toward her, his hand raised in a gesture of surprise that in the next moment can turn into a gesture of assent or one of rejection. He stands directly in the center of the picture, with the cell and the woman on either side of him like equal weights in a scale of which he is the pivot. The balance is emphasized by the fact that both objects offered him for choice are pink, the only bright color in the picture except the streak of light along the horizon. These pinks, however, clash with one another, the vermilion-pink of the shelter with the carmine-pink of the woman's robe. The woman is an exquisite little creature; the innocence of her pretty face and blond hair is denied by slits in her bodice and skirt; even her jeweled batwings are pretty, although they are hidden from the saint and revealed only to us. In contrast to the graceful and ornamental forms of the woman, the lines of the shelter are extremely severe.

The apparitional quality of the scene is created by the background, a never-never land of desert, its path sprinkled with stones to humiliate the flesh of the saint's bare feet, its odd rock-hills dotted with a few exotic trees that look like designs for jewelry, and its horizon so curved that it suggests the end of the world, the jumping-off place. Against this desolate isolation the temptress is all the more tempting.

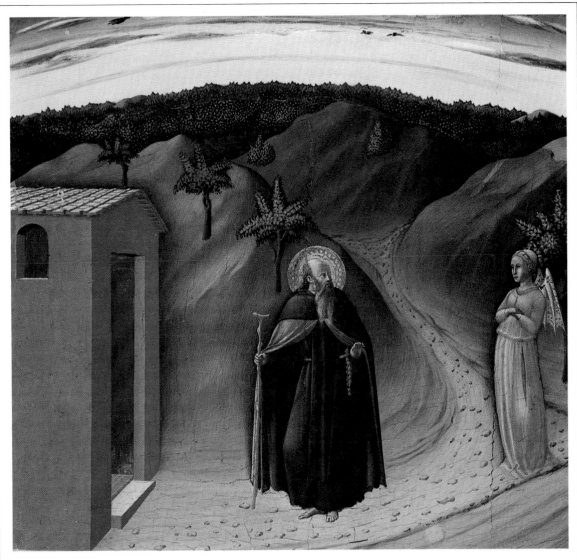

263. Sassetta. *Saint Anthony Tempted by the Devil in the Form of a Woman.* About 1430. Egg tempera on panel, 14⅞ by 15¹³/₁₆ inches. Yale University Art Gallery, New Haven, Connecticut. University purchase from James Jackson Jarves.

264. Pieter Bruegel the Elder. *Landscape with the Fall of Icarus.* About 1554–55. Oil transferred from wood to canvas, 29 by 44⅛ inches. Musées Royaux des Beaux Arts, Brussels.

This is not a complicated picture, and the story itself has been reduced to minimum terms. This minimum is reflected in the spareness of the objects represented. There are no parenthetical references, no hints of implications beyond the immediate subject. And that, of course, is where the picture might be said to fail in greatness, if it can be said to "fail" when it does not achieve something it never set out to achieve. The painting tells its little story in the most direct, succinct pictorial terms with utmost skill. Whatever else it is, or is not, it is utterly delightful—a joy.

To see how much a painter may say beyond the mere narrative of an incident drawn from a literary source, we will look at *Landscape with the Fall of Icarus* (**264**, p. 209) by the Flemish painter, Pieter Bruegel the Elder. According to Greek legend, the boy Icarus fell to his death in the sea when he flew too close to the sun on a pair of wings invented by his father, Daedalus. The wings were made of feathers and wax; the heat of the sun melted the wax in the boy's wings and they fell apart. Daedalus, also trying out his wings at a more cautious height between the sea and the sun, did not fall. The legend is given various meanings, most of them having to do with the vanity of pride or ambition.

Bruegel, however, finds its meaning in another direction. The composition of *The Fall of Icarus* carries this meaning by a kind of reverse emphasis. Whereas other compositions build every element toward a climax in the figure of the protagonist of the story, at first sight Icarus does not seem to be in the picture at all. The most conspicuous figure is a plowman, his head bent toward the soil, who is not even a part of the legend (**265**). Beyond him, looking up with mild curiosity toward an odd speck in the sky, a shepherd tends his flock. Stretching around these figures is a land- and seascape of intricate beauty. Ships move across the water, and in the cove below the plowman a particularly elaborate one is setting sail. When we have discovered this ship we have very nearly discovered Icarus at last. Our subject—or at least the small legs of our subject—is nearby, just disappearing into the water with a very small splash, lost among the details of more interesting patterns.

Bruegel's comment, then, has to do with the insignificance of personal tragedy in the great scheme of things. The death of this boy and the anguish of his father mean nothing at all in terms of a larger pattern. This could be a pessimistic conclusion, and the modern poet W. H. Auden made it one in his poem "Musée des Beaux Arts," inspired by this painting and others of the Flemish School where everyday events are combined with subjects like the Nativity and the martyrdom of saints:

> About suffering they were never wrong,
> The Old Masters: how well they understood
> Its human position; how it takes place

265. Detail from *Landscape with the Fall of Icarus.*

While someone else is eating or opening a window or
　　just walking dully along;
How, when the aged are reverently, passionately wait-
　　ing
For the miraculous birth, there always must be
Children who did not specially want it to happen,
　　skating
On a pond at the edge of the wood:
They never forgot
That even the dreadful martyrdom must run its course
Anyhow in a corner, some untidy spot
Where the dogs go on with their doggy life and the
　　torturer's horse
Scratches its innocent behind on a tree.

In Brueghel's *Icarus*, for instance: how everything turns
　　away
Quite leisurely from the disaster; the ploughman may
Have heard the splash, the forsaken cry,
But for him it was not an important failure; the sun
　　shone
As it had to on the white legs disappearing into the
　　green
Water; and the expensive delicate ship that must have
　　seen
Something amazing, a boy falling out of the sky,
Had somewhere to get to and sailed calmly on.

We have here, then, a theme from literature, transformed in painting, with a consequent literary restatement.
By this interpretation Bruegel used the Icarus legend to
comment on human indifference to the suffering of others,
the loneliness of the individual. But this idea is not in
harmony with the look of Bruegel's picture. The pattern is
of such depth and serenity, such calm beauty, such grandeur,
that we may be consoled by the knowledge that our
individual troubles are absorbed within a greater order.

In its serenity and elegance *The Fall of Icarus* is an
exception in Bruegel's work. Typically, he combines the
fantastic and the grotesque with the earthiness of peasant
life, unlikely as the combination may sound. In *Flemish
Proverbs* (266) he had a ready-made vehicle, since proverbs
grow out of the life of the people but are expressed in terms
of fantasy. The man who is enclosed in a crystal globe (at
the very bottom of the picture just right of center) illustrates
"I must stoop if I wish to go through the world" (*Ick moet
my crommen, sae ick door de werelt commen*), and the
man strewing roses before swine (*Desen stroyt roosen voor
de vercken*), just above the globe and slightly to the left, is
no stranger to us if we substitute pearls for blossoms.

Flemish Proverbs is conceived as a kind of drollery,
although in the light of Bruegel's subsequent achievements
critics like to believe that in painting it the artist intended
a compendium of human folly. Compositionally it is not
remarkable, although the job of tying together some eighty

266. Pieter Bruegel the Elder. *Flemish Proverbs.* 1559. Oil on wood, 45⅝ by 63½ inches. Staatliche Museen, Gemäldegalerie, Berlin.

267. Pieter Bruegel the Elder. *The Parable of the Blind.* 1568. Tempera on canvas, 33½ by 60¾ inches. Museo di Capodimonte, Naples.

tableaux vivants simultaneously enacted upon a large stage is admirably accomplished. *Flemish Proverbs* is a fascinating picture; but in a later one devoted to a single proverb, *The Parable of the Blind* (**267**), we see Bruegel as a mature man and a mature artist doing a great deal more with the same kind of material.

The blind men are proceeding in single file across a bit of descending ground that ends in a ditch. The leader has tumbled in. The last man in line has no suspicion of what is happening. He will continue to follow, in complete docility, until he meets the catastrophe that the other men, in graduated stages, begin to suspect. The other figures are studies in the progressive emotions of uneasy suspicion developing into terrified certainty and culminating in frantic, helpless confusion as the men are finally caught up in the disaster they failed to anticipate when they placed their trust in another no better equipped than themselves to avoid it.

If this were only a picture of blind men falling into a ditch, it would be cruel. But it is a parable of human inertia, a comment on the weakness of people who follow blindly because it is too much trouble to find a way for themselves, who would rather shift responsibility for a course of action to someone else, just anyone, than make the effort to determine one for themselves. The blind men of the picture may be pitiable, but the "blind" men of the parable are not.

For expressive reasons, the picture abandons all usual ideas of balance and catapults downward into one corner. Each man's face reflects his state of mind; in this respect the faces are a superb series of inventions. But if they were blanked out, the story would still be vividly told, since it is in the design of the figures that Bruegel has concentrated the expressive force. The last man in line is drawn in simple masses; his cloak hangs in straight lines. In each successive figure this simplicity gives way more and more to complexity and agitation, until finally the figure in the lead is a tumbled silhouette, a tumbled mass. This is not because men tumbling or falling would happen to present such forms. They might, in fact, present quite simple ones. In newspaper photographs of people falling or jumping or lying on the pavement after an accident it is a rare instance when the victim presents a shape expressive in itself. Abstractly, that is, without the attendant evidence of blood or wreckage, the form of a man who has died a violent death is not likely to be much different from that of a man lying in a drunken stupor or even one taking a peaceful nap. Nor is the form of the figure of a man in physical torment or some violent action of a tragic nature likely to be very different, objectively regarded, from that of a man dancing or engaged in sport.

The point we are making is that Bruegel's blind men are not realistically represented. They may be realistic in detail, but taken as a whole they are abstract patterns of line and form, expressively designed. If they seem realistic, it is because of Bruegel's power as a creative draughtsman.

The rest of the picture is a peaceful landscape that,

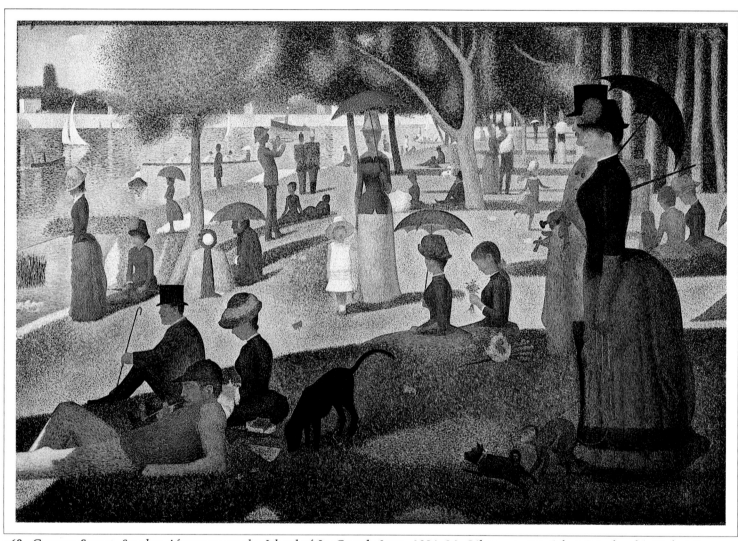

268. Georges Seurat. *Sunday Afternoon on the Island of La Grande Jatte.* 1884–86. Oil on canvas, 6 feet 9 inches by 10 feet 8 inches. The Art Institute of Chicago. Helen Birch Bartlett Memorial Collection.

269. Detail from *La Grande Jatte*.

like the one in *The Fall of Icarus*, is in emotional contrast with the tragedy being enacted. The landscape in *The Fall of Icarus* was made elaborate and fanciful to suggest the unimportance of the single detail of the boy's legs. In *The Parable of the Blind* the landscape is as simple as the procession of men is complicated. Its lines are as straight and spare as those of the hapless men are knotted. By contrast the quiet landscape emphasizes the dramatic invention of the foreground figures.

It is hardly possible to exhaust the subject of pictorial composition, since it is limited only by the number of pictures, good or bad, that exist for discussion. In analyzing some standard examples and their variations (such as Perugino's *Crucifixion* and Picasso's contrasting *Guernica*), as well as the examples of uniquely expressive or narrative compositions that we have just seen, we have made incidental reference to the part that sheer painterly technique—the method of applying the paint—may play in the structure of a composition. We saw that Poussin's *Rape of the Sabine Women* was tightly painted in a manner appropriate to the disciplines of classically static composition. In contrast, Delacroix's *Abduction of Rebecca*, a similar subject, is treated with romantic fervor in a turbulent composition where paint was so freely applied that one classically oriented critic called such brushwork the product of "a drunken broom." In the majority of our other examples there was less correlation beween painterly technique and the compositional unit, but to conclude our comments on composition we will look at a picture in which compositional structure and the sheer manual technique of paint application are interdependent to an extraordinary degree: Georges Seurat's *Sunday Afternoon on the Island of La Grande Jatte* (**268**, p. 214).

Seurat, who painted *La Grande Jatte* in 1884–86, was a Post-Impressionist, a term covering painters who, in different ways, departed from fading impressionism to seek new means of expression. (We have seen work by two other major Post-Impressionists, Van Gogh and Cézanne.) Cézanne once said that he wanted to make of impressionism "something solid and durable like the art of the museums." Seurat could have said the same thing and it would have been even more strictly to his point than Cézanne's. The Impressionists applied paint in short strokes of variegated tones and tints to increase the luminosity of the overall color. (They had an immediate ancestor in Delacroix and a remote one in Rubens.) Although impressionism thus approximated the vibration of color in light and air, the approximation was often achieved at the expense of form, which in extreme cases dissolved into rainbowed mists. Seurat stuck to the idea of using individual bits of color, but he built these bits into forms that were uncompromisingly defined. The color itself was applied with great precision instead of freely as in impressionism. A Seurat painting is composed of thousands upon thousands of individual flecks of pure color (**269**, p. 215), combined in semi-scientific proportions with others that will be blended by the eye into the desired final color. Seurat preferred the term "divisionism" to describe his chromatic juxtapositions, but the more vivid "pointillism" caught on when a critic, Felix Fénéon, referred to Seurat's "peinture au point" in an article on *La Grande Jatte*.

Seurat died at the age of only thirty-one while still involved in a program that would have demonstrated his method by representing subjects both active and static in light both indoor and outdoor, natural and artificial, and of varying intensities. Yet if he had painted nothing but *La Grande Jatte*, the first of the series, his place would still be secure as an unchallenged master of modern art. His Sunday strollers enjoying a sunny afternoon on an island in the Seine near Paris, whether we read them in two or three dimensions—as flat shapes on the surface of the canvas or as solid volumes in pictorial depth—are defined by contours distilled to such purity that the quasi-geometrical forms approach abstraction. *La Grande Jatte* is, in fact, one of the very few paintings in which insistent abstraction and explicit description of the visual world meet on equal and harmonious terms.

The composition of this, among all paintings, can be tested by trying to imagine it with any shape changed, omitted, or shifted in position—backward, which would reduce the size of the shape; forward, which would enlarge it; or to either side or higher or lower on the surface. Poussin's *Funeral of Phocion* (**260**) can serve as a key (if one is needed) to studying the structure of *La Grande Jatte*. Both are entered from the lower left corner; both express distance by means of multiple receding repetitions of the picture plane; both include figures nominally in motion that actually serve as static direction pointers. The difference between the two is that the Poussin is more subtle, with secondary structural systems discoverable within the main one, while *La Grande Jatte* is severe and uncompromising in its diagrammatic, almost ascetic, purity.

The unity of Seurat's masterpiece lies in this severity in harmony with the rigidly disciplined pointillist technique. The area of the canvas is more than 67 square feet, with every smallest fractional inch testifying to the artist's absolute control of the process of creation. One question remains: Since this process allows for no relieving improvisational stroke of the brush, since inspiration is totally ruled out in favor of calculation, since every element of the composition is forever locked immobile in its spot, what then accounts for the feeling of life that, in spite of everything, emanates from a painting which has been subjected to disciplines that could have been expected to kill it? The explanation lies in the vibrant interplay of those tens of thousands or hundreds of thousands of points of color, the colors of light fractured by a prism. If there could be such a thing as molecules of light, Seurat's points of color would correspond to them in the living compound that, together, they compose.

270. Michelangelo. *Creation of Adam* (detail above). 1511. Ceiling fresco. Sistine Chapel, Vatican, Rome.

Chapter Ten
THE PAINTER'S TECHNIQUES

In the course of the last several chapters we have enlarged on a number of answers to our original question, What is art? But we have made only incidental reference to one aspect of picturemaking that is apparent to everybody and understood by very few. This is the primary fact that a painting is a layer of pigment applied to canvas or some other surface in such a way that the manner of application becomes an integral part of the picture's expressive quality. If the application of paint were nothing more than a skilled manual procedure, there would be no point in discussing it here, any more than there would be in discussing finger exercises in an essay on music appreciation. But in a good picture there is no such thing as *mere* technique. The application of paint is more than a craft the artist learns in order to reproduce a tinted image.

In some cases the expressive quality of a painter's technique is so apparent that it need only be pointed out to be understood. (We have commented on *La Grande Jatte* in this respect.) Imagine, for instance, Whistler's *Arrangement in Gray and Black* painted in the thick, bold strokes of Van Gogh's *The Starry Night*. The image of the old lady could be presented just as accurately, and in the same harmony of quiet colors, in Van Gogh's bold style. But Whistler's paint is brushed onto the canvas so gently, so quietly, so tenderly, that the technique becomes an integral part of the expressive whole.

Likewise *The Starry Night* need not have been painted in heavy, violent strokes except as a means to its particular expressive end. The same surging pattern in the same vivid colors could have been washed onto the canvas in a diaphanous film or could have been as slick and smooth as enamel. But the dramatic texture of Van Gogh's thick, glistening swirls of paint is as expressive as the color.

Since we are going to talk about paints, pigments, and mediums, we had better define our terms. "Pigment" is simply coloring matter; a "binder" is any substance that holds pigment together and makes paint out of it; a "medium" is a modifying substance the artist may mix with his paint to bring it to the proper working consistency for his purposes. Often the word "medium" is used to cover the whole process of any kind of painting. The "oil medium" thus would cover the mixing and applying of oil paint in any of its variations. But in this chapter we will use "technique" for the whole physical process by which the painter sets down in visual terms his conception of a subject.

To illustrate our terms: The pigment called ultramarine, a magnificent dark blue with a purplish cast, is the semiprecious stone lapis lazuli ground to talcum-powder fineness. (At least it used to be; today it is usually synthesized chemically, like many other pigments.) This powdered stone could be mixed with water into a smooth paste and applied to canvas like oil paint, or thinned out and washed onto paper. But in either instance as soon as the pigment dried, it would revert to powder and drop off the canvas or paper.

But if the powder is mixed with the proper kind of oil as a binder, the pigment becomes oil paint and will adhere to canvas and other surfaces. (Acrylic, a synthetic resin, is today a popular replacement for oil, with the difference that it is very fast-drying, which is sometimes an advantage, sometimes not.) If the pigment-powder is mixed with any one of several water-soluble adhesives (gum arabic is a standard one), it becomes water-color paint and will adhere to paper upon drying. Mixed with egg, pigment becomes tempera. Pigment mixed with chalk and an adhesive is also often called tempera, but strictly speaking this is inaccurate. These are the inexpensive paints called "show-card colors" used in elementary painting classes. In more dependable form, the mixture of pigment, chalk, and a water-soluble adhesive is called gouache; it is somewhat heavier in body than water color, and somewhat bleached in tone.

Paints as they come in tubes are usually too thick for use, and the painter thins them with the proper medium. In the case of oils, the medium is likely to be the painter's favorite mixture of (linseed) oil, a varnish, and turpentine, the proportions varying according to whether the paint is to be applied in a heavy layer or a thin one. The amount and kind of varnish will depend on whether the painter wants the picture to have a glossy surface, a mat surface, or something in between. A good craftsman will know which mediums are safe to combine, when he may use a fast-drying medium and when a slow-drying one, and which mediums may be applied over which others without danger of blistering or cracking. We will see one painter, Albert Pinkham Ryder (**419**), who was so careless in combining unsympathetic mediums that his pictures are in ruinous condition. There have been others. Even the great Watteau, who painted in the early eighteenth century when artists usually learned impeccable craftsmanship as the ABC of their trade, seems now and then to have used inferior or polluted oil as a medium, to the detriment of his work. And in the late eighteenth and early nineteenth centuries, when painters found that bitumen combined with oil gave shadow tones of exceptional richness, pictures with wonderfully brilliant lights and wonderfully velvety darks were produced, soon to become miserably blackened and cracked into great scaling patches like mudflats in a summer drought.

Each painting technique has its particular quality, its special limitations, its special adaptabilities. Oil is the most versatile, the most accommodating to the painter; tempera is the most precise and offers the greatest rewards to the meticulous craftsman; water color is the most vivacious and the most sensitive. But let us say flatly that true fresco, of all forms of painting, is the noblest. It is also the most difficult.

Asked to define a fresco, the average person would

define a mural. A mural is any wall painting; a fresco is a wall painting in a special technique; and a *true* fresco is even more special. A mural may be painted on a wall in any one of several techniques, of which ordinary oil and ordinary water color are two, but not the best. Most murals today are not painted directly on the wall but on canvas in a studio and are then glued to the wall. That makes them murals; they are far from being frescoes.

True or, as it is also called, *buon* fresco, which we will distinguish shortly from other fresco, is part and parcel of the wall. The painter, working with pure pigment dissolved in lime water (pure water is also serviceable enough), paints directly on a fresh plaster coating as it dries. He must time his painting carefully. If the wall is still too wet, it will not accept the pigment from his brush. If it is too dry the pigment will not enter the plaster and will powder off later. So the painter must complete his work during the few hours when the surface is just dry enough to suck the pigment in and just wet enough to combine its own moisture with the water containing the pigment. During those few hours the plaster will absorb the pigment to a tiny fraction of an inch below its surface and hold it there. The preparation of the wall is so vital a base for fresco painting that artists who work in fresco regard their plasterers more as colleagues than as assistants.

Everyone is familiar with the beauty of a freshly plastered wall—luminously white, with an eggshell surface neither glossy nor dull. The texture and the soft luminosity of this surface are produced by a next-to-microscopic crystalline film that forms as the plaster dries. This film is in effect the binder in fresco. The pigment is bound into the wall; it *is* the part of the wall we see; it and the wall are the same. This sense of the wall is psychologically a vital element in fresco painting, and it is a sense that is lost in reproductions.

Of all techniques, true fresco is the one that forces a painter into the most direct and uncompromising attack, with no room for experiment en route. As much of the wall as he expects to cover in one day is plastered, depending on the complexity of his design and his own speed and physical stamina. Michelangelo, whose Sistine Chapel ceiling (**271**) makes him the undisputed master figure in fresco painting, completed the 5,800 square feet of the ceiling in four years without employing assistants for minor passages as most painters, faced with that vast area, would have done.

The painter in oil is free to sketch in his entire picture tentatively and work it up gradually, making as many changes as he wants while the picture takes shape. The true fresco painter is not free to come back and make even a minor change. If the color of an area must be changed, there is nothing to do but chip off the offending area and begin over again. An additional complication is that the color changes as the plaster dries, growing lighter in key. (We all know that a damp spot on a plaster wall is darker than the surrounding area.) The fresco painter is always painting two pictures at once, one in the colors he sees as

271. Michelangelo. Ceiling of the Sistine Chapel. 1508–12. About 130 feet long. Vatican, Rome.

272. Michelangelo. Preliminary drawing for *Creation of Adam.* 1511. Red chalk on paper, 7⅝ by 14⅛ inches. The British Museum, London. Courtesy of the Trustees.

273. Piero della Francesca. *The Death of Adam,* from *The Legend of the True Cross*. 1452–66. Fresco. Church of San Francesco, Arezzo, Italy.

he paints, and the other in the colors he will see the next morning when the plaster has dried. He must bear this in mind. Picking up work in a newly plastered area, he must match yesterday's colors by trying to remember how they looked before drying, something impossible for most people to do and extremely difficult for even the most practiced artist.

The painter must work from preliminary studies at full scale (these are often called cartoons) or depend on the infallibility of his draughtsmanship. Before he can begin to paint, he must find a way to transfer an adequate guiding outline from his paper cartoon to the damp plaster. In the head of Adam from Michelangelo's *Creation of Adam* (**270,** p. 218) on the ceiling of the Sistine Chapel, these guidelines show up as gouges in the plaster. Michelangelo worked in one of two ways: either he took his full-scale drawing, held it against the damp plaster, and went over the outlines with some kind of point strong enough to press the design through the paper onto the plaster; or—incomparable draughtsman that he was—he established the general dimensions and then, enlarging from a small preliminary drawing on paper, incised the guidelines directly into the plaster, probably using the wooden end of one of his brushes.

We still have a small study for the figure of Adam (272), but there may also have been a full-scale drawing of the outlines. It wouldn't have occurred to Michelangelo to save the enlargement; such cartoons were ordinarily discarded after they had served their purpose; indeed, they were usually somewhat mutilated while serving it.

In Adam's head the gouges do not provide outlines in much detail, and Michelangelo has not followed them exactly. For example, he did not draw in the hair. You will see running through the hair a line that traces the contours of the skull as if it were bald; on this skull the hair was painted in freely. The lips have also been extended a little beyond the lines of the gouged-in "sketch," and anyone familiar with the drawing of heads will recognize that the backward tilt of this one has been increased by raising the eyebrow above the first rough indication.

Another, more meticulous way of transferring a drawing to plaster is to punch the outlines of the full-scale cartoon with a series of pinholes. (This is most speedily done with a small spiked wheel called a roulette.) The cartoon is then placed firmly against the plaster, and a powder of some sort, either charcoal or a dark pigment, is rubbed over the pinholed outlines. The powder goes through the pinholes and is absorbed by the plaster, leaving the outline in a series of dots when the paper is lifted away. This is called "pouncing."

The dotted outlines are ordinarily painted over, but occasionally they remain visible, as they do in another head of Adam, now an old man (274), by Piero della Francesca. This is a detail from *The Death of Adam* (273), one panel from the series telling the *Legend of the True Cross* in frescoes running the whole height of the walls of the choir in the Church of San Francesco in Arezzo. We have already seen another subject from the same series in the chapter on abstraction (188).

In the locks of hair at the old Adam's temple and around his ear you can see what looks at first like a peppering of random dark specks. But these follow the general outlines of the locks and are obviously the kind of guidelines we have been describing. The Piero frescoes are as rigidly controlled as Michelangelo's are tempestuous. Whereas Michelangelo improvised to some extent in his head of Adam, Piero has followed a detailed preliminary drawing with unusual precision. Here and there throughout the *True Cross* frescoes the dotted lines are visible, despite the careful, thin dark outlines that have been painted over them. They are especially evident as part of the outline around Adam's ear and can still be discerned along the nose. *The Death of Adam* is the topmost panel on a high wall and from such a distance the little specks don't tell. Nor, for that matter, do the gouges Michelangelo used in his head of Adam as a magnificent youth. In both cases, the illustrations bring us unusually close to the walls.

This noblest and most difficult of all forms of painting makes no concessions to the painter; it is merciless in its revelation of his shortcomings; it offers no refuge to me-

274. Detail from *The Death of Adam.*

diocrity. True fresco is, in short, thoroughly unaccommodating. It tolerates vivacity where vivacity is appropriate, but accepts sensitivity only as an element of strength. It reflects truth rather than precision. And as for highly developed craftsmanship, that is taken for granted.

It is quite true that there are plenty of frescoes where the conception is puny or pretentious. Fresco cannot ennoble the commonplaceness or the falsity of a mediocre artist, any more than the lines of *Hamlet* can inspire a noble performance in a puny and pretentious actor. But in the history of art, true fresco has offered great painters a fulfillment in expressive depth and power that is seldom equaled in other techniques.

Fresco in one form or another has been employed since prehistoric times, but it reached its most magnificent flowering in Italy in the fourteenth, fifteenth, and early sixteenth centuries. This of course was the Renaissance, a time when man stopped regarding himself as a soul temporarily imprisoned within vulnerable flesh pending salvation or damnation in the next world, and began examining himself as a being capable of intellectual nobility in his own daily world. We have referred to the "nobility" of fresco; this may be largely a matter of association with the nobility of the Renaissance conceptions that coincided with the flowering of fresco at this time.

About the year 1305, in Padua, Giotto di Bondone lined the Arena Chapel (**279**, p. 227) with frescoes that shifted the whole current of painting away from the manipulation of mystical symbols toward the passionate investigation of the world and man's place in it. His subjects were traditional mystical ones, the lives of the Virgin and Christ, in episodes that had been painted thousands of times in terms of medieval formulas. In Giotto's retelling of the old story, the divine effigies become human beings. The Virgin (**277**) from the *Lamentation* over the body of Christ (**275**) is first of all a mother in an anguish of grief and secondly the Mother of the Redeemer. As representational drawings, Giotto's figures are awkward and full of inaccuracies—but Giotto is a beginner in the process of discovering how to represent the world in realistic images. His realism, seemingly so faulty from this side of the perfected representations of later artists (and of the camera), must have appeared almost illusionistic to his contemporaries in comparison with any other work known at the time. Painters spent the next hundred years adjusting to his break with tradition, trying to go beyond him in the direction he had set, and not quite succeeding. It was not until the appearance of another genius, Masaccio, that Giotto's achievement was extended (which does not mean surpassed), with more accurate anatomical drawing of the nude body, more convincing fall of draperies when it was clothed, more realistic representation of facial expressions, and, above all, a mastery of the newly formulated principles of perspective that allowed Masaccio to place his figures in rational relationships to nature. In spite of early training under obscure teachers, Giotto—dead for sixty-four years when Masaccio was born in 1401—was in effect Masaccio's true master, by example. After Masaccio's death at the age of only twenty-seven, his frescoes in the Brancacci Chapel in Florence (**276** and **278**) became the school for painters that Giotto's frescoes had been until then.

In the incredible century that followed, Italy produced artists with the prodigality with which we produce automobile mechanics today. Nor were they an army of hacks. In variety, vigor, invention, and profundity they topped one another's achievements, exploring every aspect of life and thought in search of the final synthesis of spiritual and intellectual perfections, whose ultimate achievement it never occurred to anyone to doubt. (We have seen Leonardo da Vinci as a towering figure of this century.)

The synthesis began to crystallize in the statuesque calm and abstract volumes of the art of Piero della Francesca; his Arezzo frescoes are the great monument of the Italian Renaissance as it neared its climax. Without being eccentric, Piero was the most individual colorist among fresco painters. It is difficult to describe any color in words, but we can try: smoky purples or lavender grays, dusty reds, pungent greens, and soft ivories dominate Piero's typical color schemes. Among these mutations, the occasional unmodified pinks and blues take on new clarity and purity.

No list of the great frescoes of the Renaissance can omit Raphael's in the Vatican's Stanza della Segnatura, of which the best known is *The School of Athens* (**280**). Raphael shares membership with Leonardo, Michelangelo, and Titian as the quartet of painters representing the moment of equilibrium called the High Renaissance, from about 1495 to about 1520, when the earlier Renaissance attained the final harmony for which it yearned. Of the four painters, Raphael comes closest to being the ideal example of the period's combinations of strength with grace, realism with idealism, and scientific principles with esthetic invention. His position in the history of art has remained unassailable for nearly five hundred years while other reputations have fluctuated, and it is customary to admire his frescoes in the Stanza della Segnatura without reservation. It is heresy, then, to suggest here that possibly these frescoes substitute grace for dignity, sweetness for elevation of spirit, facility for invention, and technical assurance for technical vigor. Perhaps it is just as well, yielding to the force of superior numbers among art historians, to let Raphael's citation as the perfect painter of the High Renaissance stand without further discussion. But even the most reverent historians concede that Raphael's harmonious synthesis is put to a severe test by the thundering frescoes that were being painted at the same time nearby in the Sistine Chapel, where Michelangelo's less optimistic message is to the effect that man in his imperfection is too vulnerable to achieve the benign harmony Raphael proclaims.

A summary of the dates for the frescoes we have been discussing might be convenient here:

275. Giotto. *Lamentation*. 1305–6. Fresco. Arena Chapel, Padua.

276. Masaccio. *Tribute Money*. About 1425. Fresco. Brancacci Chapel, Santa Maria del Carmine, Florence.

277. Giotto. Figures of Virgin and Christ from the *Lamentation*.

279. Giotto. Frescoes. 1305–6. Arena (Scrovegni) Chapel, Padua, Italy.

278. Detail from *Tribute Money*.

280. Raphael. *The School of Athens*. 1510–11. Fresco. Stanza della Segnatura, Vatican, Rome.

Giotto's Arena Chapel, about 1305–6.
Masaccio's Brancacci Chapel, about 1425.
Piero's Arezzo frescoes, 1453–54.
Raphael's Stanza della Segnatura, 1509–1511.
Michelangelo's Sistine Chapel ceiling, 1508–1512.

It is time now to distinguish between true fresco and what is sometimes called, quite justly, false fresco. The proper term is *fresco secco*, which means dry fresco. The Italian words are always used instead of their English equivalent, although, contrarily, in this country "true fresco" is generally used instead of the Italian designation for that technique, *buon fresco* or, less frequently, *affresco*.

Fresco secco is painted on the dried plaster wall, which is slightly roughened to accept more readily the pigment mixed with an adhesive or binder. Since *fresco secco* is bound only to the surface of the plaster instead of being incorporated *into* that surface, it is likely to chip, peel, or powder off, and is also more vulnerable to scratching and rubbing. It can never achieve true fresco's luminosity nor its final degree of architectural integration, the "sense of wall." It can be beautiful in its delicate tonalities, and even its disadvantage is sometimes attractive: in very old *fresco secco* that has managed to survive, the powdering of the surface gives a soft, grainy texture that has its own charm.

Secco is frequently used to touch up true fresco. A highlight may be added here, or an awkward plaster joint covered there, or a mistake corrected the easy way instead of by chipping out and beginning again. But the dedicated true fresco painter avoids retouching on several scores: the dry additions have a different character from the surrounding true fresco areas and are likely to look like what they are, afterthoughts or corrections; these additions are likely to prove temporary; and most important of all, the true fresco painter is so conscious of the integrity of his technique and the grandeur of its tradition that, all other considerations aside, he regards recourse to *fresco secco* as an unworthy subterfuge.

Fresco (whether *buon* or *secco*) continued to be an important technique into the eighteenth century, but tended to give way to oil as the creative centers shifted from Italy to the North, where damp climates and radical changes of temperature were kinder to canvas than to plaster walls. There was a significant revival in Mexico in the 1920's, as we will see in another chapter, but we must conclude our comments here with glances at pre-Renaissance frescoes from three eras—prehistoric, classical antiquity, and medieval, plus an example from the Orient.

The oldest known paintings in the world are frescoes of a kind that can be called "true." These are the cave paintings found in France and Spain (**281**), where color was incorporated with the rock wall, without so much as an intervening skin of plaster, by rubbing the pigment into the rock. Where the natural rock is either convex or concave in a form suggesting an animal's body or a portion of it, the

281. Cave painting. *Bison.* About 15,000–10,000 B.C. Lascaux (Dordogne), France.

cave artist frequently capitalized on this form as a beginning and adapted his drawing to its contours—which is one explanation for the wide variations in different photographs of the same cave painting. The natural relief is obliterated by the photographer's carefully equalized light, and shifting perspective varies the shape of the drawing in shots taken from different angles.

The pigments—browns, yellows, blacks, rusty reds—are natural mineral oxides that in some cases were probably the same as those that supplied earth pigments up until our own time. In some instances the original colors seem to have been intensified by the evaporation of moisture containing minute quantities of lime, which have imbedded the pigment within a crystalline film similar to the surface of true fresco. In other instances, unhappily, a different mineral content has obscured paintings under an opaque coating.

The tribal artists who decorated the walls of the ritual cave of Lascaux near Montignac in southern France must be included among the great painters of all time. Aside from their fascinating evocation of a life infinitely removed from ours—one they manage to bring overwhelmingly close when you are in their presence—these are great paintings. They would be great paintings if they had been done yesterday.

They swarm over the walls of the cave, magnificently alive. How passionately the artist has observed animals! He sums up the idea of "bison" in the most acute and economical way: the powerful forequarters, the small, taut hindquarters, the contrasting bony delicacy of hoofs and shins, the brutishness of the head, the menacing curve of the horns.

If there is any question as to whether or not the prehistoric artist who executed this expressive masterpiece was a creative painter in the most demanding definition of that term, his bisons need only be compared with a painting of a bull done in mid-thirteenth-century Japan during the Kamakura period, a time when technical mastery and esthetic sophistication produced corresponding master-pieces of Oriental art (282). The close stylistic resemblance across a gap of at least eleven thousand and perhaps as much as sixteen thousand years is more than a fantastic coincidence; it is accounted for by the fact that the prehistoric artist, whatever his expressive impulse and source of skill, and the Japanese artist, working within a highly developed tradition for an esthetically demanding audience, understood the essential quality of the subjects they were painting and expressed that quality by the most effective degree of selection and emphasis.

In ancient Greece and Rome, walls were often covered with rich painted decorations, generally referred to as frescoes, though it is not often possible to determine exactly what techniques were employed. The largest group of ancient wall paintings to have come down to us, many of them in good condition, are Roman, paradoxically preserved

282. Unknown Japanese painter. *One of the Ten Fast Bulls.* Kamakura Period (thirteenth century). Hanging scroll, ink and slight color on paper, 10¾ by 12⅝ inches. The Cleveland Museum of Art. Purchased by John L. Severance Fund.

283. Unknown Roman painter. *Woman Playing the Kithara.* Before A.D. 79. Fresco from villa at Boscoreale, 73½ inches square. The Metropolitan Museum of Art, New York. Rogers Fund, 1903.

284. Early Byzantine. *Empress Theodora and Attendants.* About A.D. 547. Mosaic. San Vitale, Ravenna.

285. Master of Pedret, early twelfth century Spanish. *Virgin and Child Enthroned.* About 1130. Fresco, height approximately 11 feet. The Metropolitan Museum of Art, New York. Cloisters Fund, 1950.

286. Unknown Russian painter. *Saint George, Bishop.* Late sixteenth century. Tempera on wood, 43½ by 17 inches. Elvehjem Museum of Art, the University of Wisconsin, Madison. Gift of Joseph E. Davies.

by the cataclysmic eruption of Vesuvius in A.D. 79 that buried Pompeii and Herculaneum under volcanic ash. Paintings on any walls that withstood the disaster were safe from an even more destructive force—changes in fashionable taste.

As Pompeii and Herculaneum were provincial cities, it is unlikely that the very best Roman painters bothered to work so far from the capital. But even if that is so, we can deduce from the work of these painters of second rank the general character of classical painting elsewhere. *Woman Playing the Kithara* (283, p. 230), showing a seated woman holding a musical instrument while her daughter or handmaiden peers from behind the chair, is one of a series from a villa at Boscoreale, outside Pompeii. It differs from the Italian Renaissance frescoes we have seen in the intimacy and informality of its subject, as well as in its size, which is relatively small.

The woman and child shown here are probably portraits; certainly they are not identifiable as mythological or historical characters, and the painter has tried with some success to enliven and individualize them by casual poses. As portraits they fall somewhere between the classical formula for the ideal head and the subjects' own features. The formula calls for an oval face, a small, full mouth, a straight, high-bridged nose, a rounded chin, and perfect regularity of features. Here the variations from formula are slight, but the personality of the subject, whoever she was, is tantalizingly suggested. By current standards the image is somewhat ponderous and, accepting the probability of its being a portrait, not acutely individualized. But there is no denying the person's matronly force and dignity, the paramount virtues of a Roman wife prosperous enough to have a handsomely decorated villa at Boscoreale.

Certain formulas serve their purposes so effectively that they are not dulled by endless repetition. *Virgin and Child Enthroned* (285), an early twelfth-century fresco by an artist known as the Master of Pedret, follows one such formula. Originally it covered the semidome of the central apse of the Catalan Church of San Juan de Trédos; at present it is reassembled on a panel in the Metropolitan Museum, but thanks to modern technicians it could be reassembled at any time on a reconstruction of the original apse. If we imagine it in the church, with the Virgin—more than 10 feet in height—surmounting the vista of the nave, we may have some idea of the impressiveness of this representation of the Queen of Heaven.

Stylistically, this example is not much different from hundreds of other representations of the Madonna, Child, saints, and angels in frescoes, mosaics, altarpieces, panel paintings, and manuscript illuminations of the early Middle Ages. The conventionalized face with the black-rimmed, staring eyes, the angular patterning of the robes, the crisp linear contours and strong outlines everywhere, were repeated with local variations from generation to generation from the sixth century into the twelfth, all the way from Byzantium to England.

Considering that the ancient world had left to the early Middle Ages a legacy of realistic painting that could easily have been adapted to Christian subjects (and which we have seen exemplified in *Woman Playing the Kithara*), where did this very unrealistic style come from? It is not enough to say that in isolated parts of the early medieval world artists had no classical models to follow, or even that during the first centuries of confusion after the fall of Rome the arts declined. Both explanations can be supported to some extent, but this style flourished most vigorously in Byzantium, the greatest seat of money, power, and art at the time.

We owe the perpetuation of the stylistic formula in large part to a drastic theological schism, the famous Iconoclastic Controversy of the eighth and ninth centuries inspired by the Bible's specific injunction against the making of images in the Second Commandment: "Thou shalt not make unto thee any graven image, or any likeness of any thing that is in heaven above, or that is in the earth beneath, or that is in the water under the earth" (Exodus 20:4). The body of ecclesiastics called the iconoclasts—literally, "image-breakers"—not only forbade the making of images, either painted or sculptured, but destroyed existing ones, including scraping mosaics off the walls.

In 787 the Empress Irene convened an ecumenical council at Nicaea, in which it was declared that images were acceptable for veneration (as opposed to idolatrous worship) and were ordered restored to churches. But in the Eastern branch of the Church the iconoclasts remained stubborn for another century, and when they finally yielded they did so with a strong feeling of unease. Images were again tolerated, but the unease was assuaged if the images were unrealistic. The flat, bodiless, almost diagrammatic style of the Byzantine icon (286), which holds in the Eastern branches of the Church to this day, was a compromise with realism that, in addition, carried with it an otherworldly air that made it appropriate for holy subjects even in places where there was no objection to imagery.

Byzantine style reached its most opulent expression in mosaics. The technique of decorating walls or floors with patterns and pictures made from thousands of small pieces of colored marble was inherited from pagan antiquity. With the addition of gold and opaque glass "tesserae" of brighter colors (a tessera is any one of the small pieces used in mosaic work), the Byzantine mosaic became the most opulent form of wall decoration ever known in Europe and the Near East. The flat, severely outlined forms inherent in the limitations of picturemaking in mosaic were perfectly compatible with Byzantine conventionalizations. The Emperor Justinian took advantage of the hieratic grandeur of a style usually devoted to religious subjects to portray himself (with a halo) and his Empress Theodora in a pair of famous mosaics in the Church of San Vitale in Ravenna,

287. Head from *Emporess Theodora and Attendants.*

288. Head from *Virgin and Child Enthroned.*

Byzantium's Italian stronghold. The empress with her attendants (**284**, p. 230) could almost be the Queen of Heaven herself surrounded by her court of saints. If we compare the head of Theodora (**287**), done about the year 547, with that of the Virgin in the Catalan fresco (**288**) done nearly six centuries later, we see the continuation of a style from regal Byzantium to an obscure church in the Pyrenees. (The Master of Pedret had probably never seen a large mosaic, and mosaic workers in any case would not have been available in that part of the world to decorate the church; but in many churches fresco was used as a substitute for mosaic, which was extremely expensive even when available.)

It was natural that the Byzantine style, ubiquitous in one variation or another throughout the early medieval world, should make its most significant compromise with the realism of antiquity in Italy, where Roman art was still a visible influence even when in ruins. A thirteenth-century *Enthroned Madonna and Child* (**289**) now in the National Gallery in Washington is a fine example of the beautiful hybrids bred by the union of East and West, Byzantium and classical Rome. At first glance, the strongest inheritance is Byzantine, with the rich color and liberal use of gold. But the faces of the Virgin and Child are softly modeled—so much so that they rather break away from the rest of the picture—and the golden lights on the Virgin's robe, for all their Byzantine crispness, recall the naturalistic modeling of Hellenistic drapery.

At this point we are not far from Giotto's revolution. The rebirth of realism in Italian painting was anticipated by such immediate predecessors of Giotto as the painter Cimabue, but for our purposes we may compare the head of the Virgin by the Master of Pedret (**288**) with the one by Giotto we saw some pages back (**277**). The earlier painter accepts the mystery on faith and cuts directly through to it without question; hence he is satisfied with a conventionalized effigy not much different from hundreds of others. If the divine mystery is there without question, then an accepted symbol of it is sufficient as an object for our contemplation. But almost two centuries separate these two representations of the Virgin, and Giotto belonged to a time and an intellectual circle for which blind faith was no longer enough. It was necessary for him to search for the divine, which we can only sense, by way of the world, which we know. By bringing the Queen of Heaven down to earth and subjecting her to the agony of human grief, Giotto ennobled the human condition and made humanity worthy of divine compassion.

In China and India the tradition of wall painting stretches back until it is lost in hypothetical origins. We must include one example—from China—as a token representative of a vast, still inadequately studied field. Our knowledge of existing, ancient Oriental frescoes is often limited by their inaccessibility; through neglect or vandalism many have been lost, and many are still disappearing.

289. Byzantine school. *Enthroned Madonna and Child.* Thirteenth century. Tempera on wood, 51⅝ by 30¼ inches. National Gallery of Art, Washington, D.C. Gift of Mrs. Otto Kahn, 1940.

Some of the earliest records of wall paintings in China tell that they were done on silk and then stretched on the walls, or hung there like tapestries. Wall painting could have originated as a substitute for these fragile and expensive decorations, just as fresco in the West was often a substitute for preferred but expensive mosaics.

Around the fourth century, when Buddhism became a powerful force in China, there was a strong development of mural decoration. Not only the walls but the ceilings of temples were completely covered with paintings of religious subjects in a conventionalized style based on flowing line and monumental, formalized silhouettes. Our example, which by coincidence happens to have been painted at about the same time as the Arena Chapel, is in *fresco secco* on a base of mud and sand, miraculously removed in sections from an ancient temple wall in Shansi Province and reassembled in the Metropolitan Museum (290). A detail of a head, if compared with the two we have just seen, is a miniature visual essay on comparative esthetics. The anonymous Chinese painter's absolute control of the brush line in describing forms with maximum economy and maximum sophistication is the inheritance of generation upon generation of artists who refined a tradition of decorative pictorial narration to the point of insuperable formal elegance. The play of color across this great wall, while softened by time and the slight powdering of the surface, gives us a hint of the full richness of a temple interior covered with a thousand multiplications and variations of the colors and rhythms of this fragment.

· · ·

290. Unknown Chinese painter, Yuan Dynasty (1200–1368). *Buddhist Assembly* (detail of a head, opposite). Wall painting, watercolor tempera on mud and sand. The Metropolitan Museum of Art, New York. Gift of Arthur M. Sackler, 1965.

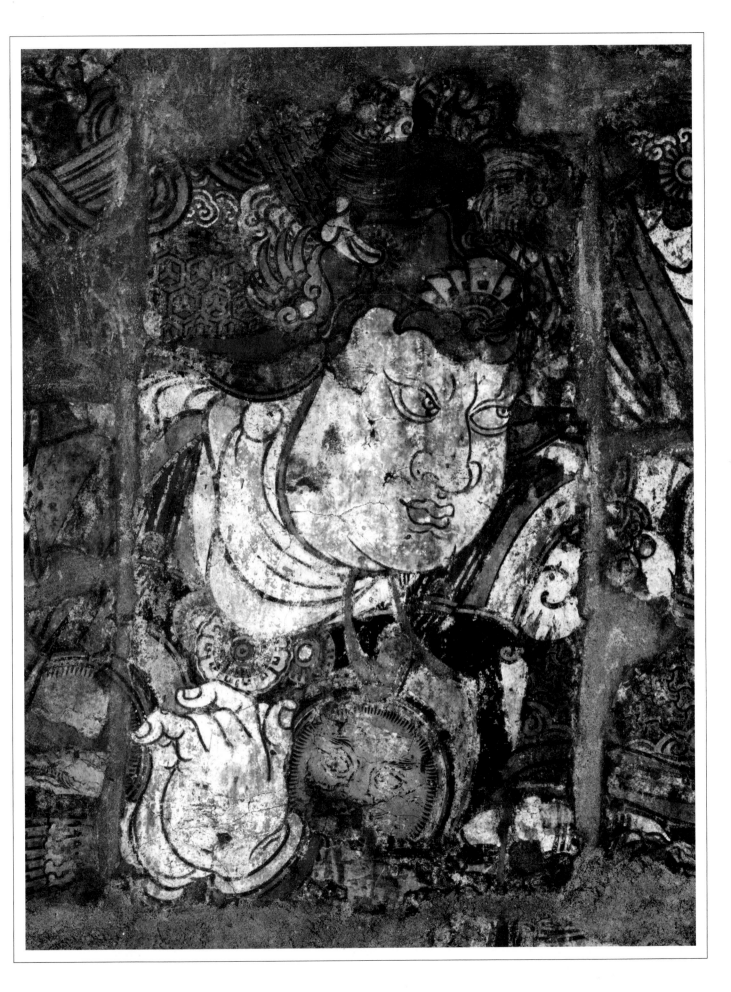

We said that the fresco from Shansi Province was "miraculously" removed. The word is hardly too strong. Modern techniques account for the presence of frescoes that are now found in museums all the way across the world from the walls on which they were originally painted. James J. Rorimer, who was director of the Metropolitan Museum at the time the Chinese fresco was reassembled there, supplied the following description of the process:

> The process of removing frescoes from old walls begins with the cleaning of the surface of the fresco; then canvas or some other cloth is applied to the surface with a paste that binds the fresco more closely to it than to the wall. The canvas and fresco are then cut and the fresco loosened from the wall with a knife or spatula and rolled [291]. A layer of canvas is attached to the back of the fresco, and the protecting canvas on the front is removed with a solvent which affects neither the fresco nor the paste of the lining canvas. The canvas with the fresco on the front is then ready for mounting in one of various ways, often being kept on a stretcher as in the case of a painting on canvas.

If fresco imposes a broad, vigorous, unhesitating execution, tempera is demanding in another way: it requires extreme precision, absolute control in minutiae, and patience. It is slow. It does not allow for suggestion; each fractional bit of the area of a large painting must be covered as meticulously as that of a small one. But tempera rewards the artist with its combination of adaptability to grand themes and of tolerance for statements of secondary importance. Most of the greatest pictures of the early Renaissance, aside from frescoes, were painted in pure egg tempera, but this is also, of all the periods of painting, the one in which minor masters appear to best advantage. Even the painter who did not have a great deal to say was likely to say his little bit with order and clarity. Even the painter with nothing to say, if he managed to become a painter at all, was able to turn out pictures that offer at least the satisfaction inherent in a well-made object.

To appreciate egg tempera painting as a technique, we must abandon the picture of an artist standing before his easel at work on a canvas, improvising as he paints, covering large areas rapidly with a stout brush, manipulating pigment as he pleases, smoothing it, blending it with other colors, applying it thickly or thinly as seems best. We must visualize instead a painter at a workbench applying color in small, thin strokes that dry immediately. And he is at work not on a canvas but on a panel whose preparation in itself demands conscientious craftsmanship. When he was an apprentice, the artist learned to prepare panels in the master's studio. As he proceeded in his training, he was allowed to work on more and more important stages of the many through which an egg tempera painting progresses on its way to completion. As he grew more proficient, he was allowed to paint some of the preliminary passages or even to execute some of the minor figures in the master's commissions. He would eventually paint entire pictures

291. Technician removing fresco from wall of the church of Santa Maria, early twelfth century, Tahull (Lérida), Spain.

under the master's instruction, and by these degrees would attain recognized status as a full-fledged painter, a member of the guild with his own studio in which he trained the next generation of painter-apprentices.

Several stages of the production of a large tempera panel painting are revealed in the *Madonna Enthroned Between Saints Peter and Leonard* (**292**), executed about the third quarter of the thirteenth century by a painter of the Tuscan School. (A very conservative painter, his work sticks to established traditional formulas and gives no hint of changes in the air that would produce Giotto's Arena Chapel in 1305.) In its present condition the panel is an exceptional examination piece in the craft of egg tempera technique from the very beginning—the preparation of the wooden panel—to the completed painting. The original panel is exposed in the lower part of the area; elsewhere there are bits of the completed painting in their original condition. Between these preparatory and final stages all the intermediate ones can be seen.

When it came into the possession of the museum where it is now exhibited, the panel had experienced the normal history of many very old paintings that have suffered from alternating periods of neglect and attention. Parts of it had disappeared and been restored with varying degrees of skill from time to time. Other parts had been repainted simply to freshen them. Modern laboratory methods, including X-rays and chemical analysis, can determine with a good degree of accuracy the difference in age between the original and the restored portions of such a panel. In this case the technicians removed, fragment by fragment, every bit of matter thought to have been added to the original. Film by film, the layers of varnish and dirt were cleaned away until what remained of the original object was exposed.

Normally the next step would have been an accurate rebuilding of the lost portions and a scholarly and technically accurate restoration of the surface, a process that in skillful hands can virtually recreate the original of a formula picture like this one from the clues remaining. In this case, however, the panel has been left unrestored as a study piece.

The detail illustrated here (**293**) shows the area below the hem of Saint Leonard's gown. The shred of linen visible on the right is a bit of the piece originally glued directly onto the wooden panel, not only to strengthen it but also to serve as a base for a layer of gesso, upon which the painting is done. Gesso is an extremely fine-textured, brilliant white substance, like plaster but finer and bound by glue instead of lime. It would be possible to gesso a wall instead of plastering it—possible but not practical. Gesso is not easy to prepare in large quantities and dries too fast for true fresco technique. Its virtue is that it gives the painter a wonderfully smooth, pure white panel upon which he can do work of great delicacy intended for the kind of close-range examination not ordinarily given to large surfaces of wall decoration.

Gesso is applied over the linen-covered wooden panel in several layers, which are allowed to dry between coats. It is brushed on like paint while in a warm, fluid condition. Since one of the ingredients is gelatin, it hardens upon cooling. When a thickness of one-eighth of an inch or so has been built up, the gesso is allowed to harden thoroughly, and is then sanded. The resultant surface is comparable to the smoothest eggshell and is a joy to paint on. It accepts paint readily but has just enough tooth to act as a slight brake that helps the painter control his brush.

If a tempera painting is to include a background or other passages of gold, as in *Madonna Enthroned Between Saints Peter and Leonard,* or to be painted on a panel entirely covered with gold, as in our example, a Sienese *Virgin and Child* (**295**, p. 242), the gilding is the next step once the gesso has been sanded to its perfect surface. Wherever gold is to be applied, the gesso is lightly covered with gilder's clay, which serves as an adhesive for the gold leaf and, more importantly, as a base for the necessary burnishing. Gilder's clay is brick red in color—handsome in itself. Applied like thin paint and built up in several filmy layers, it is allowed to dry, is burnished to a smooth gloss, and then dampened a bit. While damp, it is ready to receive the gold.

Gold leaf is the pure metal beaten into uniform tissue-thin leaves that, touched with the finger, disintegrate into fine powder. But a skillful gilder, using a wide, flat, brushlike instrument called a gilder's tip, can pick up sheets as large as 3 inches square. The gold leaf is attracted to the hairs of

293. Damaged area of *Madonna Enthroned Between Saints Peter and Leonard.*

the gilder's tip, but is more strongly attracted to the dampened surface of the red clay when brought close to it. If the craftsman is adept enough or lucky enough, the leaf goes on in one piece; more often, cracks or holes appear in it, one reason why several applications are necessary to get a solid coverage. Each layer is burnished with a smoothly polished agate tool before the next is applied.

With time the layer of gold partially evanesces and the reddish tint of the gilder's clay shows through. It is particularly apparent in the area around the aureole of the Virgin in our anonymous Sienese *Virgin and Child.* Fortunately the rich color of the clay is compatible with gold, and these reddish areas, which show through the surface of virtually all unrestored gilded panels as old as the ones we are seeing here, have a handsomeness of their own.

With the leaf laid on and burnished to a satisfactory sheen, the panel is ready for whatever tooling it is to receive in halos, borders, or other areas. A detail (**294**) from the border of this very ornamental little picture shows that the tooled pattern is made up by recombinations of a few elements. The tooling, or punching, is done with small instruments, frequently carved from bone, a few inches long and comparable in other dimensions to knitting needles. One end has a pattern carved into it; it is rested on the surface of the gilded gesso and the other end is given a firm tap. Inexpertly delivered, this blow may chip the gesso, a disaster. Our detail shows that, at most, half a dozen simple shapes have been combined to create a variety of patterns. Identifiable are a hollow circle repeated seven times to make the center and the six petals of the flower-like figure running along the central band, a half-circle and two arcs that are combined to make the lacy border along the inner edge, a simple blunt punch that produces a miniature crater, and perhaps one or two others. The tooling can, of course, be done after the painting is completed, but is usually done first because less is lost if the panel cracks.

Except for occasional minor details, egg tempera paintings are not improvised on the panels. Before the panel is touched by paint, a drawing at full scale is completed, finished in all its outlines, and modeled in its more important areas. To transfer the outlines to the panel, the usual practice is to scratch them lightly into the gesso surface. These scratched outlines generally become filled with paint, but you can see them now and then in a great many paintings if you look for them in a favorable light. They are more than usually apparent in the robe of the Virgin in this work by an unknown artist, which is one of several reasons we have chosen it for illustration instead of a more important painting.

Once the outlines have been scratched in, it is at last time to apply color. Egg tempera paint is composed of approximately equal parts of powdered pigment, yolk of egg, and water. White of egg is also used in some formulas. When used in the correct amount, egg is a perfect binder. If there is too little of it, however, the pigment will powder off when it dries. If there is too much, the paint is gummy and hard to work with and has an unpleasant sticky-looking

294. Indented patterns on gesso and gilt panel.

295. Sienese artist, late fourteenth century. *Virgin and Child*, left panel of a diptych *Virgin and Child with St. Jerome*. Tempera on wood, height 11¾ inches. Philadelphia Museum of Art, John G. Johnson Collection.

296. Domenico Ghirlandaio. *Francesco Sassetti and His Son Teodoro.* 1472. Tempera on wood, 29½ by 20½ inches. The Metropolitan Museum of Art, New York. The Jules S. Bache Collection, 1949.

gloss when dry. An experienced tempera painter can tell when the mixture is right by stirring it with his brush. The paint is mixed in very small quantities, a few thimblefuls at a time, since not much is required to cover a surface and it tends to thicken in the dish.

Using small, pointed brushes, the artist applies the paint stroke by stroke, not in washes or broad areas, and often in hairlines. The paint dries instantly, at least as far as workability is concerned. The only way to apply a solid area of color is stroke by stroke until hundreds of crisscrossings produce a uniform flatness.

For some reason the flat blue of the Virgin's robe has not been modeled, a curious circumstance in a picture so wonderfully complete in other passages, but a convenient omission for our purposes here. The scratched-in guidelines that were to have served as guides in modeling the robe in tones lighter and darker than the local color can be seen in our reproduction.

Modeling, like flat color areas, must be built up little stroke by little stroke until the form emerges. But difficulties increase at this point. Whereas the solid tone can be built up by crisscrossing lines in any direction, the modeling must "follow the form." Dürer's famous drawing, *Hands of an Apostle* (**298**), explains this phrase. The hands are modeled entirely in the lines; without recourse to flowing, blending, or smudging, they describe the complicated form of hands, along with all the ins and outs of secondary forms (veins, tendons, creases, the wrinkled skin over knuckles), by appearing, as it were, to lie upon the forms they describe. The result is a double definition: once in terms of light and shadow, as the camera records form; and once in terms that can be called diagrammatic, with each line describing the surface it lies on. It is a powerful way of defining form, but a technically demanding one. A misplaced line would be immediately disfiguring, with the appearance of a piece of wire or string or a hair projecting from the form, instead of a diagrammatic line following it.

A painter may "follow the form" by cross-hatching as Dürer does (especially noticeable in the cuffs), or by using lines in only one direction, as Ghirlandaio does in the head of a little boy (**297**) reproduced here at close to full size from the double portrait *Francesco Sassetti and His Son Teodoro* (**296**, p. 243). The modeling is rather shallow; the forms are treated more like low sculptural relief in color than three-dimensional forms existing in full depth surrounded by air. The red cap especially is very lightly modeled, and the delightful design of curling hair is conceived as much as a linear pattern as a three-dimensional form, so that it falls somewhere between the two. In addition to modeling the forms in only one direction, Ghirlandaio has reduced them to their simplest bases, in contrast to the method Dürer used in his drawing of the hands, in which he sought out intricacies and revealed them in linear systems that constantly shift direction with the subtlest change in the hands' multiple contours.

The greenish cast so frequent in flesh passages painted in tempera comes from the base color showing through the superimposed modeling. The tempera formula for painting

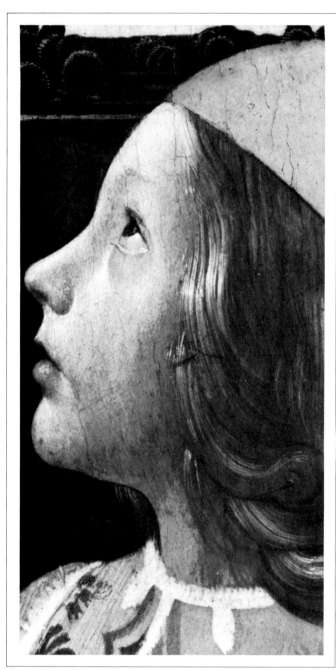

297. Head of a boy from *Francesco Sassetti and His Son Teodoro.*

flesh tones is an exception to the rule that the entire area of a color is first covered with a flat base tone of the object's local color (as we have seen in the blue robe of the Virgin with its unmodeled ultramarine area). Tempera flesh tints modeled over a pink or cream base tone appear chalky and lifeless. Inasmuch as the dominant color in flesh tones is red, its complement, green, is used as the base tone because it has a maximum vibration in opposition to red. Minute bits of the green base showing through the flesh-colored modeling bring the passage to life. The green tone was frequently left showing fairly obviously along the "shadow edge" where the light tones give way to darker ones, but seldom to the extent evident in very old temperas. Over the centuries the top film of paint tends to evanesce or become transparent; in addition, very few old temperas have escaped varnishing, which also increases transparency. Finally, any cleaning that is carried a microscopic fraction of an inch too deep will remove some of the top film, so that in many old tempera paintings the flesh tones have taken on an unhealthy greenish pallor.

The Sienese *Virgin and Child* to which we have given so much attention is a very pure example of tempera

298. Albrecht Dürer. *Hands of an Apostle.* 1508. Brush, heightened with white, on blue-grounded paper. Albertina, Vienna.

299. Sienese artist, late fourteenth century. *Virgin and Child with St. Jerome,* diptych. Tempera on wood, height 11¾ inches. Philadelphia Museum of Art. John G. Johnson Collection.

technique and has the advantage of an unfinished section for elucidation, plus the great advantage of being small enough to reproduce without drastic reduction. It is sometimes attributed to Tommaso da Modena, himself very obscure if not quite anonymous. But why choose it instead of an example by a great master—Fra Angelico, for instance, whose temperas are of exquisite purity technically and are invested, as well, with deep spirituality? The very fact that our choice could not in any way be called a great painting is one reason for its choice here. Having already said that it was painted at a time and in a medium that allowed minor masters to appear to best advantage, we will extend that point to argue that there have been times in the history of art when technique in itself, and technique alone, can become a form of expression for an artist who has nothing particularly original to say.

In the light of this preamble, let us look again at this little *Virgin and Child*. It is the left half of a diptych (**299**) whose two parts are hinged to close together face to face like the pages of a book. Being a little less than 1 foot high, it must have been a portable shrine painted for some wealthy and devout person to carry with him on his travels, with his patron saint, Jerome, occupying the right half.

In neither of these figures—and certainly not in that of the Child, which is only a pretty manikin—has the artist exercised any particular originality, force, or emotional depth of conception. These are honest, respectably executed figures, invested with whatever qualities are appropriate to the Virgin and Saint Jerome, but they appeal more by ready-made associations than by any special interpretation on the part of the artist. The Virgin bends over the Child in an attitude that is adequately tender but entirely within the formula of countless other Virgins painted by Italian contemporaries. The Child is thoroughly disappointing if we try to find anything inherently more profound than a doll-like prettiness. The little spindles of bright-colored thread are an engaging detail relating the Virgin to her household activities. Saint Jerome's lion, whose participation in such pictures is obligatory, is squeezed into a corner as an afterthought and resembles a tabby more than the king of beasts.

And yet the pictures are intensely expressive. They glitter with gold and precious pigments applied with an exquisite elaboration that becomes devotionally expressive in itself. The picture of the Virgin is as much a jewel as a painting; the craft of the jeweler, in fact, overlaps the craft of the painter in such a work. The richly tooled border with its multitude of indentations that catch the light is repeated in the halos, and around the Virgin's halo the aureole flames gently where the surface of the gold has been indented in a series of radiating lines. The gown beneath the robe is a sumptuous brocade, first modeled and painted, then scratched through to the gold in a pattern that, in turn, is tooled with minute indentations which not only increase its richness but, being delicate as threads, give the gold a brocade-like texture and differentiate it from the flat gold of the background. Otherwise it might appear that the background was showing through holes cut in a pasteboard figure. The Child's light blue robe is similarly patterned, and in addition it is modeled over his thigh and along his back with tiny scratches, which once again reveal the gold background in strokes like those of a pen or fine-tipped brush, so that the robe takes form and turns golden simultaneously.

The picture is shot through with gold in hundreds of tiny details. Gold is conspicuous along the ornamental borders of the Virgin's robe, and sparkles less obviously in the band of mosaic behind her. It shines in small details such as the stripes on the cushion upon which the Virgin is seated and on the heads of the tassels. A gold filament runs through her veil; there is a highlight of gold on the bobbin of white thread. All this rich detail is more than ornamental; it becomes devotional in character. In its psychological effect—its expressive quality—it is remindful of shrines covered with offerings of jewels, flowers, and precious trinkets from grateful worshippers.

Tempera, for all its special beauties, is a technique that makes no concessions in certain quarters where the painter could otherwise extend his range of expression. Textures can be simulated only within a narrow range. The way a robe falls—in delicate, crisp folds or in large, ample ones—may indicate that it is supposed to be of a light material like thin silk or a heavy one like thick wool, but tempera offers no really satisfactory way to simulate the difference between the sheen of silk and the nappy look of wool. While wonderfully adaptable to the description of form, tempera falls short when it comes to reproducing the quality of the light that falls on those forms, light caught and reflected in different ways by different surfaces. Flesh passages in tempera, no matter how skillfully executed, never quite take on the quality of flesh, but remain some harder, sharper substance tinted approximately the color of flesh. Fur (difficult to represent in any technique) is impossible in tempera. Individual hairs may be defined neatly, but the soft mass cannot be represented in a technique where the choice is between crisp line and mushy compromise. For instance, the lining of the robe worn by our Sienese Saint Jerome, showing at the collar and inside the sleeves, is recognizable as fur, but as for its texture, nobody is likely to grant the artist credit for more than a good try.

Tempera is an art of clearly defined edges; objects can neither fade into shadow nor loom from shadow into bright light. Tempera colors are most effective in the upper range; dark colors tend to grow heavy and turgid. And tempera is essentially an art of small scale. The large altarpieces painted in the fifteenth century may seem to refute this statement, but a large tempera painting is simply an accumulation of close-range material assembled upon a large surface, a large area of close-range painting. Dash, sweep, and free movement over large areas intended to make their effect from a distance are foreign to tempera's nature. Finally, the paint film is uniform over the surface of the gesso; the paint cannot be piled up dramatically to emphasize one passage, nor thinned out to throw another passage into the background.

For all these reasons, tempera does not appeal to many

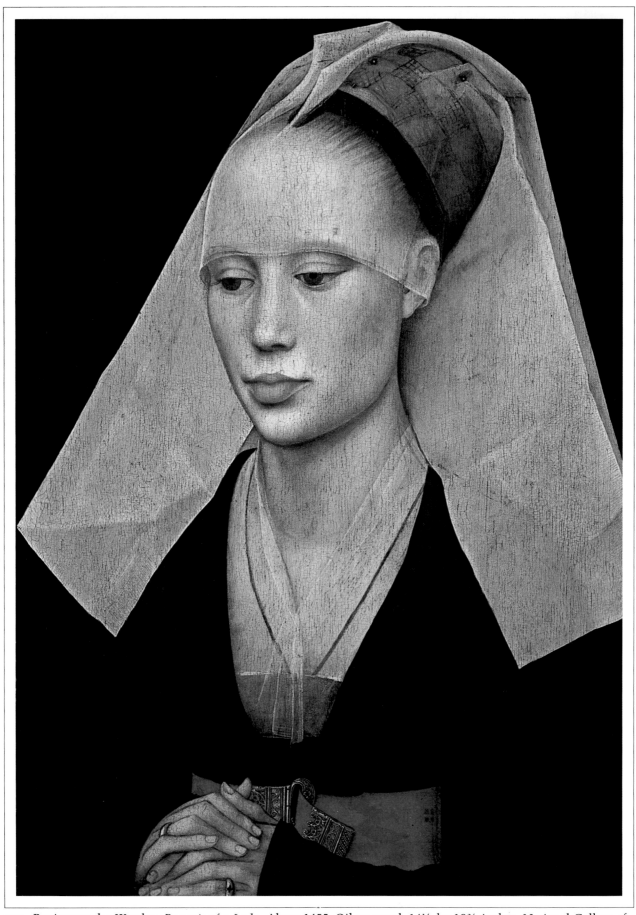

300. Rogier van der Weyden. *Portrait of a Lady.* About 1455. Oil on wood, 14½ by 10¾ inches. National Gallery of Art, Washington, D.C. Andrew Mellon Collection.

modern artists as a creative technique, no matter how much they may admire temperas of the past. Modern art usually demands the full value range from black to white and the full color range from the most brilliant primary colors (red, blue, and yellow) to sonorous secondary and tertiary mixtures. More often than not, the modern artist also wants to enhance the visual excitement of color and form by an agitated surface where uneven paint textures remain on record as witnesses to the swift passage of a brush in the hands of a skilled manipulator. Even when modern paintings are made up of flat colors held within sharply defined boundaries and within tempera's limited color range, tempera has the disadvantage of being a laborious technique outmoded by the bright, fast-drying mediums now synthesized chemically.

The most conspicuous exception to this rule among contemporary artists is Andrew Wyeth, who paints contemporary subjects realistically in the purest tradition of early Renaissance tempera technique as set down about the year 1390 by an artist named Cennino Cennini in a handbook of practical advice, *Il Libro dell'Arte.* At first glance, Wyeth's *Groundhog Day* (**301**) seems to deny what we have just been saying about tempera's limitations. Actually, it circumvents those limitations by making the most of tempera's special aptitudes.

First of all, Wyeth has painted a gentle flow of light across the landscape, into the quiet room, and across the objects on the table, apparently in direct contradiction to our having said that "tempera falls short when it comes to reproducing the quality of the light that falls on those forms." Light, indeed, is present in this tempera painting, is even its theme. According to an old tradition, the groundhog comes out of hibernation on Groundhog Day, February 2, and if he sees his own shadow, goes back to his hole for six more weeks of winter weather. The quality of the light in Wyeth's *Groundhog Day* is not only adaptable to tempera; it seems almost to demand it. The pale, cool, clear sunlight of late winter casts no strong shadows and is reflected in no brilliant highlights. In addition, Wyeth lets it spread across textures that are perfect for description within tempera's range—the cool, clean, eventless surfaces of paper, cotton or linen cloth, and lightly glazed china. Outdoors, individual twigs and blades of dry grass can be picked out by small strokes of the brush in a beautifully cohesive harmony of light, texture, and color that identifies the actuality of the scene with the magic of the technique that records and preserves it.

Tempera's characteristically dry, precise quality comes from the "lean," fast-drying nature of its binder and medium—egg and water. A "fat" medium dries slowly, allowing the painter to cover one area, brush another color into it while it is still wet, blur edges if he wishes, and to model by blending one tone into another with a soft brush instead of making the transition in a multitude of graduated tones. A fat medium can be piled thick or scrubbed thin, and can run the entire range from black to near-white without going murky in the darks or dead in the lights.

301. Andrew Wyeth. *Groundhog Day.* 1959. Egg tempera on composition board, 31 inches square. Philadelphia Museum of Art. Gift of Henry P. DuPont and Mrs. John Wintersteen.

302. Detail from *Portrait of a Lady.*

The standard fat medium is oil. Oil was used as a binder in heavy-duty paints (as for the exterior of houses) long before it was used by artists, largely because oils of sufficient purity not to discolor and deteriorate rapidly were difficult to come by. The "secret" of the earliest artists who used oil was the process of refining crude oils to a point that ensured their stability and in sufficient quantity to justify experiments.

Painters first employed oil not as an independent medium but as an adjunct to tempera. Oil's viscosity, allowing for easy manipulation of thin glazes over obdurately unmanipulatable tempera, added the advantage of easy transition between lights and darks to tempera's delightful precision, and its transparency allowed for greater depth and brilliance of colors in a wider range between black and white than tempera alone could yield. We do not know with any certainty the details of the combined oil-and-tempera technique as exemplified by its supreme master, Jan van Eyck, whose *Arnolfini Wedding Portrait* we have seen (30). But we do know that the basic formula called for thin, transparent glazes of pigmented oil over an underpainting in a leaner technique, tempera or perhaps a tempera-oil emulsion. This underpainting defined the forms in considerable detail; then the brilliant transparent oil glazes were used to "dye" the forms in the desired color, either modifying or intensifying the undercolor. Obviously there was a great deal of manipulation of the oil films, but their brilliance and variety is accounted for by the fact that they could be used essentially as dyes over forms already established.

From North European workshops, some knowledge of the new technique spread to Italy, where similar but less successful experiments had been made. Oil's attraction for the Italians is apparent if we compare the tempera portrait we have just seen, Ghirlandaio's of the boy Teodoro Sassetti, with a Northern masterpiece painted about twenty years earlier, Rogier van der Weyden's *Portrait of a Lady* (300 and 302, pp. 248 and 249). Ghirlandaio was an expert technician, but the modeling and textural variations possible in oil were beyond the range of tempera even at its most flexible. Tempera's stroke-by-stroke rendering could have *indicated* that a filmy wimple was arranged to fall across the lady's brow and ear, but could not have recreated the delicate nuances in degrees of definition and color that tell us simultaneously of the texture of flesh and the texture of the diaphanous veil that modifies the look of what we see through it. From the crisp detail of the gold buckle and the almost stylized line of the eyelids, to the imperceptibly changing gradations in the modeling of the volumes of the face; and from the rich black of the robe to the white edge of the wimple, Rogier's *Portrait of a Lady* demonstrates the range of the new technique and the limitations of the old.

Oil painting as most people think of it—a freer application of paint, with visible brush strokes and a generally more eventful surface of varying thickness—developed gradually from the early oil-and-tempera hybrid. In Venice, particularly, the taste for luxuries on the grand scale during the heyday of the hedonistic city was sympathetic to an effulgent style of painting unlike the small-scale, tightly controlled renderings we have been seeing. In the sixteenth century the development reached its apogee in the art of Titian and his followers.

Titian's *Venus and Adonis* (**303**, p. 252) is conceived to appeal first of all in sensuous terms. It relays the very feel of flesh, hair, silken gauze, jewels, foliage, and swirling balmy air, a textural symphony in which the texture of the canvas itself and the richly manipulated paint are fused with the simulation of textures in nature. The lusciousness of Titian's paint is part of the picture's expressiveness just as form and color are, and could have been achieved only in oil.

Titian's method continued to be based on underpainting that defines essential forms and overpainting in glazes to tint and develop them; but the underpainting is now brushed in freely on canvas of a natural brownish color with shadow areas defined in darker golden browns painted thinly with fluid pigment, and lights laid on in a heavy white paint that can be piled up to considerable thickness. When the underpainting was dry, the overpainting was built up in a series of glazes applied one on top of another. Orange might be produced by spreading transparent red over an opaque yellow. The resultant variety and brilliance was beyond anything that could be achieved by straight painting or by glazing in a single color over brown or gray underpainting. The uneven texture of piled-up light areas in the underpainting collects the fluid overpainting in its pits and shallows; a glaze may be applied over a large area and then rubbed off in spots. In "scumbling"—a technique in which a brush of thick, half-dry pigment is dragged over a dry, heavily textured area—the new color clings to the slightest roughness but allows the original color to show through in the shallows.

Underpainting has a function beyond its primary one as a preliminary definition of form. If executed in golden browns, it continues to affect the overall tonality of the completed picture in that direction; if in black and white, the tonality is cooler, more silvery. In either case it is always in the lights that pigment is built up and heavily worked; darks may remain hardly more than the canvas dyed by the original underpainting.

In this technique shadows have a luminosity and vibrancy, no matter how dark they are, that cannot be achieved in other ways. In contrast with these mysterious depths, forms may emerge into brilliant lights. Where Titian capitalized on the sensuous and dramatically ornamental potentials inherent in this contrast, Rembrandt found in it the means toward an opposite expression—of mystery, melancholy, and philosophical brooding. His *Aristotle with a Bust of Homer* (**304**) is typically Rembrandtian in the way forms emerge into warm, golden light from the obscurity of vibrant shadows.

The techniques of the old masters are not exactly lost, but after their abandonment it is not easy to pick them up

303. Titian. *Venus and Adonis,* with detail. Late 1560's. Oil on canvas, 42 by 52½ inches. The Metropolitan Museum of Art, New York. The Jules S. Bache Collection, 1949.

304. Rembrandt. *Artistotle with a Bust of Homer,* with detail. 1653. Oil on canvas, 56½ by 53¾ inches. The Metropolitan Museum of Art, New York. Purchased with special funds and gifts of friends of the Museum, 1963.

again even from descriptions in contemporary records. A variety of reasons account for their disappearance, including such simple ones as the appearance of oil paints ready-ground and emulsified with binder and purchasable in tubes, and commercially prepared canvases sold by the yard in art stores. Conveniences like these contributed to the demise of the idea of a painter's studio as a workshop where apprentices were trained, and to the abandonment of traditional techniques. Instead, we have the convenience of "straight" painting, where ready-made paint is applied directly from the palette to the ready-made canvas, without the preliminaries of underpainting and without any systematic glazing. Since effects of spontaneity and immediacy are typical of "straight" painting at its best, it was adaptable to the nineteenth-century Impressionist attitude of direct, unpretentious response to everyday subjects informally presented to the observer. For subject matter that was fragmentary in the first place, a style of painting dependent on suggestion rather than on detailed statement was appropriate and in harmony with a very direct attack. Manet's *Boating* (**111**) was discussed in this respect when we said that it offers us a kind of shorthand description. A detail of the woman's head (**305**) shows that the entire passage was certainly painted all at once, with the "details," if we can call them that, brushed and spotted into freshly painted areas instead of being built up over preliminary foundations by glazes, scumbling, and the like.

If we compare this head with another (**307**), a detail from Picasso's *Woman in White* (**306**), we discover that, surprisingly, the modern arch revolutionary draws more heavily from the past than Manet did. *Woman in White* is an arresting combination of paint textures involving building up in the lights of the face, glazing of a kind where the lower right section has been softened by an overscrub of white, and a free, fluid calligraphic line indicating the fall of hair—all this in connection with form as highly simplified and as sharply defined as those in a tempera painting. In a picture like *Woman in White* we can find a little bit of nearly everything: a little bit of the classical past, a little bit of the Renaissance, a little bit of impressionism, even a suggestion of Chinese painting in what we have called the calligraphic line of the hair and, of course, a great deal of Picasso and our own century.

Woman in White is not a piece of craftsmanship in anything like the sense of the earlier paintings we have seen in this chapter. It is typical, rather, of the anarchic technique of modern painting, in which individual invention takes the place of systematic procedures. Such experiments are all to the good and have tremendously enriched the painter's technical vocabulary in the twentieth century. Yet even the most experimental techniques must be based on a craftsman's knowledge of his materials. The old masters' strict observance of technical formulas in fresco, tempera, and oil was an assurance that their work would endure. Ironically, Leonardo's penchant for experiment made him an exception to the rule.

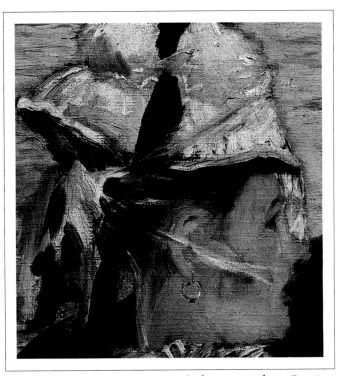

305. Edouard Manet. Head of a woman from *Boating*.

306. Pablo Picasso. *Woman in White*. 1923. Oil on canvas, 39 by 31½ inches. The Metropolitan Museum of Art, New York. Rogers Fund, 1951. Acquired from the Museum of Modern Art, Lillie P. Bliss Collection.

307. Head from *Woman in White*.

By definition water color is pigment with any one of several water-soluble gums used as a binder. It is a convenient technique, requiring no more accessory equipment than a brush, a piece of paper, and a container of water. It is also easy to clean up. For these reasons we meet water color in our first paintbox and continue to think of it as a technique for beginners. Actually, the proper manipulation of water color demands great dexterity and a sound command of the principles of picturemaking.

Water color's individuality lies in its extreme fluidity and transparency, which usually imply rapid, facile execution in pure, bright colors applied in broad washes and deft strokes with a fairly large, fully saturated brush. But water color can also be used with the precision of a pen or pencil, as John J. Audubon uses it in his combined pencil and water-color study of a family of brown rats (309)— probably the most attractive rendition ever made of these unpopular rodents, in which their not very lovely forms are caught in decorative silhouettes, and the natural growth patterns of pelt and whiskers are caught in fine individual strokes over a light water-color base tone.

A more arresting exploitation of water color's potential is made in paintings like Winslow Homer's *Sloop, Bermuda* (308). Here the preliminary drawing is limited to a few cursory pencil lines, a bare minimum indication of the picture's arrangement that leaves the forms to be described by the brush in "broad washes and deft strokes," as we have said. The effect is very "wet"; the very feel of the flowing brush is still present. The texture of the paper, which is an integral part of the effect, is revealed in two ways. In some areas, as in the sky, the pigment has been allowed to settle into the grain of the paper. (Certain heavy pigments, ultramarine blue among them, never go into complete solution, and when applied very wet they settle at the bottom of tiny puddles that form in the irregular surface of the paper.) Here and there a wavelet is defined by a relatively dry brushful of pigment dragged across the paper, leaving the grain showing as a speckling of white spots like flecks of foam or sparkles of light. Everywhere the paper is allowed to tell: in its own white brilliance beneath the transparency of the washes; in passages like the sails or the side of the sloop, where it may remain entirely unpainted or tinted with only the barest suggestion of color.

Water color thus applied has a freshness, spontaneity, and vivacity unique to itself. But the painter has no time to calculate or study, no opportunity to change or modify. Everything depends on his exact knowledge of what he is doing. He must work fast, so that passages intended to flow together may do so before the early ones dry out. The result of such speed and dexterity is a style depending on suggestion rather than complete statement, and carries with it the hazard that a painter may depend so much upon a standard bag of tricks that his water colors become sleight-of-hand performances rather than creative acts.

This was certainly not true of Homer. He thought of

308. Winslow Homer. *Sloop, Bermuda.* 1899. Water color on paper, 15 by 21½ inches. The Metropolitan Museum of Art, New York. Purchased by Amelia B. Lazarus Fund, 1910.

309. John James Audubon. *Brown Rat* (figures cropped from neutral background). 1843. Water color and pencil, full dimensions 24½ by 32⅚ inches. The Pierpont Morgan Library, New York.

his water colors as incidental to his work in oil, and it was in the oil technique, deliberately and thoughtfully developed, that his brisk water-color style was founded, as we may see if we compare *Sloop, Bermuda* with one of his most famous oils, *The Gulf Stream* (**310**), also a subject with water, a boat, and a figure. The water color is a brilliant summation, in a kind of pictorial shorthand, of principles that are fully and solidly elaborated in the oil.

The majority of painters who limit themselves to water color, no matter how technically expert they may be, fall into the trap of repetitious effects through a stock of shorthand devices. The resultant anemic productions account for the idea that the technique is without substance. To this unhappy generalization there are happy exceptions, with John Marin among the happiest. Marin is a water colorist first of all; his oils reverse the usual order and seem to be efforts to adapt to a less compatible technique what he learned about painting in water color. He used the unique advantages of water color to their fullest, forcing them to their very limits, investing the technique with a masculine force and creative originality unparalleled in its history until then.

Marin's *Boat off Deer Isle* (its rather unwieldy full title is *Maine Series No. 9: Movement—Boat off Deer Isle,* **311**) is abstract and expressionistic according to principles discussed in earlier chapters. It is not our purpose to analyze it in that way now, but to point out its identification of technique with expression. The elements we have mentioned in Homer's water color—the feel of the brush, paper, and water, the use of settling pigments, the revelation of paper texture by a dragged brush—all are present here, but with a difference. In the Homer, everything was directed toward suggesting the appearance of objects in brilliant outdoor light. In the Marin, realistic suggestion is no concern; the manipulation of water and pigment becomes a form of expression rather than a means of description. That is why it is difficult to imagine *Boat off Deer Isle* satisfactorily translated into oil, and why Marin has a claim to the title frequently awarded him as the finest and certainly the purest water colorist of them all.

Marin's water colors present the anomaly of an art combining spontaneity with a sense of complex and powerfully controlled organization. *Boat off Deer Isle* offers an unusually strong clue to the way Marin composed a picture, combining on-the-spot decisions with a general predetermined scheme. On the left side there is a strong vertical line where, apparently, a puddle collected at the bottom of the heavy, blackish stroke and then, breaking, ran down the paper. It may be taken for granted without too much risk that this was an accident that, in the ordinary water color and in most Marins, would have been ruinous. In this particular picture, however, we may deduce that Marin saw the possibility of incorporating the line thus created into his general composition, countering or echoing it with the series of five similar black strokes at the right side of the picture, and probably making adjustments in other elements that otherwise would not have had the same position or character. Admitting that the cultivation of such accidentals would hardly be a safe rule of procedure for Marin or anybody else, it is still true that in this case the result was successful. It is an exaggerated illustration of the extraordinary unity between creative invention and the manipulation of a technique in Marin's art.

Even more than water color, pastel is associated with ideas of the innocuous and the dainty. Pastel is only one of the hundreds of varieties of colored crayons made up of pigment combined with filler and pressed into stick form with enough gum to hold it together. This stick will vary in color intensity according to the proportion of pigment to the diluting filler; it varies in softness or hardness with the amount of gum. Since filler is less expensive than good pigment, the average commercial pastel is pale, sometimes having the loveliness of "pastel shades" at their best, sometimes being merely weak and flat.

Pastel may be used on any surface with enough tooth to take the crayon under light pressure. A slick paper is no good at all. There are very fine sandpapers especially prepared for pastel, and it can also be used on fine-grained canvas. If pastel is to have any life at all, the surface must have a grainy or powdery texture that accepts the pigment readily, even if this texture is close to microscopic. Beginners always overwork pastel, rubbing and smearing it to

312. Rosalba Carriera. *Personification of Europe.* Probably before 1720. Pastel on paper mounted on canvas, approximately 17½ by 13½ inches. The Cooper-Hewitt Museum, New York.

death. A skilled pastelist may rub a tone lightly here and there, or even brush a whole area lightly, but not much. Every touch, once the pastel is applied, is dangerous; passages cannot be reworked because pastel is as unpleasant when overloaded with powder as when rubbed.

A completed pastel may be "fixed" with a light spray of diluted gum, but the fixative is only a help, not a real protection, to this most delicate of surfaces. If the fixative is applied heavily enough to hold the pastel firmly to the paper, it may also spot it, deaden it, or give it an unpleasant shine. Pastels cannot be cleaned. If they are to endure, they must be sealed under glass against all dust, dirt, and surface contact.

Pastel enjoyed its liveliest vogue during the eighteenth century as a portrait medium. Its powdery, feminine tints were especially compatible with fashionable taste in decoration and costume; even the powdered coiffures of the period lent themselves to the chalkiness of pastel description. The light touch, the intimacy, and the sensitive application of pastel harmonized beautifully with the light and graceful intention of the century's décor, as well as its special kind of cultivated social personality. The reigning pastelist was a woman, Rosalba Carriera, a Venetian as successful in France and Vienna as she was at home. Her light, graceful style (312) capitalized on her patrons' desire to be invested with the rather superficial delicacy cultivated in fashionable circles.

In sporadic appearances more recently, a few artists have shown that pastel's potential for more significant statements has been neglected. Manet's portrait of *George Moore* (313 and 314) is a brilliant example. George Moore was a bright, clever, rather shallow young man, given to superficialities of social intercourse rather than to great solidity or profundity of thought. It would not take much change to turn that description into a description of pastel technique. Moore's coloring, too, so very pale of skin and so pinkish-blond of hair and beard that he was set apart from everybody else in a group, could have come straight out of a pastel box. With a subject perfectly suited to the technique, Manet did one of the most wittily revealing portraits of his century, capitalizing to the full not only on the color and delicacy of pastel but also on its capacity for quick suggestion. There are not many portraits that bring us so immediately and so freshly (and perhaps so mercilessly) into the presence of the sitter, although there are a great many, including some by Manet, in which a less eccentric subject has given the painter opportunity to explore more significant nuances of personality. But for these explorations painters usually use the more solid technique of oil.

The great exception among pastelists is Edgar Degas. From what we have already said about him in other chapters in discussing his *Woman with Chrysantheumums* (21) and *The Bellelli Family* (257), both oil paintings, it is obvious that Degas is hardly in line with the pastel tradition of superficial delicacy. His vigor, his precision, and his intel-

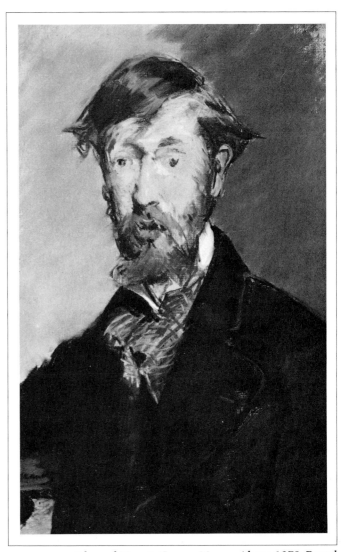

313. Edouard Manet. *George Moore.* About 1879. Pastel on paper, 21¾ by 13⅞ inches. The Metropolitan Museum of Art, New York. Bequest of Mrs. H. O. Havemeyer, 1929. The H. O. Havemeyer Collection.

lectualism are foreign to the generally innocuous run of pastels; nor was he content to turn to pastel as Manet did only for occasional use when a special subject could combine with the technique to produce an exceptional picture like Manet's of George Moore.

Still, pastel had certain advantages that attracted Degas. One of the greatest draughtsmen in the history of art, he was never altogether happy with oil paint. It is possible for a painter to draw with a brush, but a pencil or crayon is somehow closer kin to his hand and a degree closer to the surface upon which he works. In pastel Degas found satisfaction as a draughtsman, and he became the only major

314. Detail from *George Moore.*

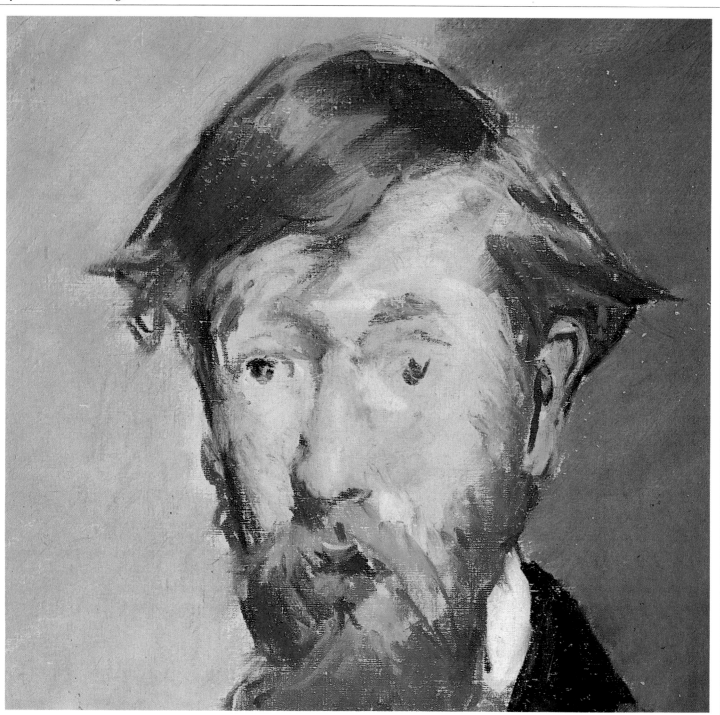

painter to produce a large body of major works in the technique, giving it a strength and solidity hitherto foreign to it. This he did by building his pigment in successive layers. Ordinarily, as we have just said, such a way of working would have resulted in an unpleasant clotting of the pastel if, indeed, it were possible at all, since there is a limit to the amount of this powdery substance a surface can retain. Degas worked with a fixative prepared specially for him from a formula that he guarded closely and that is now lost. With this fixative, successive layers could be firmly secured without loss of brilliance or the blemish of shine. Using crayons with a maximum of pigment and a minimum of filler, he avoided the obvious and limited effects of traditional pastel. *Woman Having Her Hair Combed* (**315**) is the kind of picture in which he lifted pastel from its limbo of airy effects and sporadic brilliance to a firm place among the major techniques. An examination of a detail should show the powerful drawing—in firm, decisive strokes of the crayon—that he found more possible in pastel than in oil. In color, he juxtaposed one color at full intensity with another to enhance the strength of both, and often dragged one color across another so that their intermixture vibrates with light. Diaphanous suggestions give way to solid forms that emerge with the fullness and richness of oil or fresco.

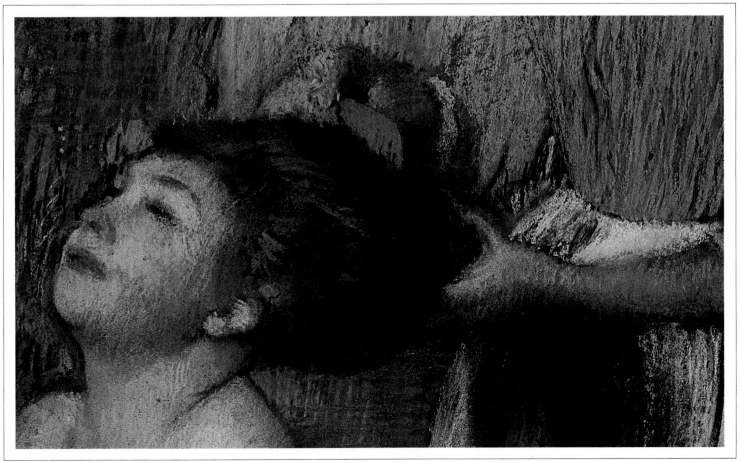

315. Edgar Degas. *Woman Having Her Hair Combed,* with detail. About 1885. Pastel on paper, 29⅛ by 23⅞ inches. The Metropolitan Museum of Art. Bequest of Mrs. H. O. Havemeyer, 1929. The H. O. Havemeyer Collection.

316. *Thousand Buddhas,* portion of a large sheet. 1212. Ink stamped on paper, height of figure 1¹/₁₆ inches. Japanese National Treasure. North Octagonal Hall of the Kōfuku-ji.

Chapter Eleven
PRINTS

Prints, with woodblocks as the oldest form, began life humbly, not as works of art but as substitutes for drawings or paintings when multiples of a single image were needed, probably as long ago as the fifth century A.D. in China. It took another thousand years for the woodblock print to come into its own as a full-fledged independent art form, which it did under the sponsorship of the great Albrecht Dürer in Germany. Dürer performed the same service for engraving, the second oldest print form, and collectors began taking etchings seriously when Rembrandt produced his wonderful ones in the seventeenth century. All three print techniques, during their rise, still served as second-class citizens in their function as reproductions of original works of art, mostly as illustrations in books and magazines. This continued well into the nineteenth century, by which time lithography had joined the print family in the same kind of double life after it was invented about 1796 by Aloys Senefelder, a Bohemian. Only in our century have prints come fully into their own as works of art, with photomechanical reproduction processes taking over their former, original function. Today fine prints are coveted as intensely as drawings and paintings.

We will take up their history in chronological order of appearance: woodblocks, engravings, etchings, and lithographs, with any appropriate offshoots as they occur.

So far as we know, the numerical record for hand-printed multiples of a single image was set in the year 770, when the Empress Shōtoku distributed one million prints of a Buddhist charm to temples throughout Japan. Since one woodblock would wear out before that number, there were no doubt many repeats of the block itself. High artistic quality was not the first goal in such prints; repeated over and over and over again into the thousands of times, and frequently placed within hollowed-out statues of Buddha, they had something like the incantatory function of the chants in which devout Buddhists repeat the same phrase over and over again for hours at a time. Our illustration (316) is a section of a sheet of a thousand Buddhas, done in the year 1212 and found inside a statue of the bodhisattva Miroku. (A bodhisattva in Buddhist lore is a person who has attained moral and spiritual wisdom in assisting suffering mankind.) The height of the figures is $1\,^1/_{16}$ inches. A related ancient form of charm-print has disappeared forever: Buddhist priests used to impress them on the wet sand of beaches, to be washed away by the tide, thus incorporating the charm with the eternal mystery of the sea.

Woodcuts did not come into wide use in Europe until the Middle Ages, when they were used in the earliest printed books, on broadsides, and sometimes as inexpensive souvenirs at religious fairs where the faithful could buy a crudely printed image of a patron saint for a few pence. In principle, the woodcut is the simplest print form—but not necessarily in execution. A drawing is first made in black ink on a smooth piece of hard wood. Then the uninked areas are cut away, leaving the drawing standing in relief, rubber-stamp fashion. Inked and printed, the block now gives, in reverse, a reproduction of the original drawing that is more or less accurate according to the skill of the craftsman who cut it. Certain characteristics of the drawing are inevitably sacrificed; even the most accurate cutting cannot entirely capture the freedom of the original. Gradations of tone are eliminated by the uniform inking and printing of the block. But in compensation, the denseness and uniformity of the printed version, and its feeling of rigidity, have their own attractions. Artists working for woodcut reproduction learn to anticipate these qualities in the original drawing.

A few artists in the early days of woodblock printing cut their own blocks, but most of them were content to put the drawing on the wood and leave the cutting to craftsmen who specialized in this work. The cutting of a fine block requires craftsmanship of excruciating precision; it is easy to draw a series of crisscrossed black lines on a piece of smooth wood, but not so easy to excise the areas between them. Dürer's *Four Horsemen of the Apocalypse* (318), shown here with an enlarged detail (317), is a woodcut conceived as a woodcut from the beginning. Hence modeling by cross-hatching (which we described in Dürer's famous drawing of praying hands, . . .) was avoided in favor of lines describing the form in only one direction and so much easier to cut. The *Four Horsemen*, one of a series illustrating the Apocalypse according to the Book of Revelation, was an early print for which Dürer himself perhaps did the cutting. That he cut the blocks for his later prints is unlikely. For one thing, he could hardly have found time to cut the number of prints he designed when they became popular. For another, the form cutter's guild became so powerful not long after the Apocalypse series that these craftsmen could have confronted Dürer with restrictions amounting to something like union troubles today. Whichever the case, the Apocalypse series was a landmark that established the woodcut as an independent art form worthy of attention by leading artists and collectors.

The general term "woodblock" includes woodcuts, as we have just described them, and wood engravings. William Blake's illustration for the *Pastorals of Virgil*, a tiny gem of a wood engraving, is reproduced here at full size (319). In contrast with woodcuts, where, as we have said, the drawing is done in black ink on the smooth block, the surface of the block for a wood engraving like this one is first darkened and the cutting then done to reveal the drawing in whites. The difference takes a moment to grasp and may seem not very important—but it is. The woodcut is conceived in blacks against whites; the wood engraving in whites against blacks. This distinction is about as close as we can get without making dozens of reservations, and unfortunately the distinction doesn't hold at all when we

317. Enlarged detail from *Four Horsemen of the Apocalypse.*

318. Albrecht Dürer. *Four Horsemen of the Apocalypse.* About 1497–98. Woodcut, 15½ by 11 inches. The Art Museum, Princeton University, New Jersey. The Laura P. Hall Collection.

319. William Blake. Illustration for Thornton's *Pastorals of Virgil*. 1821. 1⅜ by 2⅞ inches. The Metropolitan Museum of Art, New York. Harris Brisbane Dick Fund, 1921.

320. Erich Heckel. *Scene from Dostoevski*. 1912. Woodblock, 10⁵/₁₆ by 9⁵/₁₆ inches. The Metropolitan Museum of Art, New York. Gift of J. B. Neumann, 1924.

get to recent work. A modern print like Erich Heckel's illustration for a scene from Dostoevski (**320**) is obviously conceived in whites gouged out of blacks, but because they are gouged so vigorously, almost crudely, it is not by usual definition a wood engraving. Engraving always implies delicate execution with a very fine sharp point; Heckel's whites could have been hacked out with a pocket knife, and the print owes its power to this feeling of almost desperate urgency. We must be content to allow generous leeway in our definitions, especially since modern artists invent new techniques or experiment with variations on old ones every day.

Linoleum, easy to cut, has long been a substitute for wood. For purists, a linocut lacks the strength, the vigor, of the real thing, but Matisse and Picasso are among modern artists who have not disdained it. Linoleum's relative softness and its grainless texture allow for cutting more relaxed, flowing lines than are possible in wood. Matisse capitalized on this potential in a series of white-line linoleum engravings illustrating Henri de Montherlant's *Pasiphäe* in 1944 (**321**). From 1959 into early 1963 Picasso added one hundred linocuts to his always phenomenal record of production; his direct attack on the submissive linoleum was comparable to his most tempestuous manner in painting (**322**). For both Matisse and Picasso, however, these successful forays into the field of the linoleum print were temporary adventures.

So far as texture is concerned, in the scene from Dostoevski, Heckel has insisted upon what can only be called the "woodiness" of the block, and has capitalized on its gouged quality just as a water colorist might capitalize upon flow and transparency, or as a painter in oil might take advantage of glazing, scumbling, and all the other potentials of that technique. The pioneer in this contemporary attitude toward the woodblock was Paul Gauguin. Working in Tahiti, he admired the accidental irregularities of batiks and stamped tapa cloths, where the natives' primitive technical processes left their mark strongly on the finished product. He carried this idea into his woodcuts, frequently working on planks so rough that the grain reproduces in the printing. Instead of inking his blocks smoothly and printing them with uniform pressure, he allowed (or even cultivated) irregularities that printmakers before him would have regarded as defects. He was not always successful; some of his prints are blurred and smeared to the point of being indecipherable. But in many, as in *Manao Tupapao* or *She Thinks of the Spirit* (**326**, p. 269), these crudities are, by a sophisticated standard, appropriate to the primitivism of the subject. Certainly they bring us into the presence of the artist just as a painting does and as a technically perfect woodcut does not. We are close to him as he works, much closer than we are in woodblocks in which the artist has merely drawn on the surface and then left the job of cutting to an intermediary technician.

· · ·

Before commenting further on *Manao Tupapao*, we should examine some traditional color woodcuts. *Saint Christopher and Saint John the Baptist* (**325**) is a page from a book printed with wooden type and woodcut illustrations. (The inscription in the upper left corner is handwritten.) As a further embellishment the illustrations were tinted by hand—rather crudely, since handwork took time and tended to cancel out the advantages of printing. In these early printed books there is a wonderful unity between type and illustration. Both were cut by hand from wood and thus shared an identity lost in much of modern bookmaking where the type has one personality and the illustration is simply introduced with no regard for the harmony of the page as a unit. Even the relatively crude hand-tinting in our example has a vigor and directness in keeping with the rather rough cutting. A delicately and meticulously tinted picture would be out of harmony—although this could hardly have been the consideration when some apprentice was given the job of filling in certain areas with color.

The next step in the use of color was to make additional blocks from which the color areas could be printed. An early Chinese print, *Two Peaches on a Branch* (**324**), reproduces a water color after the artist Ko Chung-hsüan. The imitation of classical Chinese water-color style is successful enough to be momentarily deceptive. The shading on the gray branches and the blending of the pink tip of one peach into its yellow body are especially convincing. There is considerable speculation but no certain knowledge as to exactly how these gradations were created on the block, as we know they were, before the block was pressed onto moistened paper. The deep green leaves with dark veins are less successful imitations of the quick manipulation of the painter's brush, but the accented outlines of the peaches, which not only thicken but also darken here and there, are so brushlike that they deny their print quality, as the craftsman meant them to do.

In the two Japanese prints that we saw in an earlier chapter (**209** and **210**), the block was cut to echo the shapes of brush strokes, but the artist made no other attempt to capture brush character. Whereas *Two Peaches on a Branch* is still more painting than print, the other two examples are already more print than painting. Before long the Japanese print flourished to the point where its merits as a print superseded its attractions as a pseudo painting, crystallizing during the eighteenth century into the exquisite form in which we know it best.

After fully polychromed prints were introduced about 1765, Suzuki Harunobu emerged as the leading master of the new form, both technically and expressively. The earliest Japanese prints were of actors, courtesans, or other subjects having to do with the world of public gaiety and entertainment. Harunobu, on the other hand, developed the print as a means for representing intimate domestic scenes of the utmost delicacy. Instead of beautiful courtesans he chose modest and well-bred young girls; instead of actors and dancers, mothers and children; instead of public places

321. Henri Matisse. Illustration for Montherlant's *Pasiphäé, Chant de Minos.* (Paris: Martin Fabiani, 1944). Linoleum cut, 12⅞ by 9¾ inches. The Museum of Modern Art, New York. The Louis E. Stern Collection.

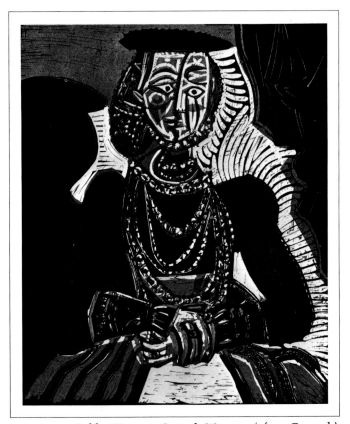

322. Pablo Picasso. *Seated Woman* (after Cranach). 1958. Linocut printed in yellow, blue, red, ochre and black, 25¹¹/₁₆ by 21⁵/₁₆ inches. The Museum of Modern Art, New York. Gift of Mr. and Mrs. Daniel Saidenberg.

323. German. *Saint Christopher and Saint John the Baptist.* Fifteenth century. Hand-colored woodcut, height 9½ inches. The Metropolitan Museum of Art, New York. Bequest of James C. McGuire, 1931.

324. After Ko Chung-hsüan. *Two Peaches on a Branch.* 1633? Color woodcut, 10 by 11½ inches. Philadelphia Museum of Art. Purchased by Seeler Fund.

325. Suzuki Harunobu. *Drying Clothes.* Mid-eighteenth century. Color woodcut, 10⅞ by 8⅛ inches. Philadelphia Museum of Art. Samuel S. White III and Vera White Collection.

326. Paul Gauguin. *Manao Tupapao* (*She Thinks of the Spirit*). 1894. Color woodcut (second plate) retouched with water color, 8⅞ by 18 inches. Philadelphia Museum of Art. Lisa Norris Elkins Fund.

327. Detail from *Drying Clothes* showing *gaufrage,* or blind printing.

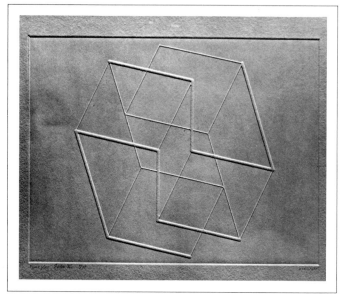

328. Josef Albers. *Solo V.* 1958. Inkless intaglio, 6⅝ by 8⅝ inches. The Brooklyn Museum.

or famous scenic spots, the interiors of homes of good families and the secluded corners of their gardens, like the charming scene *Drying Clothes* (**325**). Surely never before or since has a household chore been made more attractive than in this print epitomizing the Japanese taste for poeticizing even the least poetic aspects of daily life—in this case through the pictorial means of subtle color combinations and exquisitely graceful line.

Each color in a print of this kind represents an individual block, cut with incredible nicety to register with the other blocks within the framework of the black one that establishes the drawing and is called the "key block." Again, it is impossible to reproduce here the noticeable depressions along these hair-thin outlines that add so much life and definition to the original. Patterns are stamped into the paper here and there. In the mounds of white blossoms on the bush, detail is picked out in relief, and within the gray pattern on the curtain to the right a secondary design is incised. There are also stamped patterns on the robes of the mother and the child. Some of these markings are apparent in the detail taken in a raking light (**327**). This "blind printing," for which the French term *gaufrage* is frequently used, is done from a separate, uninked block.

A colorless impression of the cut block itself, freed from the block print's close allegiance to the art of painting, should theoretically be the final and most dramatic demonstration that prints are a totally independent art form. By this theory, Harunobu's *gaufrage* would have a large family of twentieth-century descendants in the inkless prints made by modern artists. In these, the slight relief of *gaufrage*, which is the merest fraction of an inch, is increased until a pattern tells clearly in normal light in relief alone, unassisted by inked lines and color areas. This is done by pressing thick, strong white paper, dampened for flexibility, into a pattern cut deeply into a block. When the dried paper is removed, it retains the pattern in the form of a low relief—thus, it must be admitted, shifting the print's allegiance from painting to an even stronger allegiance to sculpture. Our illustration (**328**) is a classic example of the inkless print by Josef Albers, a German artist whose emigration to the United States in 1933 and position as chairman of the Department of Design at Yale University from 1950 to 1960 made him a major force in modern American art.

It is characteristic of traditional Japanese art that it depends upon exquisitely developed craftsmanship of the most demanding kind, and in this respect Albers is sympathetically allied to that tradition. But in most aspects of modern art, traditional craftsmanship has been sacrificed to individual expression. That is one strong reason why Harunobu's *Drying Clothes* and Gauguin's *Manao Tupapao* look so very different, although we are about to say that they are alike in their authenticity as prints. Technically they are at opposite poles, but the full enjoyment of each depends upon our recognition of the uses to which the artist has put his technique.

In different good impressions of the same Japanese

print there will be certain minor differences since the process is, after all, not a mechanical but a hand one. But these differences are nothing at all compared with those in prints by Gauguin, where each print is virtually independent of others from the same blocks. Instead of applying his color uniformly over a defined area, Gauguin would smear or rub it over an area or part of an area in any way he thought might be most effective, and these differences and irregularities were exaggerated by the varying pressures of unsystematic printing. *Manao Tupapao* is Gauguin's rarest print. At an early stage he ruined the block in making some additional cuttings, and only five impressions are known. Each of the five has wide variations from the others, but in all of them the block and the process of creation is vividly, immediately present.

We may conjecture that Harunobu would have found *Manao Tupapao* unpardonably brutal, and so, in truth, Gauguin's prints seemed to most of his contemporaries. Japanese prints exerted a strong influence on Impressionist painters in the latter nineteenth century. Mary Cassatt, the American painter who joined the Impressionists in Paris, executed a particularly fine series of color prints in the manner, but not the technique, of Japanese woodblocks. *The Fitting* (329), executed in dry point, soft ground, and aquatint—techniques that we will explain a bit later— shows how she adapted the patterning, the linear delicacy, and the intimate domestic subject matter of prints like the Harunobu to the kind of everyday modern subjects so dear to impressionism. The Cassatt is more realistic than the Harunobu, but in both cases each line is beautiful quite aside from its descriptive function, and is incorporated into a flow of rhythms that in its turn defines the integrated pattern of silhouettes.

If we look for similar qualities in *Manao Tupapao*, we can find them. The line and pattern are more obvious and more direct, vigorous rather than exquisitely subtle, but ultimately they were fathered by Japanese prints, which Gauguin knew and admired and which influenced him without serving as models for imitation. In his departures from convention he committed the heresy of adding spots of color with a brush, a practice that horrifies printmakers but can be defended here. Gauguin was not touching up mistakes, but simply carrying on the creative process of a picture that he thought of in terms as individual as those involved in the execution of a painting. He was creating as he went, rather than observing the mechanical niceties involved in reproducing uniformly a predetermined pattern. There is no such term as woodblock-painting, but it could be coined to describe work like Gauguin's, not because he actually painted into his print, which he sometimes did, but because the creative process continued and developed during the production of his prints, just as it does in painting on canvas. In his prints Gauguin was, in a way, painting by means of a woodblock instead of a brush.

Have we, then, come full circle back to *Two Peaches on a Branch*, which imitated painting? No, not at all, for

329. Mary Cassatt. *The Fitting.* 1891. Color print with dry point, soft ground, and aquatint, 14¾ by 10¹/₁₆ inches. Museum of Art, Carnegie Institute, Pittsburgh.

this reason: whereas the craftsman who cut and printed *Two Peaches on a Branch* was imitating another technique, Gauguin's whole conception is stated in terms of the technique in which he is working.

Printing is ordinarily thought of in the terms we have been describing—the inking and stamping of surfaces in relief. But it is also possible to print by the reverse of this method, using the "intaglio" process, in which the drawing is incised into the surface instead of raised above it. This is the process in metal-plate engraving and in etching.

In engraving, the picture is cut into the metal plate in fine, sharp, shallow lines. (Hard metals, such as steel, are the most difficult to cut but repay the craftsman with the sharpest, cleanest lines and will yield more impressions than softer metals before wearing out.) The entire plate is then inked; special attention is given to forcing ink down into the lines. Then the plate is wiped clean on the surface, with care taken to leave the incised lines filled with ink. Next, paper is laid over the plate and put under pressure to force it down into the lines, where it picks up the ink. The drawing is thus transferred to the paper, and the plate may be re-inked and printed as long as it lasts.

Because the face of the paper is forced into the cut lines, each line is reproduced not only in ink but also in the form of a very slight ridge. This is the texture we feel when we run our fingertips over an engraved invitation or calling card, and it explains the particular character of engraved line. Properly cut and properly printed, the engraved line has a razor-sharp definition and a brilliance beyond anything that can be achieved by pen line or a line printed in relief process.

One of the finest of all engravings throughout the history of art is also one of the earliest: Pollaiuolo's *Battle of Naked Men*, done about 1465 (**330**). The reader may weary of being reminded that in reproduction the various print processes lose some of their character. But it is important to remember, because so much of the enjoyment of prints comes from an understanding of the way the artist has used the technique. The severity of Pollaiuolo's style, his passion for exact definition of anatomical contours, and the masculine force of his design are all heightened by the rigorous discipline of the burin, the pointed cutting tool used by engravers. In this great print Pollaiuolo attains maximum expression of the controlled ferocity that characterizes his art, a ferocity combined with ornamental elegance that makes no concessions to prettiness or even to grace. (We have already seen these characteristics in his *Martyrdom of Saint Sebastian*, **236**.)

The friezelike background of *Battle of Naked Men* reflects Pollaiuolo's early training in the demanding craft of goldsmithery, which must have contributed a great deal to his exceptional skill as an engraver. *Battle of Naked Men* is the only engraving known to be by Pollaiuolo, but alone it places him high in the hierarchy of an art that demands complete unity between technique and image. The finest

330. Antonio Pollaiuolo. *Battle of Naked Men*. About 1465. Engraving, 16¹¹/₁₆ by 24¹/₆ inches. The Cleveland Museum of Art. J. H. Wade Fund.

331. Detail from *Battle of Naked Men*.

332. Albrecht Dürer. Magnified details from *Melencolia I*.

engravings (including wood engravings), unlike woodcuts, are not drawn on the plate for execution by assistants. Expert engraving technicians frequently translate paintings or drawings into the form of engravings, but these are approximate reproductions quite removed from the original artist's hand.

The engraver's burin is a sharp triangular gouge that cuts cleanly into the metal plate, excising with immaculate precision the tiny channel that becomes in printing a sharp inked ridge of a line. The depth and width of the burined line depends upon the degree of pressure the craftsman applies in the cutting. A skillful engraver can accent a line by thickening it or thinning it with varying pressure, but the range is narrow because too thick a line will not print sharply. This "shaded line" has the sparkle and contrast of all engraved lines plus a suggestion of flexibility.

In a detail at approximately full size (**331**) from *Battle of Naked Men* it should be apparent that each line is produced with absolute control and that any slip throwing a single line or portion of a line out of relation to the others would have been fatal. The metal plate, engraved and ready for inking, is a beautiful thing. Each line glistens with the same quality as engraved initials on silverware, which of course are incised in the same way. Theoretically, it would be possible to reproduce (always in reverse) the initials on ordinary tableware by filling them with ink in the way described and pressing paper into them. The art of pictorial engraving probably originated in some such way when the engravers of ornamental designs on armor or other decorated metal took impressions of their patterns for future reference.

Limited as he is to thin lines, the engraver who wants to produce varieties of gray tones must do so by a multitude of crisscrossings, or a series of straight lines close together, or a stippling of tiny short strokes or dots, as Dürer has done in another masterpiece among engravings of all times and places, his great *Melencolia I* (**333**). Enlargements of two areas (**332**) show how the different textures and tonalities were produced by different combinations of burin lines.

We are indebted to Dürer more than any other single artist for the elevation of prints to the status of high art. His woodcut of the *Four Horsemen of the Apocalypse* is one of a set of fifteen subjects from the Revelation of St. John that transformed the medium by unprecedented fineness of cutting combined with design as powerfully constructed as any heretofore reserved for painting. Although he had important precursors in engraving, Dürer's transformation of that medium is hardly less impressive. It is safe to call him the greatest engraver of all, and although there might be room for argument as to which is his greatest engraving technically, most authorities would agree that *Melencolia I* is the most profound.

The subject is a complicated allegory of the human dilemma of conflict between the imaginative world of art and faith and the realistic one of science and learning. Symbols of art, science, learning, and religion are strewn in

333. Albrecht Dürer. *Melencolia I.* 1514. Engraving, 9½ by 7⁵⁄₁₆ inches. The Metropolitan Museum of Art, New York. Harris Brisbane Dick Fund, 1943.

disarray around a figure of Genius frustrated by the complexity of knowledge and skills that refute the world of faith yet leave the universe unexplained.

In his personal life Dürer himself, born at the point of change between the Middle Ages and the Renaissance in Germany, was torn between mystical faith and analytical intellectualism. We have said that Pollaiuolo's passion for exact definition (in a Renaissance world where science could be regarded as the source of ultimate realities) received perfect expression through control of the burin, a happy coincidence between stylistic preference and philosophical conviction. In Dürer's case, the engraving medium became almost an allegory of his personal struggle. The tortured complications of the artist's introspective agony are relayed to us by a kind of technical intensity in *Melencolia I,* with its thousands upon thousands of fine incisions engraved into metal, each one obsessively controlled as an infinitesimal unit in a design that has nothing less than the universe of the soul and the mind as its subject. If this is not immediately apparent in Dürer's print, compare it with a treatment of the same subject about a hundred years later in a drawing by the Italian artist Giovanni Benedetto

334. Giovanni Benedetto Castiglione. *Melancholia.* Mid-seventeenth century. Brush drawing in oil with red chalk on paper, approximately 11 by 16 inches. Philadelphia Museum of Art. Pennsylvania Academy of Fine Arts Collection.

Castiglione (334). The same symbols, although in reduced numbers, are scattered around a figure of Genius similarly clothed and crowned and, like Dürer's figure, resting a cheek on one hand and holding calipers in the other. But the similarities mean nothing; the mood in this enchanting drawing is one of graceful relaxation.

The rigorous discipline of cutting a drawing into a metal plate rules out the quick, sketchy line of free drawing. This restriction is removed—not entirely, but to a large degree—in another intaglio process, etching. The plate is similarly inked, wiped, and printed, but the sunken line is produced in a different way.

To make an etching, the artist first covers a metal plate (usually copper) with a wax coating called "ground," which is impervious to acid. Using a fine stylus (needle) point, he can draw on this ground with a freedom approaching that of pen or pencil. The sharp point removes the wax where he draws, exposing the metal to the action of an acid bath that "bites" into the surface of the plate. The artist controls the width of the line by the depth of biting. Heavy lines are produced by longer exposure to the acid. Lighter ones are "stopped out" midway by removing the plate from the bath and re-covering that area with the impervious ground.

An etched line is quite different in character from an engraved one. It is softer, warmer, richer. Whereas the engraver's burin cuts precisely, the acid eats out a little chasm with microscopically uneven edges. Rembrandt's *Christ Carried to the Tomb* (335) and a magnification of a detail (336) can be compared with *Battle of Naked Men* and *Melencolia I* to show the resultant difference after printing.

An engraved plate is always inked and wiped with maximum care to clean the surface of every trace of ink, in order that the inked lines may tell as sharply and brilliantly as possible. Some etched plates are similarly wiped, but since an etched line is softer than an engraved one, some etchers increase the effect of softness by not wiping the plate quite clean. A little film of ink may be left where a tone is desired over a certain passage. Rembrandt, among others, utilized this trick of wiping; Whistler, at the end of the nineteenth century, used it to an unprecedented extent, employing it not only as "tone" but as a pictorial element. In an etching like his *Nocturne* (337) one of many to which he gave the same title, the light on the horizon, the twilight sky, and its reflection in the lagoon are all produced by wiping. In the history of etching, Whistler's revolution was not as great as Gauguin's in woodblock printing, but it increased the freedom of etching technique and had a wide influence.

Tonalities from filmiest gray to richest black can be bitten into a metal plate by a process generally used as an adjunct to etching—"aquatint." In this technique, the plate is dusted very thinly with powdered resin. When the plate is heated from the under-side, the microscopic granules melt and adhere to its surface. Like regular etching ground, the resin is impervious to acid, so that when the plate is

335. Rembrandt. *Christ Carried to the Tomb*. About 1645. Etching, 5³/₁₆ by 4⁵/₁₆ inches. The Metropolitan Museum of Art, New York. Harris Brisbane Dick Fund, 1923.

336. Magnified detail from *Christ Carried to the Tomb*.

337. James Abbott McNeill Whistler, *Nocturne.* 1880. Etching, 8⅛ by 11¾ inches. The Metropolitan Museum of Art, New York. Harris Brisbane Dick Fund, 1917.

338. Francisco Goya. *Old Man Among Ghosts* (plate 18 from *Los Proverbios*). 1813–16. Aquatint, 9⅝ by 13¹³/₁₆ inches. The Metropolitan Museum of Art, New York. Harris Brisbane Dick Fund, 1924.

put into the bath, the acid eats into the metal only in the tiny interstices between the granules and only, of course, in areas that have not been blocked out in preparing the design. The texture and darkness of the aquatinted areas are controlled by the thickness of dusting in the first place, and the time of exposure to acid in the second. Goya's *Old Man Among Ghosts* (338) was toned with aquatint after the drawing was completely bitten in. A magnified portion (339) brings us closer to the texture.

Another intaglio process, closely related to both etching and engraving, is dry point—a technique in which lines are dug directly into the metal plate with a stylus, without benefit of biting acids. The difference from engraving is that a line gouged or scratched into the plate with a stylus is softer and more flexible than one incised with the engraver's burin. A soft metal, usually copper, is employed for dry point plates, and the stylus, like a miniature plow, throws up a ragged ridge on either side of the gouge. When the plate is wiped, these "plowed up" edges, called "burr," retain additional ink that, under the pressure of printing, squeezes out and gives a softer or even a fuzzy edge to the line. The effect of dry point can be one of great richness. But very fine, delicate lines may also be produced in dry point by polishing away the burr.

Etching and dry point are frequently combined in a single plate, most often with dry point serving as a convenient retouching technique. The combination has never been employed with more originality than in Rembrandt's *The Three Crosses* (340). Rembrandt comes closest of any artist to holding in etching the position that Dürer holds so securely in woodcut and engraving; he regarded the plate as an area for free experiment in widening the medium's range of expression, much as he regarded a canvas for painting. In his late paintings, Rembrandt's figures loom into golden light from profound shadows, an effect that had not yet been approximated in conventional etching techniques. (Aquatint could have yielded the intense blacks Rembrandt wanted, but was not invented until late in the next century.) *The Three Crosses* represents the moment following the Crucifixion when supernatural darkness spread across the sky and earth. The print exists in several "states"—a state being a print pulled from the plate in order to serve as a guide for further work. Our detail (341) of the state illustrated shows that Rembrandt took a straight edge of some kind and scored the plate heavily with lines running across the etched figures to throw them in various degrees of shadow. In some areas where the lines are close together the burr holds so much ink that an area becomes solid black, while in other passages heavy black lines separated by brilliant white give the impression of sinister gloom penetrated by miraculous rays of light.

If Rembrandt had wanted to lighten, or even eliminate, the velvety black of the heavily burred areas in *The Three Crosses*, he could have done so with a burnishing tool that eliminated the burr or, by strenuous polishing, could even have brought the plate back to a smooth surface that would

339. Magnified detail from *Old Man Among Ghosts.*

340. Rembrandt. *The Three Crosses* (4th state). 1653.
Dry point and burin, about 17¾ by 15 inches. Museum
of Fine Arts, Boston. Harvey D. Parker Collection.

print white. The erasure technique called "mezzotint" is
an application of this principle. An entire plate is given a
uniform, very fine burr (after which it would print solid
black), and the picture is then created by polishing—erasing—to produce every tone from black to white. Mezzotint
is a laborious process and has been most widely used as a
reproductive rather than a creative medium.

Woodblock printing is a relief process; engraving, etching, and the variations we have described are intaglio
processes; in between is the "planar" process, which prints
from neither a raised nor a depressed design, but from a flat
surface. Lithography—literally, "stonedrawing"—utilizes
the simple principle of the incompatibility of oil and water.
A lithograph is first drawn with greasy ink or crayon

341. Magnified detail from *The Three Crosses.*

on a slab of smooth, fine-grained limestone. (Zinc and other materials are sometimes substituted for the stone, but do not yield the same beautifully fine-grained print.) The drawing is then "fixed" on the stone with a preparation of gum arabic and nitric acid. To print, water is first applied over the entire surface. The greasy drawing repels water, but the porous stone absorbs it and remains damp. When a roller covered with lithographic ink, which has an oil or grease base, is run over the stone, the damp surface repels the ink while the grease drawing accepts it, and the stone is ready for printing. A sheet of paper is placed over it, and stone and paper are run through a press that exerts a scraping pressure. The drawing is transferred (in reverse, of course) from stone to paper, and the process can be repeated until the image on the stone breaks down from wear.

Käthe Kollwitz's *The Summons of Death* (**342**) could be mistaken for a crayon drawing as neither engravings nor etchings could be mistaken for pen or pencil; in lithographs we are particularly close to the artist as draughtsman.

As is apparent in *The Summons of Death*, lithography affords the entire range from the darkest, richest blacks to the pure white of the paper. The distinctive grainy quality of the grays comes from the texture of the stone. In the Kollwitz lithograph the drawing is exceptionally vigorous and direct. A lithographic crayon is square in section— about a quarter of an inch—and in the broad strokes at the left the various gradations within a single stroke were made by varying pressure. A stroke beginning wide and ending thin, and graduated from light to dark, like several in this example, is made in a single, sure motion, not only by varying the pressure but by turning the crayon to a different angle as it is pulled across the stone. At the opposite pole there are the delicate, tenuous lines of the hand coming into the picture from the right.

Color lithography is a rich field for the printmaker, coming closer than any other technique to the variety and flexibility of painting. Toulouse-Lautrec's lithograph of a popular Parisian clownesse, Mlle. Cha-u-ka-o (**343**), involves color as well as half a dozen different methods of applying the crayon, including its liquid form, which is called "tusche." In color lithography a different stone is prepared for each color, just as in woodblock printing. These are printed in sequence over one another. In woodblock printing two colors are sometimes printed over one another to produce a third—blue over yellow to produce a green, for instance—but the result is likely to be a little thick and heavy. In lithography, however, the grainy texture of the stone, with its peppering of tiny clear areas throughout, is wonderfully adapted to overprinting. The undercolor shows through the open spaces of the overcolor, giving an additional vibrancy to the resultant color as its two elements play against one another.

Here, the ruff, or collar, was painted on the stone with a soft brush and liquid crayon, and the spots on the floor were apparently dabbed in with the end of a stiffer brush less heavily loaded with tusche. The speckling over the

342. Käthe Kollwitz. *The Summons of Death.* 1935. Lithograph, 15 by 15 inches. Philadelphia Museum of Art. Print Club Permanent Collection.

343. Henri de Toulouse-Lautrec. *The Seated Clownesse, Mlle. Cha-u-ka-o.* 1896. Color lithograph from the series *Elles*, 20⅝ by 15¾ inches. The Metropolitan Museum of Art, New York. Stieglitz Collection, 1949.

entire stone was made by holding a stiff brush well above its surface and scraping the bristles against some rigid edge—or possibly by flipping them lightly with the thumb. This spattering was built up within certain definite areas—such as the bench and the wall back of the head—by protecting the rest of the stone with pieces of paper laid over it, stencil-fashion.

Toulouse-Lautrec's departure from conventional lithographic techniques corresponds to Gauguin's in the woodblock and is at least as important in the history of printmaking. Like Gauguin, he enlarged the scope of a limited print technique to the point where it became a flexible art form. In recent years lithography has been subject to innumerable variations, both in the studio and commercially. Other surfaces than stone have been widely adopted for convenience and, in the case of commercial printing, economy. The printing process called "offset" is an adaptation of the lithographic principle to photomechanical techniques. Lithography in all its variations, including posters and billboards, is the most ubiquitous of all print techniques today.

It has also become the most flexible as an artist's medium in which some of the commercial uses have been adapted. Robert Rauschenberg's *Centennial Certificate, M.M.A.*, 1969 (**344**), commissioned in celebration of the hundredth anniversary of the Metropolitan Museum, is a lithograph by definition; but in effect it is a collage of photographs and reproductions superimposed transparently, as would have been impossible in true collage of objects in the museum's collections, plus a piece of graph paper with signatures of museum officials and a statement of the museum's ideals at top center. The print was made from two stones and two aluminum plates in red, yellow, blue, and brown, and has the special quality of being so directly the result of special processes (such as photosensitized aluminum plates) that it could not possibly be regarded as a substitute for painting or drawing. This insistence on prints as totally independent art forms, a development of the last fifteen or twenty years, is modern art's most important expansion of the print's function.

Another planar process, the silk-screen stencil or serigraph, the newest print process, is the only one executed in paint rather than inks, which is often thought of as an advantage but which nevertheless does not eliminate the mechanical look of multiple reproduction. The stencils are made by stopping out portions of a piece of thin silk tightly stretched on a frame, leaving open the areas that are to print in a single color. The stencil is placed on top of the paper (or other material), and paint is pressed through the open areas of the silk with a squeegee. Each color demands a separate stencil unless the paints are transparent enough to yield secondary colors by overprinting. Delicately manipulated, silk screen can yield subtle variations of tone and color; but it is best adapted to bold contrasts in large, simple areas. For this reason it is widely used for posters.

Its most conspicuous use in contemporary art has capi-

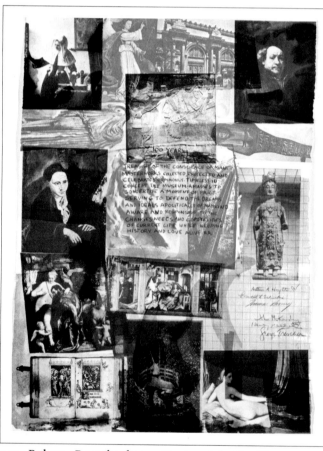

344. Robert Rauschenberg. *Centennial Certificate.* 1969. Lithograph, 35⅞ by 25 inches. The Metropolitan Museum of Art, New York. Gift of Joseph Singer, 1969.

talized on this poster-like commercial quality in the hands of Andy Warhol and the numerous studio assistants in what he calls, appropriately, not his studio but his factory. A leader in pop art, Warhol is preoccupied with that aspect of pop that finds its material in the most familiar clichés of the contemporary scene, including advertising art. His multiple portraits of Marilyn Monroe (**345**), among subjects that include other celebrities, Coca-Cola bottles, and the famous Campbell Soup cans, are at once anti-art in the conventional sense and art-innovative in another.

One other planar process is as rare as lithography and silk screen are widespread. This is the monotype, which occupies an ambiguous position between paintings or drawings and prints. The process is simple enough: a painting, in either black and white or color, is done on a nonabsorbent plate of any kind strong enough to hold up under pressure, and is then transferred to paper either in a press or by rubbing by hand. Either oil or water color may be used; oil is more common. Textures vary widely, depending on the thickness of the paint (if very thick, it may squash out rather unpleasantly on the paper) and the texture of the paper. On the plate the paint may be manipulated in many ways—by a brush, of course, but it can also be worked by hand. The paint may be scratched out over areas that the artist wants to be pure white (if he is working on white paper).

The only major artist who has regarded the monotype as more than a novelty to be experimented with a few times was Degas, who did at least two hundred. He objected to the term "monotype," saying that his were "drawings done with greasy ink and printed." The monotype, as the term indicates, yields only one good print; a second, much paler, can sometimes be pulled, or even a third, very pale indeed. Ordinarily, the plate has to be touched up, refreshed, after the first print is pulled.

Our example, *The Ballet Master* (**346**), was probably Degas's first experiment in monotype, but he was already investigating its full possibilities, scratching out white lines, "erasing" soft white and light gray areas, and, in the upper right and upper left, smearing the paint to suggest stage scenery, all, of course, on the plate before printing. When he pulled a second impression, Degas often touched up the weak passages on the paper, sometimes with pastel.

A monotype, by the very meaning of the word—"single print"—is unique, and hence has the rarity of a painting. We pointed out at the beginning of this chapter that prints owed their early development to the fact that they could be produced in multiples. This not only made them adaptable for use as illustrations or ornamentations in books but also gave artists a chance to produce a desirable low-priced product for people who could not afford such unique works as paintings or drawings. Originally regarded as second-best works of art for this reason, prints were given less care than paintings or drawings. Hence the few surviving examples

345. Andy Warhol. *Marilyn Monroe,* diptych. 1962. Silk-screen enamel on canvas, each panel 82 by 59 inches. Collection Mr. and Mrs. Burton Tremaine, Meriden, Connecticut.

346. Edgar Degas. *The Ballet Master.* About 1874. Monotype in black ink, 22 by 27½ inches. National Gallery of Art, Washington, D. C. Rosenwald Collection.

of some fairly large printings now have rarity value for collectors. It is not known how many prints were pulled from Pollaiuolo's wonderful plate of the *Battle of Naked Men* (which, incidentally, is often found under the title *Battle of Ten Nudes*), but if one of the existing prints should come onto the market today, it would be competed for by every museum and collector in the field with enough money to make a bid.

Recognizing that prints could have rarity value, printmakers in the nineteenth century began limiting their editions. Instead of printing until the plate wore out, they deliberately destroyed the plate or disfigured it—for example, scoring the surface of an etching plate (**347**)—after pulling a predetermined number of prints. Prints thus arbitrarily limited in number (as virtually all prints are today) bear a notation, usually just below the lower left corner of the impression, consisting of two numbers, such as 20/75, which would mean that the print in hand was the twentieth pulled in an edition of seventy-five. In place of the numbers there may be the written words "Artist's Proof," which means that this is one of an undesignated number pulled in addition to the edition proper. Obviously, each artist's proof reduces the rarity of each of the numbered proofs, but there is no very good way of telling how many such additional proofs have been pulled.

Finally, this leaves us with the question, What is an "original print"? The term is a recent one, coined to distinguish between mere reproductions and prints like those we have been discussing, in which the artist either created the plate and printed it, or created it and supervised the printing by a technician. Unfortunately some reproductions are numbered, implying that this photographically manufactured product is the work of the artist's hand. Serious confusion is created in a few instances where artists have unwisely "OK'd" the quality of reproductions of their work by examining them for defects and then signing them. The amateur print collector must be wary; but with a little practice, his eye will soon learn the difference between a good impression of an original print, a poor one pulled after the plate had deteriorated, and the print that is not an original print at all but only a pretender.

347. Edgar Degas. *Portrait of Tourny.* 1857. Etching. Print from canceled plate, 9 by 5⅝ inches. Courtesy Associated American Artists, New York.

348. Honoré Daumier. *Rue Transnonain, April 15, 1834.* 1834. Lithograph, 11½ by 17⅝ inches. Boston Public Library, Print Department.

Chapter Twelve
THE ARTIST AS SOCIAL CRITIC

By popular conception the artist is an individual at odds with society (the artist as a rebel), or free from its conventions (the artist as a bohemian), or a dweller in some Cloud-Cuckoo-Land where he is less than half conscious of the world and its practical demands. He is ordinarily thought of as a person unconcerned with the social problems of the time.

In general the history of art bears out this last assumption. The most enduring paintings are not likely to be comments on the passing scene, simply because that is what it is—passing, and art is concerned with permanent values, not transient ones. Great art's ultimate statement is general, not specific, even when it is couched in specific terms. But spotted through the history of art there are instances when contemporary events associated with violent injustice and social cruelty have inspired artists to specific protests that, with time, have taken on the character of judgments on human folly in general. In this chapter we will see some of these instances, with the artists appearing in their least familiar guise, that of social critics and moralists.

What we call "social consciousness," the individual's awareness that he has a personal responsibility for the general good, is a relatively new idea. And it is not on the whole one that has inspired very much first-rate art, if by first-rate one means art that appeals universally instead of depending on topical subject matter for its meaning. How much a picture can change when its topical associations are no longer current is shown in Honoré Daumier's lithograph *Rue Transnonain, April 15, 1834* (**348**), which appeared in Paris that same month. Neither the name of the street nor the date means anything to most people. Quizzed, perhaps the best they might do would be to guess that April is the month the chestnut trees come into bloom along the Champs Élysées, which is hard to connect with the scene in the picture, clearly the aftermath of some appalling violence.

A man and woman lie dead on the floor of a bedroom. There has been a struggle; furniture is overturned, blood is spattered here and there and trickles from the bodies. Under the man lies the body of a child; the head of another corpse, an older man, whom we take to be the grandfather, shows at the right. It is a sobering picture, but anybody who looks at it without detailed knowledge of the period will see first of all a sordid story of murder, unexplained.

On its appearance in 1834 with no other explanation than its title, the picture's association was entirely different. Workmen in Paris had been rioting in sympathetic demonstrations connected with a general strike called at Lyons. In this state of near–civil war, troops patrolling the streets were fired upon from a window or windows of number 12, Rue Transnonain. In retaliation the soldiers went through the building and killed every person in it, innocent or guilty. Thus to Parisians, still shocked by this crime, the picture, when it appeared a few days after the event, was not the record of a sordid anecdote but a monumental accusation. And understood in this light the picture changes character for us; the very room in which the bodies lie seems to grow more quiet, the bodies themselves acquire the stature of martyrs.

Rue Transnonain, then, loses its original point if we don't know its story. But without the key to its subject the picture may gain even more, going beyond its topical reference to become a universal statement of our mortal vulnerability to anonymous violence.

A work of art may rise above topical limitations even when its subject is clearly defined. Goya's *The Executions of the Third of May* (**349**) is based on events that took place in 1808, the year of the Napoleonic conquest of Spain. The king and the army had hardly resisted the French invasion, which was accomplished with a maximum of pointless brutality, if we are to trust Goya's records of it, and the French occupation was regarded with a minimum of concern by an incomparably contemptible Spanish ruling class.

349. Francisco Goya. *The Executions of the Third of May.* 1814. Oil on canvas, 8 feet 8¾ inches by 11 feet 3⅞ inches. Museo del Prado, Madrid.

But then, in Madrid, the people learned that the son of the king was to be carried away to France. Whether he stayed or went made no practical difference, but to the people he was a symbol. Thus the Madrileños, protecting the monarchy whose members were doing their best to ingratiate themselves with Napoleon, attacked the invaders in the streets. This was the Second of May, the date that marked the beginning of Napoleon's expulsion.

The uprising of the Second of May was followed the next day by frightful reprisals. Civilians were executed in group lots without much regard for their guilt or innocence as participants in the fighting. Possession of a penknife was called carrying arms, and, according to one account, even the ownership of a pair of scissors was enough to establish guilt and bring a sentence of death.

Goya shows one of the civilian executions in *The Executions of the Third of May*, in which a group of Madrileños face the firing squad. At their feet sprawl human carcasses, while beyond them the next lot of victims stands in line. The scene takes place against a barren rise of ground; in the distance the outlying buildings of the city are spectral.

Now, while all these elements are historically identifiable, and while the scene is specific enough to be read as a political execution even without the historical background, the picture goes beyond the immediate circumstance to make a statement applicable at any time in history. For a Spaniard, the historical context no doubt endows the painting with particular excitement. Yet this context also imposes a limitation. If we know nothing about the Third of May as a historical event, the picture's dramatic power is at least as great. It is even more inclusive, for the picture's effectiveness is widened when the connotations are no longer tied to a single event or a single country.

The picture centers upon a young man who flings up his arms and thrusts his body forward as if to proclaim his vulnerability as an individual and yet to defy the soldiers with the jibe that this execution will not affect the cause for which he stands. He is the spirit of a revolt that will continue against all odds because it is beyond personal defeat or annihilation. At his shoulder a half-brutish companion senses this conviction. Half-comprehending, he too thrusts himself forward to receive the bullets. The other figures and those in line stare or hide their faces in various reactions of horror, despair, or resignation.

In contrast to the excitement, variety, and humanity of the figures of the victims, the executioners are ranged in identical poses suggesting automatons, their faces hidden so that they are further deindividualized. Thus they become figures of blind force, ultimately incapable of victory because they are not endowed with passion and perception.

If Goya had chosen to make us aware of the psychological state of each soldier as an individual, the point of the picture would be lost. If the soldiers were represented as a group of unmitigated villains, we would sense that the artist was stacking the cards. Soldiers selected as members of a firing squad are human beings also; they react in a variety of ways to the job at hand. But Goya wants no interplay of human emotions here. He is painting unquenchable passion for freedom in the face of any force attempting to stem it, and he does it by ranging human beings against symbols of insensate power.

Goya painted *The Executions of the Third of May* in 1814, six years after the event. Daumier published his lithograph of the massacre on the Rue Transnonain immediately following that infamy in 1834. As the nineteenth century progressed, "socially conscious" art appeared with increasing frequency, and then in the twentieth found vehement expression during and after the Great Depression of the 1930's in America, with artists becoming political activists. But if we trace in the other direction, backward from Goya and Daumier, the opposite is true. Art as social comment, except in terms of storytelling and picturesque scenes of poverty, gradually disappears. It is surprising, then, to find an indictment of political injustice painted at the end of the fifteenth century in Italy. We will compare this extraordinary picture with another on the same theme painted more than four hundred years later in America.

The first is Botticelli's *Calumny* (**351**), painted just before the year 1500 in Renaissance Italy. The second is a contemporary American picture, Ben Shahn's *Passion of Sacco and Vanzetti* (**352**) one of a series painted only a few decades ago, in 1931–32. On the surface the two pictures appear to have no similarities at all, yet they have unexpected parallels when examined more deeply.

Botticelli's *Calumny* is a curious picture and not altogether a pleasing one. The extreme complications of line are an exaggeration of Botticelli's earlier style, which we have already seen at its happiest in his *Primavera* (**219**).

In the center of the composition we see an innocent victim dragged by the hair to judgment by Calumny, who carries a torch, false symbol of her love of truth. Two other female figures flank her and twine roses in her hair. These are Calumny's attendants, Fraud and Deception. The standing male figure in this central group, dressed in rags, is Envy, who makes his false accusations to the Judge.

Although the Judge wears a crown and carries a scepter, he also has ass's ears. Ignorance whispers into one ear, Suspicion into the other, and he listens.

All these figures are snarled and knotted into groups with lines of such complication that the effect they create is finally—and appropriately—grotesque and disagreeable. They occupy the major portion of the picture space, filling it with masses of twisting draperies, writhing hair, and oddly jointed limbs; lines and masses weave in and out of one another like nests of serpents. If we compare the three female figures, Calumny, Fraud, and Deception (**350**), with those of the Three Graces (**218**) from the *Primavera*, we can see how tortured confusion replaces the rhythmic linear harmony of the earlier picture. But the artist uses this disturbing line only where it is appropriate.

In one figure he gives us again a line of great simplicity

350. Sandro Botticelli. Calumny, Fraud, and Deception from *Calumny.*

351. Sandro Botticelli. *Calumny.* About 1494. Tempera on wood, height 24⅜ inches. Galleria degli Uffizi, Florence.

and purity. This is the figure of Truth, who stands naked at the extreme left, ignored and all but crowded out of the scene, connected with the other figures only by the glance of one who turns and regards her with prophetic questioning. She is Remorse, an ancient crone in black rags.

The allegory follows the description by Lucian of a vanished painting by the ancient Greek artist Apelles. Several other Renaissance artists have given us their ideas of what Apelles's *Calumny* might have looked like, but it is improbable that Botticelli painted his version simply as an exercise in the reconstruction of a lost masterpiece. Classical allegory was frequently Botticelli's vehicle of expression and, for that matter, it was the most popular means at the time for propounding moral judgments. In his *Calumny* Botticelli may have been concealing a specific accusation against contemporary society in the guise of classical symbols.

One theory is that *Calumny* allegorizes the political attacks on the Medici family, Botticelli's great patrons, that resulted in their exile from Florence after they had ruled it for several generations. The crime the artist pictures takes place within a loggia of purest classical-Renaissance design embellished with works of art, a setting that could symbolize Florence at the apogee of its cultivation under Medici patronage, now defiled by the monstrous event being enacted there. The serenity of the sea and sky opening out beyond the noble arcade is a final contrast and rebuke to the hysterical violence of the false trial.

The *Calumny* is more often interpreted as a concealed protest against the trial, conviction, and execution of the priest Savonarola. Today Savonarola would be called a revivalist; his apocalyptic sermons against the vanities of life, the corruption of power, and the moral decay of Italy in general made him for a while the most influential man in the city-state of Florence. A scholar and a man of God, he was also a fanatic so zealous that his power waned through the sheer exhaustion of his followers, who were unable to sustain his pitch of intensity. A menace to the temporal power of the Church as well as to the State, Savonarola was tried for heresy on charges that may or may not have been trumped-up. He was convicted after confessions made following an ordeal that may or may not have included physical torture, and was executed by hanging and then burned in the main public square of Florence, where not long before he had achieved his most spectacular triumphs. His pyre was built on the same spot where he had held his famous "bonfires of vanities," burning great mounds of such irreligious objects as false hair, cosmetics, rich costumes, and works of art not dedicated to the highest moral principles, all delivered up to the fire by temporarily repentant Florentines.

Although Botticelli is known to have come under Savonarola's influence, it is not likely that *Calumny* is a reference to the martyred priest's trial, conviction, and execution, since most scholars believe that the picture was painted before Savonarola was executed in 1498. But the intensity of the painting does suggest an anguished protest against the spirit of the witch-hunt, the punishment of innocent people who are sacrificed to public hysteria. Therein lies its parallel to the twentieth-century painting we are comparing with it, a picture speaking of the trial, conviction, and execution of two men, Nicola Sacco and Bartolomeo Vanzetti.

As in the case of Savonarola, the guilt or innocence of Sacco and Vanzetti was the subject of vehement controversy. The painter believed that they were the victims of a miscarriage of justice. We are not balancing the scales here, but are examining the protest made in pictorial form by an artist in the light of his own belief, in order to compare it with a similar subject approached in a different way.

Botticelli's painting accuses the Florentine government of ignorance, suspicion, envy, calumny, fraud, and deception; depicts it as unworthy of the crown and scepter of authority; proclaims the victim's innocence; and prophesies the city's remorse—all this in allegorical concealment. The modern painting makes parallel accusations with no effort whatsoever at disguising the message. In the *Passion of Sacco and Vanzetti* (352) all subtleties and indirections are abandoned for an uncompromising indictment.

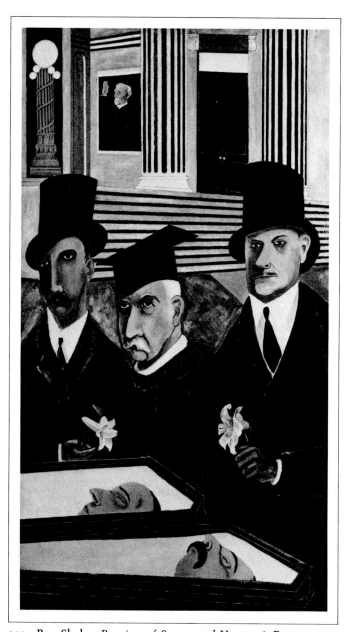

352. Ben Shahn. *Passion of Sacco and Vanzetti.* From a series of 23 paintings. 1931–32. Tempera on canvas, 84½ by 48 inches. Whitney Museum of American Art, New York. Gift of Edith and Milton Lowenthal in memory of Juliana Force.

Nicola Sacco was a fish peddler and philosophical anarchist; Bartolomeo Vanzetti a shoe-factory employee and radical agitator. In 1920 they were accused of killing two men in a payroll holdup at South Braintree, Massachusetts, and found guilty. But for six years liberals everywhere campaigned for their release on grounds that prejudice had convicted the men; essentially, that they were being convicted as an anarchist and a radical agitator rather than as killers in a holdup.

A series of sensational appeals culminated in the appointment of a committee of three, headed by President Lowell of Harvard and including the president of the Massachusetts Institute of Technology and a former judge. The opinion of this committee was that the guilty verdict should be sustained. Sentence of death on Sacco and Vanzetti was carried out in the prison at Charlestown, Massachusetts, on August 22, 1927. But a large body of considered opinion continued to believe the two men innocent.

Calumny and the *Passion of Sacco and Vanzetti* have a very close similarity of pictorial procedure beneath their primary differences of style. In the *Passion of Sacco and Vanzetti* the victims are not shown dragged naked to false judgment but are revealed in their coffins after execution. It does not take a great stretch of the imagination to associate the half-caricatured figure in academic cap and gown with Botticelli's figure of Calumny. He is flanked by two top-hatted figures holding lilies in their hands. They are certainly parallels to Fraud and Deception, the female figures who twine roses in Calumny's hair. The roses and the lilies borne by the top-hatted figures are the same false symbols of purity.

The parallel continues. Botticelli's unworthily crowned and sceptered false Judge is repeated in Shahn's painting by a framed portrait of the sentencing judge in the Sacco-Vanzetti case, his hand raised in a gesture that combines the oath of truth and a gesture of benediction, both of which are desperately ironical. This portrait hangs in the hall of a neo-classical court building corresponding to Botticelli's allegorical Renaissance palace. The only element without correspondence is the group of Remorse and Truth—if, indeed, the lamp in the upper left corner of the modern picture is not intended to be some such reference.

The four pictures we have seen so far have taken their subjects from specific instances of social cruelty or injustice. In varying degrees they accepted or overcame the limitation that can prevent this kind of picture from being an independent expression—the limitation, that is, of the observer's being dependent on knowledge of the specific event for full understanding of the picture's meaning. Even without this knowledge, even if we are left to find for ourselves their general sense, these four pictures are works of art of interpretive power or, at least, of curious fascination.

As a contrast, we may compare these pictures with John Trumbull's *The Declaration of Independence* (353)—

353. John Trumbull. *The Declaration of Independence.* 1786–94. Oil on canvas, 21⅛ by 31⅛ inches. Yale University Art Gallery, New Haven, Connecticut.

at the risk of being unfair to this worthy and much-loved painting by putting it into company that makes it look even more pedestrian than it is. Trumbull shows assembled in a room of admirable colonial style a group of dignified gentlemen conducting themselves with extraordinary decorum. The features of each participant are as true to life as Trumbull could make them; but in spite of the general solemnity and the air of consequence they have assumed, there is not much indication that the gentlemen are present at a climactic moment in the history of the modern world. They could easily be doing nothing more important than granting a charter to some minor institution, or signing one of those bothersome expressions of esteem that corporations have a habit of preparing for retiring directors. The social idealism, the political conflict, the prescience of war and sacrifice, in short, all the significant historical and emotional elements of a great moment in the course of human events are not even hinted at. Reducing our criticism to irreverent terms, the shortcoming in Trumbull's depiction of the signing of the Declaration of Independence on the first Fourth of July is that he has omitted fireworks. What do these impassive effigies have to do with the glory and the spiritual magnificence of the birth of a great nation?

Does *The Declaration of Independence* fall short because it lacks the vehemence of *The Executions of the Third of May*, the nervous intensity of *Calumny*, or the high moral purpose of the *Passion of Sacco and Vanzetti*? Unquestionably, it does—as an independent picture out of its context. But the shortcoming can be condoned, and the picture somewhat enriched, if we consider it as a reflection of the time in history—American history—when it was conceived. The subject illustrated here was one of four that Trumbull was commissioned to repeat for the rotunda of the Capitol in Washington and which he completed in 1824 (the other three being *The Surrender of Cornwallis at Yorktown*, *The Surrender of Burgoyne at Saratoga*, and *Washington Resigning His Commission*). The new nation, anxious to take its place with the established countries of the world, was more interested in proclaiming its dignity and solidity than its fire and imagination. The new Capitol was no country bumpkin of a building but a monument in the tradition of the great structures of ancient Rome, as revived and modified in the nations of the modern world. To maintain harmony with this architectural setting, it was necessary to select paintings that were imagined in the same faintly pompous spirit—a requirement that, it must be admitted, was perfectly compatible with Trumbull's shortcomings. Ideally, the four panels chosen to adorn the Capitol should have been conceived with a dignity and nobility that translated into visual terms Thomas Jefferson's masterpiece, the Declaration itself. But there was no artist in America with stature as a painter equal to Jefferson's as a statesman, and there was no European painter who could have thought and painted in terms of Jefferson's political idealism. As a result we have Trumbull's *Declaration of Independence*, a little dull and unimaginative if forced to

354. Eugène Delacroix. *Liberty Leading the People.* 1830. Oil on canvas, 8 feet 6 inches by 10 feet 8 inches. The Louvre, Paris.

355. Jacques-Louis David. *The Death of Socrates.* 1787. Oil on canvas, 51 by 77¼ inches. The Metropolitan Museum of Art, New York. Wolfe Fund, 1931.

compete with other pictures as a complete and expressive statement, yet posessing an appropriateness in the setting of its own time and of its own place that dignifies and enriches it.

Only six years later Delacroix painted his emotionalized *Liberty Leading the People* (354), a swirling, highly charged expression of the social ferment that led to revolutionary disorders in France in 1830. Both *The Declaration of Independence* and *Liberty Leading the People* are concerned with the same theme. If we try to imagine the Delacroix substituted for the Trumbull as an ornament for the national Capitol, however, it suddenly looks forced and high-flown, although no critic would seriously question its superiority over the American painting as the solution of a problem of expression.

What all this comes down to is that the essence of an event cannot be expressed simply by reproducing its circumstances. The painter with something to say about the history of his time may be wiser to forget factual appearances and depend on other ways of putting across his ideas. This is what Delacroix was doing when he painted *Liberty Leading the People,* and, less obviously, it is what Goya was doing in *The Executions of the Third of May,* which is an imagined, a created version of an actual event, not a reproduction of it.

An artist may comment on the contemporary scene without referring to it in the image he creates—and may even refer to it obliquely in images of the distant past. Jacques-Louis David's *The Death of Socrates* (355) is an instance. Although the subject is drawn from the ancient world, David's reference is to his own France. The old philosopher about to drink his cup of hemlock personifies the ideal of self-sacrifice for a principle. As a political allegory painted on the eve of the French Revolution, the picture declares that citizens who believe in the cause of liberty must accept the sacrifice of personal interests involved.

The Death of Socrates is a work of almost icy elegance, immaculately drawn and painted. Its surface is as tight and smooth as enamel, and the edges of its forms are sharp, clear, and uncompromising. In spite of a certain staginess, the arrangement is also severe—very severe in comparison with the esthetic tradition against which it revolted. A typical example of this tradition, Boucher's *The Toilet of Venus,* which we have already seen (104), shows why *The Death of Socrates* was a radically "modern" picture and why its technique was exemplary of a new social philosophy.

The Toilet of Venus was painted for an eighteenth-century French court society in which women determined much of the policy and for which they certainly dictated the taste. Fashionable décor consistently suggested the boudoir, whether applied to a bedroom, a sitting room, a court hall, or a chapel. Paintings were liberally incorporated into these decorative schemes as ornamental panels.

Boucher, with pictures like *The Toilet of Venus*, was an immense success because he developed a manner completely in harmony with the feminine delicacy of the style.

His typical female figure is a young girl of chubby proportions, with dewy lips, wide eyes, blond hair, and an air of perverse innocence suggesting more than anything else the mutual pleasures of seduction. In *The Toilet of Venus* she happens to be posed as the goddess of Love and Beauty, but even when Boucher painted milkmaids they were girls of the same cut, surrounded by the same opulent, fashionable swirls of taffetas, flowers, and ornamental paraphernalia. *The Toilet of Venus* suggests every feminine refinement of erotic pleasure; it is a perfumed, sweet-flavored painting, at once as fresh as the blossoms strewn about in it, as expensive as the jewels of the goddess, and as calculated as the wiles of a professional courtesan. It is a superb, professional job created for a limited audience, an audience of specialized cultivation with the means to indulge itself in the acquisition of every accessory to this cultivation, from desirable partners to fine or fashionable works of art.

Indirectly, a picture like *The Toilet of Venus* is a social comment even though the painter had no trace of such an idea in mind. In earlier chapters where we have insisted that painting is inevitably an expression of its time, we examined a painting by one of Boucher's contemporaries, Chardin. His still life of simple homely objects (**105**) was conceived in a spirit the reverse of Boucher's slick and superficial one. The two painters represent opposing factors in eighteenth-century culture: Chardin, the new philosophical interest in the common man and the nobility of simple things; Boucher, the tag end of the Renaissance period of luxury and power concentrated in inherited position. It was this conflict, we know, that at the end of the century would tear France apart in the Revolution.

In the light of the burgeoning French Revolution, David's *Death of Socrates* begins to make new sense. The revolutionary spirit was a denial of every quality of the *ancien régime* summarized in *The Toilet of Venus*: it was a proclamation of new social standards. Masculine decision must dominate feminine sensitivity; self-sacrifice must replace self-indulgence. Moral force becomes the paramount virtue, opposing its parallel vice, the cultivation of sensuous pleasures. Opulence gives way to austerity, fashionable invention to philosophical order.

When *The Toilet of Venus* and *The Death of Socrates* are placed side by side, it should be apparent that *The Death of Socrates*, for all its elegance, proclaims these new ideals. Its revolutionary approach is more apparent if we know that as a student young David was greatly influenced by Boucher and even did a competition picture, *The Combat of Minerva and Mars* (358, p. 301), in a windy adaptation of Boucher's style. But as a fledgling painter in Rome he departed from this manner to develop the severe, highly disciplined style that helped make him one of the powerful figures in the revolutionary government.

356. Detail from *The Death of Socrates.*

357. François Boucher. Detail from *The Toilet of Venus.*

358. Jacques-Louis David. *The Combat of Minerva and Mars.* 1771. Oil on canvas, 45 by 55 inches. The Louvre, Paris.

Instead of the seductive adolescent goddess in her boudoir, David paints a philosopher surrounded by his loyal followers. But subject matter aside, the choice and delineation of forms in the two pictures contrast correspondingly. As an instance, some of the drapery passages in the David are of great beauty (356), but it is a beauty of discipline and order as opposed to the profligate gaiety of Boucher's taffetas (357). Compositionally, the antithesis continues. The Boucher is designed in swirls and graceful curves; forms play coquettishly in and out of the picture depth; objects are piled and strewn about with wanton abandon. But the David gives an immediate impression of absolute control. Each figure is placed uncompromisingly, posed almost rigidly, in a scheme where every detail is calculated to the last degree. *The Toilet of Venus* is just as skillfully and even more subtly organized; the point is that its organization is directed to give an impression of lightness and spontaneity, whereas *The Death of Socrates* insists upon formal order as a virtue and calls our attention to the fact that every element in the picture is subject to its unyielding discipline.

Compared with the half-illustrative, half-symbolical approach of the *Passion of Sacco and Vanzetti*, the social statement of *The Death of Socrates* seems to be made in a roundabout way. But in the long run—and art is always a matter of the long run—the *Passion of Sacco and Vanzetti*

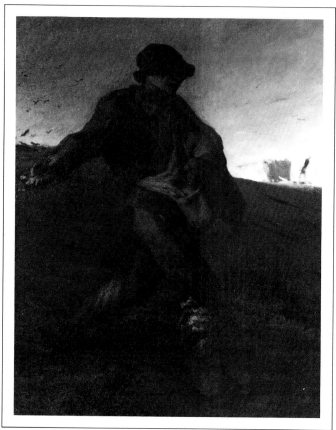

359. Jean François Millet. *The Sower.* 1850. Oil on canvas, 39¾ by 32½ inches. Museum of Fine Arts, Boston. Gift of Quincy A. Shaw.

will grow more and more enigmatic, while *The Death of Socrates* will continue to speak of high idealism, dedication, and sacrifice, whether or not any connection is made between it and the events that once surrounded it.

We referred a few paragraphs ago to the eighteenth-century philosophical conception of the innate nobility of simple things and the common man. In the nineteenth century this idea was given enough sentimental flavoring to make it palatable to a wide public in the art of Jean François Millet, whose *The Sower* (359) has come to be one of the best-known pictures in the world. The figure of a full-bodied peasant played against the light of a late afternoon sky is reduced to a near-silhouette. Details of dress and features are obscured in the interest of monumental breadth; this powerful mass fills the picture space and takes on an importance that the figure would not have if it were smaller in relation to the space or if objects in the immediate background were allowed to compete with it. If, for instance, the fields were shown stretching beyond the sower on every side, as of course they would in visual fact, leaving him isolated, surrounded by earth and sky, he could have become a symbol of man's smallness in the vastness of the world. As it is, the fields behind him suggest this vastness, but he dominates it, making us aware of the fundamental importance of the man who tills and sows and reaps, without whom the structure of society could not exist. Also, working in rhythm with the cycle of nature he is presumably closer to something of ultimate significance than the rest of us are. In "Saison des Semailles," a standard romantic poem that French schoolchildren are required to memorize, Victor Hugo eulogizes the peasant who throws the grain afar, dips his hand, throws again, and strides as rhythmically as the cycle of the seasons themselves across the plain in silhouette against deepening shadows that "seem to extend to the very stars the noble gesture of the sower."

The romantic ideal of the peasant as a kind of earth-symbol is all very well, but the lot of the nineteenth-century peasant was a little less than ideal when he was thought of as a human being. At close range, Nature's Nobleman had a distressing way of looking more like Society's Victim, a variation on Millet's theme that did not escape him even if he seldom dealt with it. In at least one picture, however, he showed the peasant as a creature brutalized by labor and poverty, the famous *Man with the Hoe* (360), which inspired another poet, Edwin Markham, to a comment different from Hugo's:

> Bowed by the weight of centuries he leans
> Upon his hoe and gazes on the ground.
> The emptiness of ages in his face,
> And on his back the burden of the world.
> Who made him dead to rapture and despair,
> A thing that grieves not and that never hopes,
> Stolid and stunned, a brother to the ox?
> Who loosened and let down this brutal jaw?

360. Jean François Millet. *The Man with the Hoe.* About 1863. Oil on canvas, 32 by 39½ inches. Private collection, San Francisco.

Whose was the hand that slanted back this brow?
Whose breath blew out the light within this brain?

Is this the Thing the Lord God made and gave
To have dominion over sea and land;
To trace the stars and search the heavens for power;
To feel the passion of Eternity?

The position of the French peasant some hundred years ago was neither as desperate as that of *The Man with the Hoe* nor as pleasant as that of the rest of Millet's simple folk, but the position of the Mexican peon at the beginning of this century was without question subhuman. In *The Liberation of the Peon*(**361**), Diego Rivera commemorates the social rescue of the Mexican peasant by the Agrarian Revolution.

Rivera, a leader in the only significant revival of fresco painting in two centuries, was commissioned to paint a

361. Diego Rivera. *The Liberation of the Peon.* 1931. Variation of a fresco in Ministry of Education, Mexico City, 1923–27. Fresco, 74 by 95 inches. Philadelphia Museum of Art. Gift of Mr. and Mrs. Herbert C. Morris.

362. Courtyard, Ministry of Education, Mexico City. Murals by Diego Rivera.

series of murals for the Ministry of Education (**362**) in Mexico City, an undertaking he started in 1923. He conceived the murals as a combination of historical fact, ancient legend, and sociological and political propaganda—a combination just as original but more harmonious than it sounds. The standard approaches for such commissions for the ornamentation of public buildings had crystallized into two familiar, threadbare forms. The more familiar was the obvious series of stuffy storytelling scenes in which historical figures stand around in costume like so many dummies in waxworks tableaux of famous events. The second approach might be called the routine-symbolical, in which groups of well-built male and female models are painted in decorative attitudes, holding cornucopias, shields, torches, scrolls, parts of machines (very advanced), and so on for the amount of wall space to be covered, and labeled Prosperity, Law, Justice, Art, Industry.

Rivera fell victim to neither of these bromides. His frescoes cover walls around open courts, where, read in sequence, they constitute a propagandistic textbook for the illiterate, who may read the history of Mexico in pictorial terms of agrarian-revolutionist ideology. *The Liberation of the Peon* symbolizes the end of an era of persecution and exploitation for the common Mexican, and the beginning of his liberation in the sense of political rights, land ownership, and education.

In the background, a hacienda of the oppressive landowning class is in flames. The revolutionists who have overthrown this régime are grouped around the peon, whose body is striped with whip marks. One man symbolically cuts a rope that binds the peon's wrists; another supports the body gently; a third covers its nakedness.

Rivera's murals are effective decorations aside from and often in spite of the insistent propagandistic fervor that sometimes defeats itself. It does so in *Dinner of the Millionaires* (**364**), where John D. Rockefeller, J. Pierpont Morgan, and Henry Ford are shown in caricature that overshoots the mark and gives us a newspaper cartoon rather than a work of art with expressive extensions beyond its immediate subject.

The Liberation of the Peon has these extensions. Compositionally, the scene is built along a sweeping line running diagonally through the picture along the limp body of the victim. This line is countered by the head and neck of the horse in upper center, which turns the line back and leads us again toward the right. On both sides the movement is stabilized by standing figures with strong vertical axes—the horse on the left, the man holding a horse on the right. Within this framework there are secondary rhythms of highly geometrized loops made by the ammunition belts, the ropes, saddles, hats, and the simplified, rounded forms of the figures. In places this decorative geometry is strong enough to distract our attention from the whole, as it should not have been allowed to do. The pattern on the chest of the horse to the left, for instance, is too conspicuous for so incidental a detail; the crisscrossed loops of ammu-

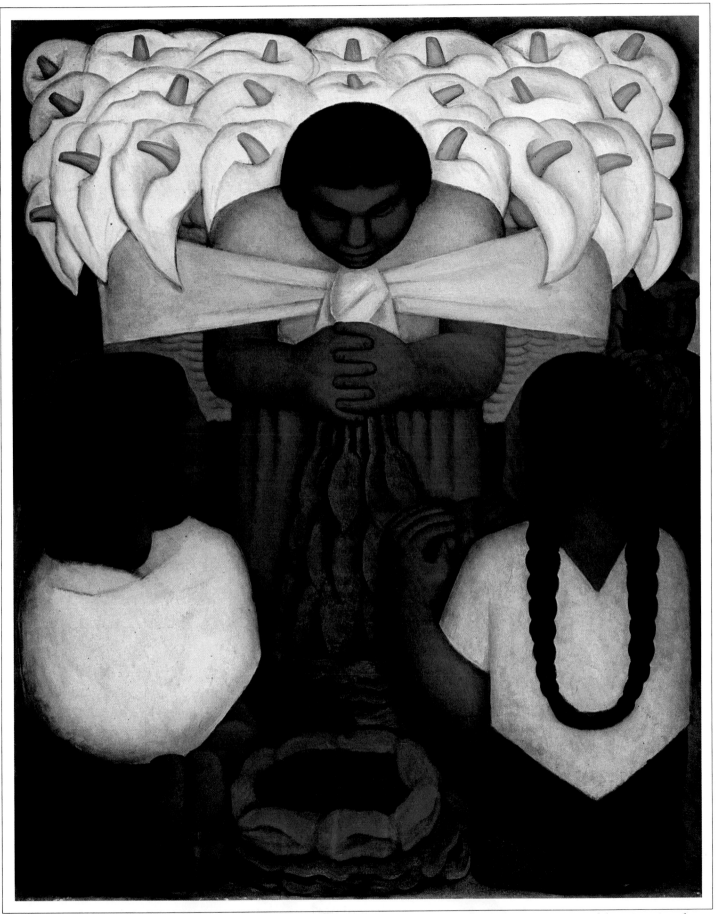

363. Diego Rivera. *Flower Day.* 1925. Oil on canvas, 58 by 47½ inches. Los Angeles County Museum of Art. Los Angeles County Funds.

364. Diego Rivera. *Dinner of the Millionaires.* 1923–27. Fresco. Ministry of Education, Mexico City.

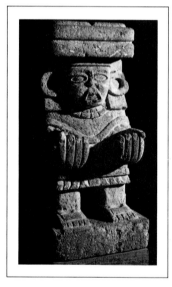

365. Central Mexico. *Standing Goddess.* A.D. 250–650. Volcanic stone with traces of green and red paint over stucco, height 36 inches. Philadelphia Museum of Art. Louise and Walter Arensberg Collection.

366. Aztec. *Rattlesnake.* 1200–1521. Rhyolite porphyry, diameter 23¾ inches. Dumbarton Oaks, Washington, D.C. Robert Woods Bliss Collection.

nition around the neck and chest of the standing figure at the right, the knot in the shirt, the design of the ropes, are also attractive enough to exist for themselves rather than as adjuncts to the whole. But in singling these out, we are finding flaws in a generally successful arrangement.

In beginning the murals, Rivera experimented with the juice of a Mexican cactus plant as his medium, an idea with special attractions for this particular commission, but it was not successful. He employed instead the pure fresco technique of fourteenth- and fifteenth-century Italian painters, also borrowing heavily from their pictorial tradition; the forms and the composition of *The Liberation of the Peon* are directly comparable to those of Giotto's *Lamentation* (**275**) in the Arena Chapel in Padua, painted in 1305. But it is one thing to depend parasitically upon a great tradition like that of early Renaissance Italy and another to use it as a point of departure, as Rivera did. Rivera's stature has been drastically reduced by most critics during the years after 1923 when he painted the Ministry of Education frescoes; yet *The Liberation of the Peon* stands as a legitimate work of art, whatever its borrowings from the Italians and its reduction of the forms of ancient Mexican art to a decorative formula.

To Rivera's way of thinking, a revival of the forms of native Mexican art, the gods and symbols of the pre-Columbian cultures and civilizations destroyed by the Spaniards, would revitalize the spirit of independence in Mexico's oppressed majority—the peons, in which the Indian strain was ethnically dominant over the European, and often quite pure. Rivera's identification of social reform with esthetic principles had a good sound, but not quite so good a look. In *Flower Day* (**363**) the figure of the gentle Indian with his load of calla lilies reflects the stylistic symmetry and conventionalizations of not at all gentle Aztec gods of death and destruction (**365**), while the wreath-like form at lower center is a similarly sweetened echo of another frequent Aztec motif, the coiled rattlesnake (**366**). There is not much evidence that the Mexican peasants understood Rivera's implication that the great traditions of their ancestors were still alive and legitimate in everyday life. But the wealthy Mexicans and gringo millionaires who were excoriated in Rivera's socialistic murals were attracted by the decorative sophistication of his synthesized style and became avid collectors of his paintings and drawings, an unhappy backfire in the art of social consciousness.

The "Mexican Renaissance" of the 1920's and 30's is the only important instance of an art movement created by artists themselves, dedicated to propagandizing the ideals of a political system—unlike the official art of the Soviet Union, where artists have been obliged to adhere to themes dictated by the government or subsist as esthetic outlaws. Rivera and the two other leading Mexican artists of the day—José Clemente Orozco and David Alfaro Siqueiros—were strong individualists, so strong in fact that in spite of the didactic humanitarian goal that they shared, their "renaissance" was finally defeated by intramural squabbles.

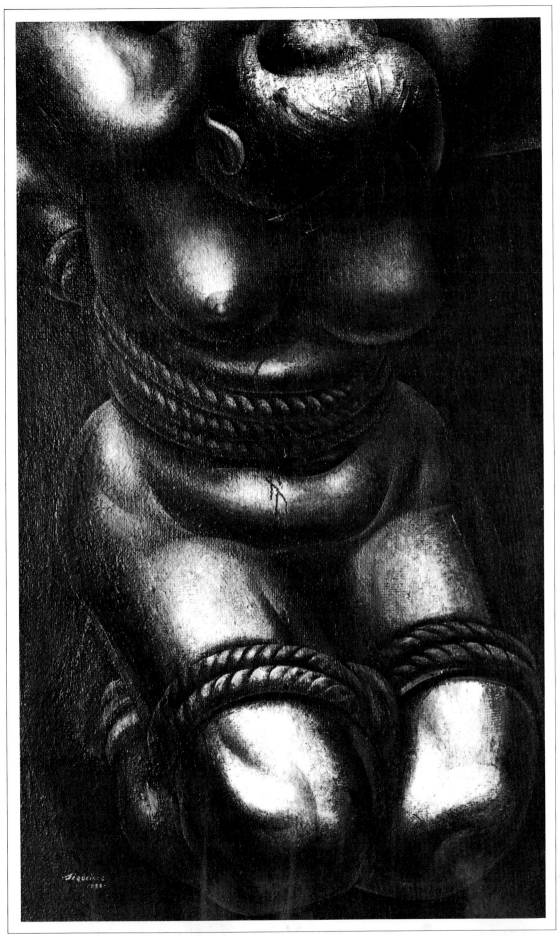

367. David Alfaro Siqueiros. *Proletarian Victim.* 1933. Duco on burlap, 6 feet 9 inches by 3 feet 11½ inches. The Museum of Modern Art, New York. Gift of the Estate of George Gershwin.

368. José Clemente Orozco. *Law and Justice.* 1921–24. Fresco. National Preparatory School, Mexico City.

369. William Hogarth. *The Rake's Progress.* First episode: *The Young Heir Takes Possession of the Miser's Effects.* Engraved version, published June, 1735. 14 by 16 inches. Boston Public Library, Print Department.

A strong element of satire characterizes much of Orozco's work, and we will show here an early example, *Law and Justice* (with the reminder that Orozco's noblest works are murals fusing Aztec mythology with the history of the Spanish conquest in the formation of the Mexican people and nation). *Law and Justice* (**368**) is a ribald condemnation of legal corruption, in which a tipsy lawyer bearing all the earmarks of the prosperous bourgeoisie whom Orozco despised as enemies of the proletariat cavorts with an equally tipsy Justice. Her sword is broken, her scales are out of whack, and the blindfold over the eyes that assures equal justice before the law has slipped to one side. One may wonder which is more effective as propaganda, this bitterly amusing satire, or the pretentious *Proletarian Victim* (**367**) by Siqueiros, who more often than not weakened his point by melodramatizing it.

In 1732 the English painter William Hogarth published *The Harlot's Progress,* a set of six engravings following the misadventures of an innocent country girl from her seduction upon arriving in London through a career embracing prosperity, poverty, prison, disease, and finally death. Partly fiction with overtones of soap opera and partly social comment on evils of the day, the series was a financial success. Although Hogarth secretly regarded them as hack work, he published two more sets, *The Rake's Progress* and *Marriage à la Mode,* the latter detailing the misfortunes of a young couple in a loveless marriage arranged by selfish and ambitious parents.

These pictorial tracts have become classics in the history of art and cornerstones in the history of art as social comment. They are an amalgam of rather fuzzy moral preachments, lively satire, and explicit records of the contemporary scene, lifted to significance by the sudden appearance here and there of episodes castigating social cruelties. We will follow the eight episodes of *The Rake's Progress* in some detail.

The first scene, *The Young Heir Takes Possession of the Miser's Effects* (**369**), is worth examining closely as an example of Hogarth's narrative method. We are told what is going on by pictorial signposts such as letters, open diaries, and other written matter that we must actually read to understand the action. This method is a most unpainterly way of going about the job, as Hogarth very well knew, but he was working for popular response from a not very art-minded public, and he found the formula to be a successful one.

The signposts show us a very young man, Tom Rakewell, called home from Oxford by the death of his father. There are a dozen indications that the father was a miser who managed to save a considerable fortune, and just as many that Tom is getting ready to spend it. A strongbox full of silver has been broken open; beside it are heaps of securities—mortgages, bonds, and indentures. A diary (lower right), conveniently open at an appropriate page, tells us under the date "May 5th, 1721" of the old miser's joy at having got rid of a bad shilling. The shabby furniture, the unused fireplace, and the contents of a dusty wardrobe, as well as a pair of old shoes resoled with leather from a family Bible, show that the father wasted no money. The young heir has hastened to change all this: at his direction a servant builds a fire, and a tailor measures Tom for new clothes.

The walls are being draped with black mourning cloth, disturbing a rotten molding that drops a fall of gold coins. Near the window the miser's escutcheon shows three vises clamped tight, with the motto "Beware!" The jack and spit, symbols of hospitality, have been carefully kept locked up in a cubbyhole (upper right).

Tom is arguing with an irate mother, who holds an apronful of his letters to her pregnant daughter, Sarah Young. Sarah, a good girl with whom Tom has had his way, weeps, holding his ring in one hand. Tom will pay her off with the sack of gold behind him, from which his lawyer filches a coin, a prophecy of the assaults he will make on the young rake's fortune on a larger scale after they get to London.

In the second scene, *The Levée* (**370**), Tom is in London holding a gathering in the French (and to Hogarth, everything French was contemptible) manner. He is cultivating all the fashionable graces; hence his entourage, with identifiable portraits of London figures, including a dancing master, a French fencing master who lunges with the shortsword, an English instructor in quarterstaff who looks on disapprovingly, a landscape architect, a professor of music at a harpsichord, a jockey with a trophy in the form of a silver bowl presumably won by one of Tom's horses, and in the background tailors, perukemakers, hatmakers, and a poet who hopes for Tom's patronage. Portraits of fighting cocks on the wall show that the young blade is also interested in that sport.

Skipping the third scene for the moment, we find in the fourth scene, *The Arrest* (**371**), that our rake has made the grade socially and is on his way to be received at court. Or at least we learn it if we identify the palace of Saint James in the background and if we recognize, as Hogarth's contemporaries would, two figures of Welshmen wearing enormous leeks, a symbol that fixes the day as March 1, sacred to the titular saint of Wales and one observed by a reception at court. (If this seems farfetched, think how easily today we would identify a date as March 17 if a picture included an Irishman appropriately displaying a shamrock emblem and, perhaps, lining up for a parade.) It is easier for us to identify a bailiff who stops Tom's sedan chair and threatens him with arrest for debt. Bankrupt, Tom is saved by Sarah Young, the girl he had wronged. Her reappearance at this particular moment, fortunate for Tom, is a plausible coincidence. We see by her costume that she is now a milliner and has come to observe the dress of the people arriving at the reception. She pays the bailiff from her own purse.

This is Tom's chance for repentance and redemption; but in the next scene, *The Marriage* (**372**), we find him marrying a hideous old woman, obviously rich, who has

370. *The Rake's Progress.* Second episode: *The Levée.*

371. *The Rake's Progress.* Fourth episode: *The Arrest.*

372. *The Rake's Progress.* Fifth episode: *The Marriage.*

accepted his proposal with such alacrity that her maid is still arranging her wedding gown at the ceremony. Tom is hardly able to hide his repugnance for his bride. Sarah, holding Tom's baby, stands in the background while her mother tries to battle her way into the chapel.

The story goes on with Tom's losing his new wife's fortune in a gaming house (373) and follows him to debtors' prison (374), where Sarah Young, unable to help him further, falls in a faint while his hag of a wife berates him. In the last scene, *The Madhouse* (375), Tom ends up in Bedlam, London's insane asylum, a maniac among maniacs, not even recognizing his faithful Sarah, who still stands by.

As a narrative, *The Rake's Progress* is lively enough; as a moral lesson, it is ambiguous because while vice is punished, virtue is not rewarded. As social comment, it is largely satirical; but in the last two scenes, the debtors' prison and especially Bedlam, the story rises above itself.

In debtors' prison Tom has tried to write a play to recoup his fortunes. A rejection note lies beside him on the table. Behind him the turnkey presses for his prison fees, and an errand boy refuses to leave a mug of beer Tom has ordered but cannot pay for. The other inmates are so picturesque as to confuse the issue somewhat. The man who helps support Sarah is identified by a scroll as one "J.L. now a prisoner in the Fleet" (London's notorious debtors' prison), who has been working on "a new scheme for paying the debts of the nation." And in the background another prisoner operates a chemical apparatus, possibly tied up with alchemy, while on the canopy of the bed (upper right) a pair of wings designed to be worn by a human being are a third symbol of visionary foolishness. In spite of these distractions, our attention is called to the squalor and hopelessness of the Fleet.

The scene in Bedlam (a corruption of Bethlehem) Hospital is more appalling. The inmates are a roster of standard insanities—the religious maniac, the naked man with delusions of grandeur, the hopeless depressive seated on the stairs, and various gibbering manic types. The two women in the background are visitors. Bedlam was open as a kind of sideshow for the public, and according to contemporary records was a notorious meeting place for sexual intriguers.

To what extent was Hogarth actually protesting against the cruelty of social institutions in these pictures of Fleet Prison and Bedlam? Although he reveals them in all their foulness, he does not do much more than record the actual state of things. But the state of things was so bad that any truthful record had to constitute a protest.

Although another artist might have treated these subjects humorously or with the morbid, callous curiosity of the two women visitors to Bedlam, it must have been quite possible for Hogarth's contemporaries to miss the point of his implied criticism of the institutions, for the pictures did not reveal any conditions not well known to everybody. If *The Rake's Progress* is a moral lesson, and if Fleet Prison and Bedlam, for all their horrors, are only the hells to which

373. *The Rake's Progress.* Sixth episode: *The Gaming House.*

374. *The Rake's Progress.* Seventh episode: *Debtor's Prison.*

375. *The Rake's Progress.* Eighth episode: *The Madhouse.*

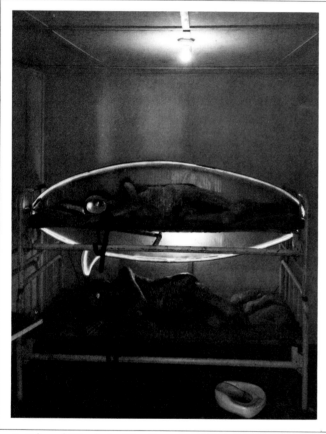

376. Edward Kienholz. *The State Hospital.* 1966. Construction—plaster, neon, glass, fibers, metals, light bulb—approximately 8 feet high, 14 inches wide at front. Moderna Museet, Stockholm.

our sinner is legitimately damned, then Hogarth's social protest is confused with his moral warning that his rake is getting no worse than he deserved. But since Hogarth once said that he would rather have "checked the progress of cruelty than have been the author of Raphael's cartoons," we may take it that he had some such protest in mind.

We have omitted one episode from *The Rake's Progress,* which we will see in a moment, but first we might look parenthetically at a twentieth-century American artist's version of a madhouse to compare it with Hogarth's Bedlam. The eighteenth-century artist's social protest in the story of a foolish young man's career is adulterated by its lively appeal as a pictorial novelette and its confusion between personal morality and society's obligation to care for its wayward or incompetent members. But Edward Kienholz's *The State Hospital* (**376**) can leave no question in the observer's mind as to the horror of the situation represented and the brutal side of a society in which that situation can exist.

Kienholz worked in a mental institution in 1948. In 1964 he described his project of *The State Hospital,* based on his memory of cruelties and indifference to the suffering of inmates that he had witnessed, as follows:

> This is a tableau about an old man who is a patient in a state mental hospital. He is in an arm restraint on a bed in a bare room. (The piece will have to include an actual room consisting of walls, ceiling, floor, barred door, etc.) There will be only a bedpan and a hospital table (just out of reach). The man is naked. He hurts. He has been beaten on the stomach with a bar of soap wrapped in a towel (to hide tell-tale bruises). His head is a lighted fish bowl with water that contains two live black fish. He lies very still on his side. There is no sound in the room.
>
> Above the old man in the bed is his exact duplicate, including the bed (beds will be stacked like bunks). The upper figure will also have the fish bowl head, two black fish, etc. But, additionally, it will be encased in some kind of lucite or plastic bubble (perhaps similar to a cartoon balloon), representing the old man's thoughts.
>
> His mind can't think for him past the present moment. He is committed there for the rest of his life.

Kienholz's "tableaux," as he calls his combinations of sculpture and real objects, are extensions of the "assemblage" idea that we have already seen used for esthetic purposes (**70**). In *The State Hospital*—which was executed in 1966 with a few variations from the concept written out in 1964—the combination of sculptured figures (cast from life) with actual paraphernalia accentuates the horror of a situation that would have been lessened if all the objects had been translated into sculpture.

The episode we omitted from *The Rake's Progress* is the third, an early station on Tom's road to ruin. Hogarth's engravings for the popular market were first created as

377. William Hogarth. *The Orgy,* third episode of *The Rake's Progress.* About 1733. Oil on canvas, height 24½ inches. Sir John Soane's Museum, London. Courtesy of the Trustees.

378. Henri de Toulouse-Lautrec. *Salon in the Rue des Moulins.* 1895. Oil on canvas, 43⅞ by 52½ inches. Musée Toulouse-Lautrec, Albi, France.

paintings; we are illustrating the painting of *The Orgy* (377). The details are largely self-explanatory, except for the portraits of Roman emperors (each but Nero's with its head cut out) and the staff and lantern by Tom's chair (probably trophies of some drunken prank). The woman spitting gin across the table at her rival is not an invention. Hogarth witnessed the incident while visiting Moll King's Tavern with an artist friend, one Francis Hayman. Hogarth knew these brothel-taverns and their inmates well; if the bawds in the picture are not portraits, they are close to it.

The brothel scene is chosen for illustration to make a comparison with Toulouse-Lautrec's *Salon in the Rue des Moulins* (378), painted in 1895. Hogarth's painting, whatever its moral content in other ways, is unconcerned with his prostitutes except as accessories to the narrative of Tom's adventures. He tells us that loose company leads a foolish young man to a bad end, but does not indicate that the women are engaged in anything more distressing than a rollicking, profitable evening at Tom's expense. In other words, the human condition is not involved in this illustration of a social evil except in the most roundabout way.

But beneath its apparently callous objectivity as reportage on sordid aspects of Parisian life, Lautrec's art makes compassionate observations on contemporary social values—much more so than Hogarth's, of which the reverse is true. *Salon in the Rue des Moulins*, referring to a brothel frequented by the artist, is an intensely moral picture in spite of its "immoral" theme, and subjective in spite of its air of casual detachment from anything more profound than a bit of journalistic on-the-spot description. And indeed each figure in the painting is a portrait of an inmate of this particular *maison close*; the seated one facing us is the madam of the place. But instead of Hogarth's hilarious orgy, we have here an expression of infinite lassitude, a suggestion of stagnant air where the spirit languishes, a mood that has as little to do with hope as it does with hopelessness. Hogarth preaches that the wages of sin are madness and death; in Lautrec's world, they are infinite boredom, the desiccation of the human spirit, and stultification into brutish semiconsciousness.

Hogarth's "moral comedies" take place in the fashionable half-world of the early eighteenth century; Lautrec concentrates on Parisian bohemia at the end of the nineteenth. Both men are quite specific in their incidental references. (Lautrec's salon is now taking on the air of a period room, as Hogarth's interiors have long since done.) The difference we find in the painters, when we compare the brothel scenes, is that Hogarth is interested in people typed as social phenomena, while Lautrec is interested in people as individuals affected by the structure of society.

There comes a point where what we have been calling social consciousness merges with a more general consciousness of the human condition within the complexities of the world. Lautrec's *Salon in the Rue des Moulins* reaches this point; it would be difficult to say whether it is more a comment on prostitution or more a comment on human beings who happen to be prostitutes. In that respect it stands midway between Hogarth's social observation and a disturbing comment on humanity painted by an American in 1929–30—Ivan Albright's *Into the World There Came a Soul Called Ida* (**379**).

This mass of flesh, luminous with decay, pitted, scarred, and swollen with time, partially covered with bits of cheap imitation silk—this piteous image may or may not be that of a prostitute, but it is certainly an image of the mortality of the flesh and of the spirit. By the clothes, dressing table, and knickknacks, all of them shoddy machine products of the most painful ugliness and repellent vulgarity, this double mortality is linked to some evils of our civilization—its crassness and especially its exploitation of mediocrity. To that extent, the picture is a social comment whether it was intended as one or not. The picture is not a tragic one since the subject is without nobility, a pathetic creature mercilessly painted. But the social implications are no less disturbing for being inherent in the subject rather than propounded by the artist.

The theme of frustration and loneliness in individual lives within a society that is supposed to offer them everything—the theme that we called "the exploitation of mediocrity" in the case of the soul named Ida—has been a recurrent one in American art of our century. We have already examined the head of a sculpture by Duane Hanson as an example of extreme realism in presentation. But extreme realism is also typical of the effigies in waxworks museums. Just where does a sculpture like *Couple with Shopping Bags* (**380**) become something more than pore-by-pore reproduction of nature? What is the social or humanistic comment beneath this exaggerated realism?

Here are two people who must have been normally attractive in their youth, and normally high-spirited in their confidence of finding their place in the best of all possible worlds. In early middle age they are defeated—the woman sullen, the man despairing. Confronted by these faces, a poet could ask variations on the questions Edwin Markham asked about the *Man with the Hoe*. What turned youthful rapture to despair, what extinguished the light within these spirits? What has gone wrong? Economically, this couple is secure enough somewhere in the middle brackets of a society that has offered its middle class more material benefits than any other in the history of the world. They are dressed in wonder fabrics that they will wash in a wonder washing machine with the new wonder detergent that competes with other wonder products for their attention every night on the TV. Their shopping bags must contain food with what the manufacturer calls new wonder ingredients, and they are probably dosing themselves with new wonder cures for colds, aches, pains, and upset stomachs. The commercials on their set tonight will tell them of the latest new wonders available to make their lives dirt-free, care-free, and work-free, from cat food to automobiles. And yet nothing wonderful ever seems to happen for them.

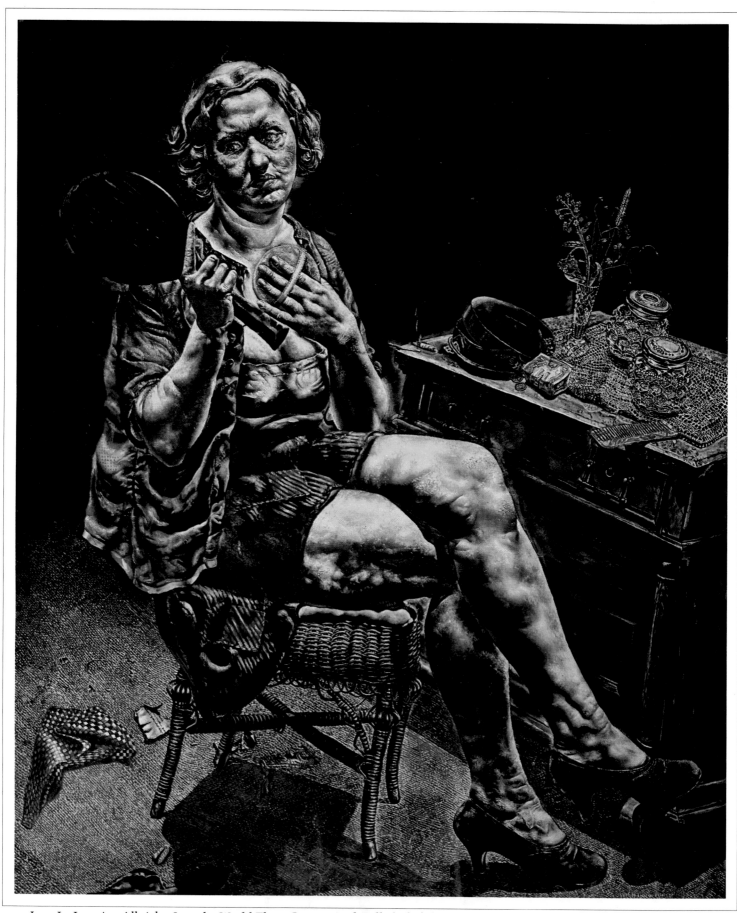

379. Ivan Le Lorraine Albright. *Into the World There Came a Soul Called Ida* (*The Lord in His Heaven and I in My Room Below*). 1929–30. Oil on canvas, 55 by 46 inches. The Art Institute of Chicago. Gift of the artist.

380. Duane Hanson. *Couple with Shopping Bags.* 1976. Polyester resin and fiber glass, polychromed in oil, with clothing and accessories, life size. Courtesy O. K. Harris Gallery, New York.

381. George Segal. *Subway.* 1968. Construction—plaster, metal, glass, rattan, electrical parts, light bulbs—90 by 114½ by 53 inches. Collection Mrs. Robert B. Mayer.

382. Peter Blume. *The Eternal City.* 1937. Oil on composition board, 34 by 47⅞ inches. The Museum of Modern Art, New York. Mrs. Simon Guggenheim Fund.

The realization that American life is not perfect shattered our national complacency in the 1920's with the appearance of books like Sinclair Lewis's *Main Street* and Sherwood Anderson's *Winesburg, Ohio.* But the locales were small towns, implying that life in the cities, with their cultural advantages, was different. In 1949 Arthur Miller wrote one of the masterpieces of the American theater, *Death of a Salesman,* in which an honest man finds himself lost at the end of a career based on the false values promulgated as basic virtues in a materialistic consumer society. Hanson's people (it is easier to think of them as people than as sculptures) are the current victims of a society now, in effect, completely urbanized, yet as unrewarding to them as the small-town cultures of their grandfathers. Hanson calls up the couple with shopping bags as witnesses for the prosecution in his indictment of a persistent aspect of our society, which has failed to offer the inner satisfactions of human life that less advanced civilizations seem to have offered generously.

The theme of urban loneliness that runs through modern American art is all the more poignant because this loneliness persists in the crowd, seems even to be generated by the crowd. In George Tooker's *The Subway* (**383**), this most hectic area of New York is composed of interlocking prison cells; each person, for all the presence of others, is isolated, uncertain, fearful. Three men in telephone booths are clones of one another, symbolical of the conformity imposed on members of a supposedly individualistic society. In sculpture, George Segal brings an almost spectral loneliness to his subway passenger (**381**). We have already mentioned the American artist Edward Hopper as a painter of loneliness, and we may refer back to that brief passage (**113**). But there is a difference between Hopper and the artists we have been discussing here, which is that Hopper's interpretation of a commonplace city scene is his expression of a personal loneliness that permeates all his work, rather than a deliberate social comment.

With the exceptions of Botticelli's allegory and Tooker's nightmare subway, the paintings and sculptures we have examined as social comment or record have been on the whole realistic. Their realism has ranged from Shahn's near-caricature to David's neo-classical idealism, from Daumier's broad generalization of form to Albright's microscopic detail, from Trumbull's prosaic reconstruction to Rivera's decorative patterning. Their realism is not surprising; fantasy by definition should be useless to the artist as social critic. An exception is Peter Blume's *The Eternal City* (**382**), where fantasy and sociopolitical content are inseparable.

The painting was completed in 1937 after several years of work following the artist's visit to Rome in 1932. It was the heyday of Mussolini's power as Il Duce. His Fascist state was presenting every surface indication of Italian rejuvenation. Trains ran on time, as they had never done before in Italy. Tourists regarded this miracle a bit uncomfortably, finding the practical convenience rewarding in

383. George Tooker. *The Subway.* 1950. Egg tempera on composition board, 18 by 36 inches. Whitney Museum of American Art, New York. Juliana Force purchase.

spite of the brutality and violence they read of but never met face to face. The full Fascist potential had not yet been revealed by events in Germany that were to make Mussolini's Italy only an amateurish preface to Hitler's demonstration of man's full capacity for evil.

Blume's picture shows Mussolini as a scareface leaping out of a jack-in-the-box. Weightless upon its paper stalk, the head was inspired by a papier-mâché statue of the dictator seen by the artist in Rome. With brilliant green face and bright red lips it is a shocking dissonance (the painter's own word) in the color scheme. Blume writes: "It hurt me aesthetically to paint the head but . . . the question of harmony was superseded by other considerations."

What these other considerations are should be apparent in the surrounding elaborate fantasy-allegory. Anyone who has visited Rome—and most who have not—will recognize that *The Eternal City* is a composite of familiar elements: the underground corridors of the Colosseum, the pillared monuments of the Forum, the vaults of the catacombs, a late baroque shrine, and the bell tower of an early medieval church. These references to the past do not insist on Rome's grandeur; corruption and decay are everywhere, culminating in a pile of broken sculpture and architectural fragments in the foreground, where a miserable beggar sits. Yet all of it is more substantial than the Hallowe'en jack-in-the-box Duce springing from it. The luxuriant vines and the tree may symbolize the city's eternal vitality, its capacity for rebirth from age to age, just as the peaks in the background, which define Italy's geographical entity, suggest an eternity and indestructibility that reduce the Fascist régime to an affair of the moment.

Unfortunately fascism could not be taken that lightly. In April 1937, while Blume was finishing *The Eternal City*, Fascist planes bombed the Spanish city of Guernica and gave the world a sinister prophecy of what World War II was going to be like. This crime generated the most powerful indictment of war that our war-ridden century has produced, a painting worthy to stand with Goya's *Executions of the Third of May*—Picasso's *Guernica*, which, for convenience, we will repeat in illustration here (**394**).

In a landmark essay of the early 1920's, *The Dehumanization of Art*, the Spanish philosopher José Ortega y Gasset commented that the new forms of art, including cubism, were not adaptable to humanistic expression, but could only serve the pleasures of an élite class interested in art for art's sake. This seemed true until Picasso, in his anguish and rage after the bombing of Guernica, produced virtually overnight a painting in Cubist-derived forms that stands as a humanistic statement accessible to an audience innocent of any knowledge of esthetic theory and uninterested in—or even opposed to—modern art.

Suddenly the Cubist deformations were no longer formal exercises for analysis by estheticians but seemed to have been produced by the physical violence and emotional intensity of the subject. It was as if the whole history of cubism, since Picasso's innovational *Les Demoiselles d'Avignon* (**169**) thirty years earlier, had been directed toward this unexpected consummation, by which a form of horror peculiar to our century—bombing from the air—had been represented in a form of art invented to express it.

Confronted by *Guernica*, who can imagine this painting redone realistically? Earlier in this chapter we spoke of pictorial style as an element of social statement, citing David's iciness in *The Death of Socrates* and Boucher's playfulness in *The Toilet of Venus* as examples. If Picasso's *Guernica* stands in the future as the masterpiece of the twentieth century, as is quite possible, it will be because of the triple coincidence of a subject of profound significance, an artist passionately involved, and a formal style appropriate to the release of expression at full force.

After *Guernica*, it seems unfair to conclude this chapter with a painting that, although excellent, must bear comparison with Picasso's masterpiece as an ambitious treatment of a closely related subject, James Rosenquist's *F-111* (**395**); but chronology dictates the necessity. During the twenty-eight years that elapsed between the two paintings, the technology of mass murder from the air produced the atom bomb, and Rosenquist's painting is a protest against the production of an experimental bomber, the F-111 (F-One-Eleven), highly publicized in the years of the "cold war" with Russia. Produced at vast expense, the F-111 proved faulty and was scrapped. Paradoxically, the best thing that came from the program was Rosenquist's painting protesting it.

Measuring 10 feet high and 86 feet long, *F-111* was designed to be installed as a mural on three walls. Rosenquist was a prominent practitioner of pop art, the move-

384. Pablo Picasso. *Guernica.* 1937. Oil on canvas, 11 feet 5½ inches by 25 feet 5¾ inches. Estate of the artist.

385. James Rosenquist. *F-111* (central portion and portion at right of center). 1965. Oil on canvas with aluminum. Entire work, 10 by 86 feet. Private collection.

ment, then at its peak, that drew its images from the most commonplace mass-produced aspects of America's consumer society, everything from soap boxes to the standard formula for glamour girls. Routine advertising art of the magazine and billboard type was often adapted satirically in deadpan social comment. Rosenquist himself had worked as a signpainter on the gigantic billboards above Times Square. One passage in *F-111* is adapted from advertising for canned spaghetti with tomato sauce. Rosenquist gives it a double meaning: juxtaposed as it is with a representation of an atomic explosion, the spaghetti becomes the bloody entrails of a bombing victim. (The "umbrella" of the atomic cloud is accompanied by the commercial image of a real umbrella, to less point.)

The pros and cons of the merits and shortcomings of *F-111* can be rationalized back and forth indefinitely, and we might reach the conclusion that in this case the means offered by pop art were inadequate to the magnitude of the theme. But *F-111* would remain an important work of sociologically oriented art even if we had nothing but the climactic image of the little girl under a hair dryer. There is another double reference here, first to the vulgarity of a culture that sends little girls to beauty parlors, and second to the horror of a civilization that murders little girls along with everybody else from the air—for the hair dryer is also the nose cone of a bomber.

Postscripturally, we might ask why the art of protest has inspired no monumental sculptures comparable to *Guernica*. One good reason is that monuments are not likely to be commissioned until years after the events they commemorate, and by that time the topicality of an event has faded. The victors, whether of war or some other social struggle, are more interested in celebrating the heroism of leaders or martyrs than in raging against forces that, after all, have been defeated. One recent sculpture of rage that must inevitably bear comparison with Picasso's *Guernica*, since the subject and intention are so nearly parallel, is Ossip Zadkine's *The Destroyed City* (**386**), in Rotterdam. The entire center of that city was destroyed by German air bombardment in 1940 several hours after the city had capitulated. In angular, twisted forms, less abstract than Picasso's, a figure shouts defiance to the sky, arms extended in a pose that recalls the defiant figure in Goya's *Executions of the Third of May*—but is less real.

Here a critic is on uneasy ground—or, at least, one who finds Zadkine's sculpture unequal to its theme must feel uncomfortable in saying that for all its admirable, even noble, intentions, he finds the statue little more than a mannered exercise in semi-abstraction, neither tragic nor wrathful. The total effect of rebuilt Rotterdam is deeply moving; it must depend on personal responses whether the monument is ennobled by association, standing as it does against that background, or whether it is not only an intrusion in the first place but an inadequate expression of its theme as well.

Somehow, in either case, the fire is gone.

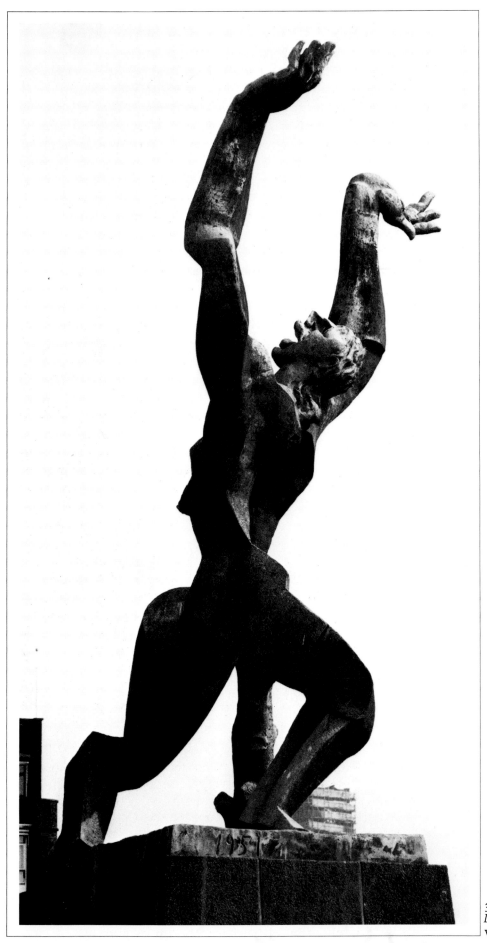

386. Ossip Zadkine. *The Destroyed City (The Destruction of Rotterdam)*. 1954. Bronze. Leuvehaven Quay, Rotterdam.

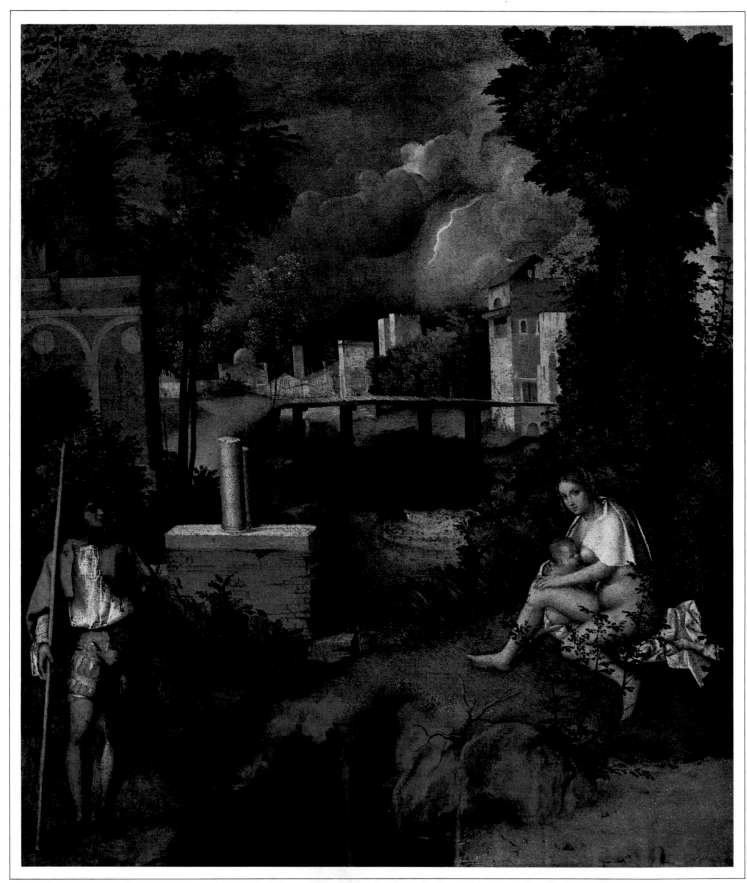

387. Giorgione. *The Tempest*. About 1505–10. Oil on canvas, 30¼ by 28¾ inches. Galleria dell'Accademia, Venice.

Chapter Thirteen

THE ARTIST AS VISIONARY

We have defined realism, expressionism, and abstraction, and have offered enough examples of each to indicate that the variations and overlappings of each classification may be infinite. We have analyzed composition as pattern, as structure, and as a relationship of forms determined by special problems of expression and narration. We have seen that the various techniques available to artists are not only the means of bringing a work of art into existence but may be in themselves elements of expression.

If these discussions have succeeded in their purpose, then anyone who has followed them should have found ways of looking at works of art to discover within them some meanings not apparent on the surface. But it should also be clear by now that in spite of the general principles we have outlined, formula must always take second place to invention for the artist—which means that formula must always take second place to perception for the observer. In outlining general principles, we have tried to give some kind of basis for the speedier development of individual perception. In the end, a work of art is a communication between artist and observer, in which a guide or interpreter is only in the way.

We have thought of these discussions as an introduction to art, but all acquaintance with art is an introduction to it, since each new work of art is a new experience. If by a miracle it were possible for one person to have universal knowledge of art up to this moment, everything he knew would be only an introduction to what will be created tomorrow, whether good or bad, false or sincere, conventional or revolutionary. Art is so various that once we have begun its exploration we are always in midstream.

Since we have been engaged in something like a course of study, it might seem reasonable to devote this last chapter to an exposition of some knottier problems than any we have tackled so far, basing the explanations on what we have learned from preceding examples. But this would suggest that the understanding of art depends more than it does on the application of rules and systems. Instead, we will be concerned with some subjects that are essentially unexplainable in any specific sense. Visionary, grotesque, fantastic, or mystical, they depend to the utmost on that communication between a work of art and its observer that may be facilitated by acquaintance with rules and general principles but is finally determined by the unique reaction of the individual to a unique image.

Giorgione's *The Tempest* (**387**) is—partly by accident—a perfect example of such a situation because, though its subject has been lost, the picture is so provocative that it must take on meaning of some kind for anyone with a grain of imagination. The meaning must be entirely personal; the title is an arbitrary one, since we have no idea what Giorgione originally called it. (It is also sometimes called *Soldier and Gypsy,* a title that presumes more than we can actually know about the two figures.) The painting is beautifully composed; its individual elements are quite irrational and contradictory in any narrative or psychological connection that we can perceive, yet they are integrated into a perfectly unified pictorial whole.

To one side of the picture, a young woman suckles a child. She is nude except for a length of cloth draped across her shoulders. Her attitude is not particularly one of maternal tenderness; she seems rather to be engaged in some casual, indefinable reverie. Her presence in the countryside upon this grassy bank, amid luxuriant sprays and clumps of foliage, is unexplained yet appears inevitable. She seems unaware of the other figure or of the gathering storm; although she glances in our direction, she does so without any response to our presence. It is important to the extraordinary impression of isolation created around her that she is separated from us by a delicate filigree of leaves and branches springing from the rock in the immediate foreground.

The figure on the opposite side is a very young man, hardly more than an adolescent, sometimes described as a knight, sometimes as a shepherd, who carries a staff that is not quite appropriate to either. The figure is graceful and assured, alert in contrast to the half-meditative, half-enchanted young woman. He regards her attentively, and his position in the extreme foreground and his graceful pose suggest an awareness of the observer. He is the only element that invites our participation in the picture. We are barely admitted to the right foreground, and we are fenced out of the left, as soon as we have encompassed the figure of the youth, by a barrier of foliage, water, and architectural ruins, beyond which some buildings of a town or city rise in spectral illumination against a dark sky breached by a streak of lightning.

Giorgione, a Venetian, painted *The Tempest* about 1508. It is a typical Venetian Renaissance painting in its transmutation of sensuous luxury into pastoral idyllicism. In Giorgione's other paintings and in works by his contemporaries we find the same combination of soft golden flesh, tender foliage, gleaming velvets and satins, mellowed stones, the same sense of the touch of air, the same glowing lights and vibrant shadows. But *The Tempest* somehow remains outside the formula. There is no other picture anywhere quite like it. Compare it, for instance, with *Pastoral Concert* (**388**), a superb painting frequently attributed to Giorgione as a compound expression of the delights of the flesh and the senses that rises above salaciousness or vulgarity because it is conceived in the spirit of pagan worship of sensuous delight, rather than commonplace indulgence.

The difference between the two pictures, which has led some authorities to reject the attribution to Giorgione, is that in *The Concert* our curiosity is satisfied by the completeness we find in it. Its greatness lies there, in the

388. Giorgione, attributed. *Pastoral Concert.* Before 1510. Approximately 43 by 54 inches. The Louvre, Paris.

rich fullness of its statement. But the fascination of *The Tempest* lies in its atmosphere of lyrical mystery. Someday the subject may be discovered, but it seems probable that Giorgione deliberately invented a mysterious picture, a probability supported by the fact that X rays have revealed that the figure of the "knight" was originally that of another woman. Such a change would be difficult to account for if the picture illustrates a lost poem or an episode from an ancient Greek story, as has been conjectured. A more likely explanation is that the subject is an allegory, which would account for the curious combination of figures and setting but would change the picture from a poetic mystery into a didactic illustration.

Nothing, of course, could quite do that. No explanation, however precise and irrefutable, could transform *The Tempest* from a poetic masterpiece into the collection of symbols that make up an allegory. For the poetry does not lie in the objects themselves, nor does the mystery lie entirely in the strangeness of their combination. It is their unification as forms in light and their harmony as sensuous experiences that lift this collection of miscellaneous and itemizable elements to the level of an experience not to be explained in terms of the world. It would not be proper or safe to wonder whether *The Tempest* is a more expressive picture for having lost its subject. But it is probably a different picture. Its details remain explicit while the total statement Giorgione intended them to make remains mysterious, so that its meaning is of necessity a matter of personal response to all the suggestions involved. *The Tempest* may have begun as an allegory; it has become a dream. When we look at it the dream becomes our own, and our own interpretation of it becomes the legitimate one.

What is the image of a dream? By popular conception it is fuzzy, misty, half-formed, and wavering—no doubt because of the quickness with which dreams fade from memory, their elusiveness when we try to describe them. But in actual experience a dream may be and usually is acutely vivid. When painters set about exploring this otherworld, the best of them have usually chosen to do so in forms of exceptional clarity, sharper than reality, so that the fantasy and unreality of the visionary forms are intensified.

William Blake, the late eighteenth/early nineteenth-century English painter and poet whose *The Wise and the Foolish Virgins* we have already seen (**220**), wrote:

A spirit and a vision are not, as the modern philosophers suppose, a cloudy vapour or a nothing; they are organized and minutely articulated beyond all that the mortal and perishable nature can produce. He who does not imagine in stronger and better lineaments and in stronger and better light than his perishing and mortal eye can see, does not imagine at all.

Blake's "perishing and mortal eye" was frequently indistinguishable from his imagination. At the age of four he told his parents that he had seen God's head at the window, an incident frequently related to indicate his visionary nature but one common enough in children at that age. But at the age of seven his vision of the prophet Ezekiel in the fields surrounded by angels in trees was more exceptional. The wings of the angels were "bespangling the boughs like stars." Even if this description, as quoted much later by his wife, has the benefit of hindsight, it is quite in the spirit of Blake's art and temper. From his wife, too, we have the description of Blake's death, certainly as jubilant a passing as has ever been recorded. He was seventy years old and confined to bed, where he worked on a set of drawings illustrating Dante. On the day of his death he called his wife and told her, "Kate, you have been a good wife; I will draw your portrait." He proceeded to do so for an hour as she sat by the window and then, according to her account, "he began to sing Hallelujahs and songs of joy and triumph, loudly and with ecstatic energy. His bursts of gladness made the walls resound," and then he died. This was a man who had suffered poverty and scorn and had been forced to live on the thinly disguised charity of friends.

Like many artists of extreme individuality, Blake must be accepted without question or completely rejected. His paintings and engravings are ecstatic and thrilling visions, or they are conscientious but obvious and labored illustrations based on forms cribbed from Raphael and Michelangelo. In everything Blake did, his naïveté is a primary characteristic. In *The Archangel Raphael with Adam and Eve* (**389**) there is not the slightest question that Adam and Eve are two specific human beings of exceptional beauty (as Blake conceived of human beauty, in terms of Renaissance idealizations). They are receiving instructions from the angel Raphael in a Garden of Eden where twining plants and exotic trees of Blake's own invention are as real as his own small garden, where he was fond of impersonating, or of confusing himself and his wife with, Adam and Eve. To Blake the word "real" described what was most real to him, whether it was of this world or another world. He appears to have made little distinction between the world around him—at least that part of it which he was willing to accept—and the world of the Bible, Milton, Dante, and Shakespeare. The world he synthesized in his art drew from all these sources.

If Blake could have known Giorgione's *The Tempest*, he might have admired it as an unexplained vision; but he would have scorned it as an explained allegory, which, for him, would have turned it into nothing but a charade. "Fable or allegory is a totally distinct and inferior kind of poetry," he wrote. "Vision or Imagination is a representation of what actually exists real and unchangeably." That he recognized no boundary between tangible fact and visionary fabrication brings Blake close to lunacy by definition. He might indeed have ended as a confined lunatic if his wife had not combined unquestioning faith in his appointed role as a spiritual messenger with an un-Blakean capacity for

389. William Blake. *The Archangel Raphael with Adam and Eve*, illustration for Milton's *Paradise Lost*. 1808. 19½ by 15⅝ inches. Museum of Fine Arts, Boston. Gift by subscription.

holding body and soul together. Kate has achieved her own special immortality in the history of art.

Blake's water colors and, of course, his engravings retain the strong lineaments in which he created them, but his tempera paintings have deteriorated to such a degree that some of them have turned to the "cloudy vapour" that so offended him as the conception of a dream or a vision. He used some form of glue tempera of his own concoction that has deteriorated badly, with much crackling and discoloration. Yet the effect is not altogether unpleasant, nor does it obscure the forms in paintings like *Zacharias and the Angel* (390). Apparently in his temperas the forms were originally even more substantial than in his water colors, even if they were not quite so sharply delineated. *Zacharias and the Angel* is filled with flame and light and smoke, filled with a spreading brilliance now visible through and exaggerated by the veil of crackling. We can guess that in their original condition these paintings, more than Blake's water colors, combined the conventional effect of apparitions in a miraculous light with the artist's insistence upon a strong and tangible image.

One modern artist who shared Blake's goal of giving reality to dreams was Odilon Redon, although his definition is frequently hazier than Blake would have tolerated. Sometimes, as in his *Evocation of the Butterflies* (391), a soft, wavering iridescence, formless or half-formed, covers the picture area; here even the butterflies scattered across such a background are only half defined. Large areas of a painting by Redon may suggest the shifting and transient glimmering of an oil film upon the surface of water. But it is a mistake to think that Redon ever composed in a haphazard manner or that his forms are insubstantial. He began as a student of architecture and later worked at sculpture, two arts in which the physical existence of three-dimensional form is, obviously, basic to the designer's conception. And when Redon said that he wanted to put "the logic of the visible to the service of the invisible," he was striking close to Blake's idea that organization and articulation are imperative to the creation of images of fantasy.

Redon's *The Chariot of Apollo* (392) bears this out. The god's chariot is drawn through an empyrean of clouds and fire dramatically expressive of flaming space. We are at the opposite pole from Blake's systematic linear rhythms, which carry us with inescapable definition from one point to another and back again over the surface of his pictures. But we can apply to a picture like this one the informal test of any composition: Can the picture's structure be changed without weakening or transforming its nature? Can we, for instance, cut down the right side, in which nothing happens, change the attitude of any one of the horses, make the chariot and Apollo larger or smaller, make the reins connecting the chariot to the horses more conspicuous or less so? The test could be pushed to the point of absurdity, but in general it is certainly true that the composition is as well articulated as one of Blake's, if less obviously, and that

390. William Blake. *Zacharias and the Angel.* Date unknown. Tempera and glue size on canvas, 10½ by 15 inches. The Metropolitan Museum of Art, New York. Bequest of William Church Osborn, 1951.

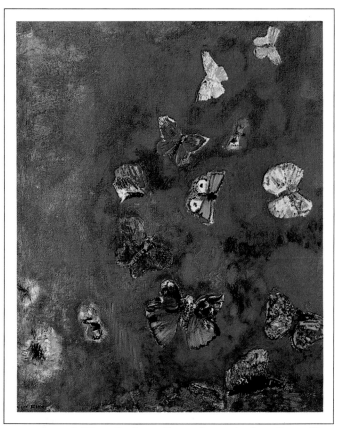

391. Odilon Redon. *Evocation of the Butterflies.* 1898–1916. Oil on panel, 16 by 29¾ inches. The Detroit Institute of Arts. City purchase.

392. Odilon Redon. *The Chariot of Apollo.* 1898–1916. Oil on canvas, 26 by 32 inches. The Metropolitan Museum of Art, New York. Anonymous gift, 1927.

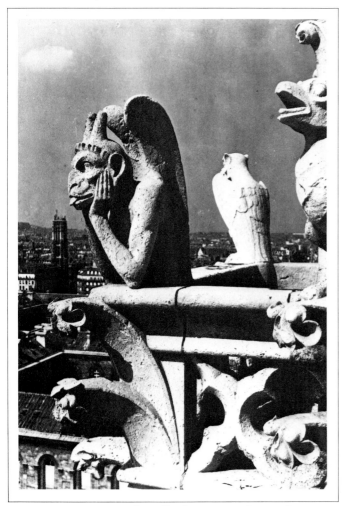

393. Eugène Emmanuel Viollet-le-Duc. *La Stryge.* Invention on medieval models. Gargoyle, mid-nineteenth century. Parapet of Notre Dame, Paris.

in the end it depends more on formal values than on ambiguous ones in its visionary description.

Blake's *The Archangel Raphael with Adam and Eve* was painted at the end of the eighteenth century, the Age of Reason, and Redon's *Apollo* at the beginning of the twentieth, the age of science, so both artists, as visionaries, fall outside the major currents of their times. But if we go back to the Middle Ages, we enter a period when reason was put into the service of the miraculous, and science was half fantasy. Hieronymus Bosch's *Creation of Eve* (**397**, p. 333) is as explicit as Blake's and as visionary, but he did not have to theorize about it. And his *Hell* (**398**) was quite naturally painted in detail as specific as that of any earthly landscape because Hell's existence was accepted, and its horrors catalogued and believed by medieval man, as easily as we may now believe a guidebook's descriptions of an exotic country we have never seen. The art of the Middle Ages abounds in fantasies—some of them symbolic, some of them accepted as literal truth, and some of them apparently the result of nothing more profound than a rollicking attraction to the grotesque. Cathedral portals were lined with statues of the saints, surmounted by Last Judgments, Resurrections, or Ascensions, and encrusted with the miraculous Christian story materialized into stone figures of unquestionable reality. And higher up on these buildings clustered the gargoyles (**393**), fantastic half-diabolic and half-humorous inventions as plausible to the medieval mind as any dog or cat in the streets. In manuscripts these little monsters appear in miniature with a kind of gaiety as part of decorative borders (**395**).

Bosch was the most terrifying of the medieval painters of the fantastic. He worked at the end of the Middle Ages, a changing time but one when, in the North at least, the conviction of sin and punishment continued to haunt men's minds in spite of all promises of forgiveness and bliss. In discussing realism, we described the infinite detail of Van Eyck's *Saint Francis Receiving the Stigmata* (**90**) and said that its microscopic description of natural objects took on spiritual meaning through the medieval conviction that every particle of matter in the world, no matter how small, was inherently significant because all existence was part of an orderly scheme created by the will of God. In Bosch's fantasies, this idea is reversed.

Bosch creates a universe as detailed as Van Eyck's, but it explores the depths of sin and evil and the damnation of the soul. Detail by detail he paints as explicitly and as naturalistically as Van Eyck; we recognize in his hellish figures parts of plants or machines or birds or animals, but these naturalistic parts are combined into outlandish and horrifying wholes. The horror of these monsters comes from their incontrovertible existence: they are true. Like Redon, Bosch puts "the logic of the visible to the service of the invisible," and, as Blake wanted to do, he organizes and articulates his inventions into something more vivid than the "perishing and mortal eye" can see.

394. Hieronymus Bosch. *The Garden of Delights*, center panel of the triptych. About 1505–10. Oil on wood, 86⅝ by 76¾ inches. Museo del Prado, Madrid.

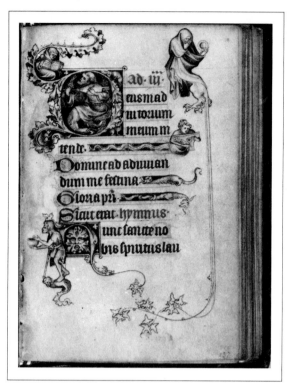

395. Jean Pucelle. Illuminated page with grotesqueries from the *Hours of Jeanne de'Evreux.* 1325–28. Tempera on vellum, 3½ by 2⅞ inches. The Metropolitan Museum of Art, New York. The Cloisters Collection. Purchase, 1954.

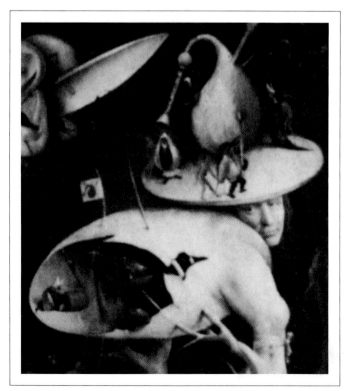

396. Detail from *Hell*, right panel of the *Garden of Delights* triptych.

Bosch's *Creation of Eve* and *Hell* are the left and right panels of a triptych, wings that tell respectively of man's creation in innocence and his consequent damnation. The Garden of Eden, where we see the creation of Eve, is like Blake's in showing against distant crags an exotic garden where the animals of the earth wander at peace with one another. The prophecy of evil in Blake's garden is made by an outsize tree in the background around which the serpent is coiled. In Bosch's the prophecy is present in a subtler and more ominous way, in the suggestion of evil taken on by the monstrously unnatural forms of the foliage, the fountain, and the crags, and by the sinister shapes and activities of some of the animals, which are like spots of infection in the terrestrial paradise.

The large central panel between Eden and Hell shows *The Garden of Delights* (**398**). The pleasures of the flesh are extolled, but with full consciousness of the medieval connotations of the sinfulness of fleshly indulgence. At virtually the same time, in the more relaxed moral climate of Venice, Giorgione was able to transmute these pleasures into idyllic reveries, as we have just seen. But Bosch's garden is a nightmarish circus where swarms of lissome naked bodies are compounded with evil grotesqueries.

In the third panel, *Hell*, all delights are abandoned in a vision of evil where logic and illogic become indistinguishable from one another. Although this is a Hell where some physical tortures take place, they are the smallest part of a Hell where the real torture is spiritual, where corruptions, deformities, monstrous growths, mutilations, and agonizing transformations are the norm. The damned soul is wracked less by physical pain than by existence in a world where all reason and order have been grotesquely transmuted by some cancerous misdirection of divine will.

In a detail from *Hell* (**396**) the head of the central figure, a concoction of parts that must be called "figure" for want of any other word, has by legend been called Bosch's own portrait. This figure looks back over its—can we say shoulder?—from beneath a disk that suggests a hat brim. Resting on the disk is a bladder-like form, terminating in a musical pipe and a spout from which issue smoke and flame. This whole invention is surrounded, in turn, by demons leading naked, condemned souls by the hand, round and round. Whether or not the head is Bosch's portrait, its sly, half-demonic, piercingly observant air suggests his spirit. The head grows from a huge eggshell-like body, hollow and broken open at one end, supported by leg-like growths. These "legs" stand in two small, rigged boats, and branch into the form of blasted trees with dead, pointed limbs that grow upward to pierce the body, whose hollow interior is infested with tiny figures, part human, part insect, that have turned this strange belly into a tavern.

In every fragment—and the scene is cumulatively effective as it is examined fragment by fragment—we are presented with a specific and concrete image of a Hell-form whose reality and whose impossibility are equally undeniable until, like the condemned souls themselves, we are

397. Hieronymus Bosch. *Creation of Eve*, left panel of the *Garden of Delights* triptych. About 1505–10. Oil on wood, 65⅝ by 38¼ inches. Museo del Prado, Madrid.

398. Hieronymus Bosch. *Hell*, right panel of the *Garden of Delights* triptych.

taken up by the force of unreason. Occasionally the figures of this mad-normal world are hideously comical. The little bird-headed, pigtailed demon walking near the front edge of the "hat brim" carrying a burning staff is such a one. These not-really-humorous figures are as horrifying as the more obviously monstrous ones; the humor is as devilish as the tortures.

Among Bosch's several followers or imitators was Pieter Huys. Although his inventions do not approach those of the master in hellish power, he is worth a parenthetical reference here to compare his *Temptation of Saint Anthony* (**399**) with Sassetta's treatment of the same subject, *Saint Anthony Tempted by the Devil in the Form of a Woman* (**263**), which might also have been included in this chapter for its dreamlike quality.

The temptation of Saint Anthony was a rich subject for the painters of diableries; Bosch himself did a large picture of this hermit saint whose mind was a battleground where his yearning to achieve grace through prayer and meditation was constantly under attack by the evil thoughts that obsessed him. Sassetta reduced the story to its essentials:

399. Pieter Huys. *Temptation of Saint Anthony.* Third quarter of sixteenth century. Tempera and oil on wood, 43 by 59 inches. The Metropolitan Museum of Art, New York. Anonymous gift, 1915.

the symbol of temptation (the woman), the symbol of meditation (the hut), the dreamlike wilderness where the drama takes place, and the saint himself.

Contrastingly, Huys shows the saint within a crowded nightmarescape centering upon the lovely figure of a nude girl but flowering all round into evil forms. The girl holds a small owl (always a witchlike bird, associated with things dark and ominous), while behind her crouches a hag with a distaff, and beside her a female monster with a platter upon which she offers what appears to be a piece of carrion. To describe the picture further would only be to continue an enumeration of the hideous visions that torment the holy man. The harmonious serenity of Sassetta's version of the subject and the agonized complications of Huys's are offered here as a reminder of one of our opening definitions of what a painting is: a reflection of the personality of the man who painted it and an expression of the time and place that produced it. The contrast in this case lies particularly between the premise that dominates Italian painting, that in spite of its evils the world ultimately is good, orderly, and beautiful, and a premise met frequently in the North, that in spite of its joys and diversions the world is basically tragic, malevolent, and mysterious.

The world we have seen in Bosch and Huys is disturbing because it operates within a set of irrational laws to which we are subject when we enter their pictures. Jumping forward four and a half centuries and substituting Freudian theory for biblical prophecies of hellfire and damnation, we enter the world of the twentieth-century Surrealists, which operates in much the same way. The sinful hallucinations besetting Saint Anthony in his wilderness are the Freudian dreams of anybody anywhere today; from them the Surrealists created a nightmare world that borrows heavily from the earlier painters. The agonized creature rending itself in Salvador Dali's *Soft Construction with Boiled Beans* (400) is obviously a relative of the eggshell figure from Bosch's *Hell*. And the same Surrealist painter's *Apparition of a Face and a Fruit Dish on a Beach* (401) is an even more curious kind of dream or nightmare picture.

Apparition is, among other things, an exercise in the invention of double images. We are all familiar with the shifting and changing of the subjects in our dreams: "I was in our old house, in the living room, and then all of a sudden it seemed to be a cave instead. There were a lot of people there, and I didn't seem to recognize them, but at the same time I realized they were all people we know."

Just so, in *Apparition* the foreground is a smooth beach that changes by imperceptible degrees into a table covered with a cloth. The apparition of the head fuses with that of a compote full of fruit—a variation on the Boschian device in which a single figure is a composite of animal, vegetable, and mineral forms—and combines, too, with objects on the shore such as the jar that does double duty as an eye. The upper right quarter of the picture is a technically exquisite landscape, crowded with inventions of corruption and de-

400. Salvador Dali. *Soft Construction with Boiled Beans: Premonition of Civil War.* 1936. Oil on canvas, 39⅜ by 39 inches. Philadelphia Museum of Art. Louise and Walter Arensberg Collection.

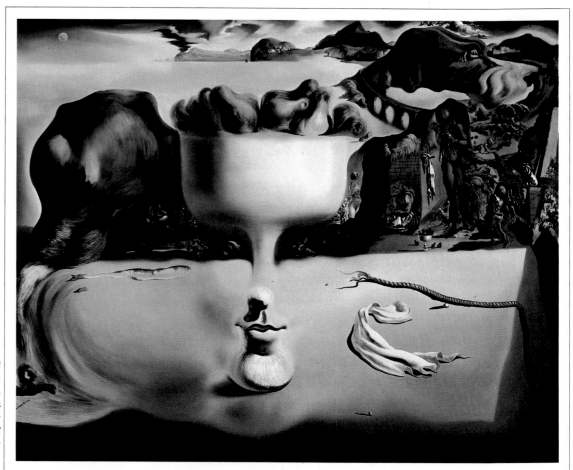

401. Salvador Dali. *Apparition of a Face and a Fruit Dish on a Beach.* 1948. Oil on canvas, 45 by 56⅝ inches. Wadsworth Atheneum, Hartford, Connecticut. Ella Gallup Sumner and Mary Catlin Sumner Collection.

402. Marc Chagall. *Birthday.* 1915. Oil on cardboard, 31¾ by 39¼ inches. The Museum of Modern Art, New York. Acquired through the Lillie P. Bliss Bequest.

cay, stretching back into a distance of magical clarity where peaks rise against the enameled sky. But with a sudden reversal of scale and meaning, this landscape becomes a dog's head; a tunnel becomes his eye, and a viaduct his studded collar. The animal's body merges into the apparitional fruit dish, and his hindquarters materialize from the odd shape rising at the far left. A length of frayed rope and a bit of discarded cloth lying on the beach complete the picture. Perhaps these last have an obscure and personal symbolism for the painter himself. Or perhaps, as one suspects, they are there as a demonstration of his technical dexterity as much as anything else.

This taint of exhibitionism by the artist is the flaw in surrealism and constitutes the difference between its purportedly visionary nature and that of an artist like Bosch. There is a feeling that the Surrealist synthesis of forms is arbitrary and tricky, a stunt, whereas Bosch's combinations are purposeful. One reason is that the Surrealists, particularly the one who painted this picture, indulged in so much conspicuous zaniness during their heyday that their art became suspect for much of the public. As a defense, sensationalism and shock are inherent in surrealism. Their use is conscious, open, and hence legitimate up to a point. The Surrealist may indulge in behavior that is undignified, eccentric, or outrageous by conventional standards and yet be acting within his credo. The trouble is that this liberty has so often been extended to include publicity stunts that the lay public has difficulty in regarding surrealism as a serious and thoughtful art. (Nor is it always; no "ism" has been more prostituted.) The most generous attitude to take toward the more bizarre novelties of the Surrealists is to consider that, like most modern art, surrealism is an intensely personal expression; as such it cannot be expected to achieve the same force as the art of Bosch, who worked at a time when art was an expression of unified social forces rather than a personal response to isolated and specialized fragments of social experience.

We might point out that Blume's *Eternal City*, which we saw in the preceding chapter (**382**), has certain connections with Surrealist techniques that are unexpected in a painting in which the comment is sociopolitical. But if this is surprising, it is not nearly so surprising as the general resurgence of fantastic art in this century. This is the age that has made a fetish of science, yet our artists have been more prolific and varied in exploring the worlds of pure imagination than any artists since the Middle Ages, when the otherworld was a part of daily life. Blake was all but alone in his time as a visionary painter, and his audience was small. Our fantasts are public figures, and their audience is wide and receptive. The references in the art of Marc Chagall, as in *Birthday* (**402**), are quite personal; they speak of his life as a boy in Russia, stories he has been fond of, his love and marriage, anything that gives him delight. If ever a man painted for himself alone, Chagall does. His typical painting is a private reverie that he makes no effort to explain, yet thousands of reproductions of his work are

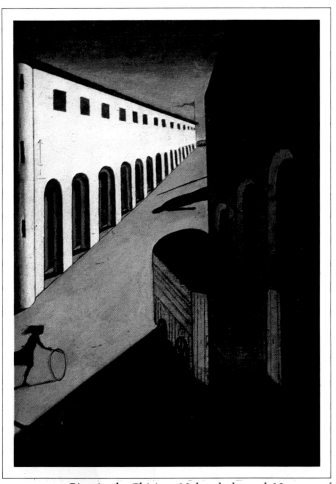

403. Giorgio de Chirico. *Melancholy and Mystery of a Street.* 1914. Oil on canvas, 34⅜ by 28¼ inches. Private collection.

sold around the world. It may be that the world being too much with us these days we are especially glad to be taken out of it for a while, and that artists, for the same reason, find satisfaction in leaving this world for excursions into worlds of their own invention.

Giorgio de Chirico created one of the first of these invented worlds and one of the most enduring. As early as 1912, ten years before the term "surrealism" was invented, he anticipated many Surrealist devices minus surrealism's morbidity and sensationalism. Again and again he painted combinations and recombinations of a limited set of motifs that, for all their repetition from picture to picture, retain undiminished their sense of mystery and melancholy touched with an ominous foreboding but mitigated by a pervading serenity. The world he creates is at once desolate and intimate, empty but filled with suggestion, deserted yet full of mysterious presences, a world that is never explained and possibly for that reason never palls.

The elements in *Melancholy and Mystery of a Street* (403), for instance, and those in *The Anguish of Departure* (404), overlap, and both pictures overlap others, yet each is individual. In the same way realistic landscapes may be individual though composed of the same set of elements—trees, hills, sky, and the other usual features. The collective mood of Chirico's dreamscapes is reflected by the titles he gives them; in addition to melancholy and mystery, anguish and departure, the titles repeat such words as "serenity," "surprise," "lassitude," "enigma," "delight" and "joy," "destiny" and "uncertainty," "torment" and "dream," "nostalgia" and "return." The words "scholar," "philosopher," and "poet" are also frequent; soothsaying and metaphysics and fatality have their visual counterparts in Chirico's repetitions of long arcades in unyielding perspective, statues in deserted squares, tiny distant figures dwarfed by their own extended shadows, towers, great isolated smokestacks, huge boxes, and wheeled vans unattended and unexplained.

The van in *Melancholy and Mystery of a Street* is empty. What was in it? Or what is it waiting to receive? In *The Anguish of Departure* the van doors are closed. What do they hide? We cannot rationalize the presence of the van nor the disposition and relationship of any of the objects in a Chirico on any kind of logical basis, yet their existence is inescapably real. The words "irrefutable logic" are familiar; in Chirico's dreamscapes there is something like an irrefutable *illogic* that accounts for the harmonious existence together in one picture of so many contradictory elements, at once so disturbing and so removed.

Chirico wrote that a painting should bring to the observer the "sensation of something new," something he had never known before. He wrote that "the strange sensations which a man can experience, faithfully reproduced by this man, can always give new joys to a sensitive and intelligent person." But in the pre-World War I years when Chirico first offered these "strange sensations" to the public

404. Giorgio de Chirico. *The Anguish of Departure.* 1913–14. Oil on canvas, 33½ by 27½ inches. Albright-Knox Art Gallery, Buffalo. Room of Contemporary Art Fund.

in paintings like the ones we have just seen, there were not many people, even among the "sensitive and intelligent" ones he mentioned, who were prepared to recognize the "new joys" of Chirico's imagined world. The most popular picture that came anywhere near to resembling that world had been painted in 1880 by a German artist, Arnold Böcklin; it is called *The Island of the Dead* (**406**, p. 340).

Böcklin held that extraordinary subject matter could best be represented in realistic images, a sound enough point of departure for an artist who can invest those realistic images with imaginative force. We have seen that William Blake held a similar conviction—that dreams should be represented in lineaments more sharply defined than nature's. But whereas Blake was a supremely imaginative artist, Böcklin's efforts at fantasy were often heavy-handed, as in this *Triton and Nereid*, where his power of invention is limited to adding stage props to models too obviously posed in the studio.

The Island of the Dead is more successful, and may make less surprising the fact that Chirico so admired Böcklin that during the years 1906–9 he adopted him as a kind of teacher by proxy (Böcklin had died in 1901), studying his paintings and even copying them. From our historical vantage point we can see the connection between two apparently dissimilar artists, but for Chirico's early audience there was no connection at all. The public's admiration for *The Island of the Dead* and its bepuzzlement in the face of Chirico's beautiful early work, followed by the dismissal of Böcklin's work and admiration for Chirico's a short generation later, is a succinct example of the turnabouts in taste that have characterized the last hundred years in art. New movements have grown so rapidly out of old ones (Chirico growing out of Böcklin, for one) that the public has suffered from a kind of esthetic jet lag.

Why did *The Island of the Dead* exert such a strong popular appeal? The best explanation is that while seeming to offer something new, it was understandable in terms of familiar experience. Unlike Chirico's deserted cities, which are both hauntingly familiar and disturbingly strange, Böcklin's island is not really strange at all. Nature is not transformed, merely somewhat refurbished. Somber and spectral the scene may be, but it could be created in hard fact, given a rocky site of the right size and an adequate body of water. It would not be difficult to pose costumed figures in a boat just as Böcklin has painted them here. In an evening light the scene would take on an appropriately eerie quality, especially if we happened to know that the island is a cemetery (just as we must know the title of the picture for it to make its full effect). Watching from the bank, as in essence we do when we stand in front of the painting, we might be stirred to certain thoughts of life, death, and afterlife, presumably the thoughts Böcklin intends to stir in us by creating a scene that never existed except as he invented it but that actually could exist, literally and concretely. Even the most practical down-to-earth person can exercise his imagination sufficiently to

405. Arnold Böcklin. *Triton and Nereid.* 1873–74. Oil on canvas, 40¼ by 75¼ inches. Bayerische Staatsgemäldesammlungen, Munich.

406. Arnold Böcklin. *The Island of the Dead.* 1880. Oil on wood, 29 by 48 inches. The Metropolitan Museum of Art, New York. Reisinger Fund, 1926.

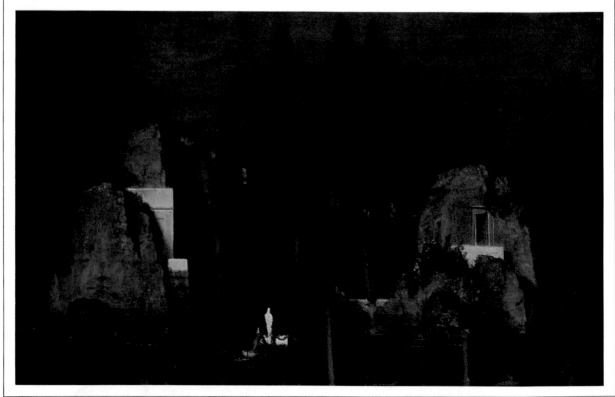

407. Washington Allston. *American Scenery: Time, Afternoon with a Southwest Haze.* About 1834–35. Oil on canvas, 18½ by 24½ inches. Museum of Fine Arts, Boston. Bequest of Edmund Dwight.

enter into the very slight exaggerations and deceptions Böcklin permits himself in this mild fantasy. With Chirico we travel in the same direction that we are taken by Böcklin, but we travel further, explore more deeply, and enter a new world instead of remaining within theatrical modifications of this one.

Böcklin was a late follower of the romantic movement that flared up early in the nineteenth century as a revolt against the desiccation of official painting. The emotionalization of romantic art ranged over a gamut of sensitivities from lyricism to violence. We have seen two of the great French romantics in Géricault and Delacroix (**245** and **246**). Géricault's *Raft of the Medusa* is a melodrama based on a contemporary event, and the emotion of *The Abduction of Rebecca* is more intellectualized than spontaneous. Neither picture can be called visionary in the sense of the pictures we have been examining, but the romantic spirit, which obviously moves toward visionary expression, produced some remarkable images we can call dreamscapes. These may appear unexpectedly, like passages of dream breaking through the more pedestrian course of a work, even a realistic one.

When Washington Allston, an American romantic, called one of his landscape paintings, *American Scenery: Time, Afternoon, with a Southwest Haze* (**407**), he certainly indicated his intention to reproduce specifically the look of a certain place, or type of place, under certain conditions. But by the evidence of the picture itself, he was painting from a deep emotional response that transfigured the subject. However specific the source of the picture may have been, it has little to do with one time or one place. Instead it becomes, with its horse and rider moving alone and silent through some golden otherworld, a vision of the isolation of the human spirit in a region beyond time and place.

The first half of the nineteenth century in America produced some of the most poetically evocative paintings of the century anywhere. As in the case of Allston's work, they are likely to have a touch of awkwardness or naïveté in comparison with their European models, giving them a special quality of their own that is extremely engaging. In his *The Flight of Florimell* (**408**) Allston was inspired by Venetian painting of the same general type as *The Tempest* and *The Concert*. The foliage of the trees, the gleaming fabric, the lush warmth of the landscape, are Venetian by parentage. But the special enchantment of *The Flight of Florimell* is its own. Instead of the openness of the Venetian pictures, we have a cave of trees into which falls a small pool of golden light. The feeling of seclusion and mysterious isolation is increased because we catch a glimpse of distant landscape beyond a small window-like opening through which we may look but may not pass. And whatever Allston intended, his slender, delicate-legged horse is motionless, as if magically transfixed, even to the regular waves of its flowing tail—as are the rider and her fluttering scarf. *The Flight of Florimell* happens to illustrate an episode from

408. Washington Allston. *The Flight of Florimell.* 1819. Oil on canvas, 36 by 28 inches. The Detroit Institute of Arts. City appropriation.

409. Thomas Cole. *The Titan's Goblet.* 1833. Oil on canvas. 19⅜ by 16⅛ inches. The Metropolitan Museum of Art, New York. Gift of Samuel Avery, Jr., 1904.

Spenser, but it is so complete in its own magical suggestion that there is little temptation to attach it to its subject. It is delightful to find in Allston's comments on the Venetians who inspired him that "the poetry of color gives birth to a thousand things which the eye cannot see," and that their pictures "leave the subject to be made by the spectator, provided he possesses the imaginative faculty." This is exactly what happens in *The Flight of Florimell*.

The Flight of Florimell is a fantasy; but American romanticism of the first half of the nineteenth century also produced a group of painters who, to an exceptional degree, revealed that a dream or a vision need not be shaped in fantasy but may exist in ordinary aspects of the world around us. This is shown in Thomas Cole's *View on the Catskill, Early Autumn* (**410**).

Cole was the leader of the group of American landscape painters called the Hudson River School. In commenting on one of these pictures, Durand's *Scene from Thanatopsis* (**23**), we noted its preoccupation with the mystery and grandeur of nature, in that instance expressed in terms merging with those of fantastic invention. Cole also painted in such terms some of the time. In one exceptional picture dated 1833, *The Titan's Goblet* (**409**), he even anticipated the Surrealist device of combining detailed realism with unrealistic reversals of scale: the goblet holds ships borne upon a vast lake.

410. Thomas Cole. *View on the Catskill, Early Autumn.* 1837. Oil on canvas, 39 by 63 inches. The Metropolitan Museum of Art, New York. Gift in memory of Jonathan Sturgis by his children, 1895.

411. Detail from *View on the Catskill.*

412. Detail from *View on the Catskill.*

But *View on the Catskill* shows Cole as less novel and more subtle, revealing the world of dream within the world we know. Without much question the landscape was painted with faithful reference to an actual panorama and might still be identifiable by its topographical features. Lyrical in a way familiar enough in landscape painting, it is more than a competent picture in this respect alone. But when we come close to it and examine it in detail as we do a Bosch, we discover something more: spotted in little openings between trees, in small valleys or upon little rises and promontories, and in a section of river emerging from concealing banks and foliage, there are human figures isolated from one another in small, intimate, enclosed worlds. A man chases horses that race through a field (**411**); another rows a boat across glassy water (**412**); a hunter approaches a fence (**413**). Ordinary enough in themselves, each little world-within-a-world grows magical because each is magically revealed. We see them as if gifted with superhuman vision; they are at once close to us and infinitely removed, at once intimate and inaccessible. Whether or not Cole held any such end or theory in mind is beside the point. The visions are there; if we want to explain their presence, we must suppose that they crystallized from the painter's innermost experience. It is this gift of crystallizing inner experience that differentiates an artist from a mere technical master, and sometimes such crystallization takes place through the chemistry of some power unwilled or even unsuspected by the artist. The most conspicuous manifestation of such a power occurs in the art of Henri Rousseau.

Henri Rousseau, usually called "Douanier" Rousseau in reference to his occupation as a French customs clerk, was what we would call today a hobby painter. An extremely simple man in his origins and in his way of life, having a next-to-incredible naïveté, he seems never to have doubted for a moment that he was a great artist. When he is called one today, it is for reasons that would hardly have pleased him. What he wrote about his pictures is often totally at variance with the impression they make. He would describe as a "genre scene" (that is, a subject from everyday life, realistically treated) a picture full of mystery and enchantment. This quality is peculiarly his own. On the surface he is one of those thousands of untrained "Sunday painters" who make pictures in their spare time for relaxation. His work bears every mark of the conscientious but inadequately trained beginner. In his *Landscape with Cattle* (**314**) we see them all: the flatness of forms intended to appear round, the labored detail, the meticulous but awkward finish, the stiffness, the inaccuracies of proportion and perspective, the trite subject (though a subject is trite only when tritely approached); in short, the Sunday painting's general air of naïveté, a natural result of technical limitations.

But the picture has something more. It has decorative flair (particularly apparent in the patterning of foliage), a pleasant if superficial virtue, and beyond that it has—

inexplicably but irrefutably—an air of enchantment. The flat, rigid objects are transfixed within some magical suspension of time; every distracting banality has been distilled away. Rousseau could not so much as copy a picture postcard (as he sometimes did) without transforming its trite realism into his own distinctive unreality.

Rousseau's exceptional quality as a "modern primitive" may be more apparent if we compare him with another who also became famous, Grandma Moses, the delightful old lady who at the age of one hundred was still painting her recollections of life in a vanished rural America (415). These are scenes of great charm in their reflection of a happy innocence that we like to think of nostalgically as a native virtue of our recent national past. (Although history tells us that those times were neither as innocent nor as happy as Grandma Moses pictures them. Perhaps they were for her.) Her paintings, for all their "primitive" quality, are acutely realistic in intention. She records the details of every visual component of her happy world with an utterly charming faith in the obvious and an absolutely invulnerable innocence that eliminates any possibility of the magical, often disturbing transmutation of reality we find in Rousseau.

It is difficult to know to just what degree Rousseau can be said to have remained innocent. He was fortunate enough to receive from established painters whom he admired the good advice to avoid formal training even when he was in a position to take advantage of it. Emulating himself, he developed a style of great polish and assurance: he performed the unlikely feat of preserving the fly of his innocence in the amber of his technical sophistication. In pictures like the well-known *The Sleeping Gypsy* (416), exotic subject matter intensifies and makes more obvious the otherworldliness inherent in all his work. This is certainly one of the master dream pictures of all time, and one that follows most decisively Blake's admonition as to "stronger lineaments" than the "perishing and mortal eye" can perceive in nature—even though one may be left wondering just where Rousseau's inborn primitivism, or naïveté, ends and where it has been supplanted by a sophisticated consciousness of the decorative values and capricious attractions of a highly developed pseudoprimitive style.

The piquant combination of innocence and sophistication in a single manner is frequent in visionary or fantastic art, but it is seldom so neatly balanced as in Rousseau. Blake was first of all an innocent, for all his theories, and the balance between his innocence and the far-from-innocent Michelangelesque and Raphaelesque forms he borrowed as a pictorial vocabulary is so precarious that he frequently teeters on the edge of disharmony. Reversing this situation is Paul Klee, a German-Swiss intellectual fantast of the most exquisite sophistication whose pictorial vocabulary is largely developed from the innocent art of children, savages, and the insane.

Klee's art is immediately comprehensible to some people, never comprehensible to some others, and a mystery

413. Detail from *View on the Catskill.*

414. Henri "Douanier" Rousseau. *Landscape with Cattle.* 1895–1900. Oil on canvas, 20¼ by 26 inches. Philadelphia Museum of Art. Louise and Walter Arensberg Collection.

415. Grandma Moses (Anna Mary Robertson Moses). *Coming Home for Thanksgiving.* 1944. Oil on canvas, 26 by 22 inches. Private collection.

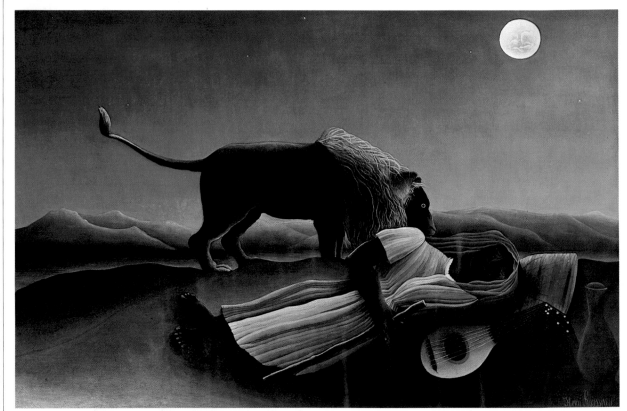

416. Henri "Douanier" Rousseau. *The Sleeping Gypsy.* 1897. Oil on canvas, 51 by 79 inches. The Museum of Modern Art, New York. Gift of Mrs. Simon Guggenheim.

to be solved for many. He is not a formula painter, and no formula can be synthesized to explain him; but if a vote were taken among modern art historians and critics as to who might be the foremost visionary artist of all time, the title would probably go to Paul Klee with William Blake as runner-up. We will approach one of his paintings by way of three others on the same subject (the ship as a symbol) and take advantage of the four to summarize in conclusion some of the points we have made about visionary painting.

Shortly before 1500 there appeared in France a certain Shepherd's Calendar, called *Le grant kalendrier et compost des Bergiers.* Like others of its kind it was an almanac combining popular misinformation, accepted superstitions, astral diagrams and astrology, medical hints, and pious comments on virtue, vice, Heaven, Hell, and the culture of the soul. It was an everyman's version of the intricate compendium of medieval learning and was illustrated with woodcuts, of which we reproduce one (**417**). The picture is an allegory accompanied by an explanation that translates to this effect:

> Mortal man living in the world is like a ship on the sea or a perilous river carrying rich merchandise which, if he can reach the desired port, will make him happy and rich. The ship from the moment of setting out clear to the end of the voyage is in great peril of being sunk or captured by enemies. Because there are always perils at sea. Thus is the body of man living in the world; the cargo which he carries is his soul, the virtues, and good works. The port is Paradise where all who arrive are wonderfully rich. The sea is the world, full of vice and sin.

> (Homme mortel vivant au monde est comparé a navire sur mer ou rivière perilleuse portant riche marchandise, lequel s'il peut venir au port que le marchant desire, il sera heureux et riche. La navire quant entre en mer jusques à fin de son voyage est en grant peril d'estre noyee ou prinse des ennemys. Car en mer sont tousjours perilz. Tel est le corps de l'homme vivant au monde; la marchandise qu'il porte est son âme, les vertus et les bonnes oeuvres. Le port est paradis auquel qui y parvient est souveraynement riche. La mer est le monde plain de vices et pechez.)

The picturization of this allegory is an engaging hybrid of explicit realistic description and symbolic conventionalizations in the service of didactic statement. The ship, the captain, the mast with its sail, and the anchor are drawn with convenient disregard of relative scale. The stormy sea is represented by conventionalized lines familiar to the medieval eye, and both God and the Devil are shown as literally as the man himself. Nothing in the picture is modified for expressive purposes; it is an allegorical diagram that must be "interpreted" in a sense as literal as its accompanying explanation's translation from one language into another for a foreign reader.

This little woodcut, of course, is without pretensions as a work of art, but the same allegory more elaborately

417. *Allegory of Man's Life,* from *Le grant kalendrier et compost des Bergiers.* French, about 1500. Woodcut, 6 by 4 inches.

rendered might be found in medieval manuscript illuminations. In either case, Blake would not approve, since "allegory is a totally distinct and inferior kind of poetry" to this visionary artist. In passing we might remember that if Blake's opinion of allegory were universally shared, we would never have had Dürer's supreme allegory, *Melencolia I* (**333**), or Botticelli's *Calumny* (**351**), among other masterpieces.

A more defendable objection to our example would be that the allegory of the ship and its pilot as symbols of everyone's passage through life is a weary one. It was certainly weary by the early nineteenth century when Thomas Cole, who also painted our admirable and genuinely poetic *View on the Catskill*, produced a set of four canvases called *The Voyage of Life* showing the passenger in childhood, youth, manhood, and old age in the company of his guardian angel, who serves as helmsman at the beginning and end and stands by on the outskirts of the drama during the two middle episodes. The third episode, *Manhood* (**418**), shows the passenger in circumstances almost identical with those in the medieval woodblock. Beset by storm, he is also threatened not by the Devil himself but by three of his representatives, the demons of lust, intemperance, and suicide, barely visible in the upper center of the picture, with God's emissary, the guardian angel, hovering in a spot of light above.

418. Thomas Cole. *Manhood,* from the series *The Voyage of Life.* 1840. Oil on canvas, 52 by 78 inches. Munson-Williams-Proctor Institute, Utica, New York.

The Voyage of Life was so successful that Cole painted it in at least three versions and made a great deal of money from engraved reproductions. The pictures are generally regarded today with a degree of condescension as reflections of the taste of an American public awakening to culture but demanding that fine art be combined with high moralistic sentiment.

We are in an entirely different domain a century and a half later with *Moonlight Marine* (**419**) by Albert Pinkham Ryder, the mystical poet of American painting. Like Blake he was an eccentric, and even more than Blake a recluse. ("The artist cannot be a good fellow," he said.) He is frequently remindful of the Van Gogh of *The Starry Night* when he writes, "I am in ecstasies over my Jonah [he was working on a painting of Jonah and the whale]: such a lovely turmoil of boiling water and everything," or, "Exultantly I painted until the sun sank below the horizon, then I raced around the fields like a colt let loose, and literally bellowed for joy."

In *Moonlight Marine* specific allegory has changed to a mystical vision that is lessened in its effectiveness if we try to pin down its component parts as symbols. The tossing sea is not meant as a specific symbol of the hazards of life in the world; even less is the frail ship meant to suggest man's body charged with the cargo of his soul, to be protected from the waters of evil. There is nothing here but a vast sea, a vast sky, a moon, the unreal shapes of some clouds, and a small boat nearly obscured. Unlike Blake with his obsession for the sharp delineation of visionary forms, Ryder believed that "The artist should fear to become the slave of detail. He should strive to express his thought and not the surface of it."

A very strong difference between *Moonlight Marine* and the ship allegories we have just seen is that Ryder's vision of a mystical voyage carries with it a sense of exhilaration. If the picture is by association an allegory of man's journey through the world, we can imagine the voyager, so small in the infinite scheme of things, feeling not threatened by the elements but exultant in his security as he keeps his tossing boat on course over the water, beneath the clouds, by the light of the moon.

So where does this bring us as an introduction to Paul Klee's *Demon as Pirate* (**420**), an example of an art that we began by calling "immediately comprehensible to some people, never comprehensible to some others, and a mystery to be solved for many"? We have approached this picture of a ship in danger from a demon by looking at two specifically explainable allegories and one painting, Ryder's, where our response is primarily unanalytical even though we may force the picture as a kind of informal allegory. With Klee, all allegory—and any other specific scheme of reference—must be forgotten; our personal response to his very personal art is everything.

Demon as Pirate, although it is a great Klee, can hardly be called a great painting. Klee is in the extraordinary position of being a major painter who never painted a major

419. Albert Pinkham Ryder. *Moonlight Marine.* 1870–90. Oil on wood, 11⅜ by 12 inches. The Metropolitan Museum of Art, New York. Samuel D. Lee Fund, 1934.

420. Paul Klee. *Demon as Pirate.* 1916. Gouache on paper, 11½ by 17 inches. Philadelphia Museum of Art. Louise and Walter Arensberg Collection.

picture to be pointed to as the summation of his genius. It is only in his total work that his scope and his expressive force become apparent. Individually his pictures may seem only witty; wit is a delightful element in all his work, and is particularly apparent in *Demon as Pirate*, but that is just part of the story. Klee's art is wider and deeper than any single one of his paintings hints; each Klee one knows enriches all the others, until eventually the individual fantasies share the psychological power of the mass. It is also true that the wider the observer's acquaintance with art in general, the richer his response to Klee's is likely to be—a good reason for putting Klee at the end of this book.

Any understanding of Klee's achievement must begin with the acceptance of two premises: first, Paul Klee is a highly trained painter of great technical skill and an esthetician of great subtlety and complication, no matter how slight his work may appear to be; second, this technical skill and this intellectualism are only the superficies of his art. To recognize them certainly adds to the interest of his pictures, but enjoyment will depend in large part on our ability to respond unanalytically.

In *Demon as Pirate* there is much that can be pointed out in partial explanation: that the fish at the left is related to hieroglyphics or sign-symbols of the kind found scratched in rocks everywhere from the American Indian's West to aboriginal Australia; that the little animals in the boat have the same character plus humorous overtones; that as pure line the pattern of the two boats and the demon connects the picture with certain Oriental traditions. The composition could be gone into at some length—the ornamental subtlety of its color, the deft placement of the three flags, the forward-swooping line of the demon, its echo in the movement of the harpoons, its stabilization by the masts and the figure in the small tublike boat. But *Demon as Pirate* is no *Raft of the Medusa*, built on traditional compositional patterns. In the long run no explanation is going to explain the most important things about *Demon as Pirate*. It is a vision and a dream, but a waking one conceived with enormous zest by an artist drawing on the full range of his complex esthetic theories, and our response to it depends finally upon complex associations that we bring to it from deep within ourselves, associations that we might be at a loss to define.

Of course this is more or less true of every picture we see. It was true of Giorgione's *The Tempest*, with which we began this discussion. The difference is that *Demon as Pirate* has only the most tenuous relationship with the world we see, and hence depends upon associations of the most inward kind. It happens also to depend upon other associations of a highly cultivated kind, ranging over the whole field of the arts. Klee stands outside the human drama and its passions, but his comments on its refinements are endlessly delightful.

When we come to sculpture, examples of visionary art by our definition become scarce. Sculpture is rich in vision-

421. *The Vision of Saint John.* About 1120–25. Tympanum, Abbey Church of Saint-Pierre, Moissac, France.

422. Jean de Bandol (Hennequin de Bruges) and Nicolas Bataille. *The Fall of Babylon the Great City* from the Apocalypse tapestries. About 1381. Approximately 6½ by 10 feet. Musée des Tapisseries, Angers, France.

ary subject matter, but that is quite a different thing from sculpture created in a visionary spirit. We gave Bernini's *Ecstasy of Saint Theresa* (**98**) as an example of dramatic realism, although its subject is a miraculous vision following the detailed description as given by the saint herself. Bernini produced a hardheaded, supremely calculated, technically breathtaking three-dimensional illustration of that vision, that is all—and that is quite enough to make this sculpture a baroque masterpiece. We also said that Bernini created an illusion of tons of marble floating in the air. But this, too, was a technical tour de force. Illusionism is the creation of optical deceptions by technical means, and is unrelated to visionary inspiration.

If visionary subject matter were synonymous with visionary art, any work illustrating any part of the Revelation of Saint John would be visionary to the point of hallucination. The images in this last book of the New Testament are so vivid as verbal descriptions that they need only be approximated in another medium to carry with them a considerable degree of visionary force. The artists of the Middle Ages were called on to illustrate this book so often, in both painting and sculpture, that a summary of their second-hand visions would require a book longer than this one.

One of the most famous examples, *The Vision of Saint John* on the tympanum of the Church of Saint-Pierre in Moissac, France (**421**), is in fact a third-hand vision, a sculpture derived from a manuscript painting derived from the text (Revelation 4) describing Christ enthroned, surrounded by the signs of the four evangelists and adored by twenty-four crowned elders. Manuscript illumination was already a highly developed art when a surge of church-building demanded quantities of sculpture unprecedented since ancient Rome, and stonecarvers became sculptors by adapting their craft to these demands, with manuscript illuminations among their models. The translation from manuscript to monumental sculpture at Moissac (originally including the bright colors and, perhaps, gold of the manuscript model) retains a visionary quality even though twice removed from Saint John's text.

The Fall of Babylon the Great City (**422**), from a series of late fourteenth-century tapestries of the Apocalypse, shows how the eerie and enchanted quality of Saint John's text is carried into another medium with, we can believe, more invention on the part of the "translator." The destroyed city—"Babylon the Great, the Mother of the Harlots and of the Abominations of the Earth"—is seen in miniature, its falling towers suspended forever in mid-air beneath trumpeting angels and the fierce, haloed eagle clutching in his beak and claws a scroll with the words "Woe, woe, woe." "And I saw," wrote Saint John, "and I heard an eagle, flying in mid heaven, saying with a great voice, Woe, woe, woe, for them that dwell on the earth, by reason of the other voices of the trumpet of the three angels who are yet to sound" (Revelation 8:13). Later (14:8) we are told that the second of the trumpeting angels says, ". . . Fallen, fallen is Babylon the great, that hath made all the nations to drink of the wine of the wrath of her fornication." Finally (16: 18–19), "There were lightnings and voices, and thunders; and there was a great earthquake, such as was not since there were men upon the earth, so great an earthquake, so mighty. And the great city was divided into three parts, and the cities of the nations fell; and Babylon the great was remembered in the sight of God, to give unto her the cup of the wine of the fierceness of his wrath."

In the tapestry the quake has torn the earth into chasms—one of them dividing the road leading into the city—with knife-edged walls, while flowers (an addition not mentioned by Saint John) continue to bloom, at an entirely different scale, on the carpeting of greensward. The saint himself, as if performing as narrator, stands at our right.

The precise definition of each visionary detail (which might have pleased Blake) may be partially a reflection of the linear manuscript style, but is primarily the enforced result of tapestry techniques of the time by which each pictorial element was woven separately from a master pattern and the parts then sewn together. Whatever the influences or borrowings involved, the Apocalypse tapestries remain, by the genius of their master designer and the unquenchable force of the Book of Revelation, one of the great visionary works in the history of art.

However, this tapestry has taken us back into the general field of pictorial art, leaving us with the question as to why sculpture has seemed ill-adapted to visionary expression. Perhaps the chief reason is that all painting offers in the first place a kind of magic in the reduction of three-dimensional images to only two, a transfiguration that is denied to sculpture by the absolute physical tangibility of three-dimensional images no matter how imaginatively conceived. Then, too, the sheer physical process of carving sculpture imposes an inflexible scheme in advance, while a painter may invent more freely as he goes, a process more compatible with imaginative wanderings.

In medieval sculpture the most popular subject for the tympanum of the main portal of a church or cathedral soon became the Last Judgment. The Last Judgment is a subject adaptable to visionary treatment if ever there was one, but it can also be treated didactically and usually was—a respectful, noninterpretive treatment of the facts as outlined in biblical texts. One of the earliest Last Judgment tympanums is an exception to this rule, in which the sculptor seems to have made the most determined effort to invest the subject with an appropriately supernatural atmosphere. This is the tympanum over the portal of the Cathedral of Autun, in France (423), by the sculptor Gislebertus, carved only a matter of five or ten years later than the tympanum at Moissac.

Gislebertus is one of the few medieval sculptors whose name we know. The fact that he signed the Autun tympanum is proof enough that he set out to create an individualistic work of art and that he recognized himself as an

423. Gislebertus. *Last Judgment.* About 1130. Tympanum, Cathedral at Autun, France.

424. Detail from *Last Judgment.*

425. Giambologna (Giovanni Bologna). *The Apennine.* About 1580. Villa Demidoff, Pratolino, near Florence.

artist rather than an exceptionally skilled craftsman, which was the status of the usual medieval sculptor. The extreme elongation of his tiny-headed figures, exceeding that of any other sculptures of the time, is the most obvious hallmark of his style. In addition he patterns these figures in expressionistic variations. On Christ's right hand (on our left as we face the sculpture) the Blessed, en route to a Paradise represented by an arched castle, are ranged in stable verticals, while the Damned on the other side, and the angel and the Devil struggling for their souls on either side of a balance, are in contorted attitudes that make the most of expressionistic angles and interruptions. On the band of the lintel, the Blessed are received by angels as they rise from their graves at the sound of the last trumpet; on our right the Damned suffer agonies of apprehension, and one unfortunate is clasped around the head by gigantic hands that lift him to judgment (**424**).

If there is anything like a school of visionary, fantastic, or demonic sculpture in Europe, it is garden sculpture of the latter sixteenth cetury. "Garden" in this context means the landscaped grounds of villas and palaces (later on to be peopled by marble gods and goddesses), which during this manneristic prelude were the playgrounds of imaginary monsters and personages of fantastic aspect. One of these is Giambologna's *The Apennine* (**425**), at once a symbol of the Apennine mountains that run from one end of Italy to the other, and of the mystical race of the peninsula's original inhabitants. The figure's identity with the stone from which it rises is intensified by the continuation of the rough-cut bank into the locks of the beard and hair—an effect of union with raw nature (in highly sophisticated terms, admittedly) that is exaggerated today by four centuries of weathering.

Modern sculpture with its extended range of materials is partially freed from the restrictions we listed a few paragraphs back that make sculpture ill-adapted to visionary expression. Alberto Giacometti's Surrealist *The Palace at 4 A.M.* is put together from wood, glass, wire, and string—materials allowing for free improvisation as the artist develops an idea, elaborates it, simplifies it, changes the relation of one part to the others, working in part from esthetic principles he knows so well that they have become inborn, but also from impulses generated by the same subconscious or unconscious forces that generate our dreams. Here we are on dangerous ground, since it is presumptuous of us, the observers, to guess how much of such a work of art is the result of the artist's studied manipulation of his means and how much is impulsive—especially in this case, where the artist by his own statement intended to leave no traces of that manipulation. But there the end product stands, dreamlike, all explanations aside.

Like most Surrealist paintings or sculptures *The Palace at 4 A.M.* needs its title for full effect, and as usual the title is enigmatic. What palace? Why 4 A.M.? But title or no title, esthetic manipulation or no manipulation, the dreamlike air, the here-but-not-here quality, comes largely from the palace's curious relationship with space. Rooms, corridors, towers: at first they seem defined for us as if this were a skeleton-palace with the walls removed for our convenience; but if we look again, there is no structural logic, no formal definition in familiar terms, no distinction at all between real space and dream space, leaving us with the choice of dismissing this fragile structure as a bit of entertaining frivolity or accepting our participation in its irreality. Looking back to the paintings we have seen, *The Palace at 4 A.M.* is most closely related to Paul Klee's *Demon as Pirate,* and most distant from Thomas Cole's *View on the Catskill,* which represent the poles of visionary conception.

Among modern art forms classified as sculpture because they are three-dimensional and fit into no other standard classification, are constructions like Joseph Cornell's, put together in shallow boxes from odds and ends (carefully selected odds and ends) of material that can include photographs, prints, stuffed birds, artificial flowers, machine parts, toys, bits of manuscript or newspapers and other printed matter, butterflies, shells, drinking glasses and glass jars, candy wrappers—anything. The term "assemblage" has been coined to apply to these and related forms of put-together-from-bits-and-pieces art, but has not been accepted in wide usage as has the earlier "collage," which is the official term for paste-ups in two dimensions. Both collage and assemblage, but especially assemblage, have been subjected to outrageous degradation by amateurs who combine disparate objects simply because they are disparate without regard for associative effects or for the esthetics (frequently traditional) of formal composition that persist within the innovative medium.

Cornell's *Medici Slot Machine* (**427**) one of several by that title) is a small box 15½ inches high, 12 inches across, and 4⅞ inches deep, with a glassed front that functions less as a physical protection for the objects within the box than as a psychological barrier that isolates those objects from the world outside and emphasizes their interdependence in the small world of which they have become the component parts. Cornell chose components with strong personal associations, combining things that delighted him as a child with others connected with his adult interests. How, then, the reader may ask, can we know what a Cornell is "about," since we don't have the same associations?

Obviously we cannot, but we have associations of our own that may be just as potent in generating the air of mystery that is fundamental to Cornell's work. Even in our own dreams we do not always understand why certain objects appear to us (although psychoanalysts may try to explain them to us) in what seem to be normal relationships until we awake and recognize their oddity.

Medici Slot Machine is an exceptional Cornell in having a strong theme identifiable to any observer—an evocation of Italy through fragments of its art. The young nobleman who occupies the central spot is a reproduction of a portrait by Sofonisba Anquisciola (now in the Walters Art Gallery, Baltimore); his head appears eight more times in shifting

426. Alberto Giacometti. *The Palace at 4 A.M.* 1923–33. Wood, glass, wire, and string, 25 by 28¼ by 15¾ inches. The Museum of Modern Art, New York.

427. Joseph Cornell. *Medici Slot Machine.* 1942. Construction, 15½ by 12 by 4⅞ inches. Private Collection, New York.

relationships with itself in vertical bands at the extreme right and left boundaries of the construction. Fragments of other Italian paintings, including a Botticelli portrait repeated four times, appear elsewhere. The column-like vertical bands on either side of the main portrait—or segment of it, since the artist has severely trimmed it—are cut from a map showing the remains of the ancient Roman imperial palace on the Palatine Hill, and the words "Italie au XVme Siècle" appear on a scrap of printed paper adjacent to the "column" on the right.

But why the division into quadrants crossing at the boy's face? Why the compass—a real compass—centered below him between the two smaller boxes with mirrored backs that reflect miscellaneous objects including jackstones, one in each box? (A third appears in the vertical band at the extreme right.)

There is no point in wondering why. If everything were explainable, this magical box would become nothing but a catalogue of objects with specific psychological relationships to one another assembled in a pleasant manner, rather than what it is—a world of its own, where disparate objects are equalized on terms mysterious to us on the outside but obviously reasonable in their own self-contained world of dream.

All painting and sculpture, we are frequently told—at least all that is worthy of the name art—is a matter of transfiguration, which usually means transfiguration of the familiar into forms that "clarify, intensify, or enlarge" our experience. This is true of Cornell's boxes, although they demand an exceptional degree of receptivity from the observer. It is certainly true of another modern American sculptor, Louise Nevelson, whose raw material for transfiguration is wood picked up at wrecking sites—parts of moldings, balusters, railings, paneling, chair arms or legs and other bits of broken furniture, and any other pieces of wood in all the variety of shapes originally determined by decorative or structural function. As the title of *Sky Cathedral* (**428**) indicates, there is a strong architectural suggestion in these sculptures, which frequently cover large walls or even become total environments.

We said, concerning *The Palace at 4 A.M.*, that it would have been presumptuous of us, the observers, to guess how much of such a work of art is the result of studied manipulation of means and how much is impulsive. In Nevelson's case, however, we know enough from recorded interviews to determine a balance between the analytical and the visionary in her creative approach. All her sculptures are either black, white, or gold, and each has for her its own mystique. Beginning with a general scheme in mind, she builds a sculpture placing this piece or that in the position that seems right, or that becomes right after adjustments. In a process where there can be no clear division between what "feels" right and what should be right according to esthetic theory and experience—esthetic discrimination attained through long study and practice—the balance in Nevelson's case does seem to be on the side

428. Louise Nevelson. *Sky Cathedral.* 1958. Assemblage—wood construction painted black—height 11 feet 3¼ inches. The Museum of Modern Art, New York. Gift of Mr. and Mrs. Ben Mildwoof.

of instinctual response, which puts her on the side of the visionaries in opposition to the intellectualizers in the eternal dichotomy that runs through the history of art.

Can there be such a thing as visionary architecture? By any puristic definition of architecture, no. But architects have played with ideas on paper that they never expected to see materialized, have invented fantastic buildings or entire architectural worlds that they are free to imagine with no engineering problems involved, and have imagined extensions of contemporary engineering into realms theoretically possible even if totally impossible from any practical point of view.

Some of the most awesome architectural visions ever recorded are the *Carceri d'Invenzione*, a series of imagined prison interiors by the eighteenth-century Italian architect and printmaker Giovanni Battista Piranesi. The few buildings that Piranesi produced as a practicing architect are of no distinction; practical architectural disciplines were too demanding for his volatile, rather violent, temperament. His talents were better adapted to the romantic glorification of architecture in pictures, and here he excelled. The 137 large etchings of his *Vedute di Roma*, views of the modern city and its ancient ruins, published from 1745 onward, were internationally popular and still are (429). But it remained for his prisons (430) to give full play to his double nature as architect and visionary. These subterranean palaces for the confinement, torture, and execution of criminals guilty, surely, of unimaginable crimes, are labyrinthine confusions of arches, vaults, piers, terraces, and monumental staircases, some complete, some half-built, some fallen, combining the wildest dramatics of hallucination with contradictory effects of architectural solidity. Actually the structural relationships are too ambiguous to allow for the possibility of construction except in terms of lath and canvas—in which terms they have inspired innumerable stage sets.

The most impressive historical example of visionary architecture designed by a professional architect who held in mind the possibility of actual construction is Étienne-Louis Boullée's project for a cenotaph for Sir Isaac Newton (431). Although best remembered for his theory of gravitation, Newton also made important contributions to mathematics and astronomy, two themes that Boullée kept in mind in designing the cenotaph. Here he was able to apply a principle that he could only partially demonstrate as an architect of buildings devoted to everyday functions: the principle that buildings should be composed of pure, simple, unornamented geometrical volumes. The cenotaph is one gigantic globe rising from circular variations of terraces and landscaping, a direct and unequivocal mathematical reference, while Newton's astronomical investigations were symbolized by the globular void of the interior, which, approached through a long, dark tunnel, was illuminated only by holes like the moon and stars, placing the observer at the center of the astral universe.

Theoretically, this enormous building could have been

429. Giovanni Battista Piranesi. *Temple of Castor and Pollux.* 1746. Etching. The Museum of Fine Arts, Boston.

430. Giovanni Battista Piranesi. Imaginary prison, from the series *Invenzione Capricciosa di Carceri.* 1745–61. Etching, 16¼ by 21½ inches. Museum of Fine Arts, Boston. Gift of Miss Ellen Bullard.

431. Etienne-Louis Boullée. Project for a cenotaph for Sir Isaac Newton, exterior and section, night effect. 1784. Bibliothèque Nationale, Paris.

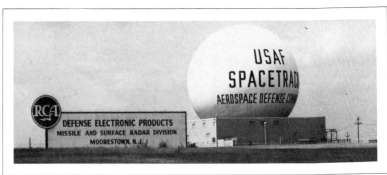

432. U.S. Air Force Radome, Moorestown, New Jersey. Destroyed.

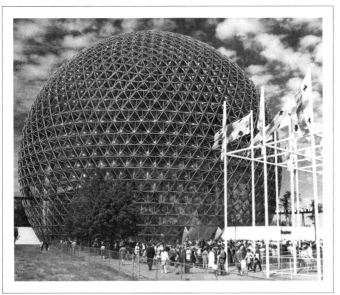

433. Buckminster Fuller. United States Pavilion, Expo 67. Montreal, Canada.

built at the scale Boullée indicated by tiny figures; certainly it could have been built at a smaller scale. Today it could be built at large scale as a concrete or opaque-plastic covered geodesic dome like Buckminster Fuller's for the United States Pavilion at Expo '67 in Montreal (**433**). But by an appropriate coincidence, the cenotaph now looks like a prophecy of the radomes, or tracking stations, whose pure geometrical forms, so like Boullée's, were developed not from any architectural premise but through the necessity of satisfying technological problems connected with the tracking of aircraft or missiles by means of radar systems (**432**). We call this an "appropriate" coincidence because the coincidence is not only one of form, but of form determined by modern scientific realizations that would have fascinated Newton the experimental physicist.

If Boullée's cenotaph for Newton was an unintentional prophecy, architects have often indulged in prophetic speculations. Leonardo da Vinci made rough sketches for a city with two-level streets several centuries before modern conditions demanded overpasses and elevated highways. And in the lively field of theatrical invention, the German expressionist movie *Metropolis* multiplied the idea many times over in sets (**434**) anticipating the planetary space stations invented for *Star Wars* half a century later (**435**).

These stations look hardly more fantastic than the "arcologies" proposed by an Italian architect now working in the United States, Paolo Soleri, as serious studies in the relationship between architecture and ecology (whence the word "arcology"). By concentrating an entire metropolis within a single arcology and leaving uncontaminated countryside between arcologies, Soleri would eliminate the blight of urban sprawl and the contamination of nature by the messy, unorganized infestation of automobile graveyards, dumps, cheap building, and decayed townships that stretches across the countryside from coast to coast with our highways as carriers of the virus.

"Babel IIB" (**436**) is at once conceivable and impossible, if it is safe to say that anything in the future is impossible. In the meanwhile, it is the vision that counts. Just as visionary painting gives a degree of materialization to intangibles and thus opens new areas of consciousness for us, so visionary architecture on the magnitude of Soleri's arcologies can affect our ways of thinking about organizing our lives on the beautiful planet that, in a sense, we have invaded.

434. Still from *Metropolis.* Germany (Ufa). 1927. Art directors, Otto Hunte, Erich Kettelhut, and Karl Vollbrecht. Sculpture by Walter Schultze. Photo, The Museum of Modern Art, New York.

435. Still from *Star Wars,* Obi-Wan Kenobi (Alec Guinness) turning off the tractor beam in the Death Star. Twentieth Century-Fox, 1977. Production designer, John Barry. Photo courtesy The Museum of Modern Art, New York.

436. Paolo Solari. *Babel IIB.* 1963. From *Paolo Solari/Arcology: The City in the Image of Man.* (Boston: MIT Press).

9. Babel IIB

Babel IIB	
(Flat land)	
Population	520,000
Density	662/hectare; 268/acre
Height	1,050 meters
Diameter of structure	3,160 meters
Surface covered	778 hectares; 1,920 acres
1,2 Section and elevation: scale	1:10,000

Comparative Arcologies
Arcodiga
Population	280,000
3. Elevation: scale	1:10,000
Arcoindian I	
Population	19,000
4. Elevation: scale	1:10,000

A hyperstructure over 1 kilometer high and 2 kilometers in diameter at the bowl base. Vertical shafts carry (1) the vertical transportation system, elevator batteries, and continental, transcontinental air transport "sleeves"; (2) services, exhausts. Anchored to the shafts are the platform-grounds of the city: (1) at the periphery, the residential spaces; (2) in the medial belt, the gardens and waste processing plants; (3) toward the center, civil facilities and work. The top platform-ground is for cultural institutions: schools, labs, studios, theaters, libraries.

At the ground is a system of parks, gardens, and playgrounds. Under the ground level develops the automated world of production and maintenance with environmental conditions dictated by the functionality of each plant division: there will, or may, thus be production (and research) in an atmosphere of vacuum, fire, cold, gas, radiation, water, pressure . . . the fusion (or equivalent) power plant at the core. Energy is served radially to plants, to the technological "city" and to the totality of the arcology, including the grounds and the atmospheric dome in which the arcology is contained.

Babel IIB floats on a mineral bed. One third of it is scooped out of the ground. From the center the hollow trunk rises 1200 meters into the air. Four major topographies ring the trunk, partly suspended. On each topography (township) is an annular park separating the outer belt of residences and the inner belt of public facilities. The light reaches deep into the core of the city, vertically from the axial well and obliquely between the four topographies. The whole bowl could be weather-controlled by means of heat-sensitive screens.

For a structure of this size and structural organization, symmetry along the vertical axis is mandatory. The center of gravity of the whole system is located exactly on the axis of symmetry.

The city could well work as a major airport with aircraft taxiing on the outer rim of the bowl within minutes' time from anywhere in the city.

EPILOGUE

Something by way of epilogue may be in order now, at the conclusion of these discussions. But it should be brief; most of it should be said by a work of art. Daumier's *The Print Collector* (**438**) makes an appropriate statement.

As a picture "of" something, *The Print Collector* shows us an ordinary man pursuing a hobby. He is going through one of the portfolios of tens of thousands of miscellaneous prints that crowd Paris bookstalls. But he might be looking at pictures anywhere, and if we ponder one question, then the inner subject of *The Print Collector* becomes apparent. The question is, Why do pictures interest this man?

Why do pictures exist at all? Why do people look at them, respond to them, grow to love some and to dislike others, argue about them, defend and attack them, collect them, explore them, starve to paint them, build museums to protect them, cross oceans to see them?

In another Daumier, *La Soupe* (**437**), human creatures devouring food with animal intensity become symbols of the cycle of birth, life, death, birth—bound to the soil, nourished by it, and returning to it.

The Print Collector speaks of our other life. This ordinary man is not a human animal but a human being who thinks, wonders, and tries to explain. He is the creature who stopped being an animal and developed into a human being when it became necessary for him to explain to himself the existence of the world and to find a reason for his presence in it. He was rubbing this explanation with colored clays onto the walls of caves at least fifteen thousand years ago and fashioning magical figures out of bone or ivory. He was creating works of art, and is still creating them, and will continue to create them as long as he continues to be a human being.

This curious, unceasing activity of the artist is defined without being explained by the dictionary—art is "Creativity of man as distinguished from the world of nature," a definition we quoted at the beginning of this book. But the impulses that force us to create, and the search for some kind of fulfillment that accounts for art's fascination—accounts for Daumier's quiet print collector—these are not quite definable, and perhaps they don't even need explaining. It is enough to say that art is a fulfillment, whether for the creator or the observer, a form of communication with our time and all times, an extension of our experience of living, sometimes profound, sometimes entertaining. The only answer to the question, What is art? is that art, whatever its definition, is an inexhaustible enrichment of life.

437. Honoré Daumier. *La Soupe.* Latter nineteenth century. Wash drawing, 11 by 15¼ inches. The Louvre, Paris.

438. Honoré Daumier. *The Print Collector.* Latter nineteenth century. Oil on wood, 13⅜ by 10¼ inches. Philadelphia Museum of Art. Purchased, W. P. Wilstach Collection.

GLOSSARY

abstract art, abstraction. Generic, nonspecific terms covering art that in various degrees departs drastically from the natural appearance of things. At its extreme, abstract art makes no reference whatsoever to nature, an aspect sometimes called nonfigurative or nonobjective to distinguish total abstraction from degrees of abstraction where objects remain recognizable in spite of distortion or reduction to geometrical equivalents. The word "abstract" is never a noun in art terminology. "Abstracts" are summaries of books, court cases, and so on, but an abstract work of art is an abstraction, not an abstract.

abstract expressionism. Movement in modern art, especially painting, in which form and color alone are the emotive forces, without recognizable reference to nature. Abstract expressionism was the dominant school of painting in the 1950's and early 1960's, centered in New York but practiced internationally.

academy, academic, academicism. "Academy" originally referred to the French Academy, founded in the seventeenth century under royal sponsorship to establish rules and supervise acceptability in literature, the arts, and the use of the French language. It and other national academies still function. The adjective "academic" is now nonspecific, and usually perjorative, referring to art that depends on established conventions rather than creative individuality.

acropolis. From Greek words for "high" (*acro*) and "city" (*polis*). Any fortified upper part of an ancient Greek city. Capitalized, the Acropolis is that of Athens, where the Parthenon and other temples were built.

acrylic. Paint in which the binder is acrylic resin, a transparent thermoplastic substance that is also the basis of such products as Lucite, synthetic fibers, and so on. Acrylic in recent years has replaced oil as the favorite paint of many artists because it dries faster.

action painting. Term invented by the American critic Harold Rosenberg emphasizing the sheer physical activity involved in the creation of large, spontaneously executed abstract expressionist paintings like those of Jackson Pollock and Franz Kline, among others.

aerial perspective. See *perspective.*

affresco (Italian). See *fresco.*

allegory. A story, play, poem, painting, or sculpture in which the participating personages and objects are the disguised components of a hidden theme, usually moralistic.

altarpiece. A painting or sculpture placed upon or behind an altar. When the subject is not a standard one such as the Crucifixion, it may be connected with the saint to whom the church or chapel is dedicated.

alto rilievo. Italian for *high relief.*

Apocalypse. The last book of the New Testament, Revelation, written on the island of Patmos about A.D. 85 by one John, probably Saint John, recounting his visions of the ultimate triumph of good over the forces of evil.

apse. A recess in a building, usually semicircular and covered with a half dome. In a church or cathedral, the semicircular end of the choir. In early medieval buildings the apse was a favored spot for mosaic or fresco decoration.

aquatint. An etching technique dating from the late eighteenth century by which tonalities approximating those of wash drawings may be produced. A plate is dusted with resin (occasionally sugar) and submerged in acid, which eats through tiny interstices between grains of the dust, biting a very fine stipple into the metal.

Archaic period. Early period in Greek art, 600–480 B.C.

architectonic, architectonics. Specifically, relating to architecture and its theories, but in general referring also to the structural quality of any art, including painting. Poussin's carefully constructed paintings are good examples of architectonic pictorial composition. (The term is also used in philosophy, where it means the systemization of knowledge.)

arcologies. Term invented by the modern architect Paolo Soleri denoting his visionary schemes for mammoth structures enclosing whole cities with open countryside between.

art brut. French term translatable as "art in the raw," invented by Jean Dubuffet to designate the art of very young children, psychotics, and the perpetrators of graffiti on public walls and monuments. Believing that spontaneous untutored art flows from basic sources more vital than timeworn standards of sophisticated, professional art, Dubuffet based his own paradoxically sophisticated style on these crude sources.

artist's proof. An unnumbered print pulled by the artist in addition to the numbered set.

art nouveau (new art). A style created in an attempt to break away from the art of the past and practiced from about 1880 to about 1910. With its sinuous lines and sharp definition it became primarily a decorative art form, but it also found expression in painting and architecture.

assemblage (a·säm·blazh'). A three-dimensional work of art (as opposed to two-dimensional collage) made up of bits and pieces from various sources, usually found objects.

baroque, baroque period. As a general term, baroque refers to elaborate, irregular, theatricalized forms, but the baroque period (roughly, the seventeenth century and the rococo sequel in the eighteenth) was also marked by schools of architecture and art based on classical models. In the same period the Netherlands produced the profoundly humanistic art of Rembrandt. Baroque cannot be given a single precise definition.

barrel vault. A vault semicircular in section.

bas relief. More frequently used than the equivalent "low relief," the term denotes sculpture in which forms are compressed from front to back into about one-quarter, more or less, of their volume in nature.

Bauhaus. State school of art and architecture founded in Germany in 1919 and headed by Walter Gropius. Most important for its theory and teaching of architecture, in which science and technology became the basis for design.

binder. The ingredient of paint that gives pigment the capacity to adhere to a surface. Binders include oil, egg (tempera), gum arabic (water color), acrylic, and others.

Book of Hours. A prayer book used by laymen for private devotions. As an illuminated manuscript in the fifteenth century, the Book of Hours was a major art form.

bravura. Bold, dashing technique that displays an artist's skill.

burin. A small, pointed tool, triangular in section, used by engravers.

burr. The uneven ridge of metal thrown up on either side of a line gouged into a plate, which collects ink and produces a soft, blurred line in printing.

buttress. A masonry support built against a wall to counterbalance the lateral thrust of an arch or vault (engaged buttress or pier buttress). A flying buttress is an arch or series of arches carrying the thrust over the side aisles to the piers of a Gothic church or cathedral.

calligraphy, calligraphic. Handwriting, and pertaining to it, especially beautiful handwriting as an art. In painting, often extended to include any freely executed linear inventions, such as Jackson Pollock's "skein" paintings.

cantilever. A large bracket, block, or beam projecting from a wall to support an elevated structural form without the use of walls, columns, arches, or other supporting forms beneath.

cartoon. A full-scale study, usually on paper, for a painting, either for reference or for transferring to the panel, canvas, or wall where the painting will be executed. Cartoons are also made for tapestries, stained glass, and other two-dimensional art forms that require a preliminary study.

cathedral. Strictly, the main church of a bishop's see, but also applied to any large, imposing church, Gothic ones in particular.

cenotaph. A monument or empty tomb honoring a dead person whose body is somewhere else.

choir. The part of a church or cathedral reserved for the clergy and choir. It occupies the space between transept and apse.

classical space. Concept of space as definable and measurable in harmoniously adjusted proportions, especially in painting.

closed form. Primarily a term applied to sculpture, but applicable to painting and architecture, denoting the entity of a form displacing a volume of space yet not fusing with it. As an extreme example, Brancusi's *The Kiss*; as a moderate one, an archaic Greek kouros. Later sculptures like the *Diadoumenos* and many others, including modern ones, are essentially closed forms in spite of the separation of legs, arms, or other units of the mass.

collage (ko·lazh'). French for "paste-up." Work of art made up wholly or in large part from bits of paper, cloth, or other material pasted onto a flat surface. The three-dimensional equivalent is assemblage.

colonnette. A small column. Because of their delicacy, colonnettes are frequently more decorative than functional.

complementary colors. In physics, any two colors of the spectrum that, combined, produce white light. In painting, however, the complementary colors (red and green; yellow and purple; blue and orange) when mixed produce browns or grays.

When juxtaposed in the right intensities, complementary colors are mutually intensifying. The principle is important in impressionism and pointillism.

composition. Arrangement; the art of arranging the component forms and colors of a painting or sculpture (sometimes architecture) in a harmonious, decorative, or expressive way.

concept art, conceptual art. Extreme phase of modern art in which ideas are presented in diagram or in description rather than in conventional execution as a painting or sculpture.

conversation piece. A group portrait of an informal gathering of relatives or companionable people disposed in their natural habitat, often a drawing room.

cubism. With fauvism, the basic revolutionary movement in modern art, initiated in 1907 by Picasso's *Demoiselles d'Avignon* . Cubism is based on two premises: first, that all forms in nature can be reduced to geometrical equivalents, usually angular; and second, that it is possible to represent multiple aspects of a figure or object simultaneously (see *space-time*). These ideas were combined in cubism's early phase, called "analytical cubism". A second phase, "decorative cubism," capitalized on ornamental shapes and patterns suggested by the analytical exercises. Since then Picasso and others have invented freely in Cubist-derived manners.

Dada. Nihilistic German anti-art movement (later French) in painting, sculpture, and literature, rejecting all established disciplines in reaction to World War I and its social upheavals. Nonsense, impertinence, and esthetic blasphemies were cultivated as a combination of protest and entertainment. The term "Dada" was selected by the poet Tristan Tzara. Marcel Duchamp remained Dada's living monument after its death in the early 1920's.

De Stijl (The Style). Journal founded in 1917 by a group of Dutch painters, architects, and sculptors proposing and practicing a system of modern design limited to rectangular forms and the primary colors (red, yellow, and blue) plus black and white. The name *De Stijl* is also given to the group and its theories.

diableries. Devilish inventions, sometimes half-homorous, frequent in Medieval manuscript illumination.

diptych. A painting or low relief sculpture in two compartments hinged to close like a book. Diptychs are most frequently met as portable shrines.

divisionism. Application of color in small spots or strokes to be blended by the eye as another color: for instance, blue and yellow to produce green, red and yellow to produce orange. The color may be applied loosely, as in impressionism, or semiscientifically according to optical rules, as in pointillism.

dome. See *vault*.

donor. Patron who commissions and pays for an altarpiece (or other work of art) and is portrayed along with saints and other religious personages in the completed work as recognition of his generosity.

drolleries. Grotesque or comical figures in manuscript illuminations.

dry point. Print technique related to etching and frequently combined with it, by which the lines of a drawing are scratched directly onto the plate with a stylus.

earth art. Form of art in which arbitrary changes with no useful reason for being are imposed on a countryside employing only the natural materials at hand. A trench a few inches deep may be dug for a distance of miles in a desert area, for instance. Basic to the ethos of earth art is a revolt against the commercialism of art galleries and the incarceration of art in museums.

egg tempera. See *tempera.*

engraving. Print made from a metal plate into which the picture or pattern has been incised with a burin.

exoskeleton, exoskeletal. As a biological term, the exterior skeletons of lobsters, turtles, and others. As an architectural term, exoskeletal refers to structural elements like flying buttresses exposed on the exterior of a building. The Pompidou Center in Paris is an extreme example of exoskeletal architecture.

expressionism. Specifically, a movement in modern art in which distortions of form and color are employed for emotive effects. Can also apply where appropriate to works of art created long before the term was invented, for instance, the paintings of El Greco.

façade. Usually the front of a building with the main entrance. Also, another side when given emphasis by architectural treatment.

fauvism. With cubism, one of the two revolutions that shifted the course of art in the early twentieth century. Never an organized movement, fauvism was a spontaneous expressionistic impulse in the use of distorted form and intense color for emotive (and decorative) effects in a happier mood than other expressionist painting. Leading Fauves (meaning "wild beasts," originally a derogatory name for the school) included Derain, Vlaminck, and the young Braque, but Matisse, the most eminent, remained fauvism's exemplar.

ferroconcrete. Reinforced concrete.

fixative. Thin solution of gum for spraying over pastels or other drawings to hold them more firmly to the paper.

flattened relief. See *rilievo schiacciato.*

flying buttress. See *buttress.*

foreshortening. Perspective as applied to the representation of objects or, especially, the human figure, by which the lines of component parts are shortened to give the illusion of proper relative sizes.

"Form follows function." Basic premise of functionalism.

found object. Any object not originally intended as a work of art, usually fragmentary and discarded, which an artist finds of sufficient esthetic interest to be treated as a work of art or to be incorporated into an assembled work of art. Old machine parts and bits of wrecked buildings serve artists most frequently.

fourth dimension. See *space-time.*

fresco. In its pure form (*buon* or true fresco), wall painting executed in pigment and water on fresh plaster. *Fresco a secco* (dry, or false fresco) is executed in tempera on dry plaster.

functionalism. The theory that a functionally perfect object or building will automatically be inherently beautiful. Although thought of as a modern concept, the functionalist idea goes back to antiquity and received its most ecstatic statement in nineteenth-century America when Horatio Greenough, a sculptor, described the beauty of a sailing ship.

futurism. Modern art movement originated by an aggressively self-publicizing group of Italian artists and literati just before World War I, which advocated the destruction of traditional art and the creation of new forms expressing the speed, energy, and violence of modern times. The automobile, railroad train, and airplane were among its symbols.

gargoyle. Strictly, a waterspout. (The word is derived from the Old French *gargoul,* "throat.") Medieval waterspouts were decorated with grotesque or monstrous heads, their mouths open to emit water. By extension, gargoyle means any grotesque projecting figure on a building.

genre painting. Subjects or scenes from daily life painted realistically, often with quaint or homely overtones.

geodesic. Form of architectural engineering in which structures are built of polygons formed by short, straight, lightweight bars. The method is particularly adaptable to the construction of large domes or globes.

gesso. Extremely fine-grained plaster used over wooden panels as a surface for egg tempera painting or on furniture as a surface for gilding and other decoration.

gestural painting. Painting in which the free action of applying paint remains apparent in the result. Not quite identical with action painting, gestural painting can be stretched to include such bravura techniques as John Singer Sargent's.

glaze. A thin, transparent film of color applied over another color to intensify or modify it.

Gothic. See *Middle Ages.*

gouache. Water-soluble paint somewhat thickened and made more or less opaque according to the degree of admixture with white.

grotesques, grotesqueries. Fanciful inventions combining human, animal, vegetable, mineral forms, usually of a humorous and decorative nature, but put to more serious use by certain late medieval Flemish painters.

ground. In etching, the acid-proof varnish with which a metal plate is covered and through which the drawing is scratched. Soft ground is a resinous mixture that remains sticky after application. In a print it yields a softer line, comparable to pencil drawing in contrast with the penlike line of etching proper.

gum arabic. A water-soluble resin obtained from several African acacias and used in medicines, candies, and various emulsions, including water-color paint, where it serves as a binder for the pigments.

happenings. Impromptu performances staged by artists, creating bizarre and ludicrous situations in which audience participation was invited. Popular in New York for a brief period in the 1960's.

hatching. A means of shading in drawing, engraving, or other graphic arts by fine lines either parallel, crossed, or systematized to describe the contours of the pictured shapes.

high relief. The degree of relief in sculpture between medium relief and full round. The term is elastic, but high relief may be thought of as the compression of the full three dimensions into about three-quarters of the front-to-back volume.

hyperrealism. Preferable to superrealism as avoiding confusion with surrealism. A movement of the 1970's in which naturalistic detail is rendered with acute fidelity, created in extreme reaction against abstraction. The term applies to both painting and sculpture.

Iconoclasts. "Image breakers." A group of members of the Orthodox Eastern Church in the eighth and ninth centuries who opposed the use of images in religious painting and sculpture, to the extent of destroying works of art in which such images appeared.

iconography. Representation of a subject, especially by interrelated symbols. See discussions of the Arnolfini wedding picture and Dürer's *Melencolia I*. Not the same as iconology.

iconology. The study and interpretation of iconography. Iconology frequently involves a kind of detective work, for instance, the discovery that the apparently casual domestic details of the Arnolfini wedding picture are interrelated as symbols.

illuminated manuscript. Manuscript decorated with pictures and designs. Initial letters and page borders are the most frequently illuminated spots, but independent miniature paintings are also encountered.

imagen de vestir. Spanish sculpture realistically carved and painted, clothed in actual garments.

impressionism. Major revolutionary art movement of the nineteenth century. Subjects from everyday life were sympathetically treated in "snapshot" compositions as if captured in momentary aspects. Effects of light and atmosphere were created by the free application of pure color in accord with loosely applied theories of physics.

intaglio, intaglio print. Print made from drawings incised into a surface, usually metal. The incised lines are filled with ink, which is transferred to paper under pressure. Engraving and etching are the major forms of intaglio prints.

jamb. The side piece of a framed opening such as a doorway, important in medieval art as the location of major sculptures, as at Chartres.

Jugendstil. German term for *art nouveau.*

Kamakura period. A.D. 1185–1333. One of the two foundation periods in Japanese art, preceded by the Heian (A.D. 794–1185). The city of Kamakura was at its most splendid during the period now given its name.

kouros (plural, *kouroi*). Greek for "young man," used in art to designate the standing nude male sculptures of the Archaic period. The female counterpart is the *kore* (maiden).

liberal arts. In art history, the medieval quadrivium (arithmetic, geometry, astronomy, and music) and the lower trivium (grammar, logic, and rhetoric). Symbolic figures of the seven liberal arts occur frequently in medieval painting and sculpture.

linear perspective. See *perspective.*

linocut, linoleum cut, linoleum print. Relief print from linoleum; otherwise same as woodblock, woodcut.

lintel. Horizontal supporting beam spanning an opening, frequently carved when on medieval portals.

lithograph. Print made from a drawing in wax crayon on special limestone (or substitute material in recent variations) by a process invented by Aloys Senefelder in 1798.

low relief. See *bas relief.*

manifesto. A public declaration of principles and intentions. Manifestos became popular with avant-garde groups of artists in the early twentieth century; the Italian Futurists made the most dramatic use of this form of publicity by scattering printed sheets from bell towers.

mannerism, mannerist. As a general term, refers to a distinctive, usually affected, mode of style or behavior. Specifically, the sixteenth-century movement in which artists departed from the ideal classicism of the High Renaissance in favor of sometimes bizarre and often neurotic stylizations.

Medieval period. See *Middle Ages.*

medium relief. See *mezzo rilievo.*

megalith. A huge stone, especially in prehistoric or ancient monuments, as at Stonehenge, but the term is also applicable to any large column, obelisk, or other architectural unit carved from a single stone.

Mexican Renaissance. Nationalistic art movement dedicated to propagandization of the Mexican Revolution, flourishing in the 1920's under the leadership of Rivera, Orozco, and Siqueiros.

mezzo rilievo. Italian term more frequently used than its English equivalent, medium relief, to denote sculptural relief where form has been compressed from front to back to about half the depth of nature's three dimensions.

mezzotint. Method of engraving by which a metal plate is uniformly roughened with an edged tool (roulette or rocker), after which it would print solid black. Smoothed with a burnisher, areas will print lighter in tones up to pure white. Mezzotint was widely used in the eighteenth century and into the nineteenth as a means of reproducing paintings, a function now served by photographic processes.

Middle Ages. The centuries between the dissolution of the Roman Empire and the Renaissance, subdivided by art historians (with vague and overlapping dates) into early Middle Ages (about 1000 to middle or late eleventh century), Romanesque (mid-eleventh century to latter twelfth), Gothic (latter twelfth to end of fourteenth) and, in the North, late Gothic (fifteenth century).

minimal art. Painting or sculpture conceived according to the modern adage "less is more," originally applied to architecture. The ultimate minimalist painting is a canvas of a single color, of which there are numerous examples; the ultimate sculpture, a simple cube, this having been demonstrated by the American artist Tony Smith.

mobile. A sculpture constructed of movable parts that change relative positions either in air currents or when motorized. Alexander Calder invented the form; Marcel Duchamp named it.

monotype. A variety of printmaking by which a painting in black and white or color is executed on metal or another nonabsorbent surface and transferred to paper under pressure. "Mono" indicates a single transfer, but a weaker second print may be pulled in some cases, or the original painting may be retouched for further impressions, all, of course, differing.

mosaic. A picture or design made by bits of stone, glass, or other material set into a floor, wall, or ceiling.

mural. A wall painting. Murals may be painted directly onto the wall or onto canvas that is then attached to the wall.

narthex. A porch, portico, or vestibule on the west end (main entrance) of a church. Penitents or others not admitted to the church itself were allowed in medieval times to enter the narthex; hence it was sometimes the size of a hall to accommodate bands of pilgrims.

naturalism. This term has been an ambiguous one in varying uses since its invention in the late seventeenth century to apply to followers of Caravaggio, who rejected idealization for the representation of people as they (more or less) are. As a literary term in the nineteenth century, naturalism was identified with the novels of Zola and with Flaubert's *Madame Bovary,* in which observation of human behavior in contemporary society was supposedly objective. In art today the term is loosely used, but basically it denotes forms of realism in which personal interpretation is avoided, such as hyperrealism and photorealism.

nave. From *navis* "ship", an early symbol of the church. The main part of a church, between the chief entrance and the choir, separated from the side aisles by piers or columns.

negative volume. Spatial volume defined by solids, but not to be confused with "void." Voids are automatically created by forms that enclose space; negative volumes are conceived as shaped spaces that are creatively introactive with the defining solids and may even be conceived as having defined those solids, as the action of natural forces can hollow out a cave. "Negative volume" refers to sculpture but is inherent in good architectural design.

Niké (Nī'-kē). In Greek mythology, the winged goddess of Victory.

nonfigurative. See *abstract art.*

nonobjective. See *abstract art.*

offset printing. A photographic adaptation of the lithographic process by which the image is set on a rubber-covered roller and then transferred to paper.

op (optical) art. A classification of abstract painting utilizing geometrical patterns that create illusions of formal displacement or motion, often in black and white, as well as chromatic juxtapositions that set up illusory color changes and pulsating vibrations.

open form. Term primarily associated with sculpture but applicable also to architecture and painting, denoting conceptions by which volumes cease to be self-contained (closed form) and, instead, project into space around them.

original print. An etching, engraving, lithograph, or other kind of print from the artist's hand rather than from mechanical reproduction. Ideally an original print is not only created by the artist on the plate or block or stone, but is also printed by him. However, printing is often left to professional craftsmen, whose work is done under the supervision of the artist, or is subject to the artist's final approval.

pastel. Finely ground pigment mixed with a gum binder and formed into a short, pencil-like stick. Pastel differs from most crayons in its dry, powdery texture, in contrast with the waxy texture of others.

pediment. The triangle (gable) at the end of a building, formed by the sloping roof. The pediment form is also applied decoratively, over windows and doors.

perspective. The art of picturing things or scenes on a two-dimensional surface in ways that represent them in three dimensions as they appear to the eye. Perspective is of two kinds, linear and aerial. In *linear perspective,* lines that are parallel in nature converge as they recede into the distance (railroad tracks being a standard example) and objects of the same size in nature become smaller in proportion to their distance from the eye. *Aerial perspective* takes into account the softening effect of distance, the diffusion or loss of detail, diminished value contrast, and the bluish color of distant scenes, all the result of atmosphere intervening between the eye and the thing or scene viewed.

photorealism. Art form of the 1970's in which artists reproduced photographs as paintings, often with maximum fidelity, at other times with certain refinements or simplifications that added a note of interpretive intent to the absolute objectivity of the earliest photorealists.

piazza. In Italy, an open public square, usually surrounded by buildings and sometimes with an architectural structure designed specifically to enclose it, as at the piazza of St. Peter's in Rome.

picture plane. The plane of the surface of a painting, most easily comparable to the glass in a framed picture, behind which the picture "recedes" in depth, often with frontal planes that repeat the picture plane.

Pietà. A representation of the Virgin Mary mourning over the body of Jesus, held upon her lap, after the Crucifixion.

pigment. The coloring matter of paint, formerly obtained from natural sources, today largely synthesized chemically. Combined with a binder (oil, egg, acrylic, gum arabic, and others), pigment becomes paint.

pointillism. Method of painting in small juxtaposed dots of chromatic colors that may be fused by the eye, at a distance, into other colors of which they are the component parts. Pointillism differs from the broken color (divisionism) of impressionism in its precision and semiscientific application of the laws of optics.

polyptych. A set of more than three panels, usually painting but sometimes carving, hinged or otherwise bound into a unit. Most frequently an altarpiece.

pop art. From "popular art." Term coined by the English critic Lawrence Alloway in the mid-1950's to denote the "vernacular culture" of comic strips, advertising, movies, and aspects of urban culture not ordinarily thought of as art. The term is expanded to include the art of painters and sculptors who have employed these motifs in commenting on the contemporary scene.

porch. An architectural structure set in front of the entrance to a building. In Gothic architecture, where it was most highly developed, the porch became as deep, wide, and high as an independent building. Heavily encrusted with sculpture and ornament, porches were dramatic introductions to the soaring vaulted cathedral interiors, as on the transepts at Chartres.

post-impressionism. Theory and practice of artists who at the end of the nineteenth century departed from impressionism in order to rectify, each in his own way, what they regarded as its shortcomings. Cézanne and Seurat rejected the free, spontaneous character of Impressionist technique for formal disciplines based on impressionism's divided color, while Van Gogh and Gauguin rejected its happy objectivity for intense personal expressionism.

predella. The base of an altarpiece, often divided into panels with paintings of subjects relating to the main subject above.

primitive art. The art of primitive societies, usually tribal.

primitive artist. Self-taught artist who has not mastered such standard means of representation as perspective, foreshortening, and the like, but who, as a result, may develop an expressive individual style.

print. A drawing or design in black and white or colors made from a master original by one of several means. Intaglios are printed from metal plates with lines incised either directly (engraving, dry point) or with acid (etching). Relief prints are made from lines or areas left standing on a master block, the blanks having been cut away (woodcut, woodblock, linoleum cut). Planar processes, from a flat surface, include lithography. Silk screen is a stencil process. See also *original print.*

psychic balance, psychological balance. Balance in a pictorial composition created by mental factors such as the degree of interest or emphasis given an element that otherwise would not hold its own in terms of size or other purely visual factors.

quadrivium. See *liberal arts.*

realism. The representation of things and people as they actually appear. Realism does not rule out personal sensitivity and acute perception, as the art of Rembrandt and Eakins among many others proves, but stops short of expressive or idealistic modifications or distortions. See also *naturalism*.

refectory. Dining hall, particularly in convents and monasteries, where the Last Supper was the standard subject for Renaissance mural paintings; Leonardo da Vinci's is the most famous.

reinforced concrete. Concrete masonry strengthened by interior steel bars or mesh.

relief. A work of sculpture in less than full three dimensions of nature. The degrees, in lessening order, are high relief (*alto rilievo*), medium relief (*mezzo rilievo*), low relief (*bas relief*), and flattened relief (*rilievo schiacciato*).

relief print. Print from a raised surface. See *print*.

rib. A masonry arch, usually molded, forming the framework of a vault.

ribbed vault. See *vault*.

rilievo schiacciato. Extremely low sculptural relief, barely rising above the surface, adaptable to the most subtle atmospheric effects. The English translation of this Italian term, "flattened relief," is seldom used.

rococo. Developing from the baroque and frequently included as its last phase, rococo was a style of extreme elaboration and delicacy. Ornamental motifs were derived from flowers, foliage, shells. (The term originated from the French *rocaille*, meaning shell work or stone work.) Paintings of similar character were widely incorporated into rococo decorative schemes.

Romanesque period. See *Middle Ages*.

romantic movement, romanticism. An international mid-nineteenth-century surge of creative energy in all the arts, with personal, emotive, and freely inventive creative approaches in rebellion against the formalized dictates of the neo-classical establishment. As contrasting examples see David's neo-classical *Death of Socrates* and Géricault's romantic *Raft of the Medusa*.

romantic space. Concept of space as limitless, mysterious, often turbulent.

roulette. A small wheel edged with sharp points that may be rolled along the outlines of a drawing on paper to puncture them, after which the outlines may be transferred to another surface by laying the punctured drawing on it and dusting with dark powder, usually charcoal.

scumbling. Heavy, rather dry paint dragged from a brush across the rough surface of another painted area so that bits of the second color adhere to the irregularities of the first. Scumbling enriches surface texture and can result in interesting color effects. Glaze is often applied over dry scumbling for further enrichment.

serigraph. A term as reasonable as "lithograph" that failed to catch on widely as a replacement for silk screen print.

show-card color. An inexpensive, opaque, water-soluble paint frequently but not quite correctly called tempera, popular in classes for beginners, especially children.

silk screen print. Print made by pressing paint through fine silk stencils onto paper. Silk screen stencils are also used on fabrics, plastics, and various other surfaces, frequently in mass commercial production.

social realism. Realism directed toward political or social comment. Nineteenth-century examples include Daumier's *Rue Transnonain* and much of his and other artists' representation of the contemporary scene, but the term is most closely associated with American painting of the period between World Wars I and II when artists cast a sympathetic eye on the anonymous members of the urban proletariat.

soft ground. See *ground.*

space-time. Concept in modern physics by which space and time are indissolubly united, the three dimensions of space being joined by the fourth of time. In art the concept is basic to cubism, in which different aspects of the same object are represented simultaneously.

state. A proof pulled at a way-point in the development of an etching, engraving, or other print, by which the artist determines what he has so far set down on the plate. States are called first, second, third, and so on, as work continues.

stigmata. Wounds or marks on a person resembling the five wounds on the body of Christ at the Crucifixion. Saint Francis of Assisi was the first stigmatist.

straight painting. The direct application of pigment to canvas in creating a picture with little or no preparatory study or guidelines.

stylus. A needle-like instrument. In art it applies to the instrument used in ancient times to incise letters, figures, or designs on clay tablets, or to the needle used by etchers to scratch their drawing into the ground on the plate.

superrealism. See *hyperrealism.*

surrealism. Movement in modern art and literature also described by its adherents as a way of life, with manifestos in 1924 and 1929 by the French poet André Breton. Surrealism in painting, where it received its widest expression, is an art of paradox where the exact pictorial description of objects and figures is paired with their irrational combination.

symbol. Something that stands for something else, especially a physical object that stands for an abstraction, such as the small dog in the Arnolfini wedding picture, symbolizing fidelity. A combination of symbols used to tell a story constitutes an allegory.

symbolism. A movement in reaction against realism based on the essential principle, proclaimed in the Symbolist Manifesto of 1886, that ideas must be "clothed in sensuous form."

tableau. French for "picture," but applied by the American artist Edward Kienholz to his verbal outlines for proposed works.

tempera. An emulsion of pigment with any of several gluey substances as a binder, yolk of egg being traditional. Egg tempera was the standard technique for panel painting in the Renaissance before the development of oil.

tensegrity. Term invented by the American artist Kenneth Snelson to denote the engineering principle of balanced tensions and compressions in suspension employed in his sculptures.

tessera (plural, *tesserae*). A small piece of stone, glass, or other material used in making a mosaic.

thrust. The outward force exerted by an arch or vault.

tight. Semicolloquial term denoting meticulous, smooth-surfaced execution of a painting.

tracery. Ornamental stonework decorating a window and holding the glass in place. Typical of Gothic buildings.

transept. The arm of a cruciform church at right angles to the nave.

triptych. A painting or carving in three compartments side by side, or three independent panels hinged so that the lateral sections, or wings, each half the width of the central panel, can be closed over it.

trivium. See *liberal arts.*

tympanum. The space over a doorway enclosed by the lintel and the arch.

underpainting. Preliminary stage of a painting, in which the forms are defined, usually in monochrome, for subsequent development in color and greater detail. Underpaintings may be in tempera, oil, or any other stable paint. A warm underpainting (browns and tans) lends a golden tone to the finished picture; a cool one (grays and whites) can yield a silvery tone.

value. The equivalent lightness or darkness of a color in terms of black and white. Yellow, for instance, tells as a light value; purple, as a dark one. Generally speaking, a black and white photograph on properly sensitized film translates color into values.

vault. An arched ceiling of stone, brick, or concrete. A *barrel vault* is semicylindrical. A *groined vault* is formed by two barrel vaults intersecting at right angles. A *ribbed vault* consists of light masonry supported by a framework of ribs. A dome is a hemispherical vault.

vedute (singular, *veduta*). Italian, meaning "views." Accurately detailed paintings of important city views, especially of Venice, popular in the seventeenth and eighteenth centuries.

wing. In painting, one of two panels of equal size flanking the central panel of an altarpiece and hinged to close over it.

woodblock, woodcut, wood engraving. Woodblock prints are of two kinds: *woodcuts,* in which the whites are cut away to leave black lines and areas standing in relief for printing, like a drawing in black ink; and *wood engravings,* in which the cutting is extremely fine and the picture is conceived in terms of white against black rather than black against white.

Photo Credits

INDEX

Abduction of Rebecca, The (Delacroix), 189–91, *190*, 207, 341

Abstract expressionism, 105, 145; improvisation in, 132, 134; and "meaning," 131–2

Abstraction, 117–43; in architecture, 140–2; Cézanne as father of, 186; and cubism, 126–7; defined, 35, 117; degrees of, 117; De Stijl, 130–1; and hyperrealism, 370; intellectualization *vs.* emotionalization, 131, 145; Mondrian's rectilinear planes, 127–30; and perspective, 121; Piero's figures, 135, 138–9; and Oriental art, 142–3, 154; proselitizing of, 142; *cf.* realism, 62–3, 119–26; rise of, 81–2; Rothko and, 135; in sculpture, 33, 35, 139–40; Seurat's *Sunday Afternoon*, 217; and Turner, 134. *See also* Abstract expressionism

Acropolis, 7, 165

Acrylic, 220

Action (motion) in art, 188–91, 205–7

Action painting, 132

Actor Dancing (Kiyotada), *155*

Advertising art, 285, 322

African, Itumba: wooden mask, *127*

Age of Bronze, The (Rodin), *45–6*

Agony in the Garden, The (El Greco), 98, 99, 101

Albers, Josef, *Solo V*, *270*

Albright, Ivan Le Lorraine, 315–16, 318; *Into the World There Came a Soul Called Ida*, 315, *316*

Allegory of Deception (Queirolo), *44*

Allegory of Man's Life, from *Le grant kalendrier et compost des Bergiers*, *347*

Allston, Washington, 340–1, 343; *American Scenery*, 340, *341*; *The Flight of Florimell*, *341*, 343

Alto rilievo (high relief), 38

American Scenery (Allston), *340*, 341

Amiens Cathedral, choir vaults, 7

Analytical cubism, 126, 368

Anatomy Lesson of Doctor Tulp, The (Rembrandt), *196*

Anecdotal realism, 77–8

Anguish of Departure, The (Chirico), *338*

Animals and Plants (Jakuchū), *143*

Anne of Cleves (Holbein the Younger), 156–7

Anti-art, 87, 285; and Dada, 48

Apparition of a Face and a Fruit Dish on a Beach (Dali), 335, *336*, 337

Appenine, The (Giambologna), *354*

Aquatint, 271, 277, *278*, *279*

Archangel Raphael with Adam and Eve, The (Blake, William), *328*

Architectonics: Brera, *cf.* Cézanne, 185–6; Nevelson's *Sky Cathedral*, 356

Architecture, 53–7; abstract values, 140–2; architectonic values, 185; arcologies, 361; bases for judgment, 54; Bauhaus, 88–9; De Stijl, 130–1; and engineering, 192–3; exoskeletal, 56–7, 192; expressionist, 114–15; façades, 165; functionalism, 87–92; geodesic, 360; materials, 54–5, 88–91, 115, 193; and mural painting, 146; negative volume, 139–42; Parthenon, 3, 5, 7–8; Renaissance churches, 66; skyscrapers, 90–2; triangular form, 167–9, 175–6; union with sculpture and painting, 9, 37–9; visionary, 358–61. *See also* Gothic period

Arcologies, 360, *361*

Arena Chapel, Padua, Giotto frescoes, 224, 226, 227, 228, 234, 236, 239, 306

Arezzo frescoes. See *Legend of the True Cross*

Aristide Bruant in His Cabaret (Toulouse-Lautrec), 158, *160*

Aristotle with a Bust of Homer (Rembrandt), 251, *252*

Arnolfini wedding picture (van Eyck). See *Marriage of Giovanni Arnolfini and Giovanna Cenami.*

Arrangement in Gray and Black, No. 1, (Whistler), 10, 12, *13*, 15, 19, 117–18, 129, 145, 219, 277

Art brut (art in the raw), 51

Artemis of Ephesus, *51*

Artist in His Studio, The (Vermeer), *116*, 118–20, *120*, 138, 182, 203

Artist's proof, 266, 287

Art nouveau, 114–15, 366

Assemblage, 46, 312, 355–6

Athenodoros, *Laocoön*, *36*

Audrey I (Snelson), *191–2*

Audubon, John J., *Brown Rat*, 255, *256*

Autun Cathedral tympanum, 353

Babel IIB (Soleri), 360, *361*

Bahram Gur in the Turquoise Pavilion on Wednesday (Muzahib), *153*, 154

Balance and counterbalance, 151, 191, 195; *Last Supper* composition, 169, 172; and motion, 36, 189–91, 198; 205–7; psychic, 206; solid forms in, 33–5, 118–19

Ballet Master, The (Degas), 285, *286*

Balzac (Rodin), 46, *47*

Bamboo arch: New Guinea *davi*, *55*

Baroque period: Bernini's *David*, *37*; churches and dynamic space, 142; dramatic realism, 70–1, 352

Bas relief (low relief), 38–9; sculpture, 164–5

Bataille, Nicholas, *Fall of Babylon*, 352–3

Battle of Lapiths and Centaurs (Greek, early classical), *36–7*

Battle of Naked Men (Pollaiuolo), 272–3, 277, 287

Bauhaus (Gropius), *88–9*

Beasts of the Sea (Matisse), 143, 151, *152*, 154

"Beaubourg." See Pompidou Center

Beaux Arts, École des, 92–3

Becket Associates, Hyatt Regency, 92

Bellelli Family, The (Degas), 195, *197*, 200–2, *201*

Bernini, Gianlorenzo: *David*, 36–7, 45; *Ecstasy of Saint Theresa*, 71, 86, 352; Saint Peter's Colonnade, *139*, 140

Binder, 219; egg, 241; in fresco, 221; and pigment, 220

Birthday (Chagall), *336*, 337–8

Bishop, Isabel, *Two Girls*, 81, *82*

Black Lines (Kandinsky), 131–2

Blake, Peter, *Form Follows Fiasco: Why Modern Architecture Hasn't Worked*, 93

Blake, William, 327–30, 339, 345, 347, 349; *Archangel Raphael with Adam and Eve,*

Blake, William (*cont.*)
328, 332; illustration for *Pastorals of Virgil*, 264, *266*; *The Wise and the Foolish Virgins*, 163–4, *327*; *Zacharias and the Angel*, *329*
Blind printing, 270
Blume, Peter, *The Eternal City*, 318–20, *337*
Boating (Manet), *80*, 81, 253
Boat off Deer Isle (Marin), *257*
Boccioni, Umberto, 44; *Unique Forms of Continuity in Space*, 41–2
Böcklin, Arnold, 341; *Island of the Dead*, 339, *340*; *Triton and Nereid*, *339*
Books, and prints, 266–7, 286
Borromini, Francesco, San Carlo alle Quattro Fontane, *141*, 142
Bosch, Hieronymus, 334–5, 337, 344; *Creation of Eve*, 330, 332, *333*; *Garden of Delights*, 331, 332, *333*; *Hell*, 330–2, *333*
Botticelli, Sandro, 31; *Calumny*, 292–6, *293*, 318, 348; *Primavera*, 159, *161*, 162–3, 195, 292
Boucher, François, *Toilet of Venus*, 75, 298–9, *300*, 301, 320
Boullée, Etienne-Louis, cenotaph for Sir Issac Newton, 358–60, *359*
Brancacci Chapel frescoes (Masaccio), 225, *226*, 227
Brancusi, Constantin, *The Kiss*, *32*, 33–5; *Torso of a Young Man*, *35*
Braque, Georges, 369; *Musical Forms*, 59–60, *62–3*
Breaking Home Ties (Hovenden), 77–78, 207
Brera altarpiece (Piero). (See *Madonna and Child with Saints and Angels.*
Bronze, sculptural, 42–6
Brown Rat (Audubon), 255; *256*
Bruegel the Elder, Pieter, *209*, *Flemish Proverbs*, 211–12; *Landscape with the Fall of Icarus*, 209, 210–11, 216; *Parable of the Blind*, 212–13, 216
Brunelleschi, Santo Spirito, 66
Brushwork: de Kooning, 132; Marin's dragging of, 106, 255, 258; Sargent, 123, 132
Buddhist Assembly (unknown Chinese painter), 236–7
Buon fresco (true fresco), 221–8, 232, 369; crystalline film, 221, 229
Burial of Count Orgaz (El Greco), *100*, 101–2
Burnham, D. H., & Co., Reliance Building, *90*
Burning of the Houses of Parliament (Turner), *133*, 134
Burr, 279–80, 367
Byzantine style, *231*, 232–4, *235*

Cabinet of Dr. Caligary, still from, *115*,
Calculation *vs.* spontaneity, 23, 96–8, 107, 192
Calder, Alexander, *Little Spider*, *42*
Calligraphy, 142–3, 253
Calumny (Botticelli), 292–6, *293*, 318, 348
Camera degli Sposi fresco (Mantegna), 146, *148*

Canaletto, *Clock Tower in the Piazza San Marco*, *5–6*
Cano, Alonso, *Saint John of God*, 86–7
Cantilever (Wright house), *54*
Caravaggio (Michelangelo Merisi), 73; *Conversion of Saint Paul*, *70*; *Musicians*, 187, *188*, 191
Card Players, The (Cézanne), 185–8, *186*
Carnival at Nice (Matisse), 151, *152*
Carriera, Rosalba, *Personification of Europe*, 258, *259*
Cartoon, 222–3
Casa Milá (Gaudí), *114*, 115
Cassatt, Mary, *The Fitting*, *271*
Castiglione, Giovanni Benedetto, *Melancholia*, 276–7
Cathedral. *See* Gothic period
Cave paintings, 228
Cennini, Cennino, *Il Libro dell'Arte*, 249
Cenotaph: Boullée's project for, 358–9
Centennial Certificate (Rauschenberg), *284*
Centennial Exposition, Philadelphia, 48–51, *49–50*
Cézanne, Paul, 26, 31, 186, 191, 216; *Card Players*, 185–8, *186*; *Mont Sainte-Victoire*, 23, *24*, 26, 131, 182, 203
Chagall, Marc, *Birthday*, *336*, 337–8
Chardin, Jean-Baptiste-Siméon, 73–5, 77, 118; *Governess*, 74–5; *Still Life*, 74, *76*, 299
Chariot of Apollo, The (Redon), 329–30
Chartres Cathedral, *7*, 39–40
Children's art, 107
Chirico, Giorgio de, 337–9, 341; *The Anguish of Departure*, *338*; *Melancholy and Mystery of a Street*, 337, *338*
Christ Carried to the Tomb (Rembrandt), *277*
Christina of Denmark, Duchess of Milan (Holbein the Younger), 155–8, *156*
Christ on the Cross (Rubens), 108, *109*, 110
Christ on the Cross with Landscape (El Greco), 110–11, *108*
Cimabue, 234
City Street (nine-year-old child), *107*
Classical composition, 202, *203*; motion and static figures, 191, 205–7; painterly technique, 216
Classicism, ideal, 66–9, 191, 232, 371
Clay, 44–6, 240
Clock Tower in the Piazza San Marco (Canaletto, *5–6*
Close, Chuck, *Nat*, *83*, 85, 86
Cole, Thomas, *Manhood* from *Voyage of Life* series, 348–9; *The Titan's Goblet*, 342, *343*, ill. 342; *View on the Catskill*, 343–4, *345*, 355
Collage, 46, 355; and lithography, 284; Matisse's *Beasts of the Sea*, 151, *152*, 152
Color: application of, 81, 134; change, and fresco painting, 221–2; Mondrian's freeing of, 127, *129*; Piero and, 137, 226; and two-dimensional composition, 147–58; warm-to-cool progression, 105–6; value of, 377
Colorism, 134–5
Colossal Head of Balzac (Rodin), *46*
Columnar forms, 40, 182, 184
Combat of Minerva and Mars, The (David), 299, *301*

Coming Home for Thanksgiving (Moses), 345, *346*
Common man theme, 298–303
Commonplace subjects, 73–5, 81, 207
Company of Captain Frans Banning Cocq and Lieutenant Willem van Ruytenburch, The (Rembrandt), *194*, 195–8
Composite work of art, 8–9
Composition, 12–13, 15; Brera masterpiece, 185–6; *Card Players*, 185–8; classical, 173, 191, 202, *203*–7; Degas, 20–1, 202, 206–7; function of, 145–6; group portraits, 195–202; *Guernica*, 177; *Last Supper*, 167–9, 172, 175, 188; linear, 159, 162–4; as narrative, 195–217; as pattern, 145–65; pictorial, 202, 216, 258, 306; pyramidal, 178; Raphael's *Transfiguration*, 172–3; rules for, 157–8; Seurat's pointillism, 217; sculptural and architectural, 191–3; spatial, 118–19, 180–4; storytelling pictures, 207–16; as structure, 167–91; testing, 12–13, 15, 61, 74, 122; triangular formula, 175–8, 188–9; two- *cf.* three-dimensional, 146–7; unbalance and motion, 188–91, 205–7; women's portraits compared, 15–23.
Composition (Mondrian), *130*
Concept art: Kienholz's *State Hospital*, 312
Construction (Stankiewicz), *46*, 47, 51
Construction of Volume Relations (Vantongerloo), 130, *131*
Constructions, 355–8; linear and spatio-dynamic, 41–3, 47
Convergence (Pollock), 132, *133*
Conversion of Saint Paul, (Caravaggio), *70*
Cornell, Joseph, *Medici Slot Machine*, 355–6
Cot, Pierre Auguste, *The Storm*, 29–31, *30*
Couple with Shopping Bags (Hansen), 85, 86–7, 315, *317*, 318
Craftsmanship and skill, 6, 30, 351; abstraction and, 121–2, 126, 132, 134; Cézanne, 26; Cot, 30; Gérôme, 77; Hicks, 27; and *buon fresco*, 224; Japanese art and Gauguin, 270–1; Marin, 106; Matisse, 150; Renoir, 17–18; and tempera, 238; Van Gogh, 97–8. *See also* Draughtsmanship
Crayons, 258, 282. *See also* Lithography; Pastel paintings
Creation of Adam (Michelangelo), *218*, 222–3
Creation of Eve (Bosch), 330, 332, *333*
Cross-hatching, 244, 264
Crucifixion, 28; old masters compared, 108–11
Crucifixion (Follower of the Master of the Saint Francis Legend), 110–*11*
Crucifixion with the Virgin and Saints (Perugino), *174*, 175–8, 216
Crystal Palace (Paxton), 89–90, 192
Cubi VII (Smith), 35–6
Cubism: analytical, 126; defined, 126; humanistic art, 320; *Les Demoiselles*, 123–7; space-time concept, 40, 126

Dada, 48
Dali, Salvador, *Apparition of a Face*, *335*, *336*, 337; *Soft Construction*, *335*
Daumier, Honoré, 288, 292, 318; *Print Collector*, 362, *363*; *Rue Transnonain*, 288, 289–90; *La Soupe*, *362*

David, Jacques-Louis, 297, 318; *Combat of Minerva and Mars*, 299, 301; *Death of Socrates*, 297, 298–9, *300*, 301–2, 320
David (Bernini), 36–7, 45
David (Donatello), 66
Davidsz de Heem, Jan, *Still Life with Parrots*, 74
da Vinci, Leonardo. *See* Leonardo da Vinci
Davis, Joseph H., *Esther Tuttle*, 147–51, *149*, 154, 157
Death of Adam, The (Piero), 222, *223*
Death of Socrates, The (David), 298–302, 320, *297, 300*
de Bandol, Jean, *Fall of Babylon the Great City*, 352
Declaration of Independence, The (Trumbull), 295–6, 298
Degas, Edgar, 20–1, 145, 195, 202, 206–7, 259–61, 285; *Ballet Master*, 285, *286*; *Bellelli Family*, 195, *197*, 200–2, *201*; *Portrait of Tourny*, 287; *Rehearsal in the Foyer of the Opera*, 202, *204*, 205–6; *Woman Having Her Hair Combed*, 261; *Woman with Chrysanthemums*, *19*, 20–2, 145, 186, 195
de Kooning, Willem, *Woman IV*, 132
Delacroix, Eugène, 216; *Abduction of Rebecca*, 189–91, *190*, 207, 341; *Liberty Leading the People*, 297–8
Demoiselles d'Avignon, Les (Picasso), 123, *125*, 126–7, 154
Demon as Pirate (Klee), 349, *350*, 351, 355
Denis, Maurice, 147
Depth, 146–7, 178, 180
de Sanctis, Francesco, *Spanish Steps*, 140, *141*
De Stijl, 130–1
Destroyed City, The (Zadkine), 112, 322, *323*
Diableries, 332–5
Diadoumenos (Polykleitos), *34–5*, 40, 45, 63
Dinner of the Millionaires (Rivera), 304, *306*
Discobolus (Myron), 207
Discovery of the True Cross (Piero), 137
Distortion: in architecture, 114–15; abstraction, 61–3; El Greco's, 101, 110; expressionism, 95–7, 99, 103, 107, 114, 145, 177; medieval *Crucifixion*, 111; Ruben's *Crucifixion* and lack of, 108; in sculpture, 111–14; and violence, 103, 177–8
di Suvero, Mark, untitled sculpture, *192*
Donatello, *David*, 66; *Saint George and the Dragon*, 40, *41*
Dramatic realism, 69–71, 108, 352
Draughtsmanship, 102–3, 222, 260, 282
Drawing: art brut, 51; full-scale, egg tempera painting, 241; monotype and, 285; on woodblock, 264. *See also* Intaglio prints
Dreamscapes: American, 341–4, 348–9; Blake, 327–30; Chirico, 338–41; Dali, 335, 337; Klee's *Demon*, 351; Rousseau, 344–5
Drying Clothes (Harunobu), *269*, 270–1
Dry point, 279
Dubuffet, Jean, *Nourrice Profuse*, 2, *3*, 5, 51
Duel After the Masquerade, The (Gérôme), 75, 76, 77, 207–8
Dufy, Raoul, *Yellow Violin*, 59, 61–2

Durand, Asher B., *Scene from Thanatopsis*, 23–6, *24, 25*, 131, 182, 203, 343
Dürer, Albrecht, *Four Horsemen of the Apocalypse*, 264, *265*, 274; *Hands of an Apostle*, 244, *245*; *Melencolia I*, 274–7, *275*, 348; and woodblock prints, 263–5

Eagle-Headed Winged Being Pollinating the Sacred Tree (Assyrian), 38
Eakins, Thomas, *Miss Van Buren*, 78–80, 79
Eclecticism, 90–1
Ecstasy of Saint Theresa (Bernini), 71, 86, 352
Egg tempera, 220. *See also* Tempera painting
Eiffel Tower (Eiffel, Gustave), 8, 56, *57*
Einstein Tower (Mendelsohn), *115*
El Greco, 31, *Agony in the Garden*, 98, *99*, 101; *Burial of Count Orgaz*, 100, *101*–2; *Christ on the Cross*, 108, *110*–12; expressionism of, 99
Empress as Donor with Attendants (Chinese), *39*
Empress Theodora and Attendants, 230, *234*
Engineering: and functional structures, 92; architectural construction, 56, 192–3; Gothic cathedrals, 6–7
Engraving: use of burin in, 272, 274, 276; defined, 263; Dürer and, 274–7; gray tones, 274; and intaglio, 272
Enthroned Madonna and Child (Byzantine school), 234, *235*
Estes, Richard, *Supreme Hardware*, 83, *84*; *Thom McAn*, 83, *84*
Esther Tuttle (Davis), 147–51, *149*, 154, 157
Etching: defined, 263; and dry point, 279; *cf.* engraving, 277; and ground, 277; and intaglio, 272; original print, 287; stylus use, 279
Eternal City, The (Blume), 318–20, 337
Evocation of the Butterflies (Redon), *329*
Executions of the Third of May, The (Goya), 290–2, 296, 320, 322
Exoskeletal architecture, 56–7, 192
Expressionism, *81*, 95–115; in architecture, 57, 114–15; color distortion, 95, 97, 99, 107; distortion, 61–3, 95, 103, 111, 145; free *vs.* calculated, 95–8; and sculpture, 111–14

"Falling Water" (Wright), *54*
Fall of Babylon the Great City, The (Bataille; de Bandol), *252–3*
Fashion and taste, 28–31, 57, 68–9, 77, 90, 95; and Beaubourg, 56; pastels, 259; reaction to Cézanne, 186; Rockwell popularity, 11–15; Sargent's portraits, 123
Ferroconcrete, 369; Nervi construction, 193, 51
Figure with Raised Arms (Wotruba), *35*
Fitting, The (Cassatt), *271*
Fixative, 259, 261
Flatness, 146–7, 149, 158
Flattened relief (*rilievo schiacciato*), 40
Flemish painting, 210–11, 330–5
Flemish Proverbs (Bruegel the Elder), 211–*212*
Flesh tones, 244–5, 247, 250
Flight of Florimell, The (Allston), 341, *343*

Florence, 66, 146, 159, 293–4
Flower Day (Rivera), 305, *306*
F-111 (F-One-Eleven) (Rosenquist), 320, *321*, 322
Foreshortening, 147
"Form follows function," 88–9, 115
Forms, 26, 74; in abstraction, 121; and cubism, 126; "follow the form" modeling, 244; Mondrian's universal, 129; ovals, 18, 22–3; Piero's abstractions, 138–9; Seurat, 216–17; solid volumes, 33, 35–6; spatial composition, 118–19; tempera painting, 247; underpainting and, 251. *See also* Composition; Distortion; "Form follows function"; Geometrical forms
Found object, 46, 48, 192
Four Horsemen of the Apocalypse (Dürer), 264–5, *274*
Fourth dimension, sculptural, 41–2; and space-time, 40, 126
Fra Angelico, 246
Francesca, Piero della. *See* Piero della Francesca
Francesco Sassetti and His Son Teodoro (Ghirlandaio), 243, *244*, 250
Freedom from Want (Rockwell), 11, *12*
Fresco: Byzantine, 234–6; Oriental, 234–6; Piero's, 135, 138, 222–5, 228. *See also* *Buon fresco*; *Fresco a secco*
Fresco a secco, 228; Chinese, 236
Fuller, Buckminster, U.S. Pavilion, 360
Fuller, Thomas, Ottawa Houses of Parliament, 90
Functionalism, 87–92, *91*
Funeral of Phocion, The (Poussin), 202–7, *204*, 217
Futurism, 41

Gabo, Naum, *Linear Construction, Variation*, *42*, 192
Garden of Delights The, triptych (Bosch), *331–3*
Gargoyle, *330*
Garnier, Charles, Paris Opéra, *90*
Gaudí, Antoni, Casa Milá, *114*, 115
Gaufrage, 270
Gaugin, Paul, 374; *Manao Tupapao*, 226, *269*, 270–2; woodblock prints, 277, 284
Gentileschi, Artemisia, *Judith and Holofernes*, 71
Geodesic method, 360
Geometrical forms, 18, 23, 117; architecture and, 53; architectonic values, 184–6; cylinders, 35; and Gothic vaulting, 6–7; and sculpture, 33; triangle, 168–9, 175–8, 189. *See also* Forms
George Moore (Manet), 259–60
Géricault, Théodore, *Raft of the Medusa*, *187*, 188–9, 341, 351
Gérôme, Jean-Léon, *Duel After the Masquerade*, 75, *76*, 77, 79, 207–8
Gesso, 240, *242*, 247, indented pattern
Gestural painting, 132, 143
Ghirlandaio, Domenico, *Francesco Sassetti and His Son*, 243, *244*, 250
Giacometti, Alberto, *Palace at 4 A.M.*, 354

Giambologna (Giovanni Bologna), *The Appenine*, 354
Gilbert, Cass, Woolworth Building, *91*
Gilding, 240–1, 242, 245, 246–7
Giorgione, *Pastoral Concert*, 326–7, 332, 341; *Tempest*, 324, 325–8, 341, 351
Giotto di Bondone, 110, 224–5, 228, 234, Arena Chapel frescoes, 224, 227; *Lamentation Over the Body of Christ*, 224, 226, 227, 306
Gislebertus, *Last Judgment*, 353
Glaze, 251, 253
Gold leaf. See Gilding
Gothic period, 114; cathedrals and churches, 6–8; exposed structure, 192; exteriors, 88; façade, 165; flying buttresses, 7, 56, 114; frescoes and mosaics, 110; gargoyles, *330*; interiors, 142; cf. New Guinea *davi*, 54–5; Orvieto façade, *165*; painted crosses, 110; sculptures, 7, 39–40, 353.
Gouache, 220
Governess, The (Chardin), 74–5
Goya, Francisco, *Executions of Third of May*, 290–2, 296, 320, 322; *Old Man Among Ghosts*, 278, *279*
Gozzoli, Benozzo, *Journey of the Magi*, 144, 146–7, 154, 164
Gropius, Walter, Bauhaus, 88
Grotesques, 325; Bosch, 330–5; Bruegel, 211; Dali, 335; expressionist sculpture, 111–12; illuminated page with, *332*
Ground, 277
Groundhog Day (Wyeth), *249*
Guernica (Picasso), *176*, 177–8, 216, 320, 321, 322
Gulf Stream, The (Homer), *257*
Gum arabic, 220, 282
Gum fixative for pastels, 258–9

Hagesandros, *Laocoön*, 36
Hands of an Apostle (Dürer), 244–5
Hansen, Duane, 118; *Couple with Shopping Bags*, 85, 86–7, 315, *317*, 318
Harlot's Progress, The (Hogarth), 308
Harnett, William Michael, 95, 117–18; *Music and Good Luck*, 58, *59*–63, 117, 122
Harunobu, Suzuki, 267; *Drying Clothes*, *269*, 270–1
Hatching, 370
Heckel, Erich, 264; *Scene from Dostoevski*, *266*
Hell (Bosch), 330–*333*
Hicks, Edward, *Peaceable Kingdom*, 27
Hogarth, William, *Harlot's Progress*, 308; *Marriage à la Mode*, 308; *Orgy*, *313*; *Rake's Progress*, 308–14, *309*, *311*, *313*
Holbein the Younger, Hans, 150; *Anne of Cleves*, 156–*157*; *Christina of Denmark*, 155–8, *156*
Homer, Winslow, *Gulf Stream*, 257; *Sloop, Bermuda*, 255, *256*
Horizontal Tree (Mondrian), 129, *130*
Hours of Jeanne de'Evreux (Pucelle), *332*
Hovenden, Thomas, *Breaking Home Ties*, 77–8, *207*

Hudson River School, 25, 343–4
Human body, 34–5, 40, 63, 66; Masaccio drawing of, 224; Rodin's bronze, 45; Rothko and, 135
Hurricane (eleven-year-old child), *107*
Huys, Pieter, *Temptation of Saint Anthony*, *334*
Hyatt Regency Hotel and Reunion Tower, Dallas (Becket Associates), *92*
Hyperrealism, 81; function of, 83, 86–7; and Hansen, 86, 315

Ideal realism, 63, 298–302
Il Libro dell'Arte (Cennini), 249
Illuminated manuscript, 232, 348, 352; *Hours*, *332*
Illusionism, 60–1, 352; mural painting, 146–7; photorealism, 83
Illustrations, for books, 264, 266–7, 285
"Image breakers," 233
Impressionism, 80; painterly techniques, 81, 216, 253
Individualism, 95, 98–9, 108, 270–1; and visionary paintings, 328, 330
Ingres, Jean-Auguste-Dominique, *Madame Leblanc*, *14*, 15–16, 19, 23
Inkless print, 270
Intaglio prints, 272–80
Internal and External Forms (Moore), 138, 140
In the Meadow (Renoir), 17, *18*
Into the World There Came a Soul Called Ida (Albright), 315, *316*
Invenzione Capricciosa di Carceri (Piranesi), *358*
I. P. Morris Blast Engine, 48, *49*
Iron, 46, 51
Island of the Dead, The (Böcklin), 339, *340*
Ivory sculptures, 43–4

Jakuchū, Itō, *Animals and Plants*, 143
Jefferson Memorial (Pope), 52, *53*
Journey of the Magi (Gozzoli), 144, 146–7, 154, 164
Judith and Maidservant with the Head of Holofernes (Gentileschi), 71

Kamakura period (Japanese art): bull painting, *229*
Kandinsky, Wassily, *Black Lines*, 131–2
Kienholz, Edward, *State Hospital*, 312
Kinetic art, 9, 42
Kirchner, E. L., *Street Scene*, 88, *106*–7
Kiss, The (Brancusi), 33–5, *367*
Kiyonobu I, Torii, 150; *Woman Dancer*, *154*–5
Kiyotada, Torii, *Actor Dancing*, *155*
Klee, Paul, 345, 347; *Demon as Pirate*, *349*, *350*, *351*, 355
Kline, Franz: action painting, 143; *New York, N.Y.*, *105*–6, 132
Ko Chung-hsüan, after, *Two Peaches on a Branch*, 267, *269*, 271–2
Kokoschka, Oscar, *Tempest*, 29–31, *30*, 61
Kollwitz, Käthe, *Summons of Death*, 282
Kouros, 34, 40, 63

Lachaise, Gaston, 44, 51; *Standing Woman*, 32, *33*; *Torso*, 32, *33*
Ladies in Waiting. See *Meñinas, Las*

Lady in Blue (Matisse), 149, *150*–1, 154
Lamentation Over the Body of Christ (Giotto), 224, *226*, 227, 306
Landscape, 81, 129; classical composition, 203–5; Hudson River School, 343–4; romantic *vs.* classic, 23–6, 131, 180–2, 344
Landscape with Cattle (Rousseau), 344–45
Landscape with Farmhouse (Mondrian), *129*
Landscape with the Fall of Icarus (Bruegel the Elder), 209, *210*–11, 216
Laocoön and His Two Sons (Hagesandros, Polydoros, Athenodoros), 36
Lascaux cave paintings, 228
Last Judgment (Gislebertus), 353–4
Last Judgment (Michelangelo), 4, 5
Last Supper (Leonardo), 167–9, 172–3, 191, 193, 195; diagrammatic scheme, *166*, *168*, 169
Law and Justice (Orozco), 308
Legend of the True Cross (Piero), 135, *137*, 138–9, 222–3, 225, 228
Leonardo da Vinci, 225, 253; architectural sketches, *360*; cf. Caravaggio, 70; *Last Supper*, 166, 167–9, *168*–9, 172–3, 191, 193, 195; *Mona Lisa*, 21–3, 106, 167; *Virgin of the Rocks*, 66–8, *67*, 80
Lever House (Skidmore, Owings & Merrill), 93
Liberation of the Peon, The (Rivera), 303–4, 306
Liberty Leading the People (Delacroix), 297–8
Lichtrequisit (Moholy-Nagy), 42
Light and dark: in abstraction, 121; Blake and, 329; Cezanne and, 26; in Degas' *Rehearsal*, 207; "follow the form" modeling, 244; in impressionist paintings, 371; and Moholy-Nagy sculpture, 42; Rembrandt and "spotlight," 79, 279; tempera painting, 247, 249; *tenebroso*, 70–1; colors used in underpainting, 251; value of color, 377; Velazquez, 72–4
Line: Blake and Botticelli analyzed, 159, 162–4, 292; engraved, 272; etched, 277; Mondrian's freeing of, 127, 129; "shaded" in engraving, 274; two-dimensional composition and, 147–9, 154–5, 159. See also Triangular formula
Linear construction, 41–2, 192
Linear Construction, Variation (Gabo), 42, 192
Linear perspective, 40
Linoleum cut print (linocut), 266
Lithography: method, 280, 282; offset printing, 284
Little Spider (Calder), 42
Low relief. See *Bas relief*
Lozenge in Red, Yellow and Blue (Mondrian), 127, *128*, 129

McArthur, Jr., John, Philadelphia City Hall, 57
Machinery, 48–51, *49*; and sculpture, 46
Machinery Hall, Philadelphia, 48, *49*
Madame Leblanc (Ingres), *14*, 15–16, 19, 23
Madonna and Child with Saints and Angels Adored by Federigo da Montefeltro (*Madonna of the Egg*) (Piero), 182, *183*–5
Madonna and Nativity paintings, 175–6

Madonna Enthroned Between Saints Peter and Leonard (Magdalen Master), *239–40*
Madonna of Mercy (Piero), *182*, 184
Maidens and Stewards (Parthenon), *165*
Manao Tupapao (*She Thinks of the Spirit*) (Gauguin), *266*, *269*, *270–2*
Manet, Edouard, 31; *Boating*, *80*, *81*, 253; *George Moore*, *259–60*
Manhood (Cole), *348–9*
Mannerism, 31
Mantegna, Andrea, *Camera degli Sposi*, fresco, 146, *148*
Man with the Hoe, The (Millet), *302–3*
Marilyn Monroe (Warhol), 285, *286*
Marin, John, *Boat off Deer Isle*, *257–8*; *Singer Building*, *103*, *105–7*, 117
Marriage à la Mode (Hogarth), 308
Marriage of Giovanni Arnolfini and Giovanna Cenami (Van Eyck), *27–8*, *29*, 250
Martyrdom of Saint Sebastian (Pollaiuolo), 178, *179*, 180, 191, 272
Masaccio, 224, 228; *Tribute Money*, *225*, *226*, *227*
Master of Pedret, *Virgin and Child Enthroned*, 231, *232*, 234
Material values, 315, 318, 322
Matisse, Henri, 369; *Beasts of the Sea*, 143, *147–8*, *150–1*, *152*, 154; *Carnival at Nice*, 151, *152*; *Lady in Blue*, *149*, *150–1*, 154; illustration for *Pasiphäe, Chant de Minos*, *266*, *267*; *Reclining Nude*, *164*
Medici family and palace, 146, 293–4
Medici Slot Machine (Cornell), *355–6*
Medieval art. *See* Middle Ages
Medium, 219–20, 249
Melancholia (Castiglione), *276*, 277
Melancholy and Mystery of a Street (Chirico), *337*, 338
Melencolia I (Dürer), *274–7*, *275*, 348
Mendelsohn, Erich, *Einstein Tower*, *115*
Meninas, Las (Velázquez), *72–3*
Metal plates: dry point, 279; aquatint tonalities, 277, 279; engraving, 272, 274; etching, 277
Metropolis, still from, *361*
Mexican Renaissance, 228, 303–4, 306
Mezzo rilievo (medium relief), *38–9*
Mezzotint, 280
Michelangelo, 135; *Creation of Adam*, *218*, *221–3*, *222*; *Last Judgment*, *4*, *5*; Sistine Chapel ceiling, *221–2*, *225*, 328
Microtemps (Schöffer), *42–3*
Middle Ages: faith, 6–8; fantasies and grotesqueries, 325, 330–5; and human body, 34; journeyman painters, 111, 238–9; mystical realism, 64–6, 330; panel painting and altarpiece formula, 232–3; Shepherd's Calendar, 347; unrealistic images, 233–4; visionary sculpture, 352–4; woodcut images, 263. *See also* Baroque period; Gothic period
Mies van der Rohe, Ludwig, *Seagram Building*, *91*
Mi Fu, "Sailing on the Wu River," *142*, 143
Millet, Jean François, *Man with the Hoe*, *302–3*; *Sower*, *302*
Miniature paintings: Persian, 154; van Eyck's *Saint Francis*, 64–5
Minor masters, 238, 246
Miss Van Buren (Eakins), *78–80*, *79*

Mobile: Calder's, 42, 51; motorization of, 42
Modeling, 147, 150, 158; by cross-hatching, 244, 264; "follow the form," 250
Modena, Tommaso da, 246
Modern art, 11, 23; anarchic techniques, 253; anti-art, 48, 87, 285; concept art, 312, 368; expressionist movement, 98–9; found objects and machinery, 43, 46, 48, 51, 192; and prints, 284; Seurat's place in, 217; straight painting, 253; and tempera technique, 249. *See also* Abstraction; Abstract Expressionism; Cubism; Futurism; Surrealism
Moholy-Nagy, László, *Lichtrequisit*, 42; *System of Dynamo-Constructive Forces* (manifesto), 42
Mona Lisa (Leonardo), *21–3*
Mondrian, Piet, 129–30, 134, 147; *Composition*, *130*; *Horizontal Tree*, 129, *130*; interview with, 127, 129; *Landscape with Farmhouse*, 129; *Lozenge in Red, Yellow and Blue*, 127, *128*, 129; *Tree*, *130*
Mondsee Gospels, 44, *45*
Monet, Claude, 31, 81
Monotype, 285
Mont Sainte-Victoire (Cézanne), 23, *24*, *26*, 131, *182*, 203
Moonlight Marine (Ryder), 349, *350*
Moore, Henry, *Internal and External Forms*, 138, *140*; *Reclining Figure*, *139*, 140
Mosaic, 232–4, 236
Moses, Anna Mary Robertson (Grandma), *Coming Home for Thanksgiving*, 345, *346*
Motion. *See* Balance and counterbalance
Motorized sculpture, 42–3
Mural paintings, 7, 146–7, 221; Chinese, 236; Rivera, 304
Murals (Rivera), Ministry of Education courtyard, *304*
Musical Forms (Braque), 59–60, *62–3*
Music and Good Luck (Harnett), *58*, *59–63*, 117, 122
Musicians, The (Caravaggio), *187*, *188*, 191
Muzahib, Mahmud, *Bahram Gur*, *153*, 154
Myron, *Discobolus*, *207*
Mystical realism, 64–5, 330
Mystical subjects, 66, 108–11, 325

Naïveté, 328, 344-5. *See also* Primitive art
Nat (Close), 83, *85*, 86
Naturalism, 60–1, 63, 108
Nature, 42, 140; and *art nouveau*, 114; classic *vs.* romantic landscape, 25–6, 343; "dynamic equilibrium" of, 129–30; transformation of, 8–9, 95
Neo-classical style: David's *Death of Socrates*, *298–302*
Neo-Gothic style, 90
Nervi and Vitellozzi, Palazzetto dello Sport, *192*, *193*
Nevelson, Louise, *Sky Cathedral*, *356–8*, *357*
New Guinea *davi* (ceremonial house), *54–5*
New Testament, 70; Book of Revelation, 264–5, *352–3*
New York, N.Y. (Kline), *105*, 132
New York school, 132
Nighthawks (Hopper), *82*, 318

Night Watch, The (Rembrandt). *See Company of Captain Frans Banning Cocq.*
Nike of Samothrace (*Winged Victory*), *41–2*
Nîmes, *193*
Nineteenth century, 7–8, 11, 37, 123, 200; in America, 25–6, 77–8, 341; architectural styles, 92–3; common and practical themes, 19–20, 75, 320; demolition, 57; French Academy and, 30–1; and machines, 48, 51; socially conscious art, 289–92
Nocturne (Whistler), *277*, *278*
Nonobjective (nonfigurative) art, 117, 127–30, 134
North Dakota missile-tracking station, *91*, 92
No Swimming (Rockwell), 11, *12*
Nourrice Profuse (Dubuffet), *2*, *3*, *5*, *8*, 51
Nude Woman (Picasso), *216*
Nydia, the Blind Flower Girl of Pompeii (Rogers), *78*

Objective optical realism, 72–3, 80–1
"Occult" balance, 206
Oil painting, 220, 250–3
Old Man Among Ghosts (Goya), *278*, *279*
Old Testament, 27
One of the Ten Fast Bulls (unknown Japanese painter), *229*
Open form, 36–7, 41–2, 139
Opéra, Paris (Garnier), *8* *90*, 92, *93*
Optical realism, 72–3, 80–1
Orange and Yellow (Rothko), 134–5, ill. *136*
Order, 22, 26; out of chaos, art function, 3–9, 64, 193; and classicism, 191, 203
Orgy (Hogarth), *313*
Orozco, José Clemente, 306; *Law and Justice*, *308*
Orvieto Cathedral, *165*
Ottawa Houses of Parliament (Fuller), *90*
Overpainting, 251

Paint: ready-made, 253; silk-screen stencil, 284. *See also* Oil; Tempera
Painterly techniques, 74, 216–17, 219–20; *buon fresco*, 221; with oil, 250–1; with tempera, 238–9. *See also* Brushwork; names of artists
Painting: and artist's personality, 11, 15, 37–8, 335; cartoons, 222–3; changing ideas and taste, 28–31; emotion *vs.* intellect, 23–6; as expression of its age, 5–8, 11, 15, 30–1, 335; journeymen and apprentices, 111, 238–9; at second level, 77–8; symbolism and disguise, 27–8; union with architecture and sculpture, 9
Palace at 4 A.M., The (Giacometti), *354–5*
Palazzetto dello Sport (Nervi and Vitellozzi), *192*, *193*
Panel painting, 232, 238–40
Parable of the Blind, The (Bruegel), *212–13*, 216
Paris, 8, 48, 57; Opera House (Garnier), *8*, *90*, 92, *93*; Pompidou Center, *54–7*; *Rue Transnonain*, 289–90
Parthenon, *3–5*, 7–8, 44; Athenian procession from frieze, *39*, *164–5*

Pasiphaë, Chant de Minos, illustration for (Matisse), 266, *267*

Passion of Sacco and Vanzetti (Shahn), 292, *294,* 295–6, 301–2, 318

Pastel paintings, 258–61

Pastoral Concert (Giorgione), 326–7, 332, 341

Pastorals of Virgil, illustration for (W. Blake), 264, *266*

"Path at Pine and Brook" (Ping-shou), *142,* 143

Pattern, 145–65; of line, 159, 162–4; of shapes and colors, 146–59

Paxton, Joseph, Crystal Palace, 89, *90*

Peaceable Kingdom, The (Hicks), 27

Peale, Charles Willson, *Peale Family,* 195, *197, 199,* 198–200, 206

Peale Family (Peale), 195, *197, 199,* 198–200

Pediments, 36–7, *38*

Persian painting, 154

Personification of Europe (Carriera), *258,* 259

Perspective, 6, 140, 147–8, 159, 185, 205; and abstraction, 121; beginnings, 224; in *Last Supper,* 167–9

Perugino, Pietro, *Crucifixion with the Virgin and Saints,* 174, 175–8, 216

Philadelphia City Hall and Tower (McArthur), *57*

Photographic art techniques, 263, 284

Photography, 5–6, 105; *vs.* abstraction, 118; capturing of space, 140, 142

Photorealism, 82–3

Piazza San Marco, 5–6

Picasso, Pablo, 11, 147; *Demoiselles d'Avignon,* 123, *125,* 126–127, 134, 154; *Guernica,* 176, 177–8, 216, 320, *321,* 322; linocuts, 266; *Nude Woman, 126; Seated Woman, 267; Studio,* 118–22, *121,* 126–7, 129, 320; *Woman in White,* 253–4

Picture plane, 205–6

Piero della Francesca, *Death of Adam,* 222–3; *Legend of the True Cross,* 135, 137, 138–9, *221–3,* 225, 228; *Madonna and Child,* 182, *183–5; Madonna of Mercy, 182,* 184

Pietà, 112–114, *113*

Pigment, 219, 374; cave paintings, 228; and mixing, 219–20; tempera, 241, 244; in water color, 255, 258

Ping-shou, "Path at Pine and Brook," *142,* 143

Piranesi, Giovanni Battista, *Invenzione Capricciosa di Carceri, 358; Temple of Castor and Pollux, 358*

Planar process, prints, 280–5

"Plane surface," 147, 205

Plaster: drying of, 221, 229; *cf.* gesso, 240. See also *Buon fresco*

Plus and minus compositions, 130

Pointillism. *See* Seurat

Pollaiuolo, Antonio del, *Battle of Naked Men, 272, 273,* 274, 276; *Martyrdom of Saint Sebastian, 178, 179,* 180, 191, 272

Pollock, Jackson, 132–4; *Convergence, 132, 133*

Polydoros, *Laocoön, 36*

Polykleitos, *Diadoumenos, 34–5,* 40, 45, 63

Pompeiian wall painting, 229–32

Pompidou Center, 54–7, 192

Pont du Gard, Nîmes, *193*

Pop art, 285, 322

Pope, John Russell, Jefferson Memorial, *52*

Portals, 39–40

Portrait Head of a Man, Roman, 63–4

Portrait of a Lady (van der Weyden), *248–9,* 250

Portrait of Madame Renoir (Renoir), 16–23, *17,* 30, 33, 186

Portrait of Tourny (Degas), 287

Portraits: pastels, 259; of women compared, 15–23; *Miss Van Buren,* 78–80, *79*

Poster art, 158–9, 284

Post-Impressionism, 216–17

Pouncing, 223

Poussin, Nicholas: *Funeral of Phocion, 202–7, 204,* 217; *Rape of the Sabine Women, 171, 173,* 191, 203–5, 216

Première Pose, La (Roberts), 48, *50,* 51

Primavera (Botticelli), 159, *162;* "Three Graces" from, *161,* 162–3, 195, 292

Primitive art, 148; *Esther Tuttle,* 149–50

Print Collector, The (Daumier), *362, 363*

Prints, 263–87; development of, 263–4, 284–5, 287; limited edition, 287; original, 287. *See also* names of various techniques, *i.e.,* Engraving; Etching; Lithography

Proletarian Victim (Siqueiros), 308, *307*

Prometheus Bound (Rubens), 69–70, 207

Propagandist art, 304, 306, 308

Psychic balance, 206

Pucelle, Jean, *Hours of Jeanne d'Evreux, 332*

Quadrivium, 371

Queirolo, Francesco, *Allegory of Deception, 44*

Radome, U.S. Air Force, *360*

Raft of the Medusa, The (Géricault), *187, 188–9,* 341, 351

Rake's Progress, The (Hogarth), 308–314

Rape of the Sabine Women (Poussin), *171, 173,* 191, 203–5, 216

Raphael, 312, 328; analysis of, 225; *School of Athens, 225, 227,* 228; *Transfiguration, 170, 172–3,* 175

Rattlesnake (Aztec), *306*

Rauschenberg, Robert, *Centennial Certificate, 284*

Ready-made paint, 253

"Ready-made" sculpture, 46–8

Realism, 59–93; *cf.* abstraction, 60, 62–3; anecdotal, 75–8; architectural, 57, 87–93; and Byzantine style, 233; commonplace themes, 73–5, 79–80; dramatized, 68–71; *cf.* expressionism, 59, 61–2, 95; Giotto frescoes, 219; hyperrealism, 83, 86–7, 315, 318; ideal, 63–4, 177; illusionism, 60–1, 74; impressionism, 80–1; mystical, 64–5, 110–11; objective, 72–3, 83; photorealism, 82–3; Renaissance, 66–8; sculptural, 86–7; *See also* Social criticism and realism

Reclining Figure (Moore), *139,* 140

Reclining Nude (Matisse), *164*

Red and Blue Chair (Rietveld), 130, *131*

Redon, Odilon, *Chariot of Apollo,* 329–30; *Evocation of the Butterflies, 329*

Refectory, 375

Rehearsal in the Foyer of the Opera (Degas), 202, *204,* 205–6

Reliance Building (Burnham & Co.), *90*

Relief, 38–40

Relief print, 263–71, 280

Rembrandt, *Anatomy Lesson of Dr. Tulp, 196; Artistotle with a Bust of Homer, 251, 252; Christ Carried to the Tomb, 277; Company of Captain Frans Banning Cocq, 194,* 195–8; etchings, 263, 277, 279–80; humanistic art, 11; realism, 70; "spotlight" effect, 79, 279; *Three Crosses,* 279–280, *281*

Renaissance, 9, 175, 306, 372; frescoes, 224–5, 232; High, and painters of, 71–2; ideal classicism, 22, 66–9; tempera panel paintings, 238–45; three-dimensional composition, 180. *See also* Baroque period; names of artists

Renoir, Pierre Auguste, 31; *In the Meadow, 17, 18; Portrait of Madame Renoir,* 16–23, *17,* 33, 117, 186

Reproductions, 15, 78, 284, 372; bronze sculpture, 44; literal, 87; original prints, 287. *See also* Prints

Resin, 277, 279

Restoration technique, 239–40

Rietveld, Gerrit, *Red and Blue Chair,* 130, *131;* Schröder House, 130

Rilievo schiacciato, 40

Rivera, Diego, 303; *Dinner of the Millionaires, 304, 306; Flower Day, 305,* 306; *Liberation of the Peon, 304,* 306; murals, *304,* 306, 318

Roberts, Howard, *La Première Pose,* 48, *50,* 51

Rockwell, Norman, *Freedom From Want,* 11, *12; No Swimming,* 11, *12;* and *Whistler's Mother,* 12–13, 15

Rodin, Auguste, *Balzac, 46, 47; Colossal Head of Balzac, 46; The Age of Bronze,* 45–6

Rogers, Randolph, *Nydia, 78*

Romantic movement (Romanticism), 23, 189–92; in America, 25–6, 341–3; peasant ideal, 302

Romantic space, 182; *Abduction of Rebecca, 189*

Rome: architecture, 8, 140–2; Blume's *Eternal City,* 318–20

Rosenquist, James, *F-111,* 320, *321,* 322

Rothko, Mark: colorism, 134–5; *Orange and Yellow, 136*

Röttgen Pietà, 112–14, *113*

Rouault, Georges, *Two Nudes,* 102–3, *104*

Rousseau, Henri "Douanier," *Landscape with Cattle,* 344–5; *Sleeping Gypsy, 345, 346*

Rubens, Peter Paul, 73, 80; *Christ on the Cross, 108, 109,* 110; *Prometheus Bound,* 69–70, 108

Rue Transnonain, April 15, 1834 (Daumier), *288,* 289–90

Ryder, Albert Pinkham, 220; *Moonlight Marine, 349, 350*

Saarinen, Eero, TWA Terminal, *115,* 193

"Sailing on the Wu River" (Mi Fu), 142–3

Saint Anthony Tempted by the Devil in the Form of a Woman (Sassetta), 208–209, 334–5

Saint Christopher and Saint John the Baptist, German hand-colored woodcut, 267, 268

Saint Francis Receiving the Stigmata (Van Eyck), 64, 65, 68, 72, 80, 86, 330

Saint George, Bishop (Byzantine, unknown Russian painter), 231

Saint George and the Dragon (Donatello), 40, 41

Saint John of God (Cano), 86–7

Saint Matthew (*Mondsee Gospels* miniature), 44, 45

Saint-Nectaire Church, 88

Saint Peter (Stwosz), 86

Saint Peter's, Rome, 7; Colonnade (Bernini), 139, 140

Saint Peter's Cathedral, Beauvais, choir vaulting, 6

Salon in the Rue des Moulins (Toulouse-Lautrec), 313, 314

San Carlo alle Quattro Fontane, Rome (Borromini), 141, 142

Santo Spirito (Brunelleschi), 66

Sargent, John Singer: and gestural painting, 132, 134; *Wyndham Sisters*, 122–3, 124, 132, 134

Sassetta, *Saint Anthony Tempted by the Devil*, 208–209, 334–5

Savonarola, 294

Scene from Dostoevski (Heckel), 266

Scene from Thanatopsis (Durand), 23–6, 24, 25, 131, 182, 294, 343

Shöffer, Nicholas, *Microtemps*, 42–3

School of Athens (Raphael), 225, 227

Schröder House (Rietveld), 130, 131

Script, ornamental, 154

Sculpture, 33–51; Baroque theatricality, 71; closed vs. open forms, 34–7, 139; composition, 146; constructions, 42, 192, 355–8; degree of relief, 38–40; De Stijl, 130; expressionist, 111–14; fertility symbols, 33–6; found objects, 46, 48, 192; fourth dimension, 40–2; "garden," 354; Gothic cathedrals and, 7, 38–40; Greek and Roman, 34–5, 63–4; Hansen, 86–7; low relief and two-dimensions, 164–5; mobiles, 42–3, 51; modern vs. traditional, 42–51; negative volumes, 139–40; of protest, 322; Renaissance, 66; with sound, 43; surrealist, 354–5; visionary, 351–5; woods and stone used, 43–4. *See also* Relief; Realism

Seagram Building (Mies van der Rohe), 91

Seated Clownesse, Mlle. Cha-u-ka-o, The (Toulouse-Lautrec), 282, 283

Seated Woman (Picasso), 267

Seeon Monastery *Pietá*, 112, 114

Segal, George, *Subway*, 318

Semi-abstraction, 117, 322

Serigraph. *See* Silk-screen print

Seurat, Georges, 374; *Sunday Afternoon on La Grande Jatte*, 214, 215, 216–17

"Shaded line," 274

Shahn, Ben, *Passion of Sacco and Vanzetti*, 292, 294, 295–6, 301–2, 318

Sienese *Virgin and Child*, 240–1, 242, 244, 245, 246–7

Silk-screen print, 284–5

Singer Building (Marin), 103, 105–7, 117

Siqueiros, David Alfaro, 372; *Proletarian Victim*, 307, 308

Sistine Chapel ceiling (Michelangelo), 5, 225, 328

Skidmore, Owings & Merrill, Lever House, 93

Skyscrapers, 9, 90–1, 93

Slab architecture, 91–2

Sleeping Gypsy, The (Rousseau), 345, 346

Sloop, Bermuda (Homer), 255, 256

Smith, David, 46, 51; *Cubi VII*, 35; *Volton XV*, 47

Smithson, Robert, *Spiral Jetty*, 8

Snelson, Kenneth, *Audrey I*, 191–2

Social criticism and realism, 289–323; American urban loneliness, 82, 292, 312, 315, 318; in France, 289–90, 298–301, 302–3, 314; Germany, 106–7; Hogarth's *Rake's Progress*, 308–14; injustice, 292–8; Mexico, 303–8; politics and war, 290–2, 318–22; morality and prostitution, 102–3, 310, 312, 314–315

Soft Construction with Boiled Beans: Premonition of Civil War (Dali), 355

Soleri, Paolo, *Babel IIB*, 360, 361

Solid volumes: interpenetration of, 41–2, 184; *Card Players*, 186, 188; De Stijl, 130; spatial composition and, 118–19.

Solo V (Albers), 270

Sound sculptures, 43

Soupe, La (Daumier), 362

Soviet art, 306

Sower, The (Millet), 302

Space: architectonic values and, 185–8; classical, 182, 189, 203; closed form, 33–4, 36–7; depth and three-dimension, 147, 180, 182; fourth dimension, 40–2; dynamic, 142; negative volume, 139–40, 184; open form, 36–7; romantic, 182, 189; shaped in architecture, 140–2

Space-time concept: and cubism, 126; in sculpture, 40–3

Spanish Steps, Rome (de Sanctis), 140, 141

Spatial composition, 118–19, 180, 182, 184–6, 188

"Spatiodynamic" construction, 42, 43

Spiral Jetty (Smithson), 8

Spotlight effect, 79

Stained glass, 7, 367

Standing Goddess (Aztec), 306

Standing Women (Lachaise), 32, 33

Stankiewicz, Richard, *Construction*, 46, 47, 51

Starry Night, The (Van Gogh), 94, 96–9, 101, 219, 349

Star Wars, still from, 360, 361

State Hospital, The (Kienholz), 312

Steinberg, Saul, 91

Stencil, 284

Stigmata: *Saint Francis* painting, 64–65

Still-life painting, 73–5, 118

Still Life with a White Mug (Chardin), 74, 76

Still Life with Parrots (Davidsz), 74

Stone drawing. *See* Lithography

Stonehenge, 52, 53, 55

Storm, The (Cot), 29–31, 30

Storytelling paintings, 207–16

Street Scene (Kirchner), 88, 106–7

Stryge, La (Viollet-le-Duc), 330

Studio, The (Picasso), 118–22, 121, 126–7, 129

Stwosz, Wit, *Saint Peter*, 86

Stylus, 277, 279, 376

Subway (Segal), 318

Subway, The (Tooker), 318, 319

Summons of Death, The (Kollwitz), 282

Sunday Afternoon on the Island of La Grande Jatte (Seurat), 214, 215, 216–17

Superrealism, 81

Supreme Hardware (Estes), 83, 84

Surrealism, 81–2, 335, 337; Giacometti's *Palace*, 354–355; realism with fantasy, 343

Symbols: Arnolfini wedding picture, 28; Botticelli's *Calumny*, 293; Dürer cf. Castiglione, 276–7; in Goya's *Executions*, 292; medieval, 142, 347; Renoir's universal, 18, 21

Tableau, 312

Taliesin East (Wright), 54

Tapestries, 7, 146; Chinese, 236; *Fall of Babylon*, 352–3

Tempera painting, 249, 329; preciseness and technique, 220, 238–50

Tempest, The (Giorgione), 324, 325–8, 341, 351

Tempest, The (Kokoschka), 29–30, 61

Temple of Castor and Pollux (Piranesi), 358

Temptation of Saint Anthony (Huys), 334

Tenebroso, 71

Tensegrity, 192

Tessera, 233

Textures: and aquatints, 279; Braque's use of, 62; Harnett's illusion of, 60; Marin and water color, 106; monotype print, 285; and oil painting, 250; of paper, water color, 255, 258; for pastel, 258; Picasso, 7, 121, 253; swift brushwork and, 249; in tempera painting, 247

Theatricality, 115. *See also* Dramatic realism

Thom McAn (Estes), 83, 84

Thousand Buddhas (Japanese), 262, 263

Three Crosses (Rembrandt), 279–80, 281

Three-dimensional composition, 146, 150–1; Brera altarpiece, 184–5; Caravaggio and Cezanne cf., 185–8; depth in space, 178, 180, 182, 184; techniques of, 159; triangular composition, 178; vs. two-dimensional, 147, 184

Three-dimensional relief, 38, 40

Time, 56; and space, 40

Titan's Goblet, The (Cole), 342, 343

Titian, *Venus and Adonis*, 251, 252

Toilet of Venus, The (Boucher), 75, 298–9, 300, 301, 320

Tooker, George, *The Subway*, 318, 319

Torso (Lachaise), 32, 33

Torso of a Young Man (Brancusi), 35

Toulouse-Lautrec, Henri de, *Aristide Bruant*, 158, 160; lithographs, 284; posters, 158–9; *Salon in the Rue des Moulins*, 313, 314; *Seated Clownesse, Mlle. Cha-u-ka-o*, 282, 283

Transfiguration (Raphael), *170, 172–3, 175*
Transparent sculpture, 42, 192
Tree (Mondrian), *130*
Triangular formula: altarpieces, 175; *Guernica*, 177; *Last Supper*, 168–9, 175; *Martyrdom of Saint Sebastian*, 178; off-balance and motion, 189; *Perugino's Crucifixion*, 175–7
Tribute Money (Masaccio), *225, 226, 227*
Triptychs, 177, 182, 331, 332, 333
Triton and Nereid (Böcklin), *339*
Trivium, 7
Trumbull, John, *Declaration of Independence*, 295–298
Turner, J. M. W., *Burning of the Houses of Parliament*, *133, 134*
Tusche, 282
TWA Terminal (Saarinen), *115, 193*
Twentieth century, 11, 270; American artists, 82–7, 106–7, 292, 312, 315, 318; *Guernica*, 278, 320; New York as composite work of, 8–9; sculptural materials, 43; Van Gogh's *Starry Night*, 98–9; visionary art, 337–43
Two-dimensional composition, 146–65; linear design, 159, 162–5; Oriental, 154–5; portraits compared, 149–58; primitive, 147–9; shift from, 178, 180
Two Girls (Bishop), *81, 82*
Two Nudes (Rouault), *102–3, 104*
Two Peaches on a Branch (Ko Chung-hsüan), *267, 269, 271–2*
Tympanum, *352–3*

Underpainting, 251, 253
Unique Forms of Continuity in Space (Boccioni), *41–2*
Unmodeled space, 158
U.S. Pavilion, Expo '67 (Fuller), *360*

Van der Weyden, Rogier, *Portrait of a Lady*, *248–9, 250*

Van Eyck, Jan, *Marriage of Giovanni Arnolfini*, *27–8, 29, 250*; *Saint Francis Receiving Stigmata*, *64, 65, 72, 80, 86–7, 330*
Van Gogh, Vincent, 216, 219; *Starry Night*, *94, 96–9, 349*
Van Ruisdael, Jacob, *Wheatfields*, *180, 181, 182*
Vantongerloo, Georges, *Construction of Volume Relations*, *130, 131*
Vaults: bamboo *davi*, 54–5; and buttresses, 56–7; engineering of, 6–7
Velázquez, Diego, 74, 80–1, 83; *Las Meñinas*, *72–3*
Venus and Adonis (Titian), *251, 252*
Venus of Willendorf, *32, 33, 35–6, 46, 51*; grotesqueness of, 111–12
Vermeer, Jan, 207; *Artist in His Studio*, *116, 118–22, 120, 138, 182, 204*
Verrazano-Narrows Bridge, *193*
View on the Catskill, Early Autumn (Cole), *343–4, 345, 355*
Violence in art, 289–92
Viollet-le-Duc, Eugène Emmanuel, *La Stryge*, *330*
Virgin and Child Enthroned (Master of Pedret), *231, 232, 234*
Virgin and Child with Saint Jerome (Sienese artist), *240–1, 242, 244, 245, 246–7*
Virgin Mary, 111, 374; Giotto and, 224, 234; Pietà sculptures, 112–14. *See also* Madonna and Nativity paintings
Virgin of the Rocks (Leonardo), *66–8, 67, 80*
Vision of Saint John, The (Saint-Pierre Church Tympanum), *352*
Visionary paintings, 325–61; Bruegel, 211–13, 216; Klee, 345, 347, 349–51; Middle Ages and, 330–5; Surrealists, 335, 337, 354–5. *See also* Dreamscapes
Vitellozzi and Nervi, Palazzetto dello Sport, *192, 193*
Void, 139–40, 184
Volton XV (Smith), *47*

Warhol, Andy, *Marilyn Monroe*, *285, 286*
Water-color painting, 220, 254, 255, 257–8;

Water-color painting (*cont.*)
Blake, 329; and Chinese woodcut, 267. *See also* Marin, John
Watteau, Jean Antoine, 220
Wax: and bronze, 44; and etching, 277
Wheatfields (van Ruisdael), *180, 181, 182*
Whistler, James Abbott McNeill, *Arrangement in Gray and Black*, *12, 15, 19, 117–18, 129*; composition, *10, 13, 145*; painterly technique, 219; *Nocturne*, *227, 278*
Whistler's Mother. See Arrangement in Gray and Black, No. 1
Winged Victory, *41–2*
Wise and The Foolish Virgins, The (Blake), *163–4, 327*
Woman Dancer with Fan and Wand (Kiyonobu I), *154–5*
Woman IV (De Kooning), *132*
Woman Having Her Hair Combed (Degas), *261*
Woman in White (Picasso), *253–4*
Woman Playing the Kithara (unknown Roman painter), *230, 232–3*
Woman with Chrysanthemums (Degas), *19, 20–2, 145, 186*
Woodblock prints, *154–5*, 263–72; color development and Gauguin, 267–72; Dürer and, 264; medieval allegory, 347–8
Woodcut and wood engraving, distinction, 264–5
Woolworth Building (Gilbert), *91*
Wotruba, Fritz, *Figure wtih Raised Arms*, *35*
Wright, Frank Lloyd, "Falling Water," *54*; Taliesin East, *54*
Wyeth, Andrew, *Groundhog Day*, *249*
Wyndham Sisters (Sargent), *122–3, 124, 132*

Yellow Violin, The (Dufy), *59, 61–2*
Young Horseman (classical Greece), *38*

Zacharias and the Angel (Blake), *329*
Zadkine, Ossip, *Destroyed City*, *112, 322, 323*

A Note About the Author

John Canaday was born in Fort Scott, Kansas, and educated at the University of Texas and Yale University. He has taught art history at various universities. For six years he worked as an administrator and lecturer at the Philadelphia Museum of Art, where he directed the Division of Education. From 1959 to 1976 he was the art critic for *The New York Times.* In 1977 he toured South America lecturing on North American art for the State Department. He is the author of fourteen other books, including *Mainstreams of Modern Art* (1959), *Embattled Critic* (1962), *Culture Gulch* (1969), and seven mystery novels published under a pseudonym. He lives with his wife in New York City.

A Note About the Type

The text of this book was set in *Trump Mediaeval.* Designed by Professor Georg Trump in the mid-1950's, Trump Mediaeval was cut and cast by the C. E. Weber Typefoundry of Stuttgart, West Germany. The roman letterforms are based on classical prototypes, but Professor Trump has imbued them with his own unmistakable style. The italic letterforms, unlike those of so many other typefaces, are closely related to their roman counterparts. The result is a truly contemporary type, notable both for its legibility and versatility.

This book was composed by Monotype Composition Company, Inc., Baltimore, Maryland, who also shot the black-and-white illustrations. The color reproductions were separated by Offset Separations Corporation, New York and Turin, Italy. The book was printed and bound by the Kingsport Press, Kingsport, Tennessee.

Typography and binding design by Robert Aulicino.